Shojo Beat

S·A
Special A

Kei & Finn
9 years old

Volume 9

Story & Art by
Maki Minami

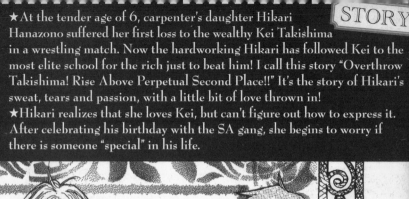

★At the tender age of 6, carpenter's daughter Hikari Hanazono suffered her first loss to the wealthy Kei Takishima in a wrestling match. Now the hardworking Hikari has followed Kei to the most elite school for the rich just to beat him! I call this story "Overthrow Takishima! Rise Above Perpetual Second Place!!" It's the story of Hikari's sweat, tears and passion, with a little bit of love thrown in!

★Hikari realizes that she loves Kei, but can't figure out how to express it. After celebrating his birthday with the SA gang, she begins to worry if there is someone "special" in his life.

Kei Takishima

Ranked number one in SA, Kei is a seemingly flawless student who not only gets perfect test scores but also runs his family business, Takishima Group, from behind the scenes. He is in love with Hikari, but she doesn't realize it.

Ryu Tsuji

Ranked number seven in SA, Ryu is the son of the president of a sporting goods company...but wait, he loves animals, too! Megumi and Jun are completely infatuated with him.

Megumi Yamamoto

Megumi is the daughter of a music producer and a genius vocalist. Ranked number four in SA, she only talks to people by writing in her sketchbook.

Jun Yamamoto

Megumi's twin brother, Jun is ranked number three in SA. Like his sister, he doesn't talk much. They have both been strongly attached to Ryu since they were kids.

S•A CHARACTERS

Hikari goes to an elite school called Hakusenkan High School. This school divides each grade level into groups A through F, according to the students' test scores. Group A includes only the top seven students in each class. Then the top seven students from all grades' A-groups are put into a group called Special A, which is considered much higher than all others. Known as SA, they are "the elite among the elite."

What is "Special A"?

Sakura Ushikubo

Sakura's family set her up with Kei via a matchmaker. But if she married Kei, it would only be for her family's convenience. Right now she is head-over-heels for Jun. ♥

Tadashi Karino

Ranked number five in SA, Tadashi is a simple guy who likes to go at his own pace. He is the school director's son, which comes in very handy. He likes the sweets that Akira makes.

Hikari Hanazono

The super-energetic and super-stubborn heroine of this story! She has always been ranked second best to Kei, so her entire self-image hinges on being Takishima's ultimate rival!

Yahiro Saiga

A childhood friend of Kei and Akira, Yahiro is even wealthier than Kei. He seems to really care for Akira, but he's got a mysterious side as well. What is his real objective?

Akira Toudou

Ranked number six, Akira is the daughter of an airline president. Her favorite things are teatime and cute girls...especially cute girls named Hikari Hanazono!

Contents

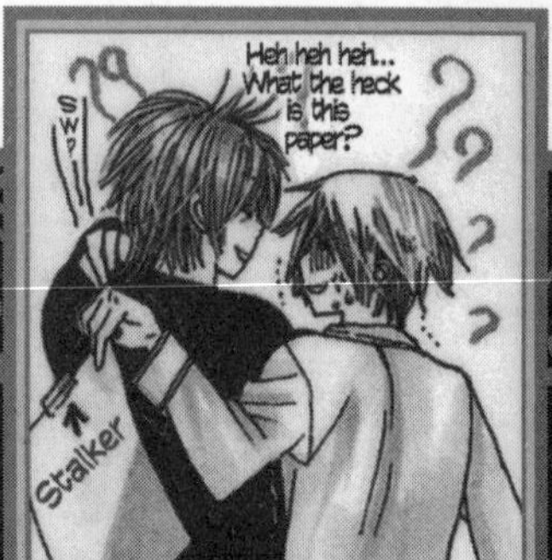

Heh heh heh... What the heck is this paper?
Stalker

Chapter 47

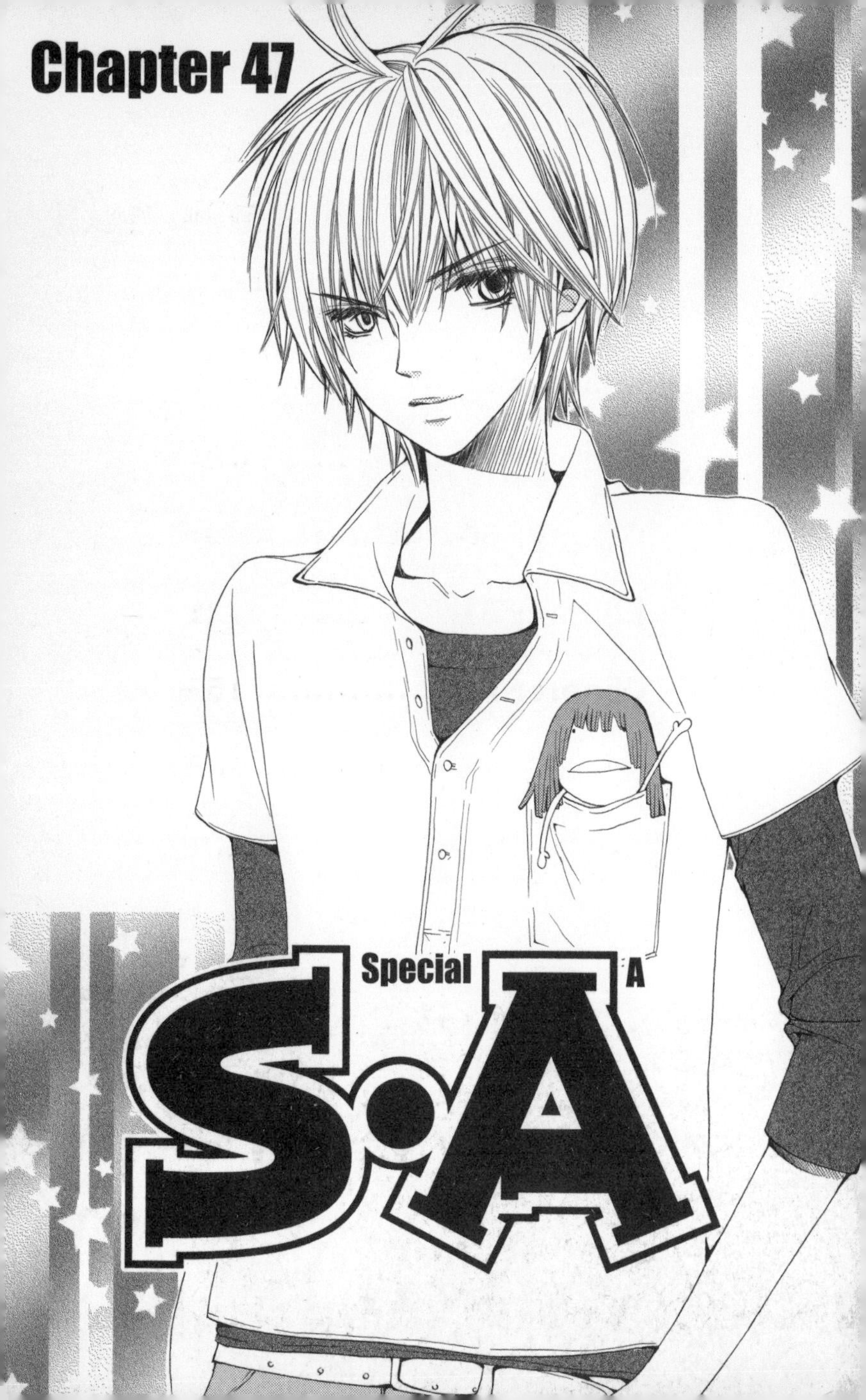

Special
S·A

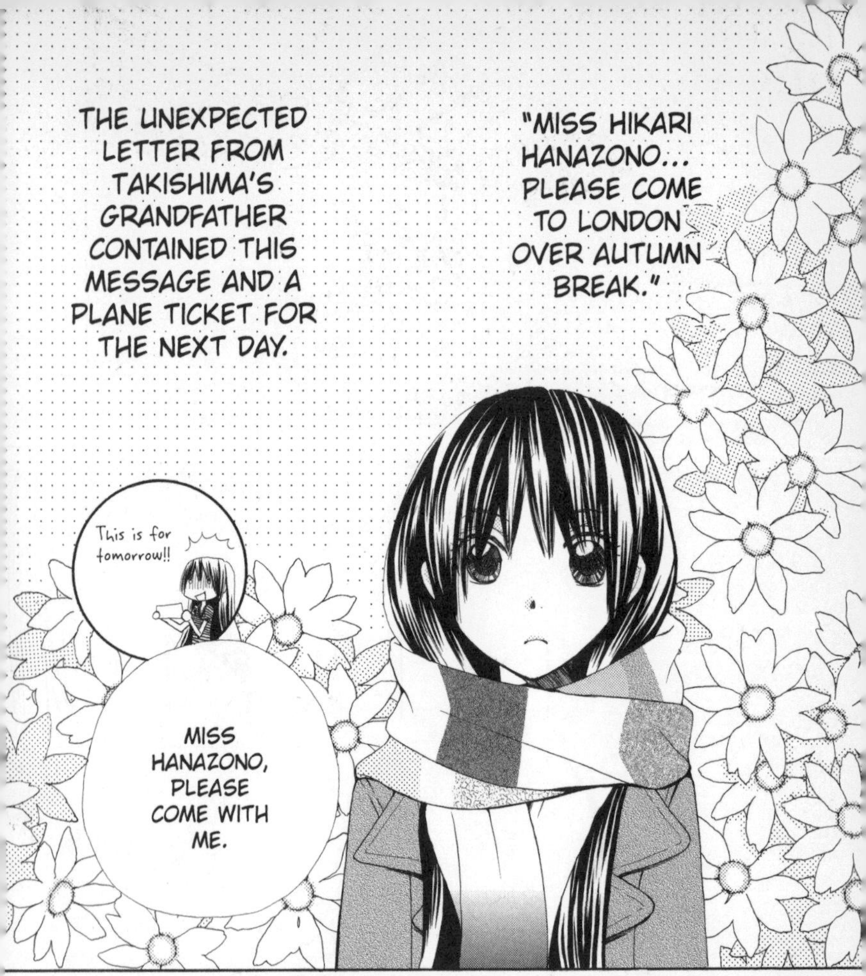
"MISS HIKARI HANAZONO... PLEASE COME TO LONDON OVER AUTUMN BREAK."
THE UNEXPECTED LETTER FROM TAKISHIMA'S GRANDFATHER CONTAINED THIS MESSAGE AND A PLANE TICKET FOR THE NEXT DAY.
This is for tomorrow!!
MISS HANAZONO, PLEASE COME WITH ME.

•COVER AND THIS AND THAT•

- KEI AND FINN ARE ON THE COVER THIS TIME. THE CHARACTER OF FINN APPEARS FOR THE FIRST TIME IN THIS ISSUE. BY THE WAY, IT TURNS OUT THAT "FINN" MEANS "WHITE." HA HA! THE FLOWERS ON THE COVER ARE ANEMONES AND THEY'RE ONE OF MY FAVORITE FLOWERS. I LIKE THE PERSIAN BUTTERCUPS AND CHINESE PEONIES TOO. FLOWERS ARE GREAT!

- THIS ISSUE ALSO INCLUDES A SHORT MANGA ABOUT YAHIRO AND SAKURA. I HOPE YOU ENJOY IT!

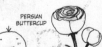

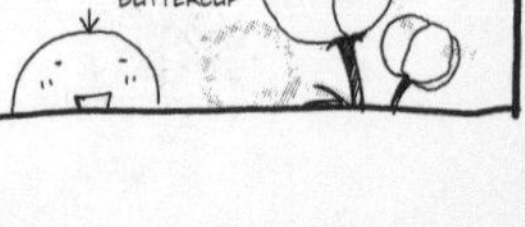
PERSIAN BUTTERCUP

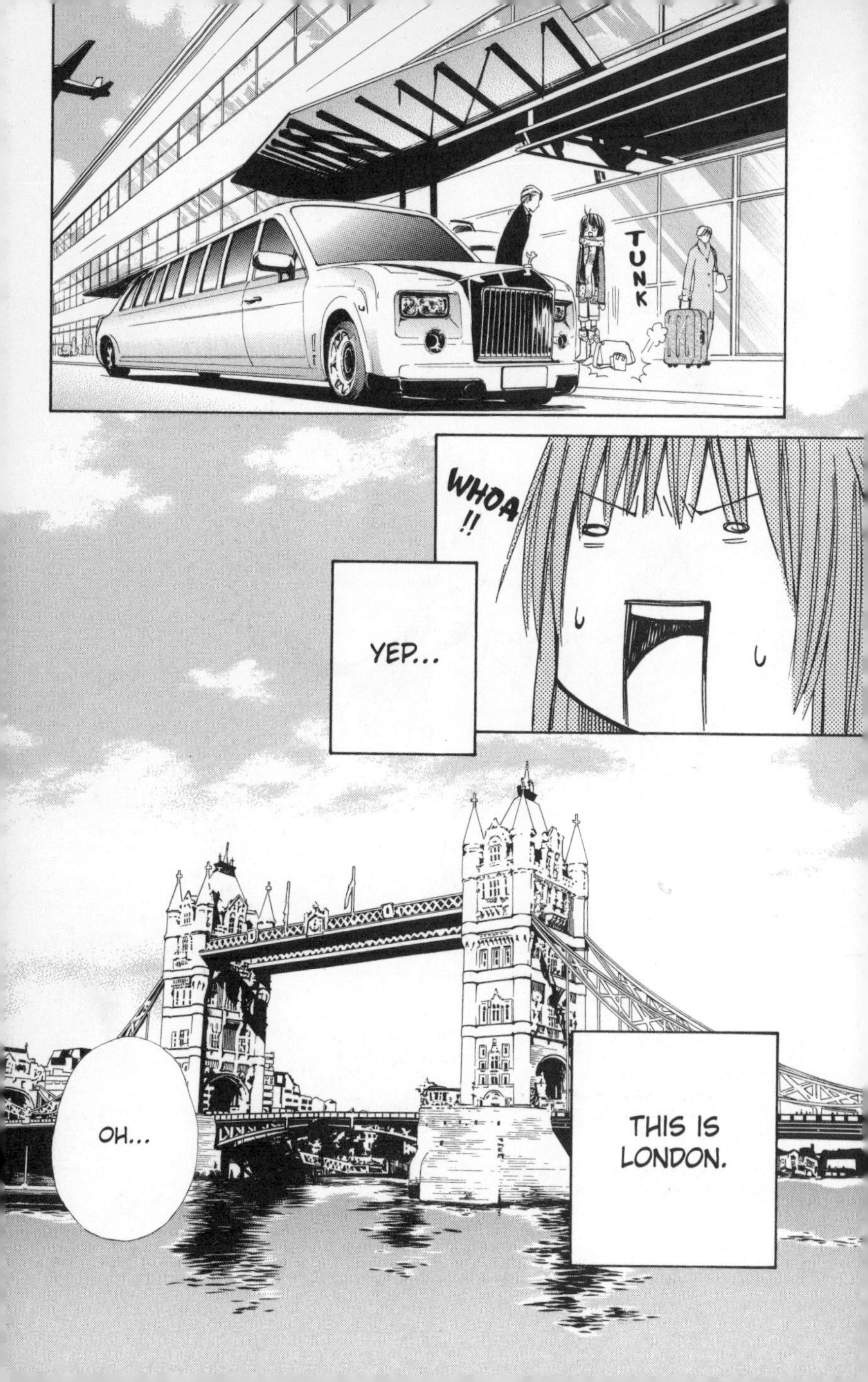
TUNK
WHOA!!
YEP...
THIS IS LONDON.
OH...

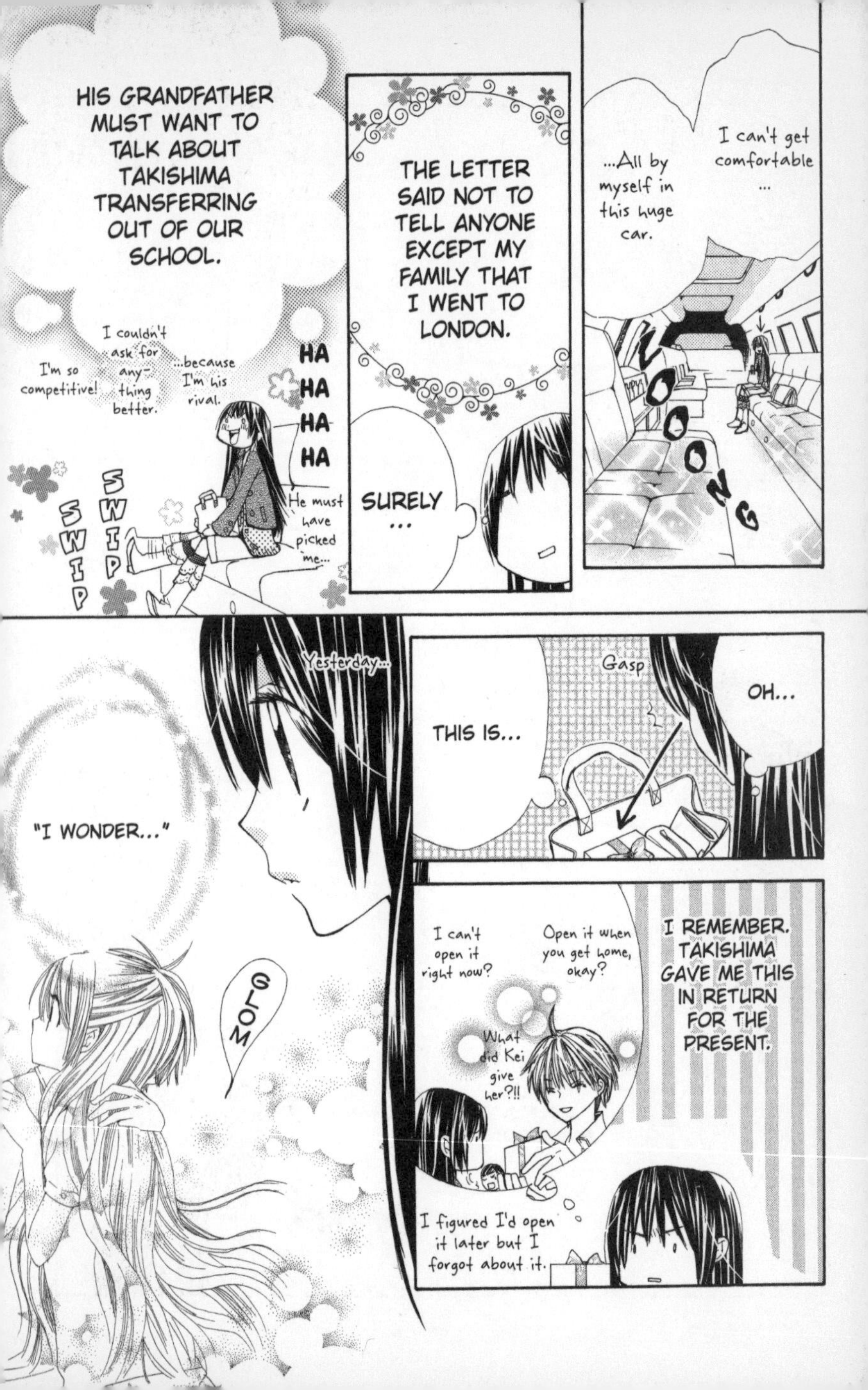
I can't get comfortable...
...All by myself in this huge car.
VOOONG
THE LETTER SAID NOT TO TELL ANYONE EXCEPT MY FAMILY THAT I WENT TO LONDON.
SURELY...
HIS GRANDFATHER MUST WANT TO TALK ABOUT TAKISHIMA TRANSFERRING OUT OF OUR SCHOOL.
HA HA HA HA
...because I'm his rival.
I couldn't ask for anything better.
I'm so competitive!
He must have picked me...
SWIP
SWIP
OH...
Gasp
THIS IS...
I REMEMBER. TAKISHIMA GAVE ME THIS IN RETURN FOR THE PRESENT.
Open it when you get home, okay?
I can't open it right now?
What did Kei give her?!!
I figured I'd open it later but I forgot about it.
Yesterday...
"I WONDER..."
GLOM

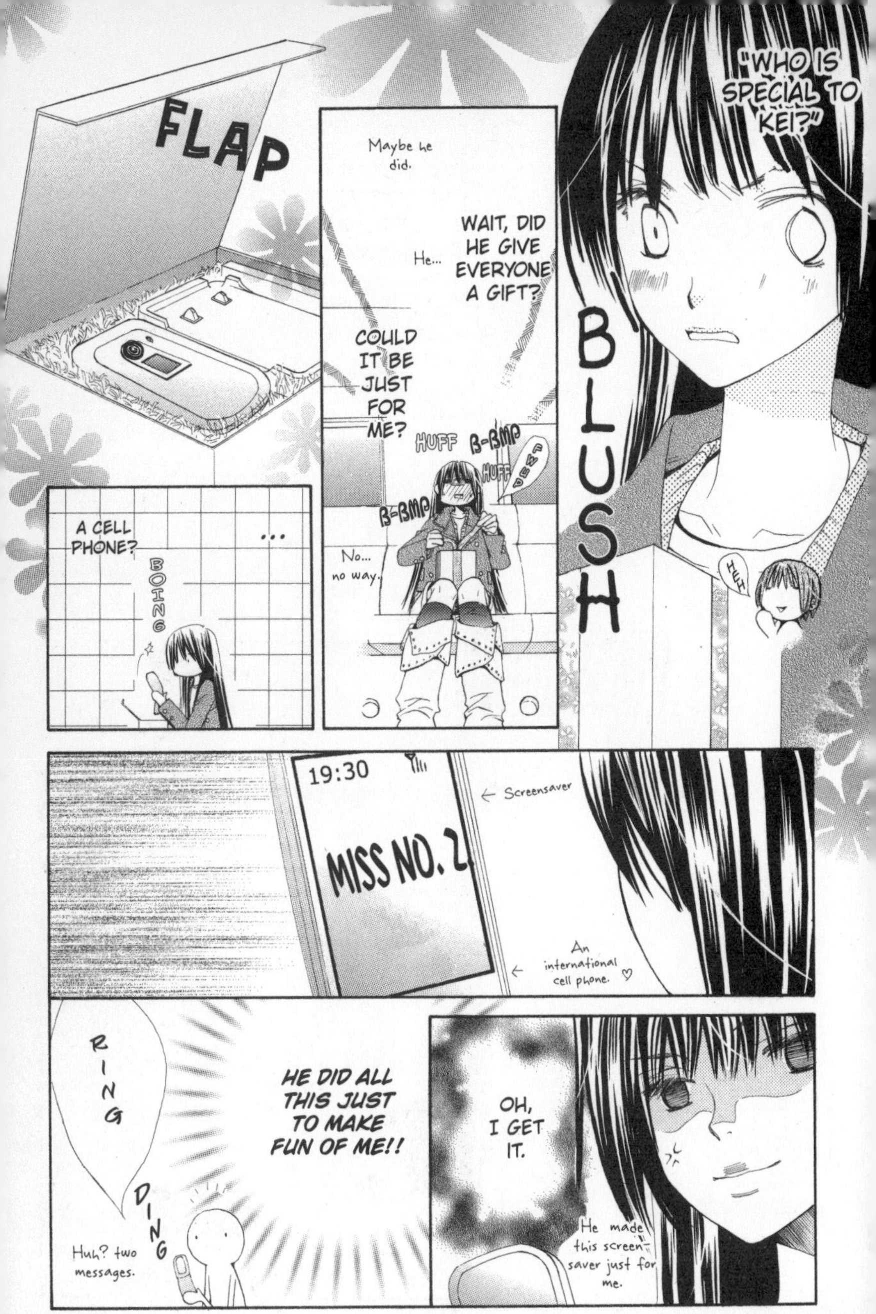
"WHO IS SPECIAL TO KEI?"
BLUSH
HEH
WAIT, DID HE GIVE EVERYONE A GIFT?
He...
Maybe he did.
COULD IT BE JUST FOR ME?
HUFF
B-BMP
HUFF
FWEP
B-BMP
No... no way.
FLAP
...
A CELL PHONE?
BOING
19:30
MISS NO. 2
← Screensaver
← An international cell phone. ♡
OH, I GET IT.
He made this screensaver just for me.
HE DID ALL THIS JUST TO MAKE FUN OF ME!!
RING
DING
Huh? two messages.

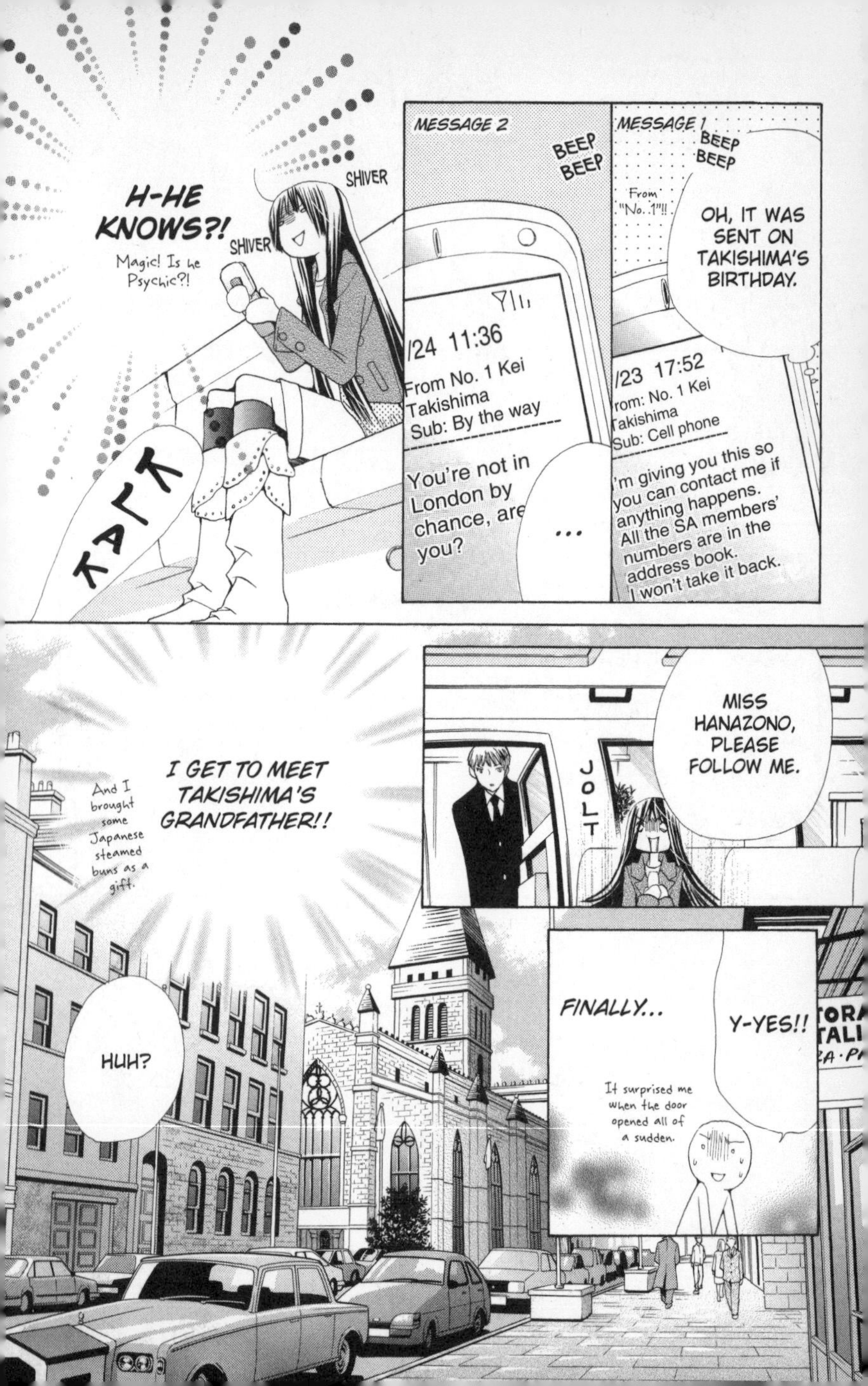

MESSAGE 1
BEEP BEEP
From "No. 1"!!
OH, IT WAS SENT ON TAKISHIMA'S BIRTHDAY.
/23 17:52
rom: No. 1 Kei
akishima
Sub: Cell phone
'm giving you this so you can contact me if anything happens. All the SA members' numbers are in the address book. I won't take it back.
MESSAGE 2
BEEP BEEP
/24 11:36
From No. 1 Kei Takishima
Sub: By the way
You're not in London by chance, are you?
...
SHIVER
SHIVER
H-HE KNOWS?!
Magic! Is he Psychic?!
TALK
MISS HANAZONO, PLEASE FOLLOW ME.
JOLT
Y-YES!!
FINALLY...
It surprised me when the door opened all of a sudden.
I GET TO MEET TAKISHIMA'S GRANDFATHER!!
And I brought some Japanese steamed buns as a gift.
HUH?

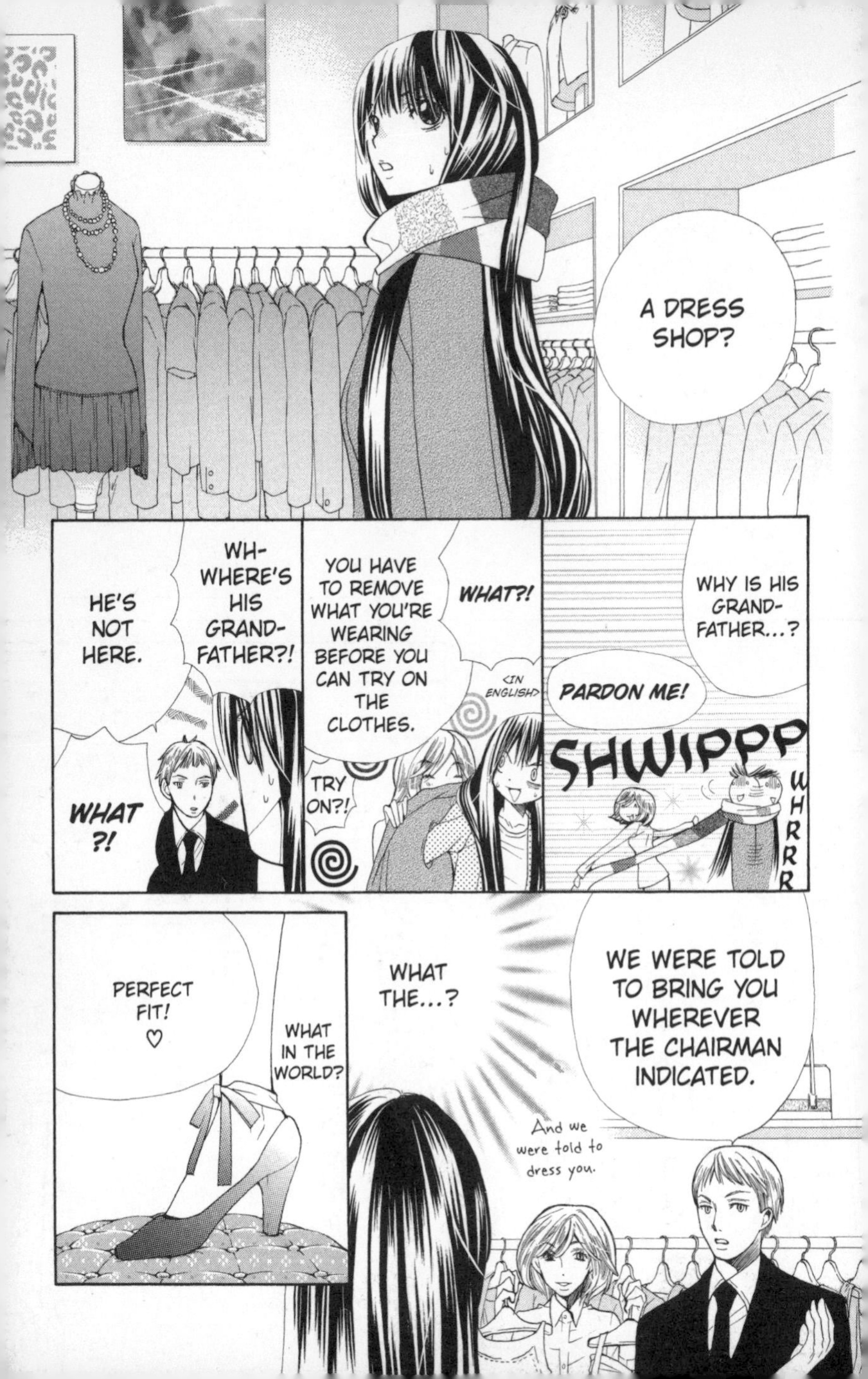
A DRESS SHOP?
WHY IS HIS GRAND-FATHER...?
PARDON ME!
SHWIPPP
WHRRR
WHAT?!
<IN ENGLISH>
YOU HAVE TO REMOVE WHAT YOU'RE WEARING BEFORE YOU CAN TRY ON THE CLOTHES.
TRY ON?!
WH- WHERE'S HIS GRAND-FATHER?!
HE'S NOT HERE.
WHAT ?!
WE WERE TOLD TO BRING YOU WHEREVER THE CHAIRMAN INDICATED.
And we were told to dress you.
WHAT THE...?
WHAT IN THE WORLD?
PERFECT FIT! ♡

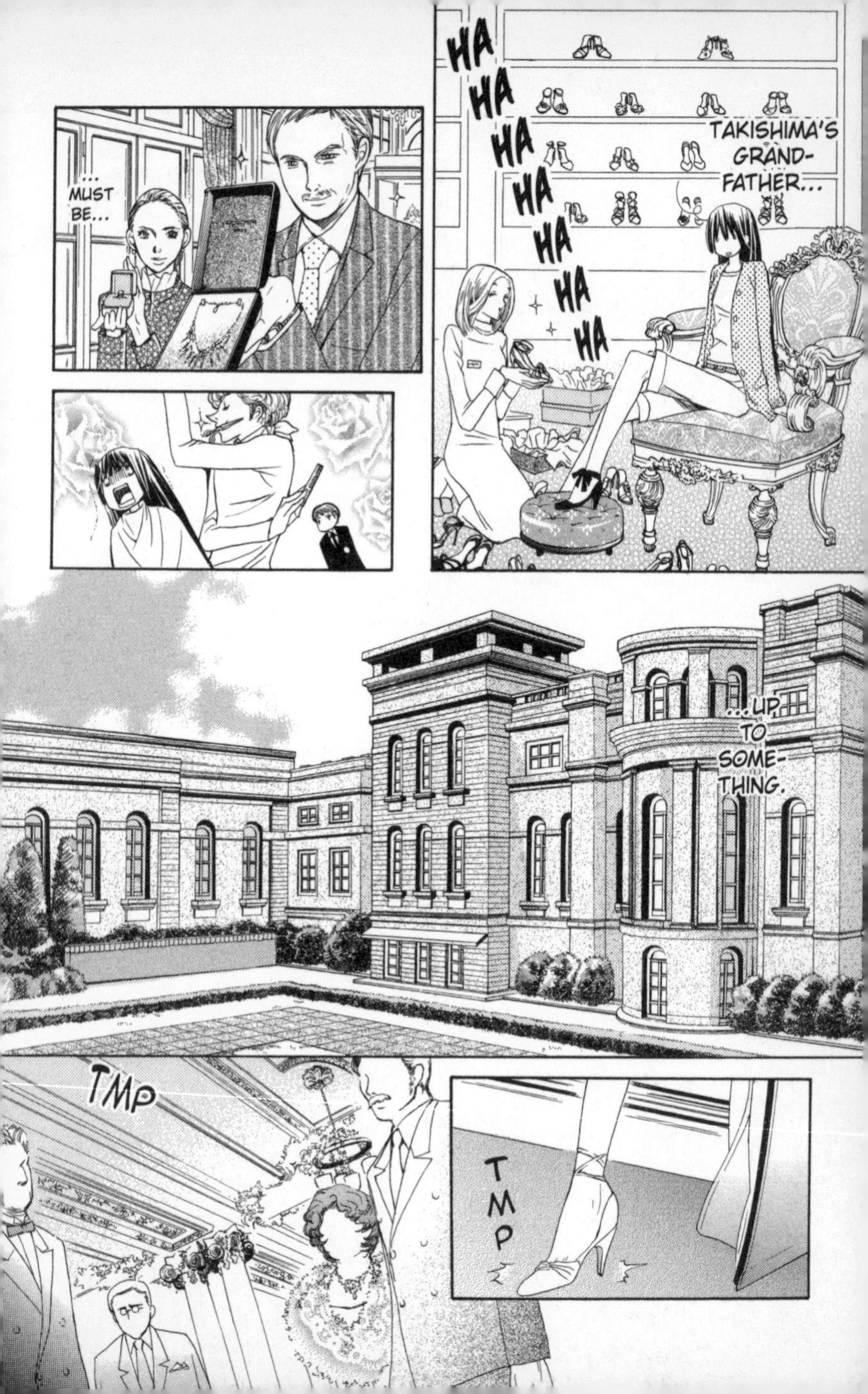
HA HA HA HA HA HA HA
TAKISHIMA'S GRAND-FATHER...
...MUST BE...
...UP TO SOME-THING.
TMP
TMp

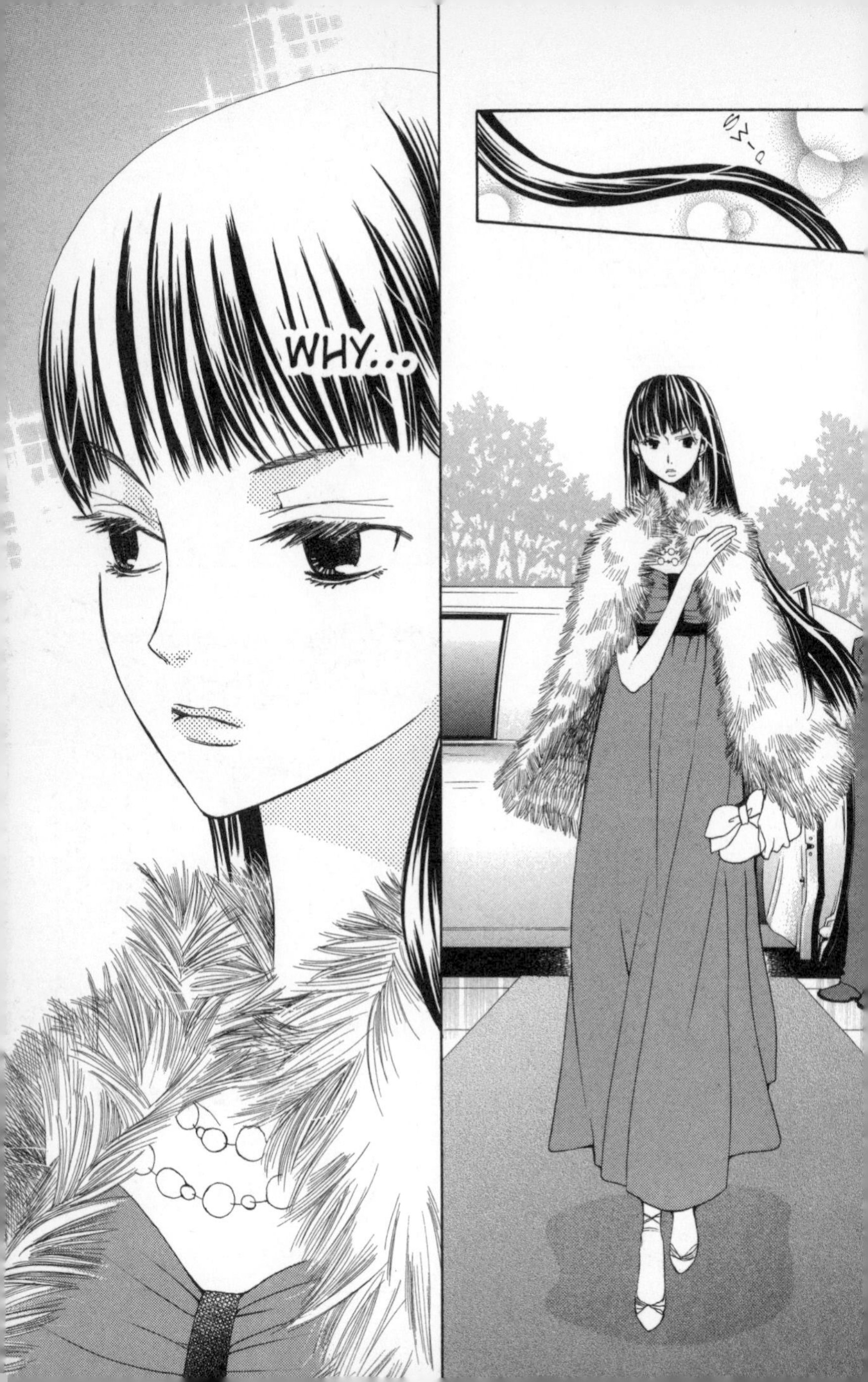
WHY...

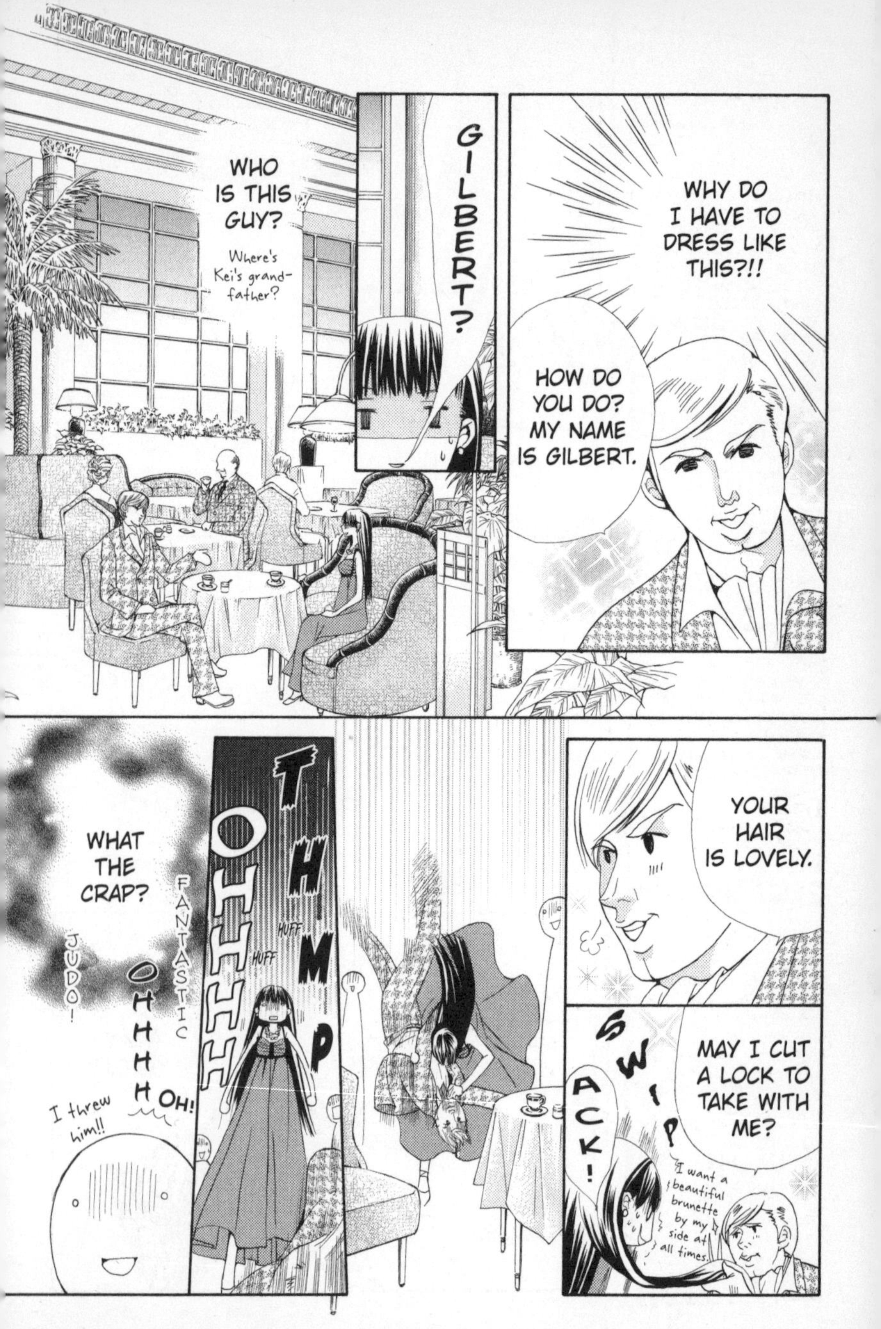
WHY DO I HAVE TO DRESS LIKE THIS?!!
HOW DO YOU DO? MY NAME IS GILBERT.
GILBERT?
WHO IS THIS GUY?
Where's Kei's grand-father?
YOUR HAIR IS LOVELY.
MAY I CUT A LOCK TO TAKE WITH ME?
SWIP
ACK!
I want a beautiful brunette by my side at all times.
THUMP
OHHHHH
HUFF
HUFF
WHAT THE CRAP?
FANTASTIC
JUDO!
OHHHHH OH!
I threw him!!

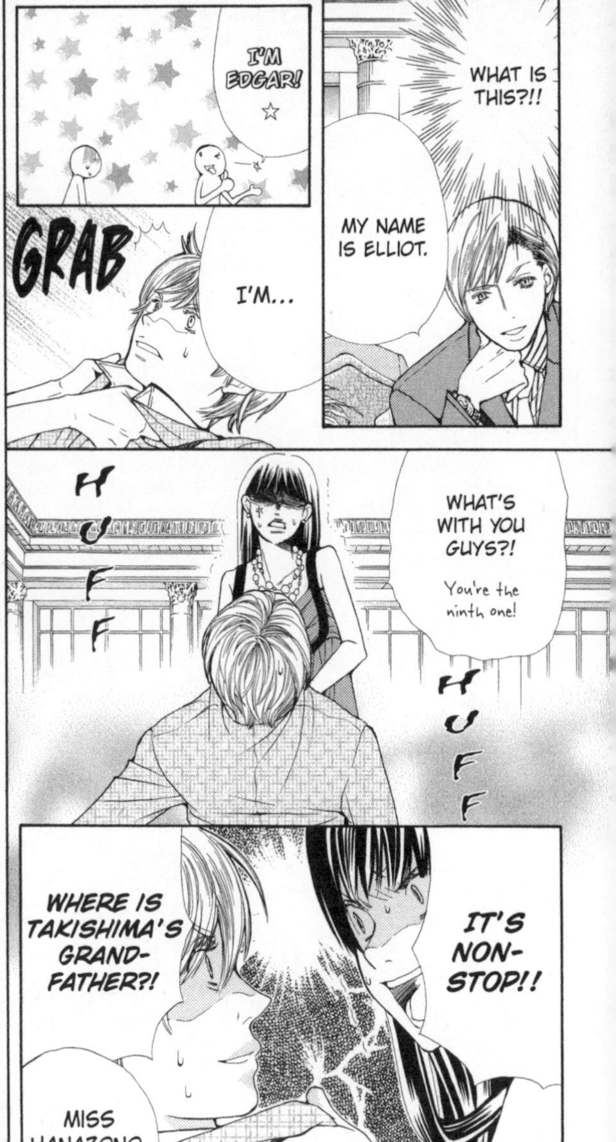
WHAT IS THIS?!!
MY NAME IS ELLIOT.
I'M EDGAR! ☆
GRAB
I'M...
WHAT'S WITH YOU GUYS?!
You're the ninth one!
HUFF
HUFF
IT'S NON-STOP!!
WHERE IS TAKISHIMA'S GRANDFATHER?!
MISS HANAZONO.

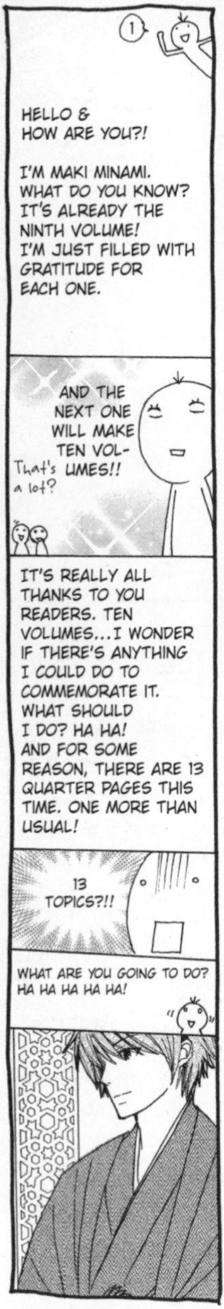
1
HELLO & HOW ARE YOU?!
I'M MAKI MINAMI. WHAT DO YOU KNOW? IT'S ALREADY THE NINTH VOLUME! I'M JUST FILLED WITH GRATITUDE FOR EACH ONE.
AND THE NEXT ONE WILL MAKE TEN VOLUMES!!
That's a lot?
IT'S REALLY ALL THANKS TO YOU READERS. TEN VOLUMES...I WONDER IF THERE'S ANYTHING I COULD DO TO COMMEMORATE IT. WHAT SHOULD I DO? HA HA! AND FOR SOME REASON, THERE ARE 13 QUARTER PAGES THIS TIME. ONE MORE THAN USUAL!
13 TOPICS?!!
WHAT ARE YOU GOING TO DO? HA HA HA HA HA!

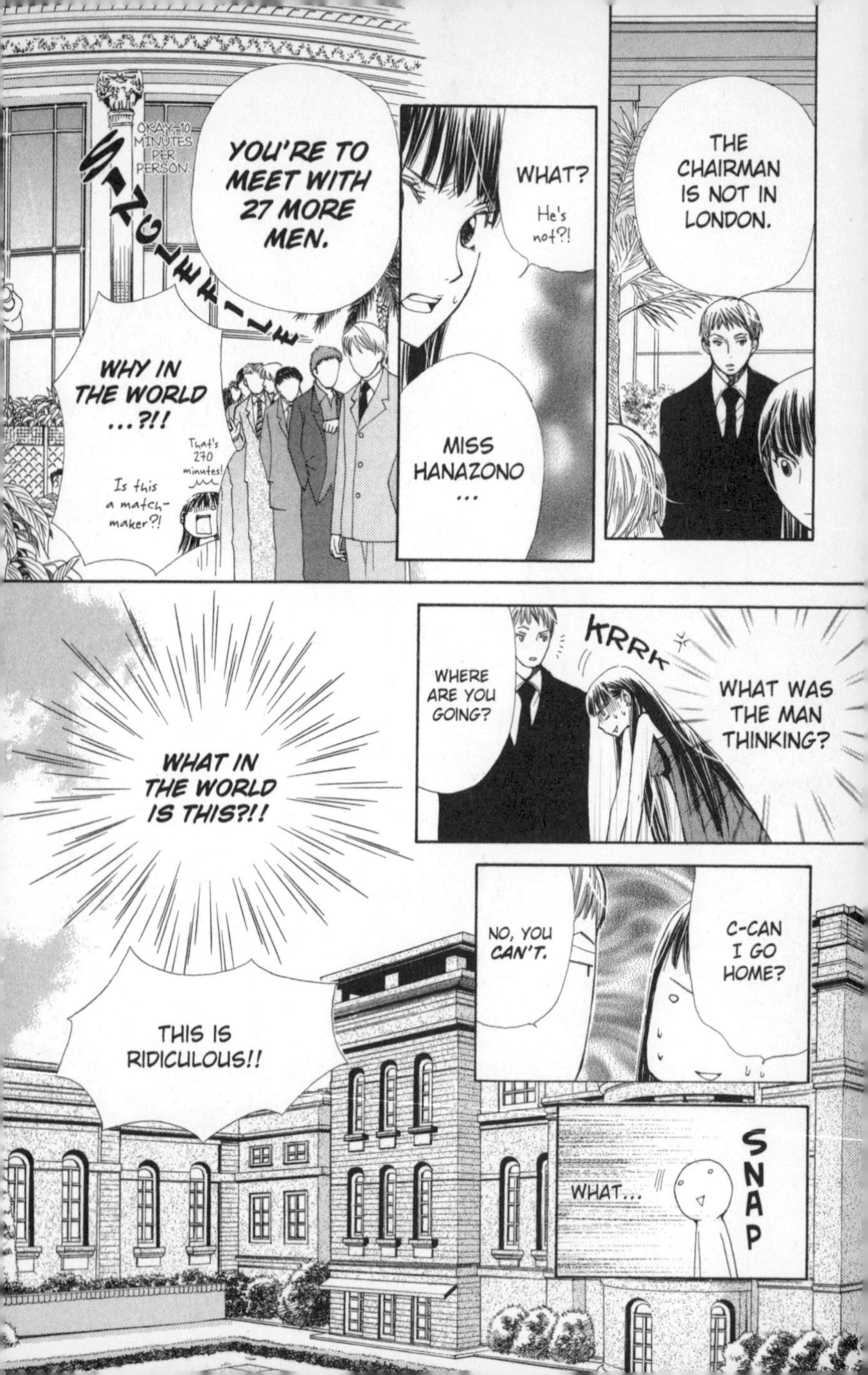
THE CHAIRMAN IS NOT IN LONDON.
WHAT?
He's not?!
MISS HANAZONO ...
YOU'RE TO MEET WITH 27 MORE MEN.
OKAY—10 MINUTES PER PERSON.
WHY IN THE WORLD ...?!!
That's 270 minutes!
Is this a match-maker?!
WHAT WAS THE MAN THINKING?
KRRK
WHERE ARE YOU GOING?
WHAT IN THE WORLD IS THIS?!!
C-CAN I GO HOME?
NO, YOU CAN'T.
SNAP
WHAT...
THIS IS RIDICULOUS!!

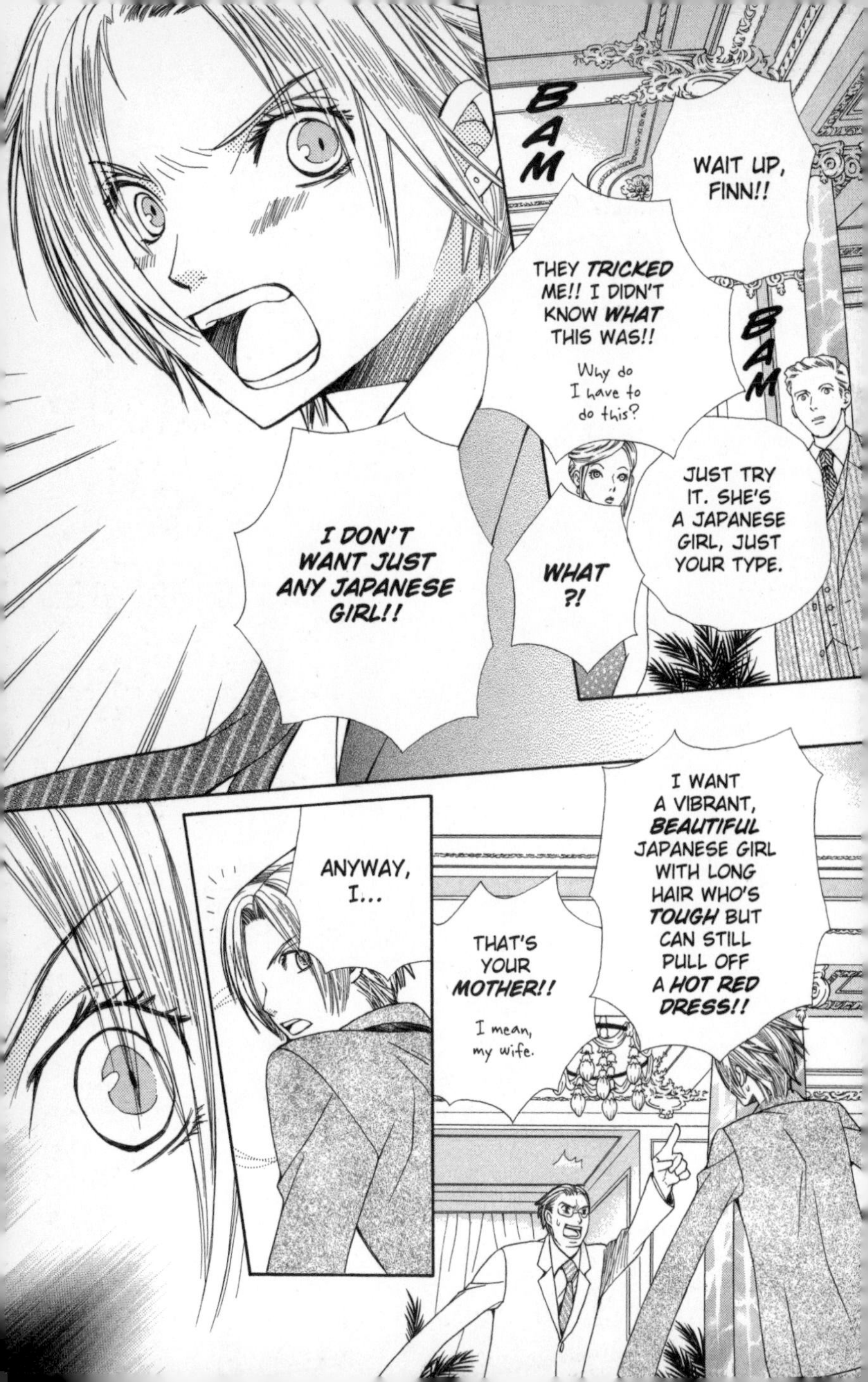
BAM
WAIT UP, FINN!!
THEY TRICKED ME!! I DIDN'T KNOW WHAT THIS WAS!!
Why do I have to do this?
BAM
JUST TRY IT. SHE'S A JAPANESE GIRL, JUST YOUR TYPE.
WHAT?!
I DON'T WANT JUST ANY JAPANESE GIRL!!
I WANT A VIBRANT, BEAUTIFUL JAPANESE GIRL WITH LONG HAIR WHO'S TOUGH BUT CAN STILL PULL OFF A HOT RED DRESS!!
THAT'S YOUR MOTHER!!
I mean, my wife.
ANYWAY, I...

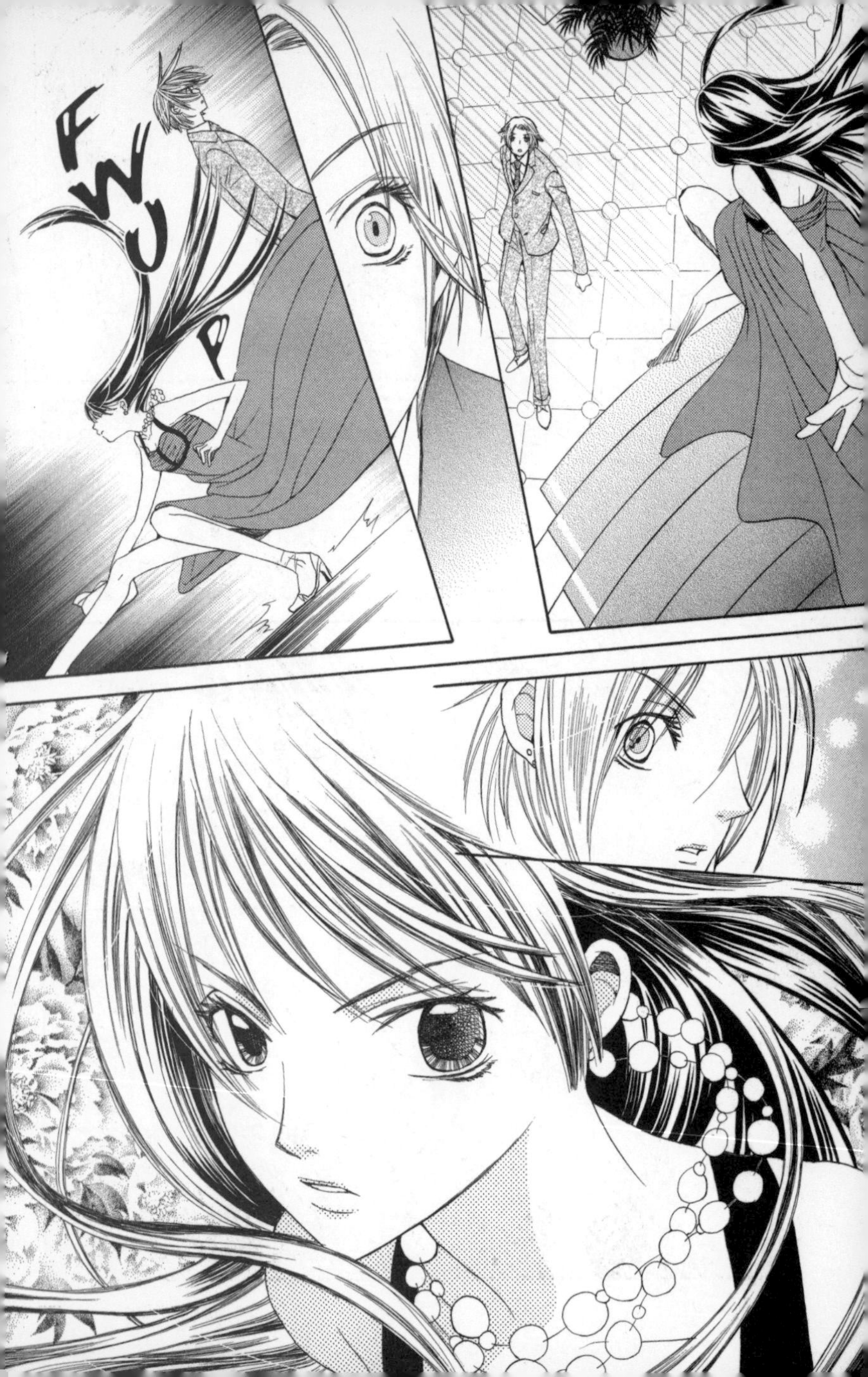
FWUP

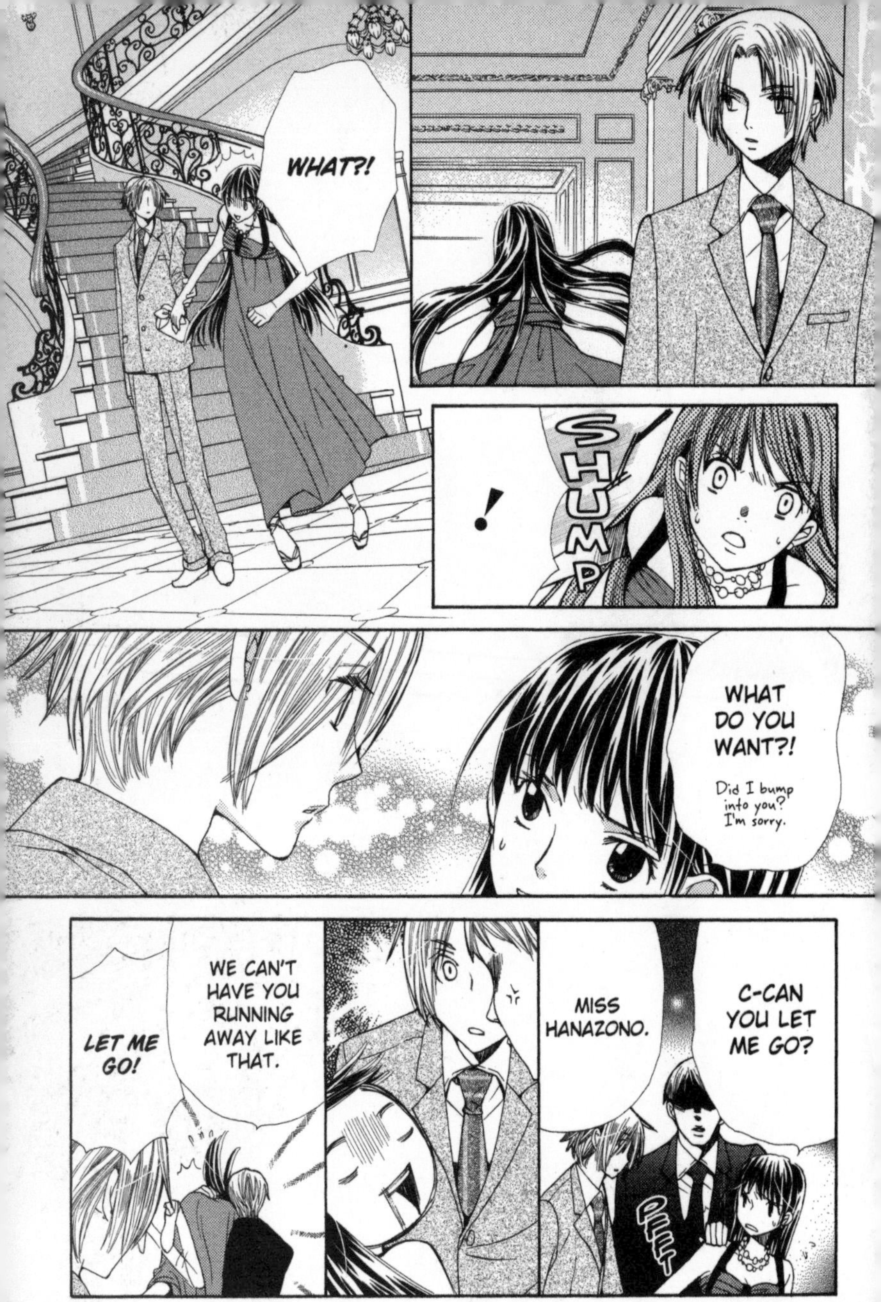
SHUMP
!
WHAT?!
WHAT DO YOU WANT?!
Did I bump into you? I'm sorry.
C-CAN YOU LET ME GO?
MISS HANAZONO.
WE CAN'T HAVE YOU RUNNING AWAY LIKE THAT.
LET ME GO!

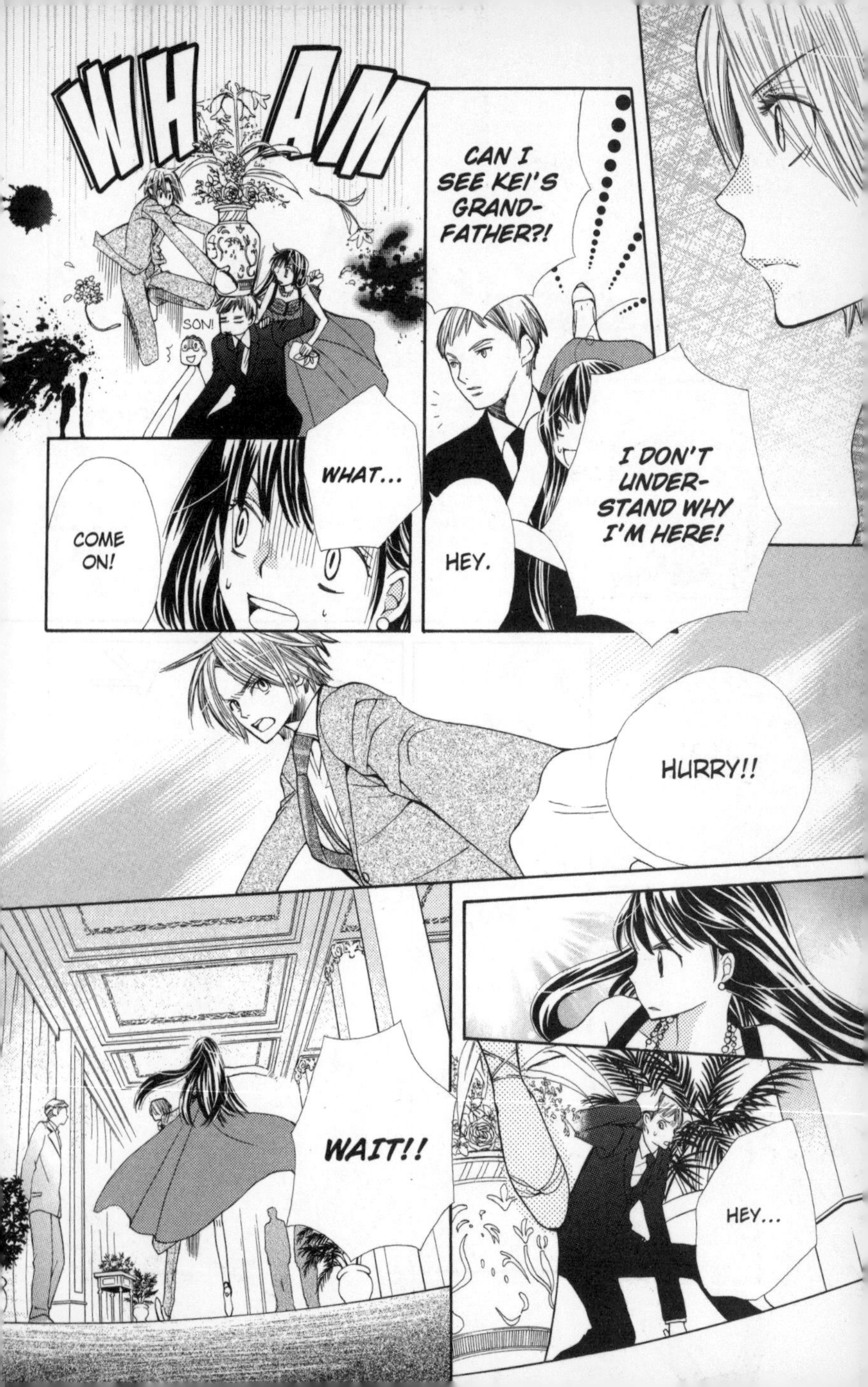

I DON'T UNDERSTAND WHY I'M HERE!
......
CAN I SEE KEI'S GRANDFATHER?!
HEY.
WHAM
SON!
WHAT...
COME ON!
HURRY!!
HEY...
WAIT!!

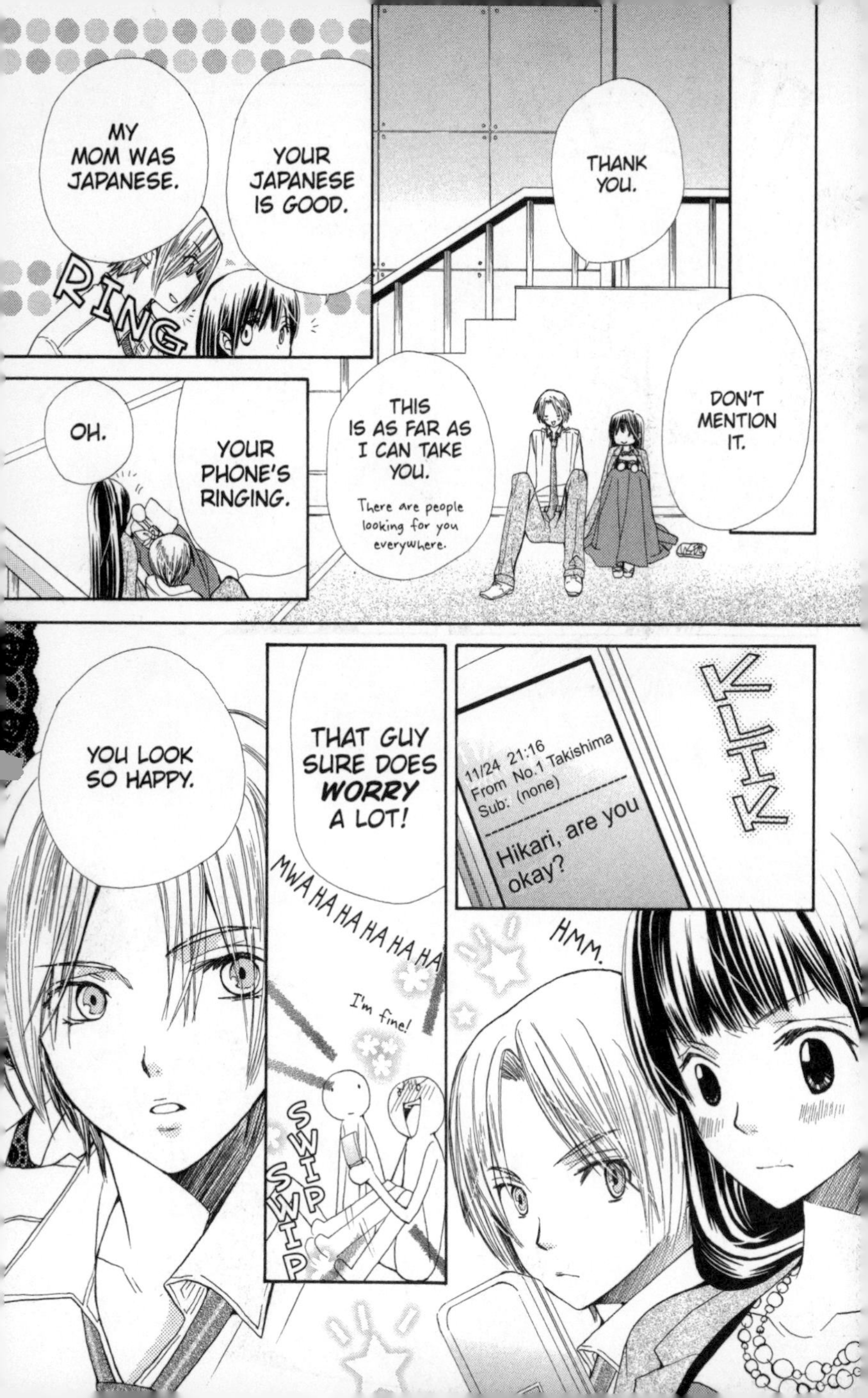
THANK YOU.
DON'T MENTION IT.
THIS IS AS FAR AS I CAN TAKE YOU.
There are people looking for you everywhere.
YOUR JAPANESE IS GOOD.
MY MOM WAS JAPANESE.
RING
YOUR PHONE'S RINGING.
OH.
KLIK
11/24 21:16
From No.1 Takishima
Sub: (none)
Hikari, are you okay?
HMM.
THAT GUY SURE DOES **WORRY** A LOT!
MWA HA HA HA HA HA HA
I'm fine!
SWIP SWIP
YOU LOOK SO HAPPY.

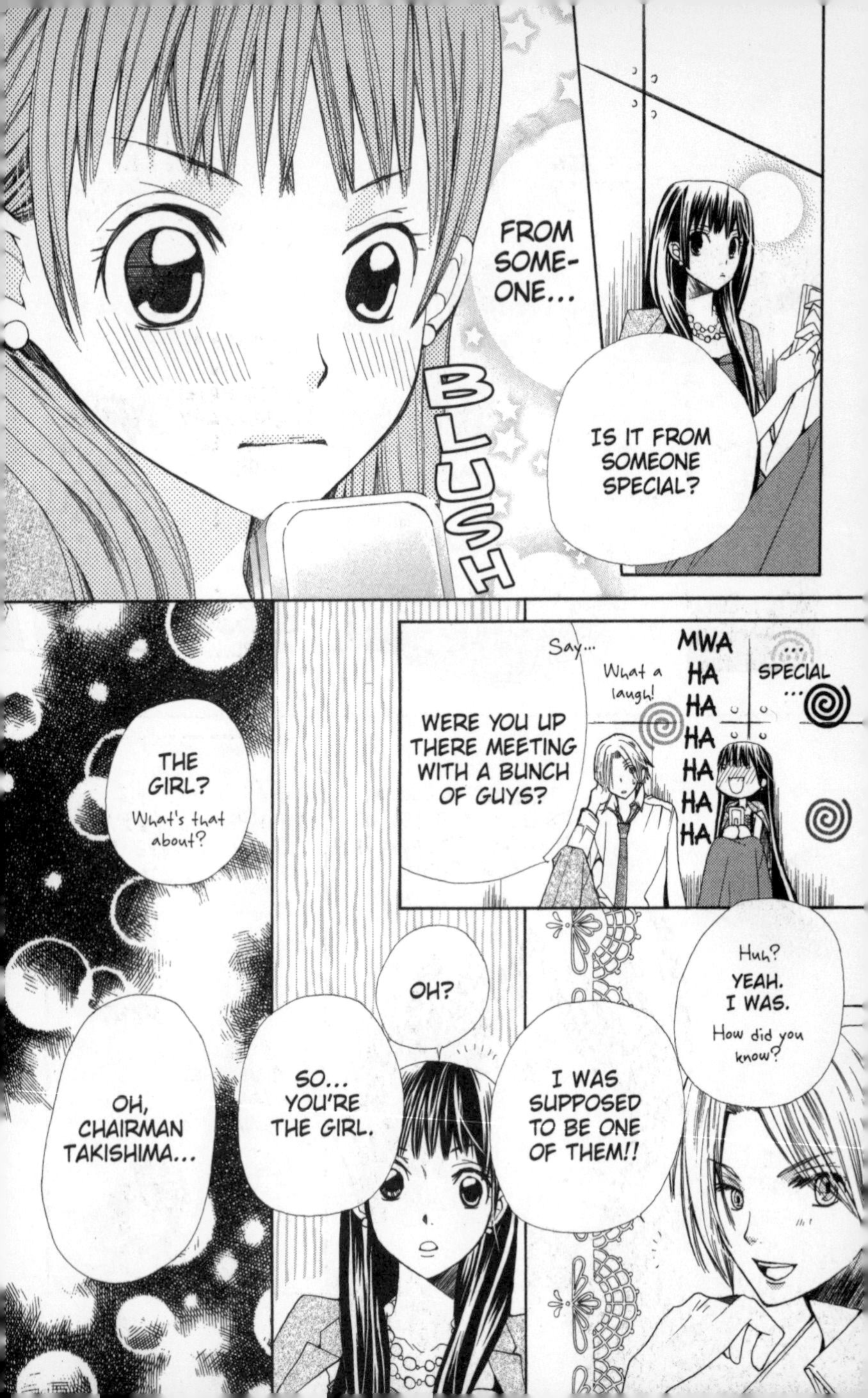
IS IT FROM SOMEONE SPECIAL?
FROM SOME-ONE...
BLUSH
SPECIAL...
MWA HA HA HA HA HA HA
What a laugh!
Say...
WERE YOU UP THERE MEETING WITH A BUNCH OF GUYS?
Huh? YEAH. I WAS. How did you know?
I WAS SUPPOSED TO BE ONE OF THEM!!
OH?
SO... YOU'RE THE GIRL.
THE GIRL? What's that about?
OH, CHAIRMAN TAKISHIMA...

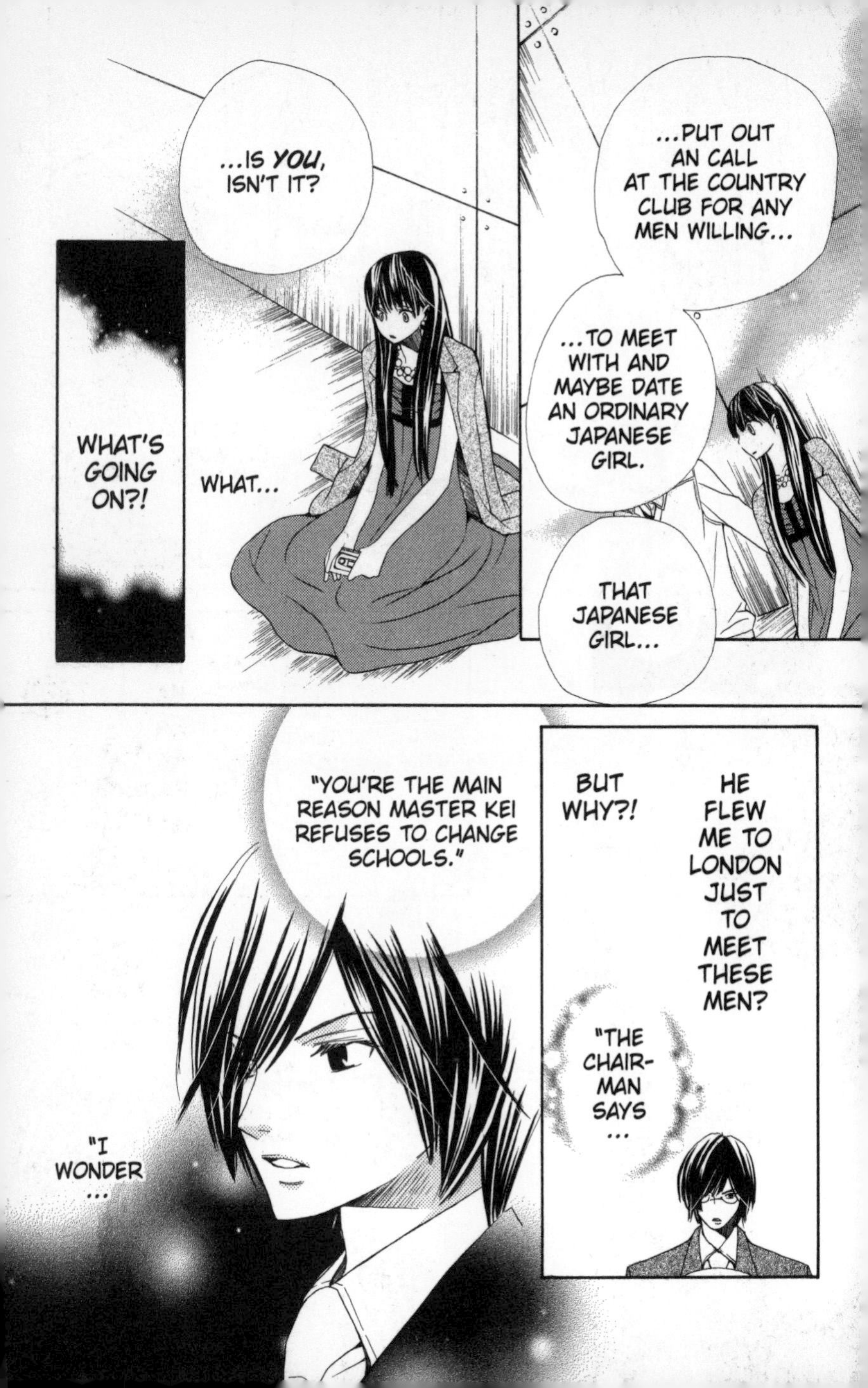
...PUT OUT AN CALL AT THE COUNTRY CLUB FOR ANY MEN WILLING...
...TO MEET WITH AND MAYBE DATE AN ORDINARY JAPANESE GIRL.
THAT JAPANESE GIRL...
...IS *YOU*, ISN'T IT?
WHAT...
WHAT'S GOING ON?!
HE FLEW ME TO LONDON JUST TO MEET THESE MEN?
BUT WHY?!
"THE CHAIR-MAN SAYS ...
"YOU'RE THE MAIN REASON MASTER KEI REFUSES TO CHANGE SCHOOLS."
"I WONDER ...

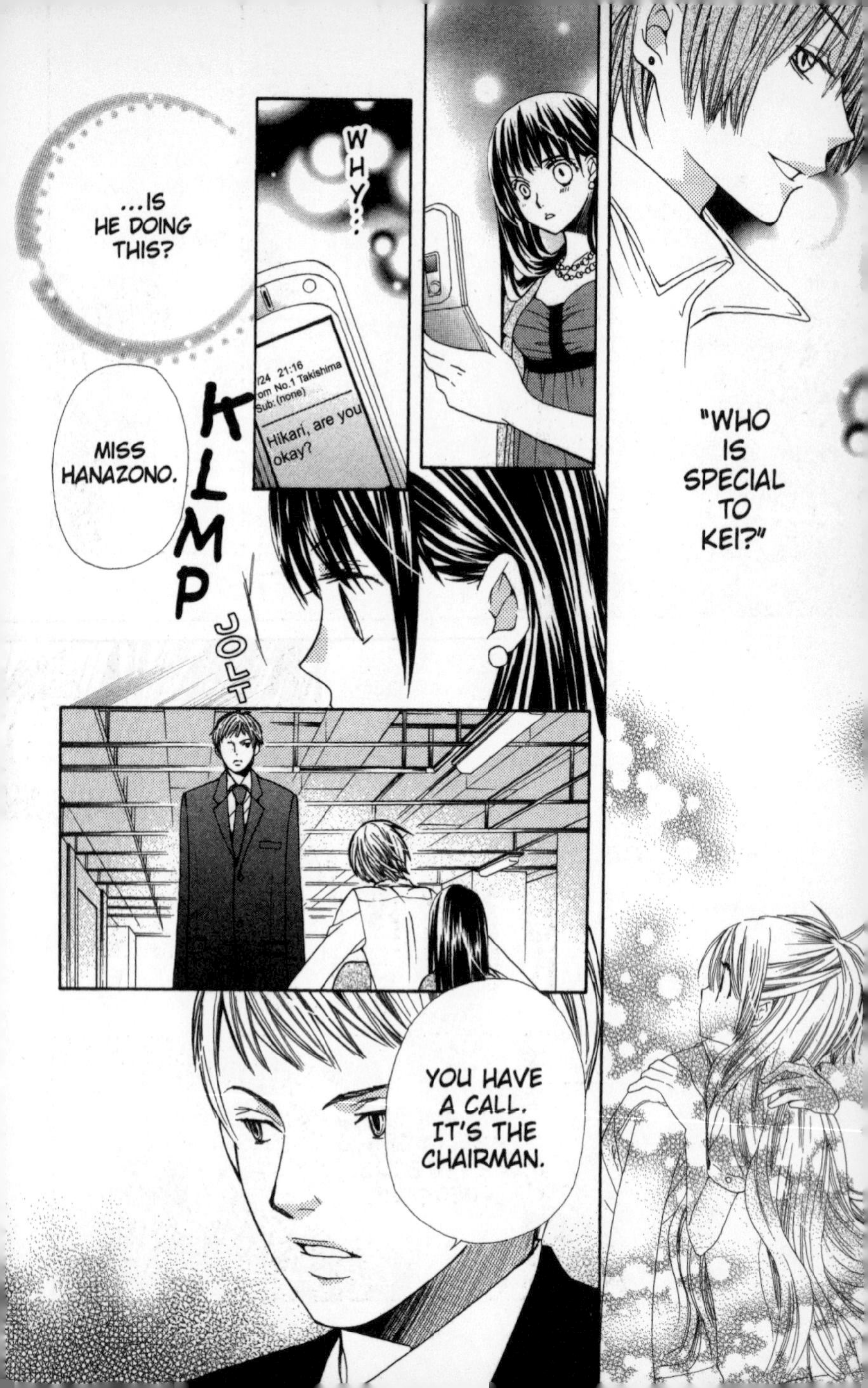
"WHO IS SPECIAL TO KEI?"
WHY...
/24 21:16
om No.1 Takishima
Sub: (none)
Hikari, are you okay?
...IS HE DOING THIS?
KLMP
MISS HANAZONO.
JOLT
YOU HAVE A CALL. IT'S THE CHAIRMAN.

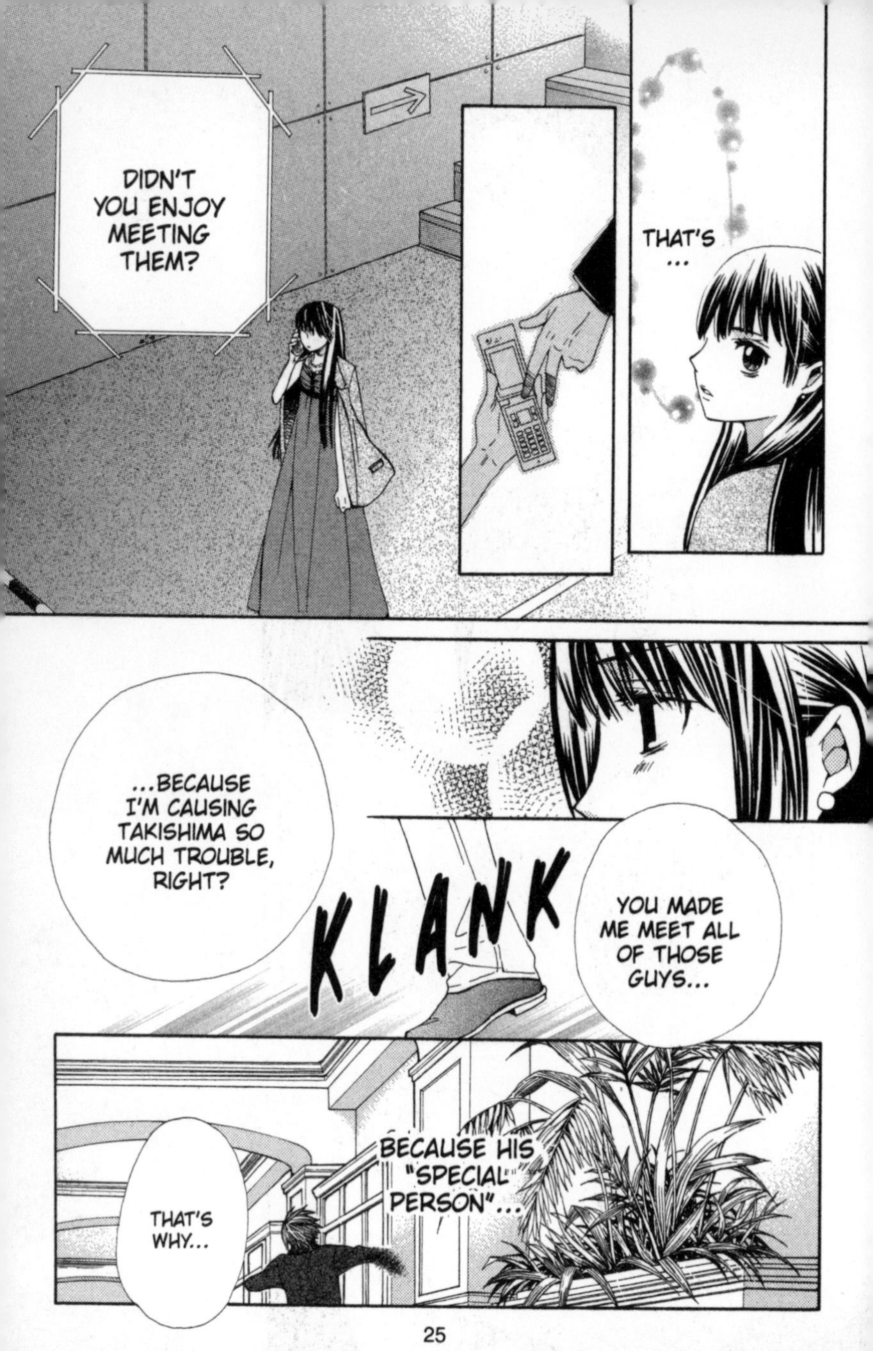
DIDN'T YOU ENJOY MEETING THEM?
THAT'S ...
YOU MADE ME MEET ALL OF THOSE GUYS...
KLANK
...BECAUSE I'M CAUSING TAKISHIMA SO MUCH TROUBLE, RIGHT?
BECAUSE HIS "SPECIAL PERSON"...
THAT'S WHY...

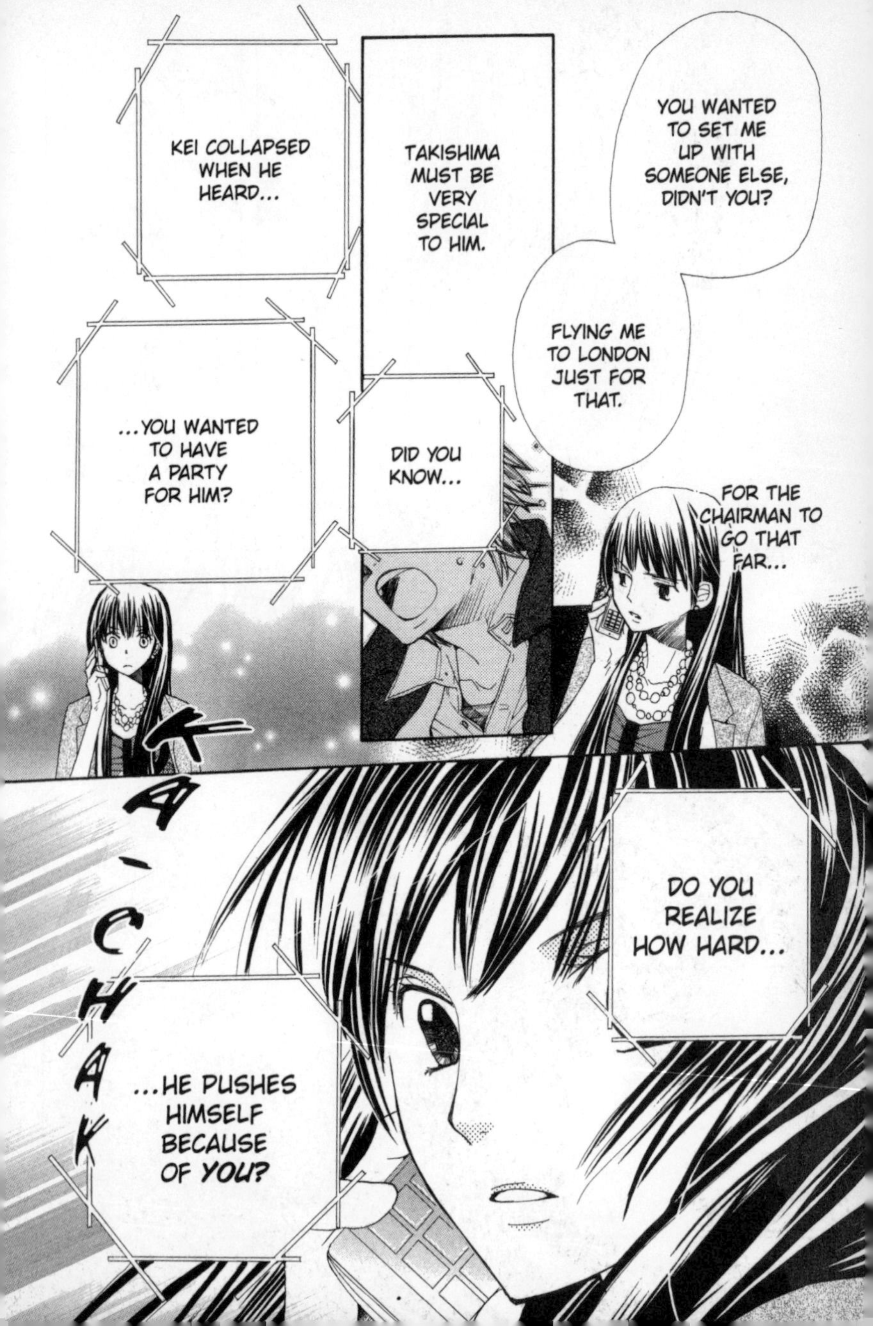
YOU WANTED TO SET ME UP WITH SOMEONE ELSE, DIDN'T YOU?
FLYING ME TO LONDON JUST FOR THAT.
FOR THE CHAIRMAN TO GO THAT FAR...
TAKISHIMA MUST BE VERY SPECIAL TO HIM.
DID YOU KNOW...
KEI COLLAPSED WHEN HE HEARD...
...YOU WANTED TO HAVE A PARTY FOR HIM?
K
DO YOU REALIZE HOW HARD...
...HE PUSHES HIMSELF BECAUSE OF *YOU*?
A-CHAK

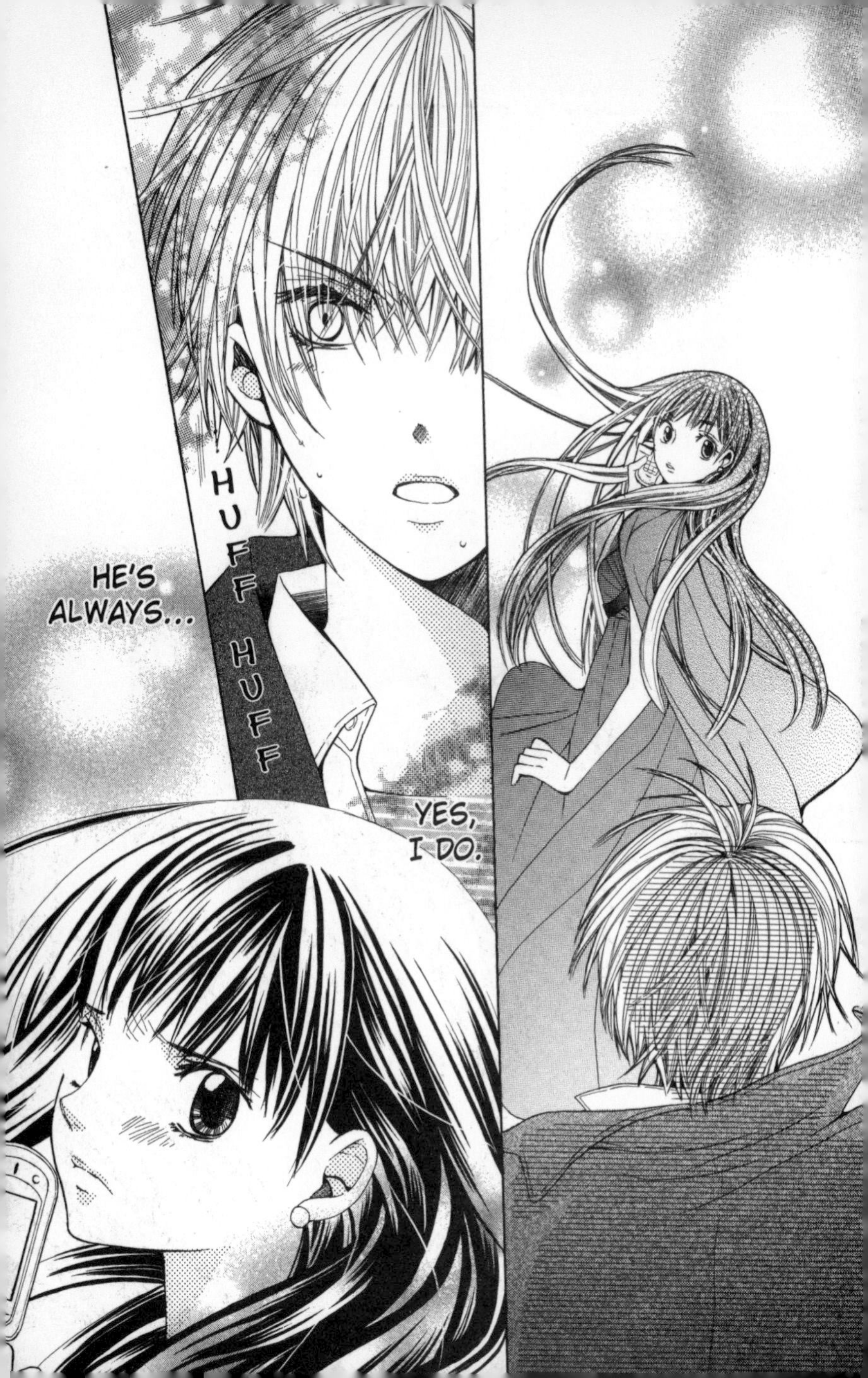
HUFF HUFF
HE'S ALWAYS...
YES, I DO.

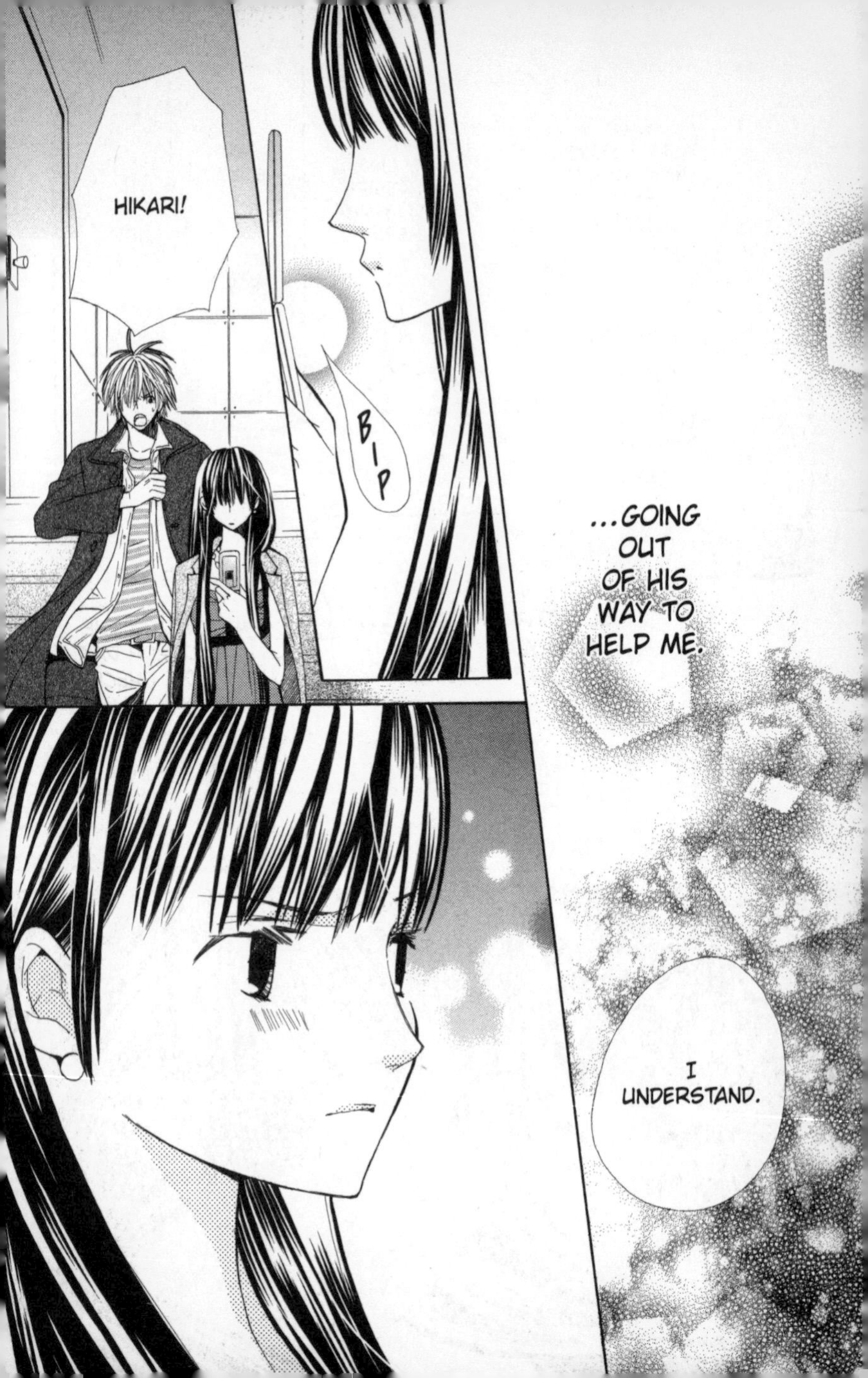
...GOING OUT OF HIS WAY TO HELP ME.
I UNDERSTAND.
BIP
HIKARI!

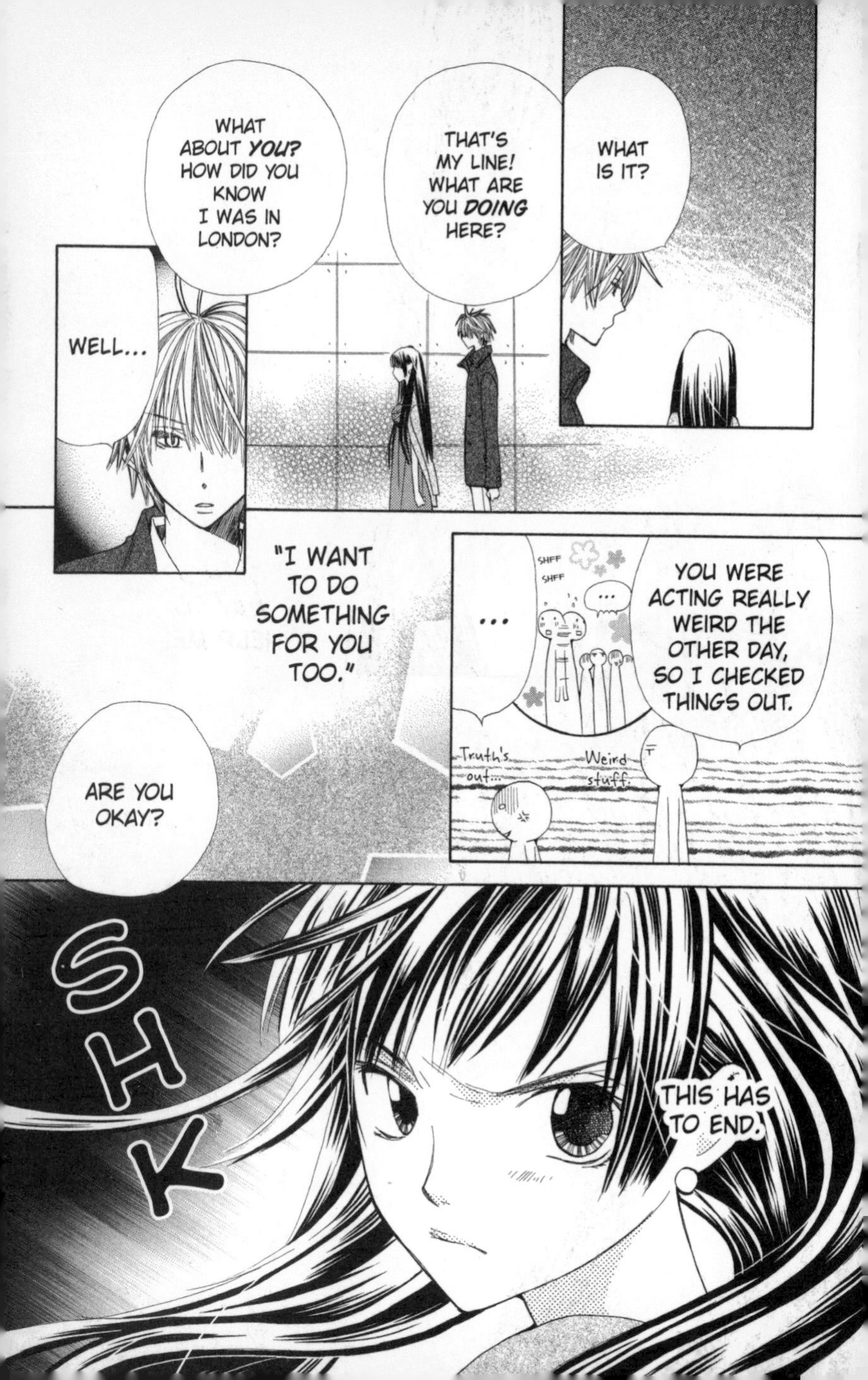
WHAT IS IT?
THAT'S MY LINE! WHAT ARE YOU DOING HERE?
WHAT ABOUT YOU? HOW DID YOU KNOW I WAS IN LONDON?
WELL...
YOU WERE ACTING REALLY WEIRD THE OTHER DAY, SO I CHECKED THINGS OUT.
SHFF
SHFF
...
...
Weird stuff.
Truth's out...
"I WANT TO DO SOMETHING FOR YOU TOO."
ARE YOU OKAY?
THIS HAS TO END.
SHK

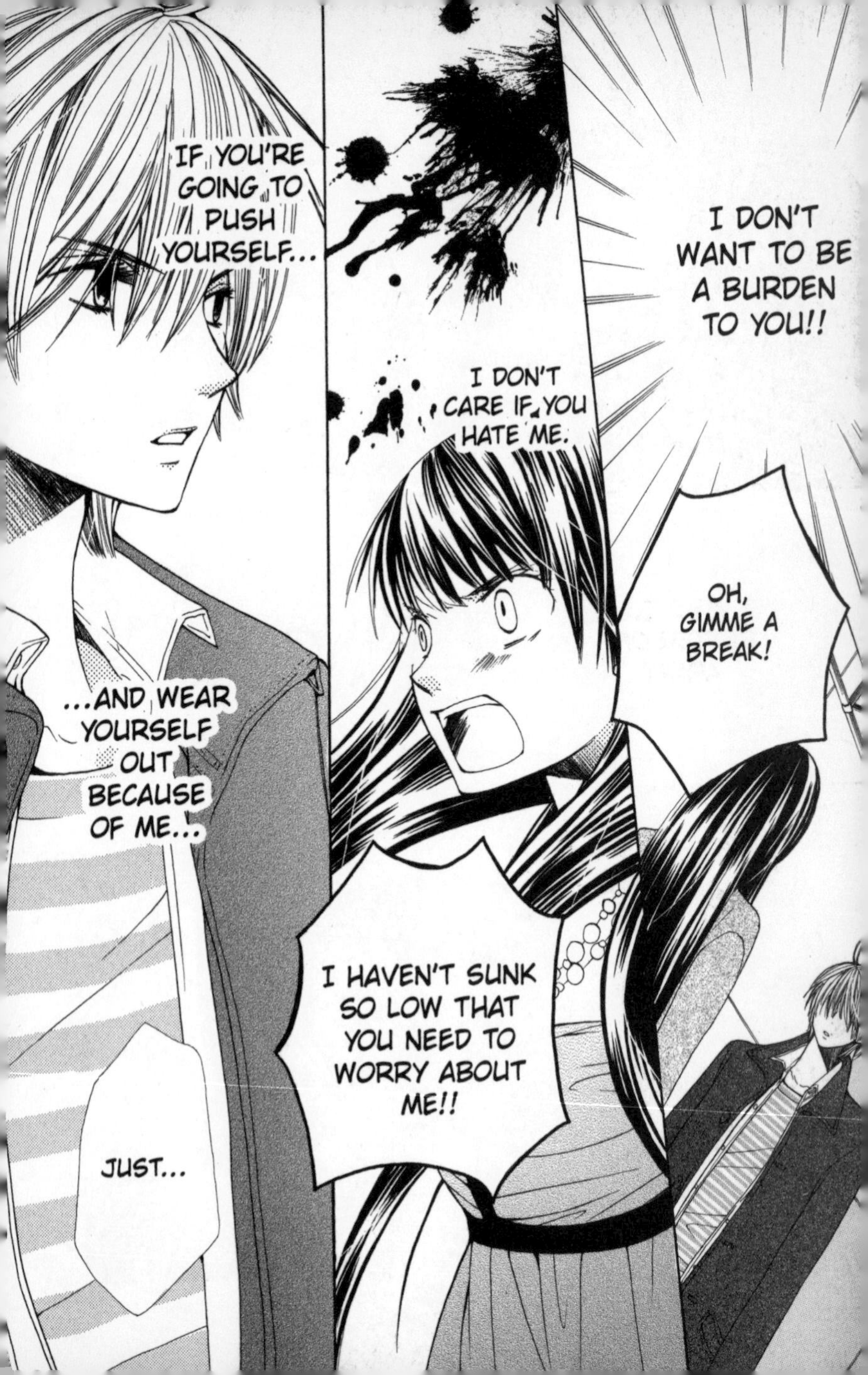
I DON'T WANT TO BE A BURDEN TO YOU!!
OH, GIMME A BREAK!
I DON'T CARE IF YOU HATE ME.
I HAVEN'T SUNK SO LOW THAT YOU NEED TO WORRY ABOUT ME!!
IF YOU'RE GOING TO PUSH YOURSELF...
...AND WEAR YOURSELF OUT BECAUSE OF ME...
JUST...

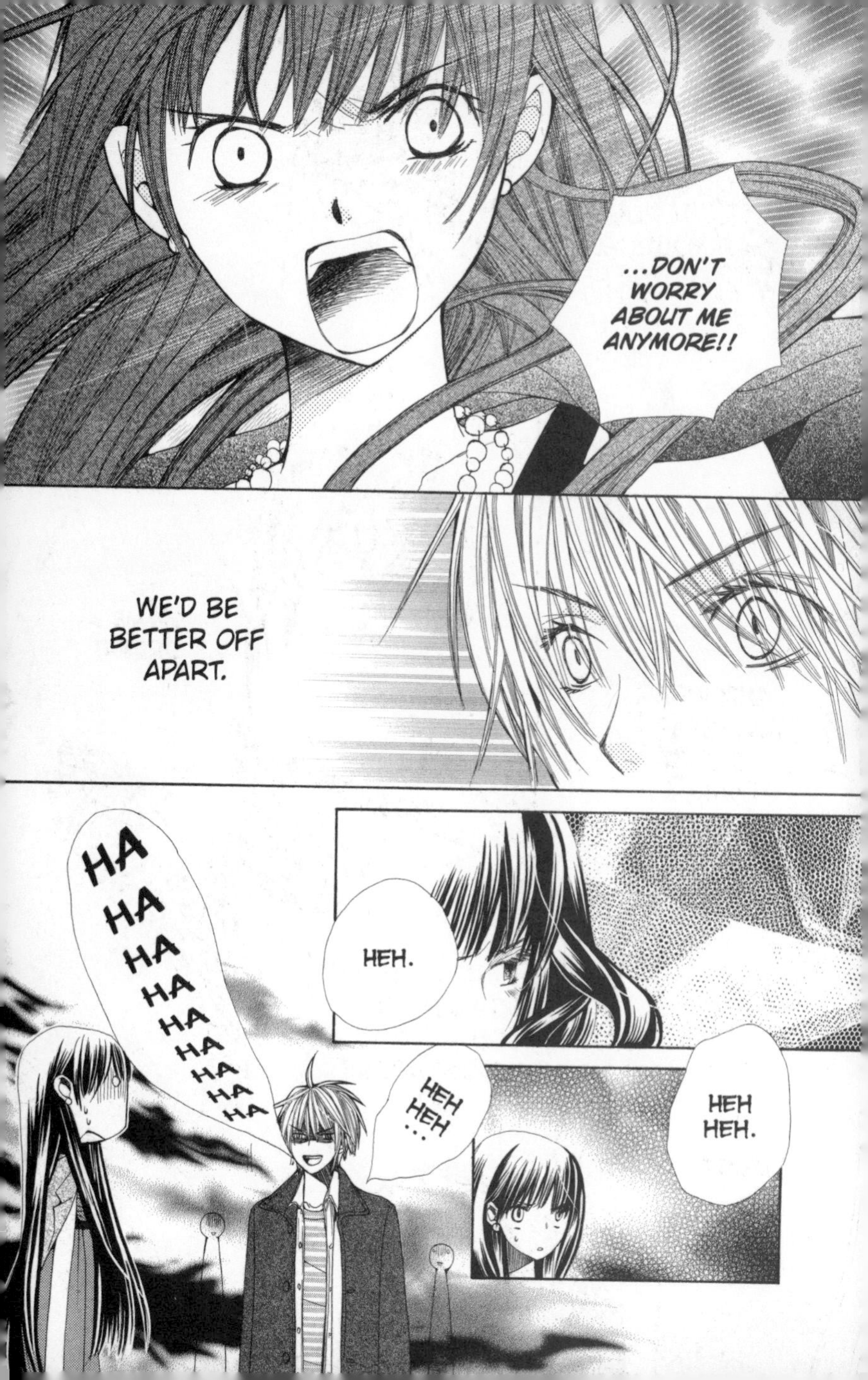
...DON'T WORRY ABOUT ME ANYMORE!!
WE'D BE BETTER OFF APART.
HEH.
HEH HEH.
HEH HEH...
HA HA HA HA HA HA HA HA HA

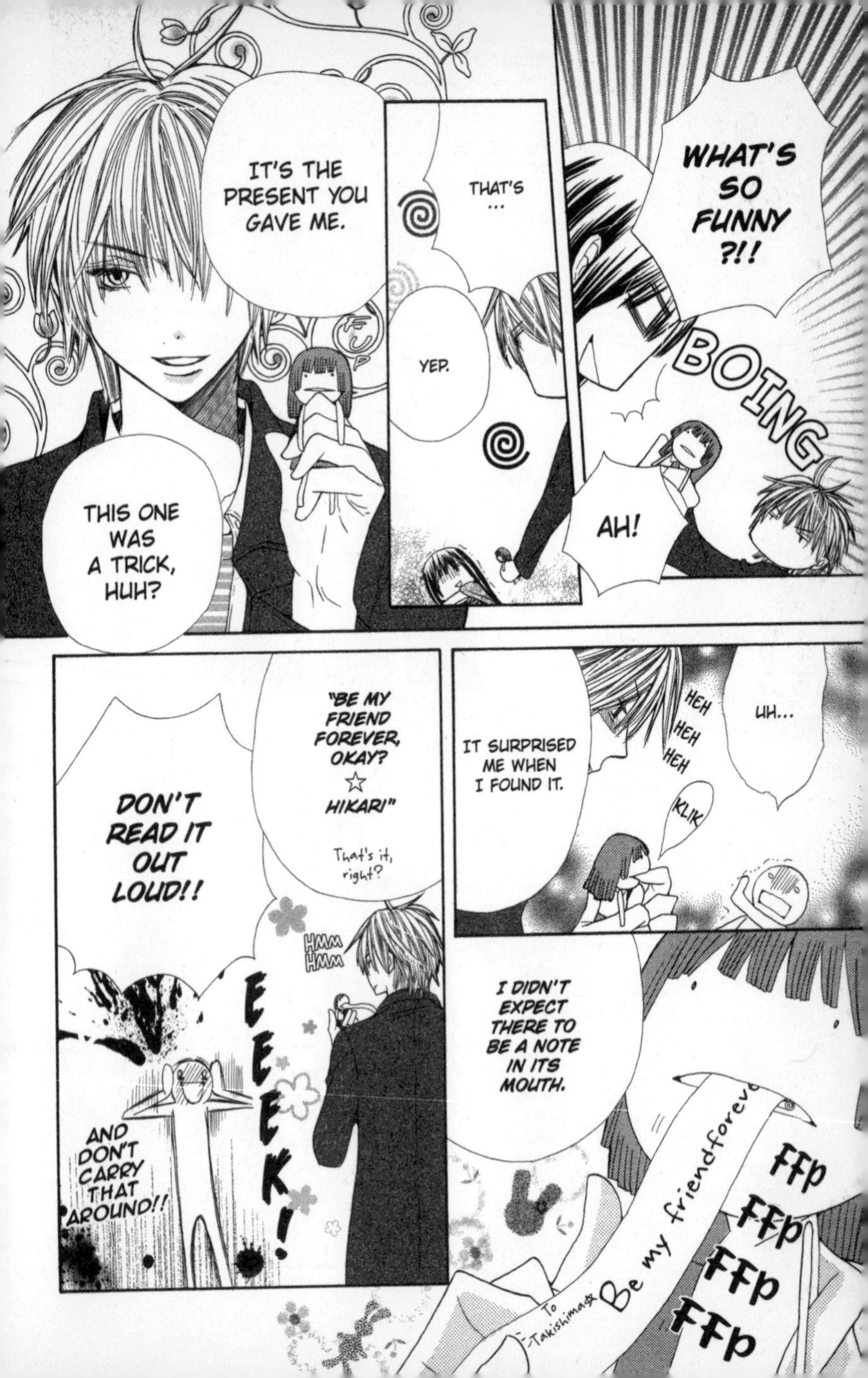
WHAT'S SO FUNNY ?!!
BOING
AH!
THAT'S ...
YEP.
IT'S THE PRESENT YOU GAVE ME.
THIS ONE WAS A TRICK, HUH?
UH...
HEH HEH HEH
IT SURPRISED ME WHEN I FOUND IT.
KLIK
I DIDN'T EXPECT THERE TO BE A NOTE IN ITS MOUTH.
FFp FFp FFp FFp
To Takishima☆
Be my friend forev
"BE MY FRIEND FOREVER, OKAY? ☆ HIKARI"
That's it, right?
DON'T READ IT OUT LOUD!!
HMM HMM
EEEK!
AND DON'T CARRY THAT AROUND!!

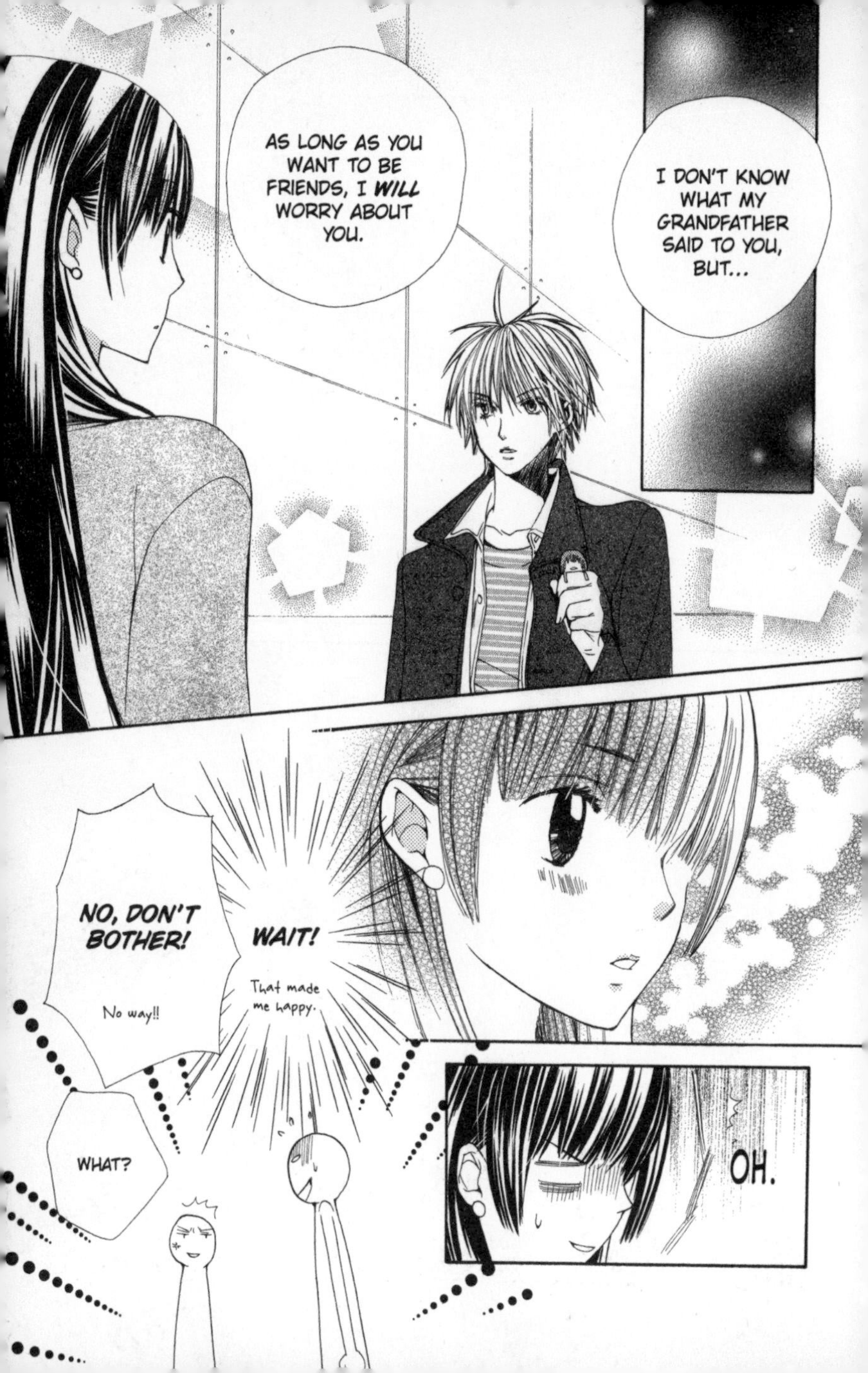
I DON'T KNOW WHAT MY GRANDFATHER SAID TO YOU, BUT...
AS LONG AS YOU WANT TO BE FRIENDS, I *WILL* WORRY ABOUT YOU.
WAIT!
That made me happy.
NO, DON'T BOTHER!
No way!!
WHAT?
OH.

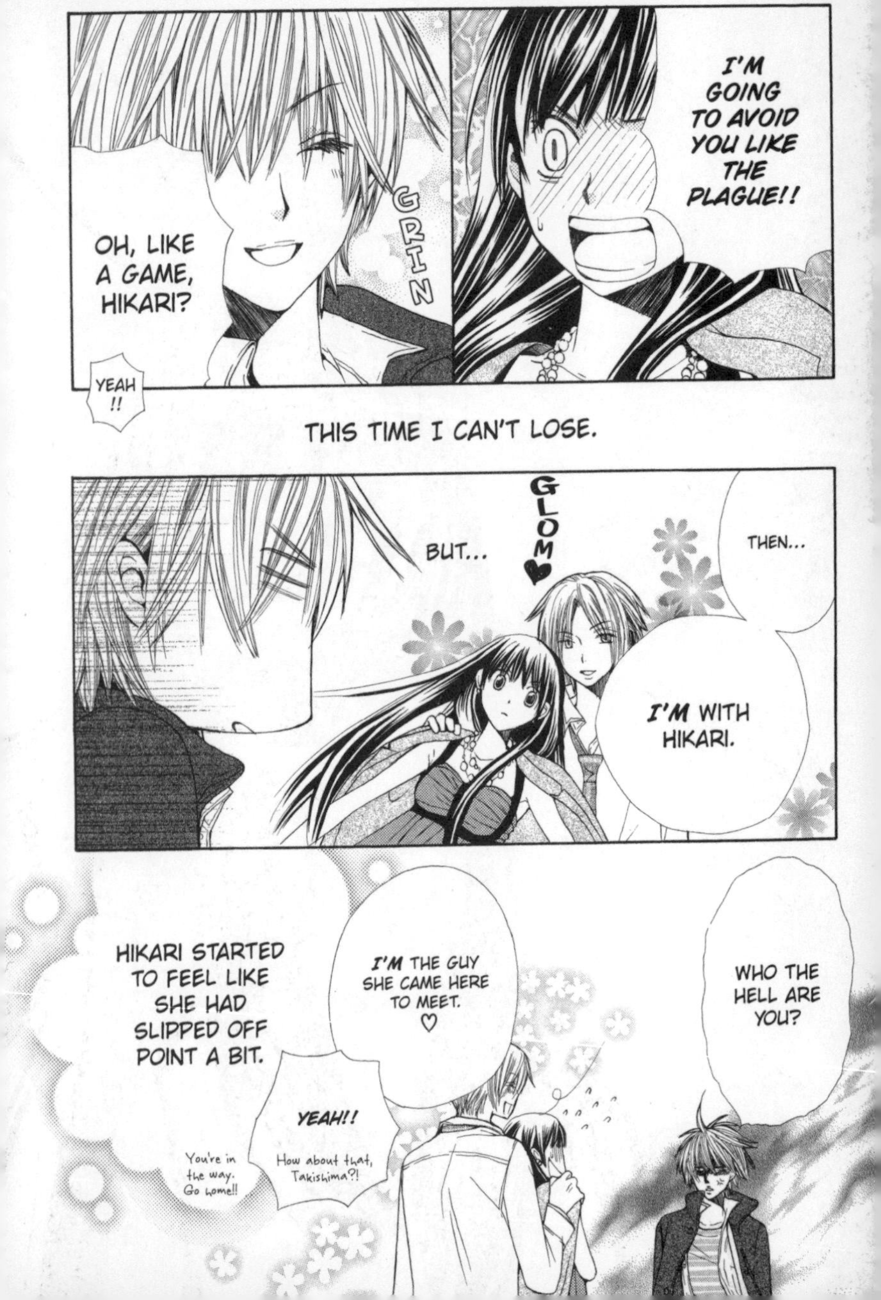
I'M GOING TO AVOID YOU LIKE THE PLAGUE!!
GRIN
OH, LIKE A GAME, HIKARI?
YEAH !!
THIS TIME I CAN'T LOSE.
THEN...
I'M WITH HIKARI.
GLOM
BUT...
WHO THE HELL ARE YOU?
I'M THE GUY SHE CAME HERE TO MEET. ♡
YEAH!!
How about that, Takishima?!
You're in the way. Go home!!
HIKARI STARTED TO FEEL LIKE SHE HAD SLIPPED OFF POINT A BIT.

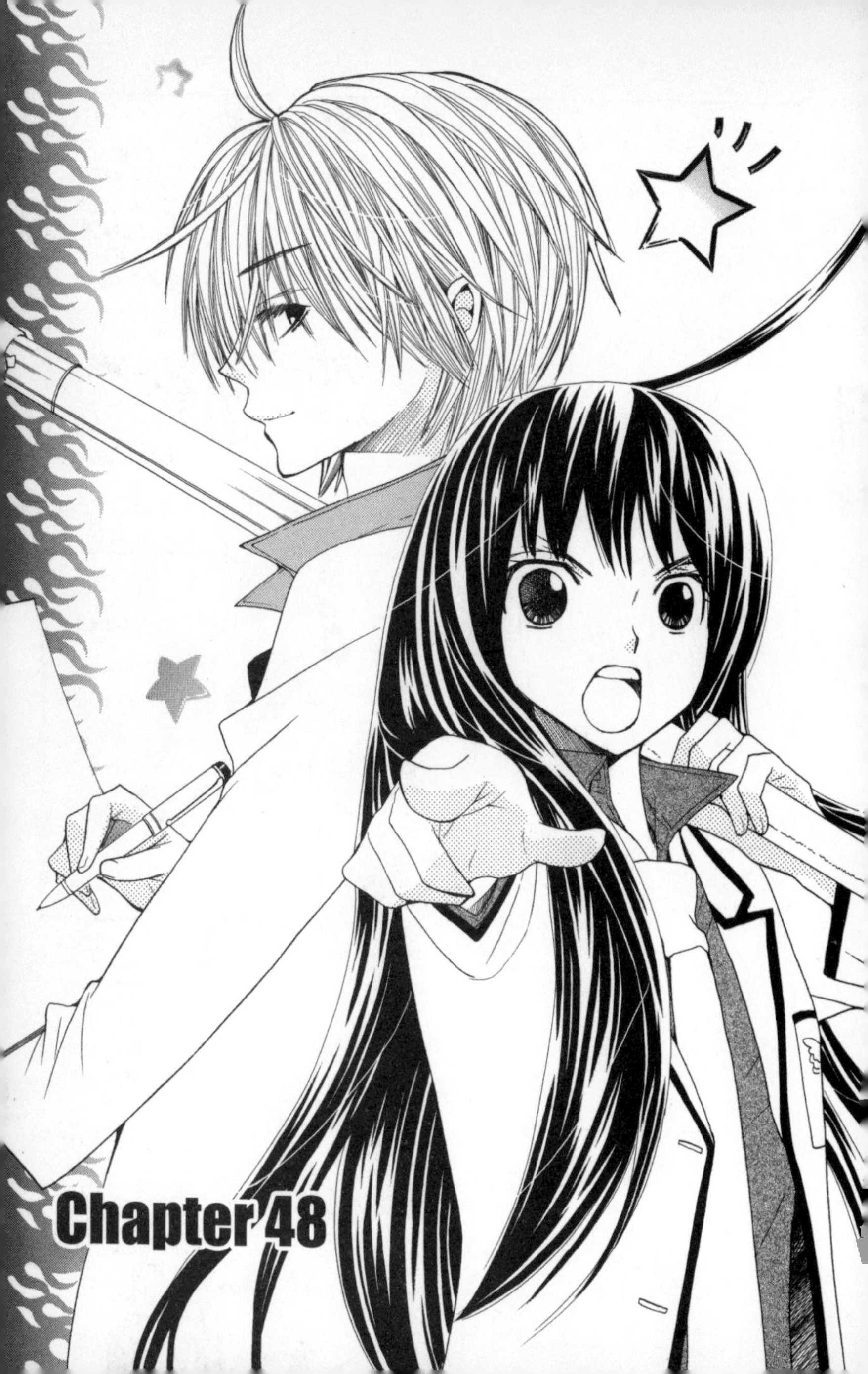
Chapter 48

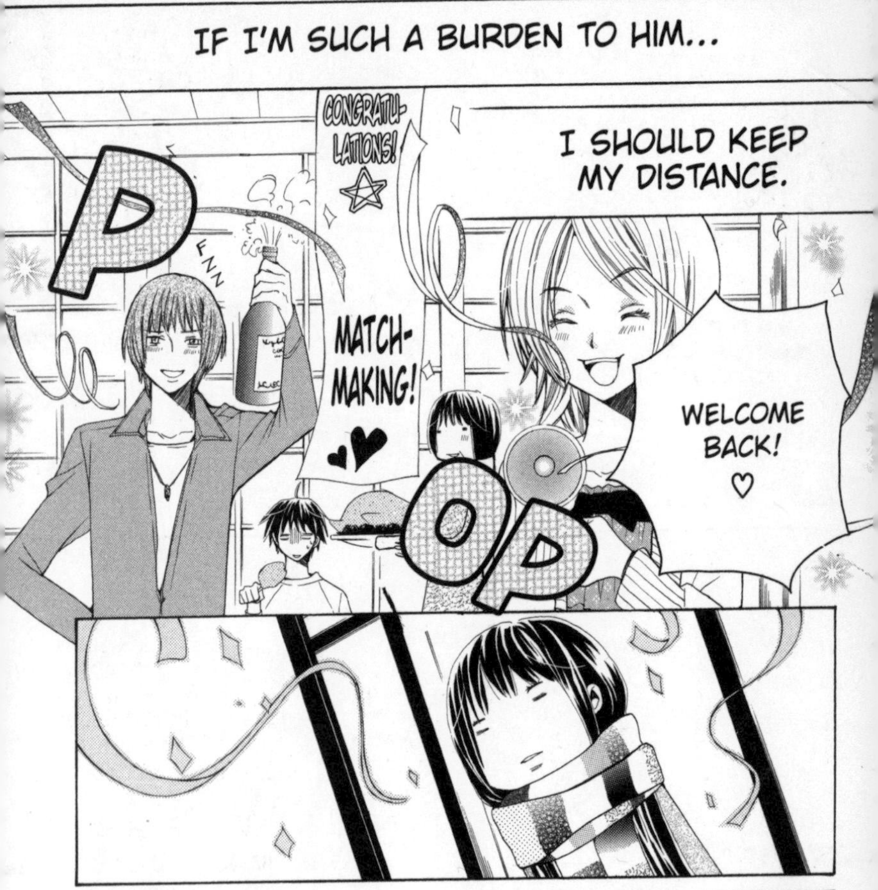
IF I'M SUCH A BURDEN TO HIM...
I SHOULD KEEP MY DISTANCE.
CONGRATULATIONS!
WELCOME BACK! ♡
MATCH-MAKING!
FZZ
POP

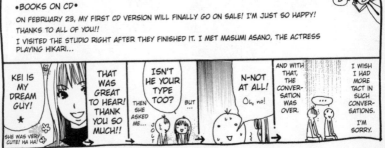

•BOOKS ON CD•

ON FEBRUARY 23, MY FIRST CD VERSION WILL FINALLY GO ON SALE! I'M JUST SO HAPPY! THANKS TO ALL OF YOU!!

I VISITED THE STUDIO RIGHT AFTER THEY FINISHED IT. I MET MASUMI ASANO, THE ACTRESS PLAYING HIKARI...

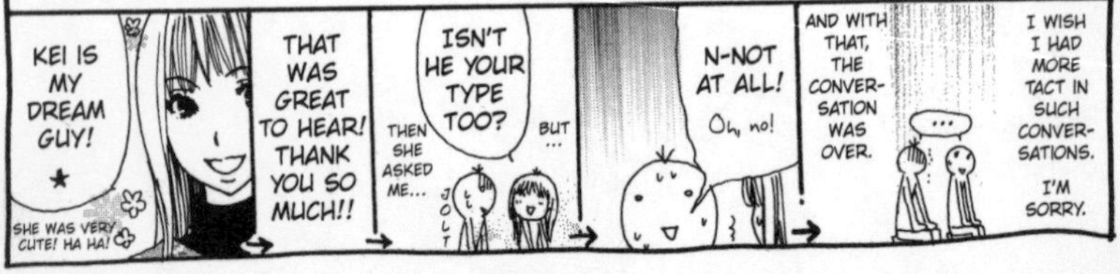
KEI IS MY DREAM GUY! ★
SHE WAS VERY CUTE! HA HA!
THAT WAS GREAT TO HEAR! THANK YOU SO MUCH!!
THEN SHE ASKED ME...
ISN'T HE YOUR TYPE TOO?
BUT ...
JOLT
N-NOT AT ALL!
Oh, no!
AND WITH THAT, THE CONVERSATION WAS OVER.
...
I WISH I HAD MORE TACT IN SUCH CONVERSATIONS.
I'M SORRY.

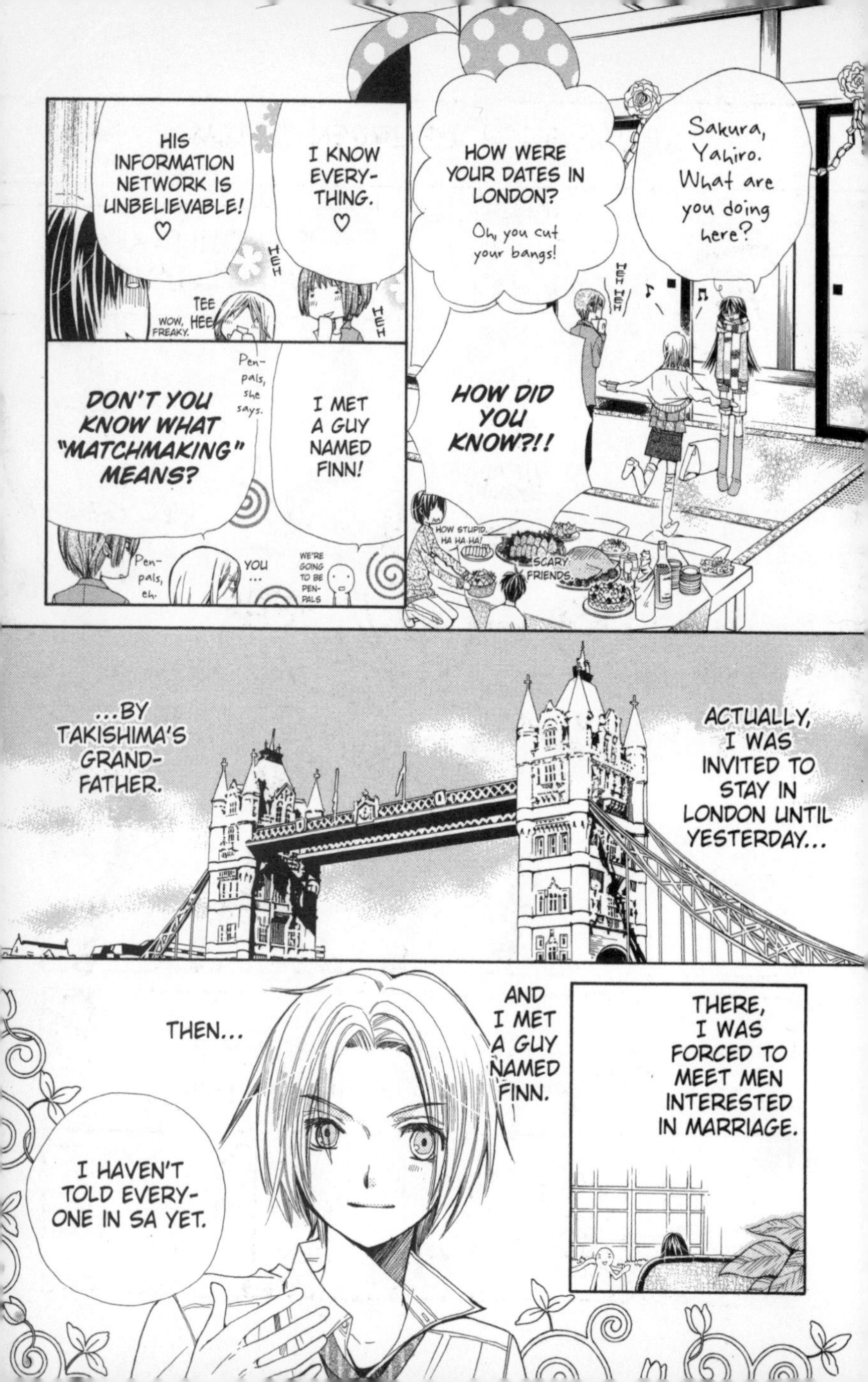
Sakura, Yahiro. What are you doing here?
HOW WERE YOUR DATES IN LONDON?
Oh, you cut your bangs!
HEH HEH
HOW DID YOU KNOW?!!
HOW STUPID. HA HA HA!
SCARY FRIENDS.
I KNOW EVERY-THING. ♡
HEH HEH
HIS INFORMATION NETWORK IS UNBELIEVABLE! ♡
TEE HEE
WOW, FREAKY.
I MET A GUY NAMED FINN!
Pen-pals, she says.
DON'T YOU KNOW WHAT "MATCHMAKING" MEANS?
WE'RE GOING TO BE PEN-PALS
YOU ...
Pen-pals, eh.
ACTUALLY, I WAS INVITED TO STAY IN LONDON UNTIL YESTERDAY...
...BY TAKISHIMA'S GRAND-FATHER.
THERE, I WAS FORCED TO MEET MEN INTERESTED IN MARRIAGE.
AND I MET A GUY NAMED FINN.
THEN...
I HAVEN'T TOLD EVERY-ONE IN SA YET.

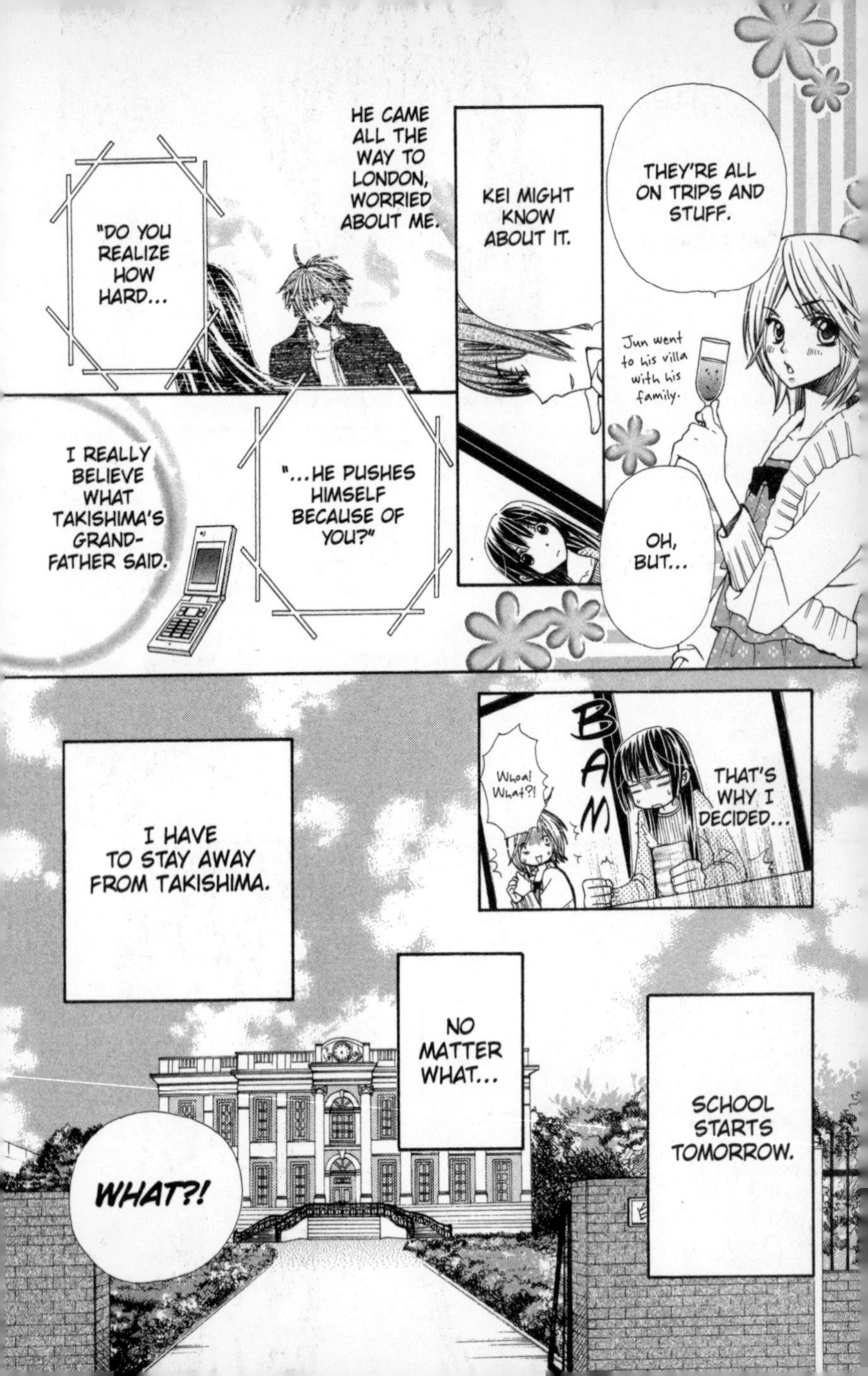
THEY'RE ALL ON TRIPS AND STUFF.
Jun went to his villa with his family.
OH, BUT...
KEI MIGHT KNOW ABOUT IT.
HE CAME ALL THE WAY TO LONDON, WORRIED ABOUT ME.
"DO YOU REALIZE HOW HARD...
"...HE PUSHES HIMSELF BECAUSE OF YOU?"
I REALLY BELIEVE WHAT TAKISHIMA'S GRAND-FATHER SAID.
BAM
THAT'S WHY I DECIDED...
Whoa! What?!
I HAVE TO STAY AWAY FROM TAKISHIMA.
NO MATTER WHAT...
WHAT?!
SCHOOL STARTS TOMORROW.

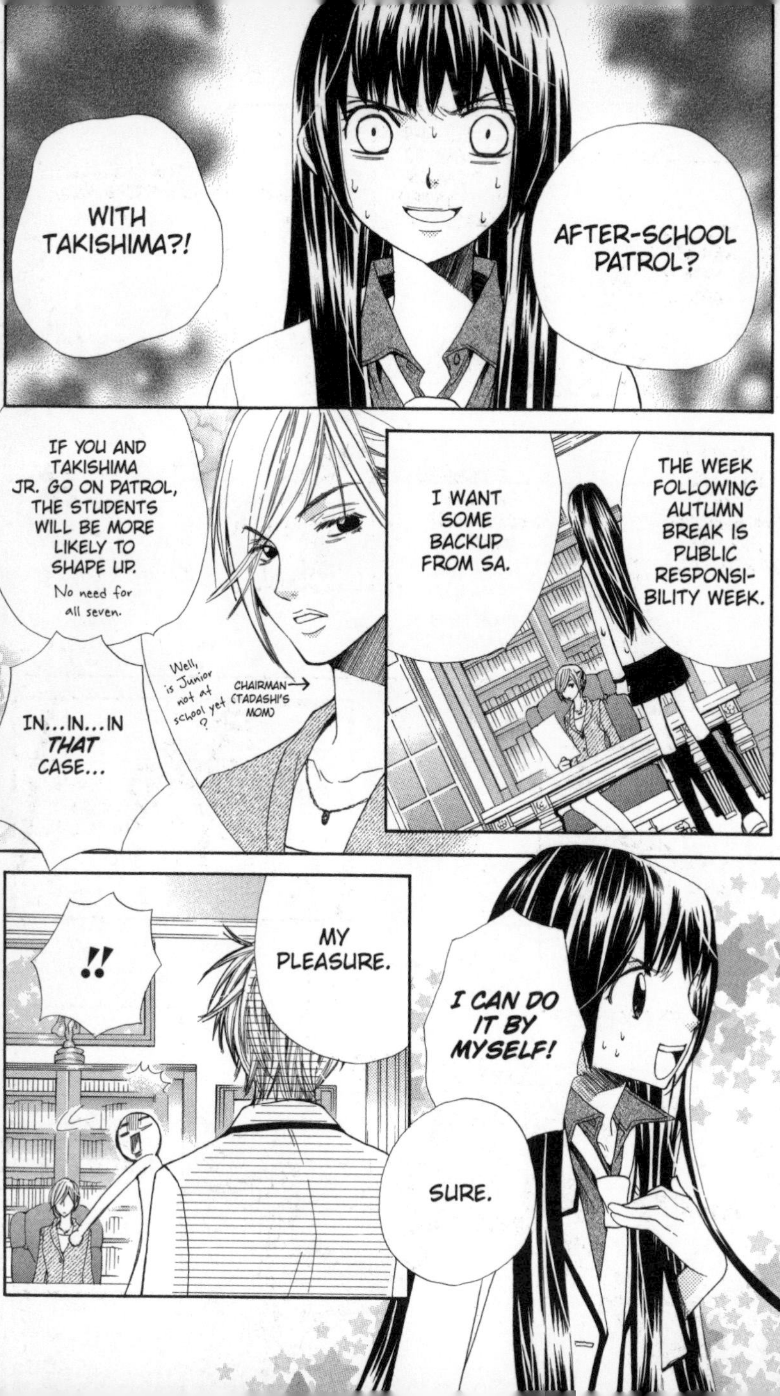
AFTER-SCHOOL PATROL?
WITH TAKISHIMA?!
THE WEEK FOLLOWING AUTUMN BREAK IS PUBLIC RESPONSI-BILITY WEEK.
I WANT SOME BACKUP FROM SA.
IF YOU AND TAKISHIMA JR. GO ON PATROL, THE STUDENTS WILL BE MORE LIKELY TO SHAPE UP.
No need for all seven.
CHAIRMAN (TADASHI'S MOM)
Well, is Junior not at school yet?
IN...IN...IN *THAT* CASE...
I CAN DO IT BY MYSELF!
SURE.
MY PLEASURE.
!!

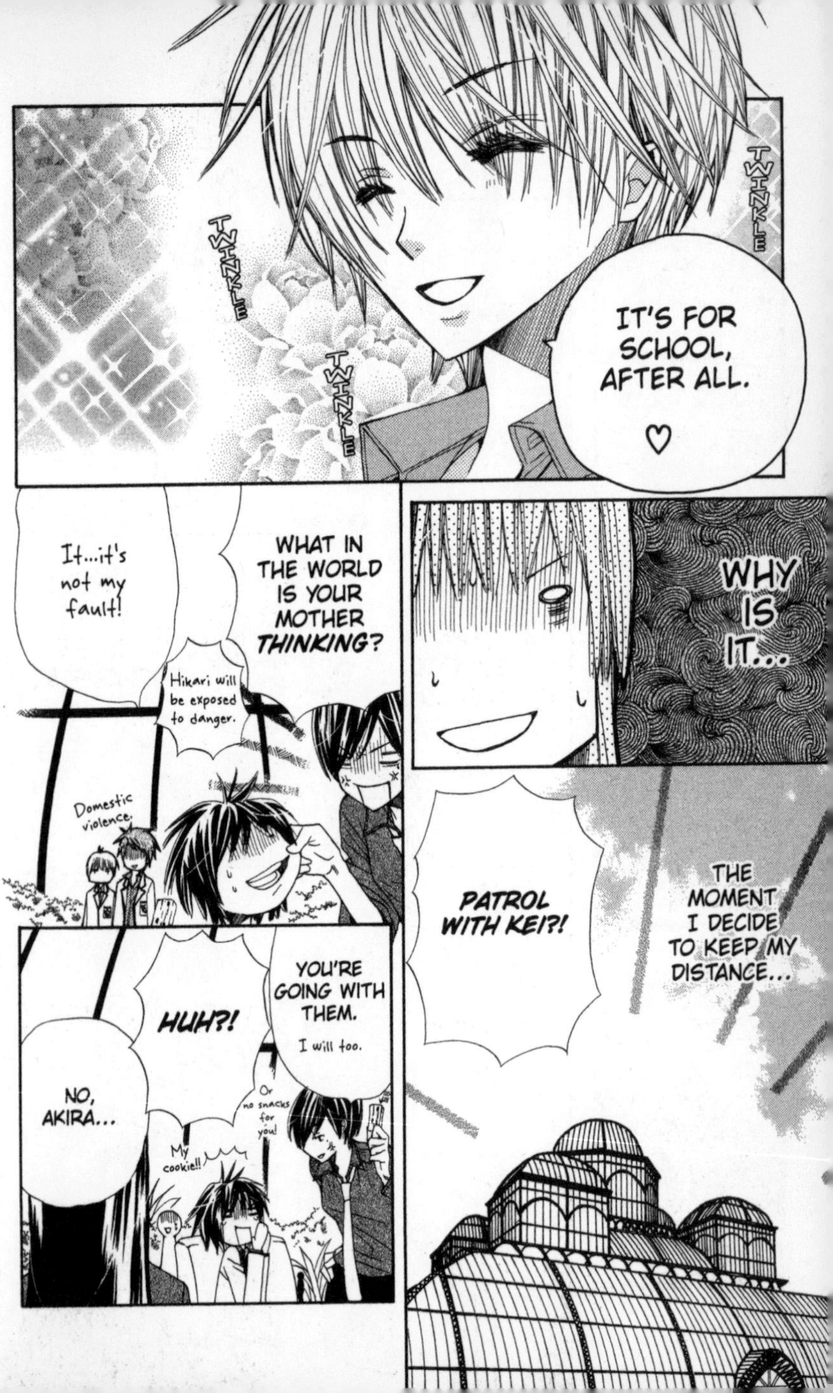
TWINKLE
TWINKLE
TWINKLE
IT'S FOR SCHOOL, AFTER ALL. ♡
WHY IS IT...
THE MOMENT I DECIDE TO KEEP MY DISTANCE...
PATROL WITH KEI?!
WHAT IN THE WORLD IS YOUR MOTHER *THINKING*?
It...it's not my fault!
Hikari will be exposed to danger.
Domestic violence.
YOU'RE GOING WITH THEM.
I will too.
HUH?!
NO, AKIRA...
Or no snacks for you!
My cookie!!

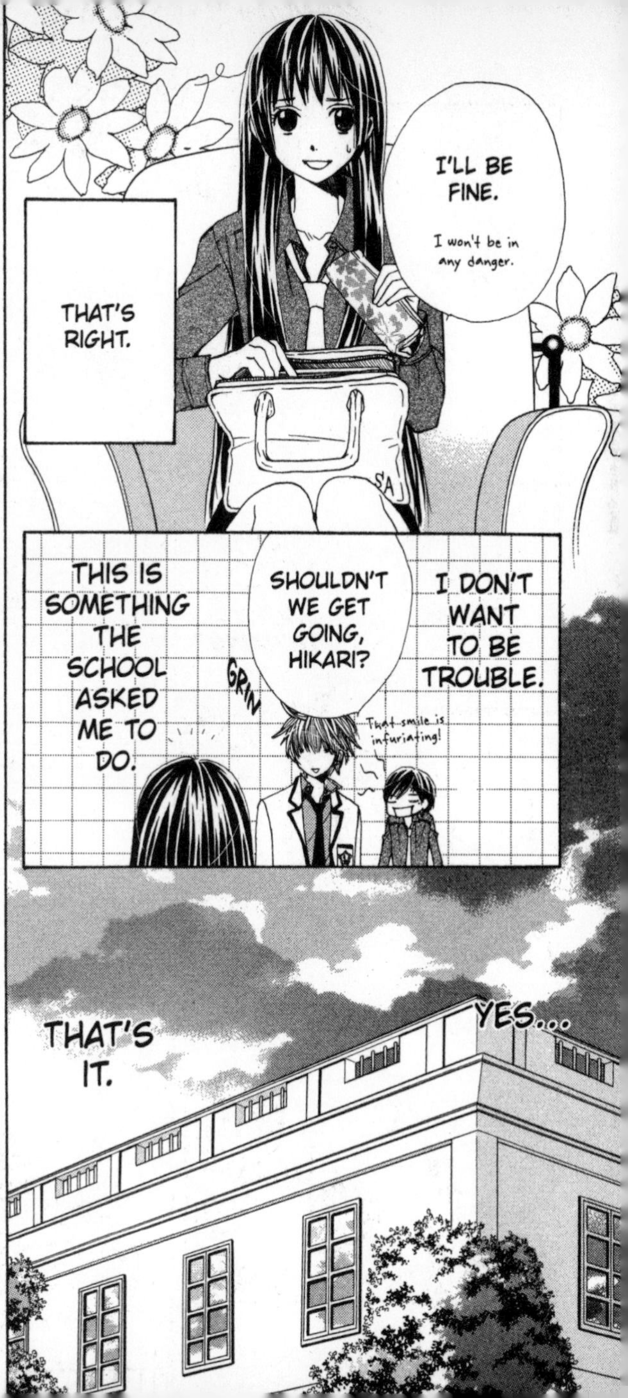
I'LL BE FINE.
I won't be in any danger.
THAT'S RIGHT.
I DON'T WANT TO BE TROUBLE.
SHOULDN'T WE GET GOING, HIKARI?
That smile is infuriating!
GRIN
THIS IS SOMETHING THE SCHOOL ASKED ME TO DO.
YES...
THAT'S IT.
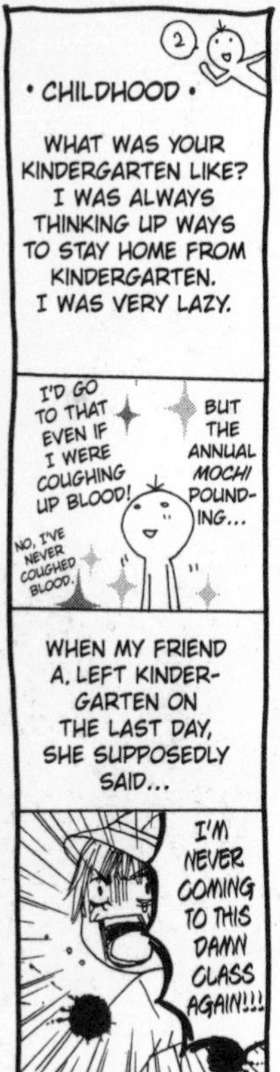
2
• CHILDHOOD •
WHAT WAS YOUR KINDERGARTEN LIKE? I WAS ALWAYS THINKING UP WAYS TO STAY HOME FROM KINDERGARTEN. I WAS VERY LAZY.
BUT THE ANNUAL MOCHI POUNDING...
I'D GO TO THAT EVEN IF I WERE COUGHING UP BLOOD!
NO, I'VE NEVER COUGHED BLOOD.
WHEN MY FRIEND A. LEFT KINDER-GARTEN ON THE LAST DAY, SHE SUPPOSEDLY SAID...
I'M NEVER COMING TO THIS DAMN CLASS AGAIN!!!
WHAT IN THE WORLD WOULD MAKE HER SAY THAT? I WONDER... AND WHERE DID SHE LEARN THAT LANGUAGE?

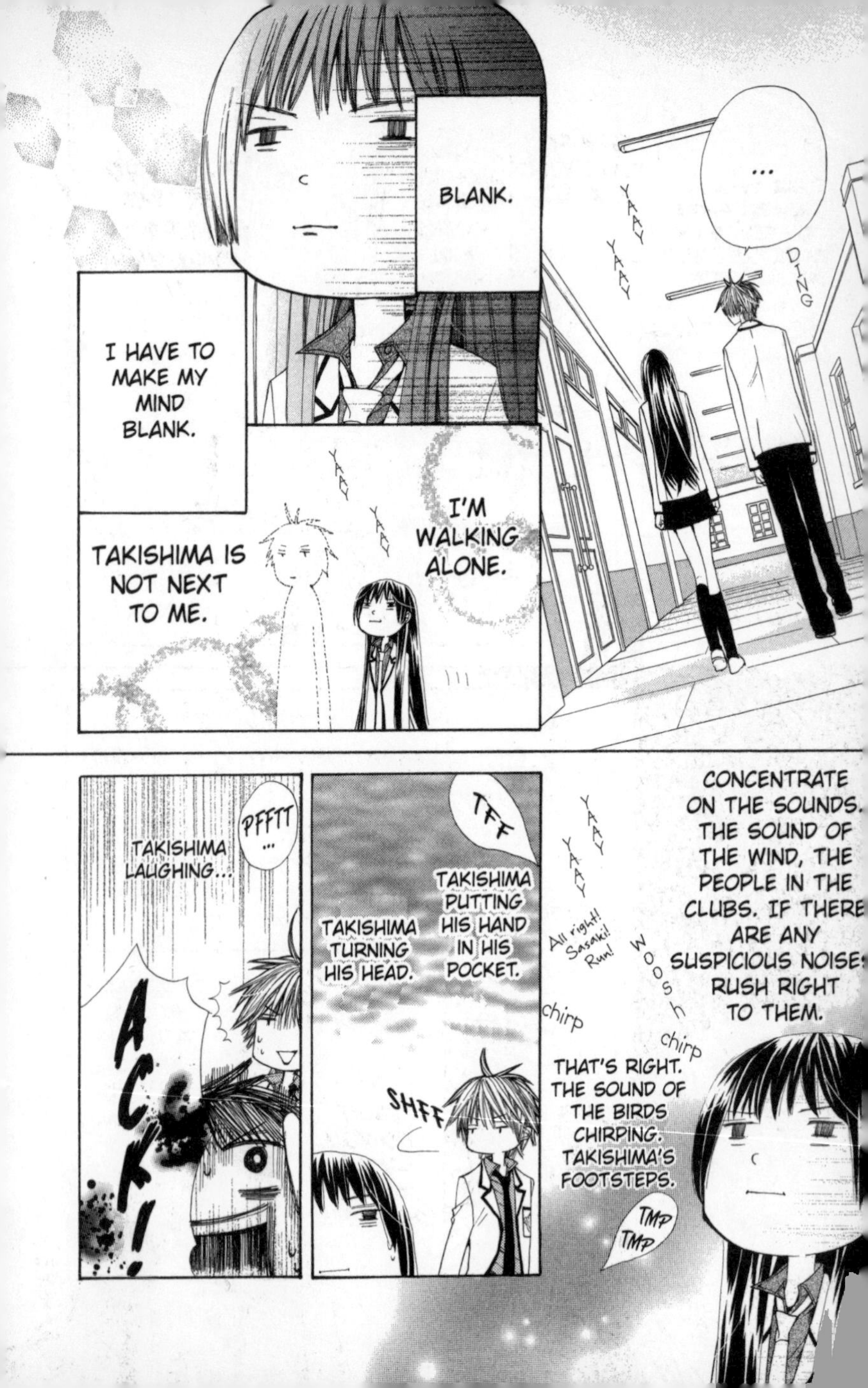
...
YAAY YAAY
DING
BLANK.
I HAVE TO MAKE MY MIND BLANK.
I'M WALKING ALONE.
TAKISHIMA IS NOT NEXT TO ME.
YAAY YAAY
CONCENTRATE ON THE SOUNDS. THE SOUND OF THE WIND, THE PEOPLE IN THE CLUBS. IF THERE ARE ANY SUSPICIOUS NOISES RUSH RIGHT TO THEM.
YAAY YAAY
All right! Sasaki! Run!
WOOSH
chirp
chirp
THAT'S RIGHT. THE SOUND OF THE BIRDS CHIRPING. TAKISHIMA'S FOOTSTEPS.
TMP TMP
TFF
TAKISHIMA PUTTING HIS HAND IN HIS POCKET.
TAKISHIMA TURNING HIS HEAD.
SHFF
PFFTT...
TAKISHIMA LAUGHING...
ACK!!

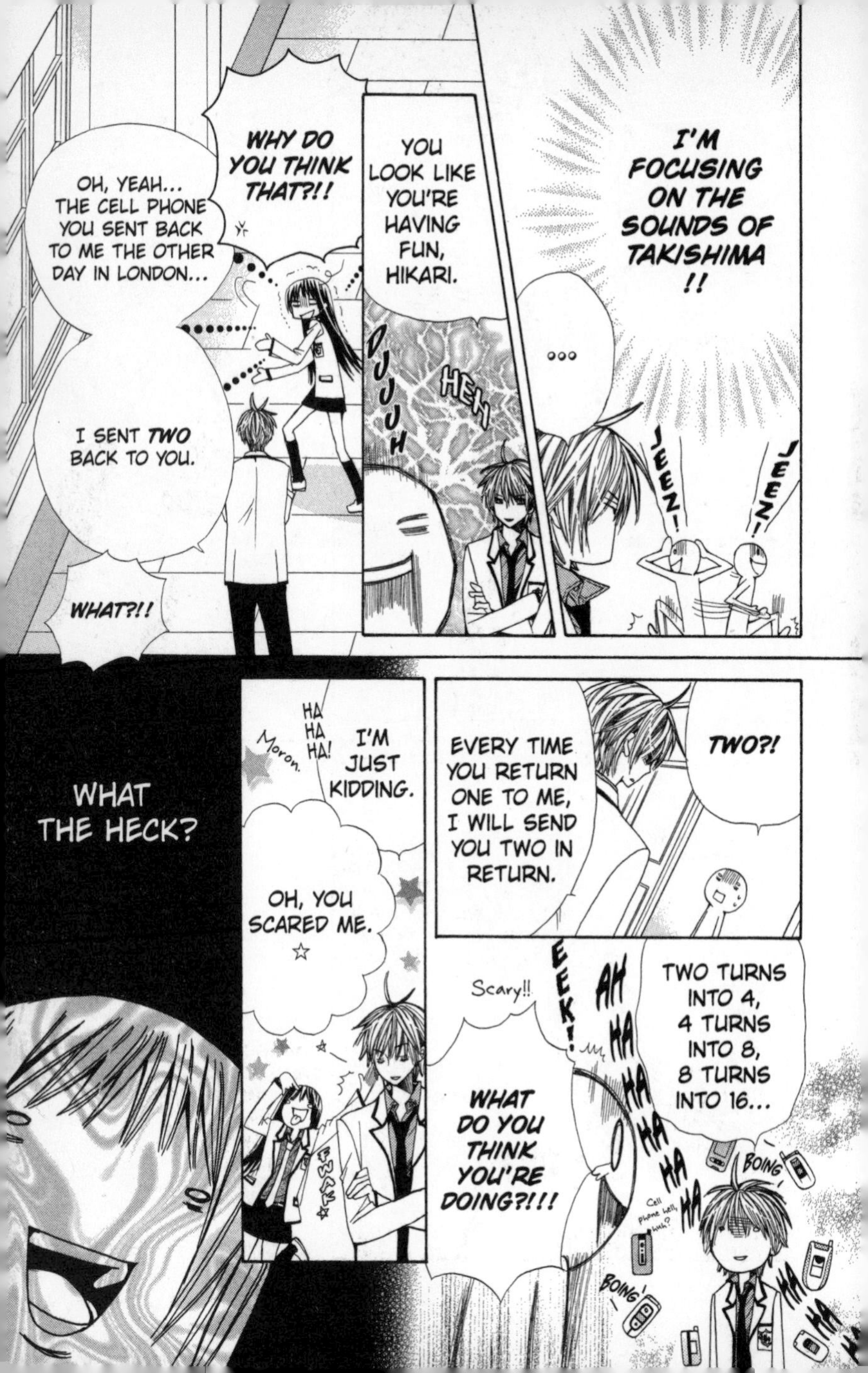
I'M FOCUSING ON THE SOUNDS OF TAKISHIMA!!
...
JEEZ!
JEEZ!
YOU LOOK LIKE YOU'RE HAVING FUN, HIKARI.
DJUUUH
HEH
WHY DO YOU THINK THAT?!!
OH, YEAH... THE CELL PHONE YOU SENT BACK TO ME THE OTHER DAY IN LONDON...
I SENT TWO BACK TO YOU.
WHAT?!!
TWO?!
EVERY TIME YOU RETURN ONE TO ME, I WILL SEND YOU TWO IN RETURN.
TWO TURNS INTO 4, 4 TURNS INTO 8, 8 TURNS INTO 16...
AH HA HA HA HA HA HA HA HA
EEK!
WHAT DO YOU THINK YOU'RE DOING?!!!
Cell phone hell, huh?
BOING
BOING
HA HA HA! I'M JUST KIDDING.
Moron.
OH, YOU SCARED ME.
Scary!!
WHAT THE HECK?

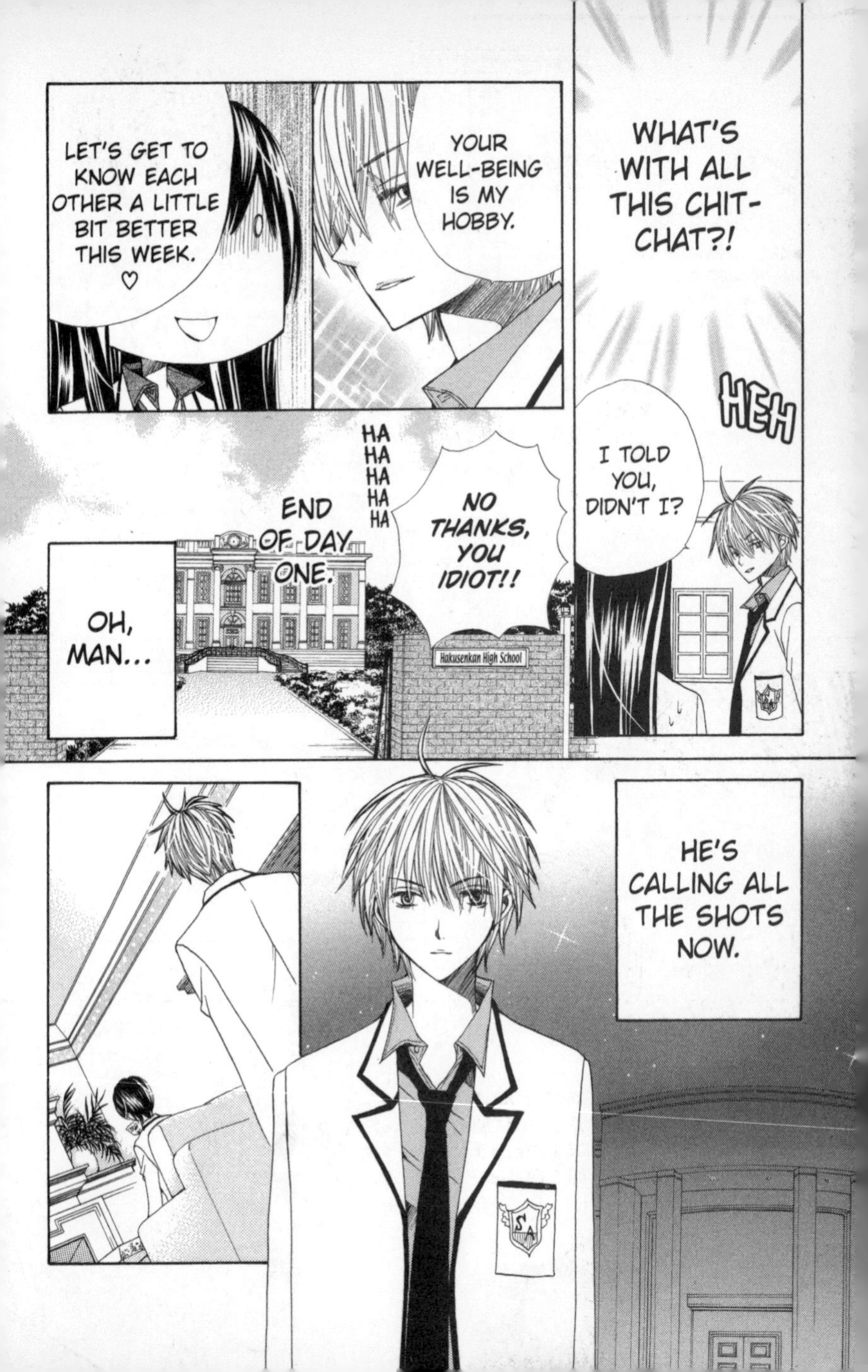
WHAT'S WITH ALL THIS CHIT-CHAT?!
YOUR WELL-BEING IS MY HOBBY.
LET'S GET TO KNOW EACH OTHER A LITTLE BIT BETTER THIS WEEK. ♡
HEH
I TOLD YOU, DIDN'T I?
NO THANKS, YOU IDIOT!!
HA HA HA HA HA
END OF DAY ONE.
Hakusenkan High School
OH, MAN...
HE'S CALLING ALL THE SHOTS NOW.

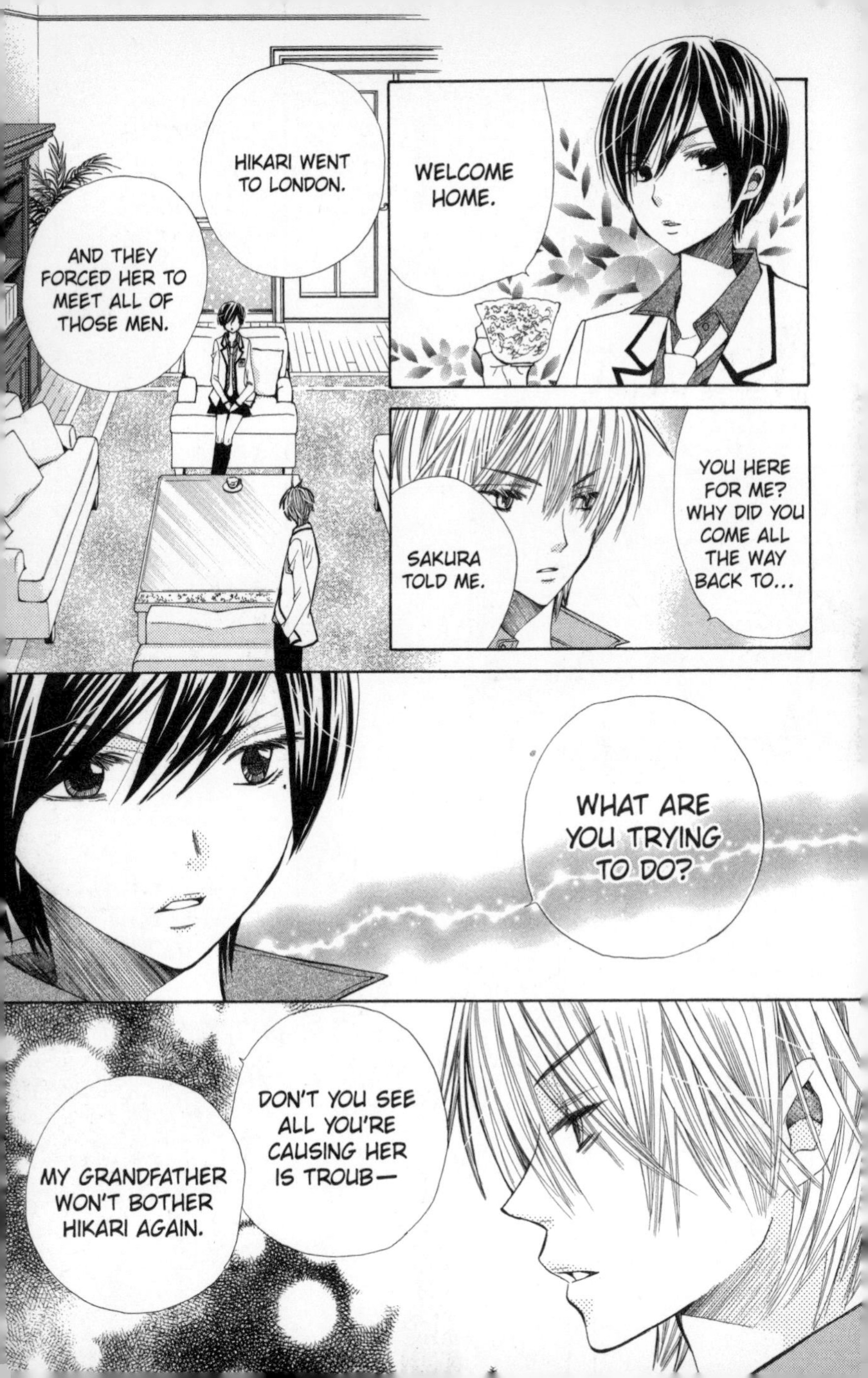
WELCOME HOME.
YOU HERE FOR ME? WHY DID YOU COME ALL THE WAY BACK TO...
SAKURA TOLD ME.
HIKARI WENT TO LONDON.
AND THEY FORCED HER TO MEET ALL OF THOSE MEN.
WHAT ARE YOU TRYING TO DO?
DON'T YOU SEE ALL YOU'RE CAUSING HER IS TROUB—
MY GRANDFATHER WON'T BOTHER HIKARI AGAIN.

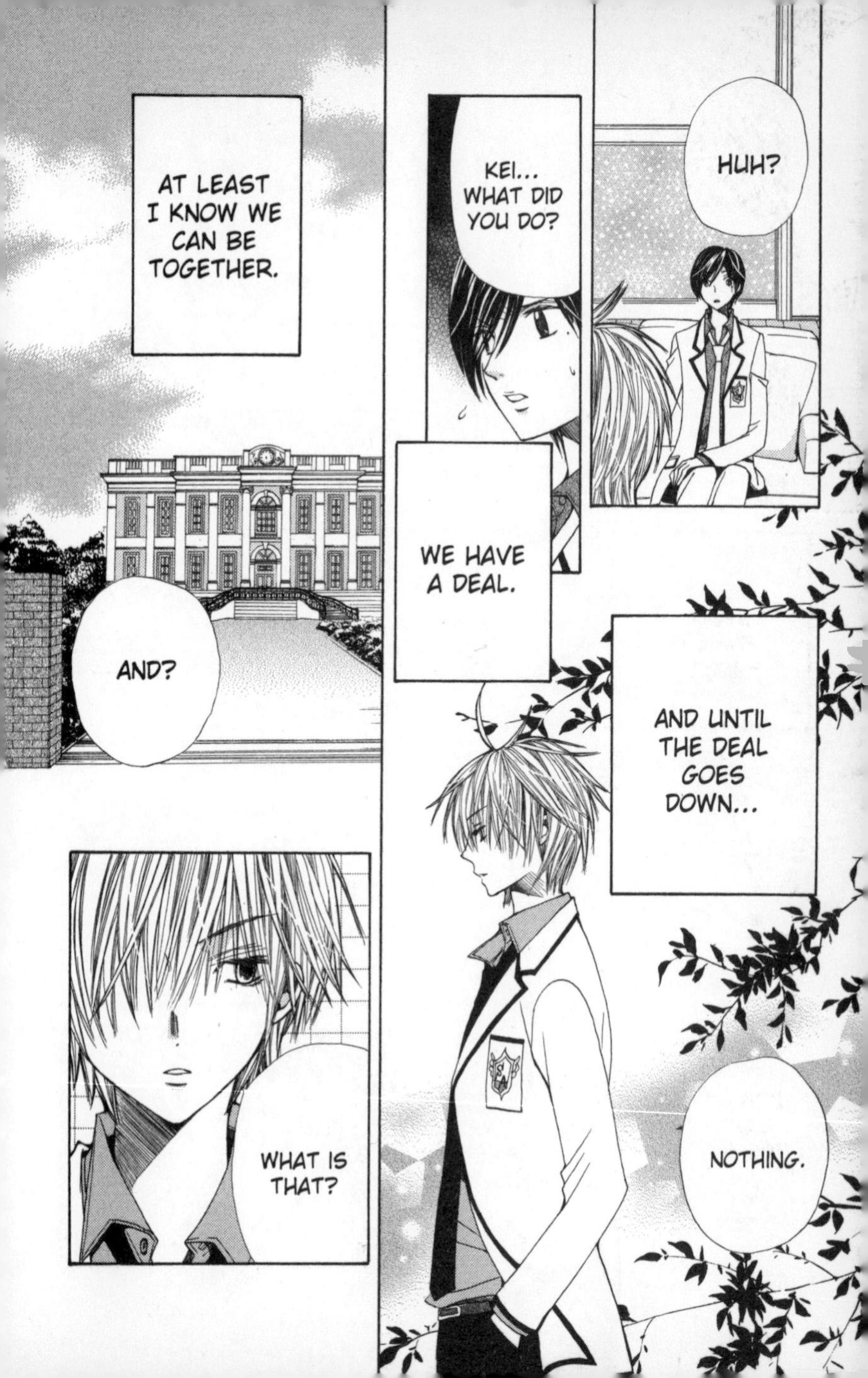
HUH?
KEI... WHAT DID YOU DO?
WE HAVE A DEAL.
AND UNTIL THE DEAL GOES DOWN...
NOTHING.
AT LEAST I KNOW WE CAN BE TOGETHER.
AND?
WHAT IS THAT?

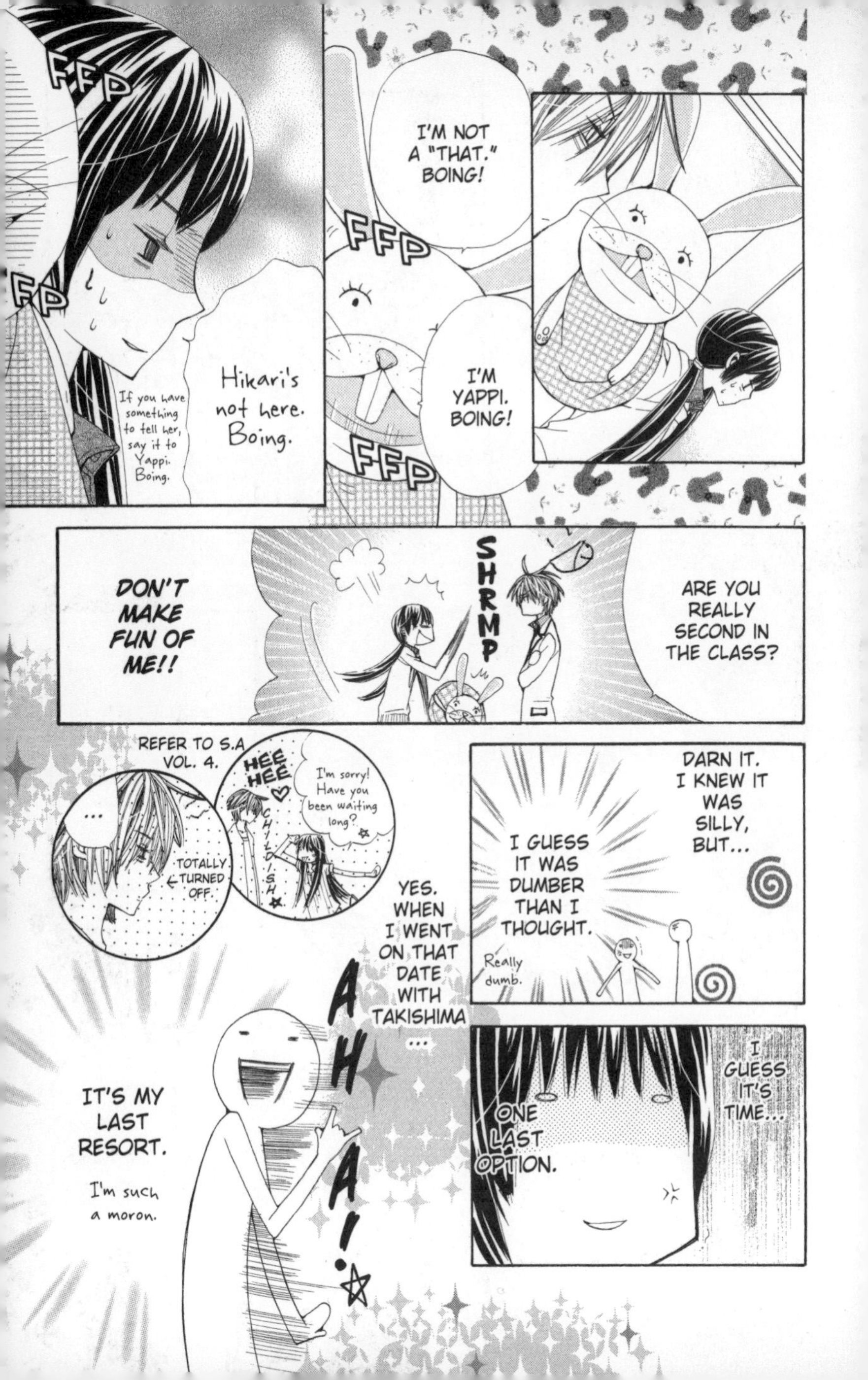
I'M NOT A "THAT." BOING!
FFP
I'M YAPPI. BOING!
FFP
FFP
FP
Hikari's not here. Boing.
If you have something to tell her, say it to Yappi. Boing.
ARE YOU REALLY SECOND IN THE CLASS?
SHRMP
DON'T MAKE FUN OF ME!!
DARN IT. I KNEW IT WAS SILLY, BUT...
I GUESS IT WAS DUMBER THAN I THOUGHT.
Really dumb.
YES. WHEN I WENT ON THAT DATE WITH TAKISHIMA...
REFER TO S.A VOL. 4.
HEE HEE
I'm sorry! Have you been waiting long?
CHILDISH
TOTALLY TURNED OFF.
...
I GUESS IT'S TIME...
ONE LAST OPTION.
AHAI!
IT'S MY LAST RESORT.
I'm such a moron.

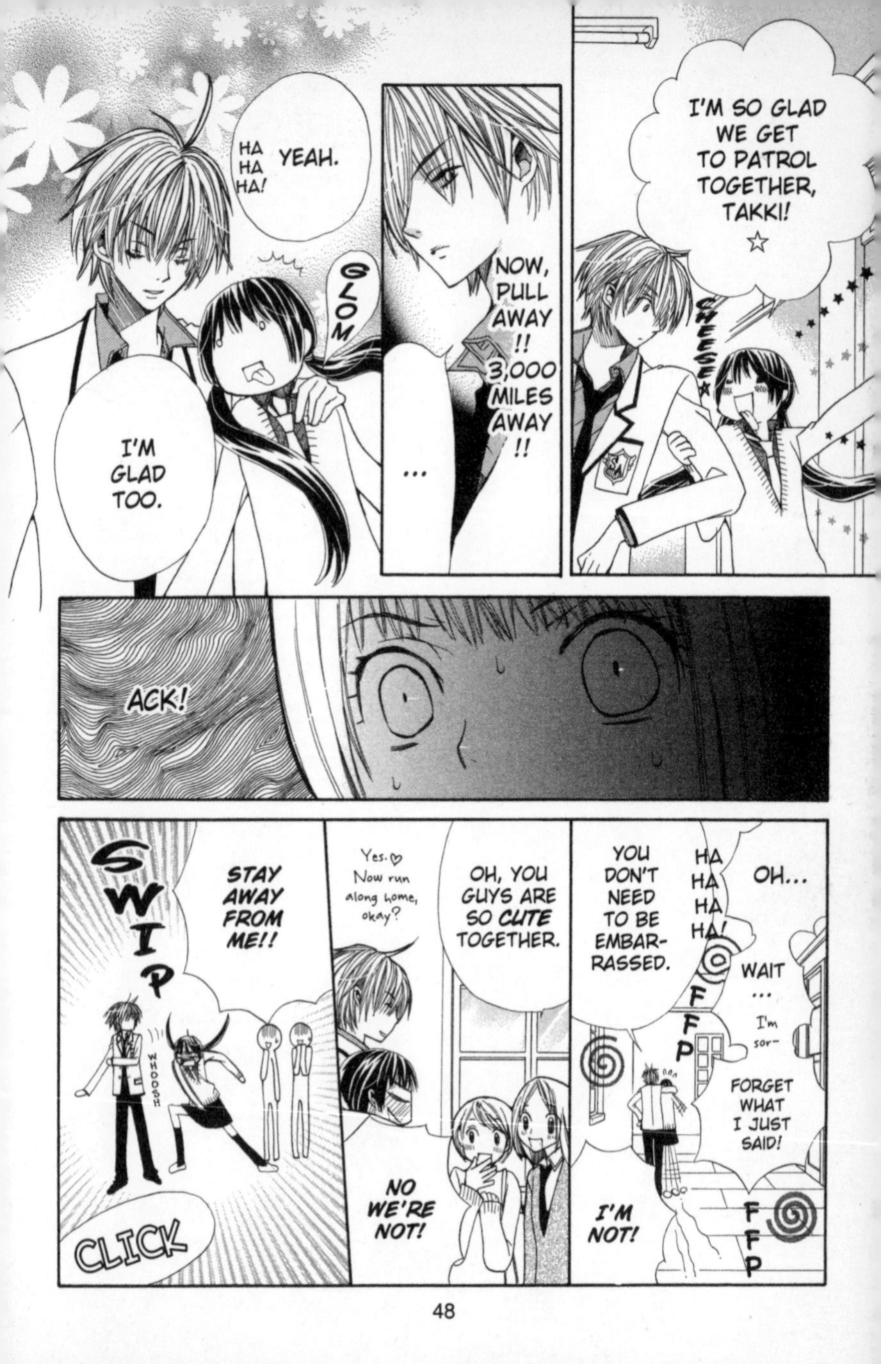
I'M SO GLAD WE GET TO PATROL TOGETHER, TAKKI! ☆
CHEESE☆
NOW, PULL AWAY!! 3,000 MILES AWAY!!
...
HA HA HA!
YEAH.
GLOM
I'M GLAD TOO.
ACK!
OH...
HA HA HA HA!
YOU DON'T NEED TO BE EMBARRASSED.
FFP
WAIT... I'm sor-
FORGET WHAT I JUST SAID!
FFP
I'M NOT!
OH, YOU GUYS ARE SO CUTE TOGETHER.
Yes.♡ Now run along home, okay?
NO WE'RE NOT!
STAY AWAY FROM ME!!
SWIP
WHOOSH
CLICK

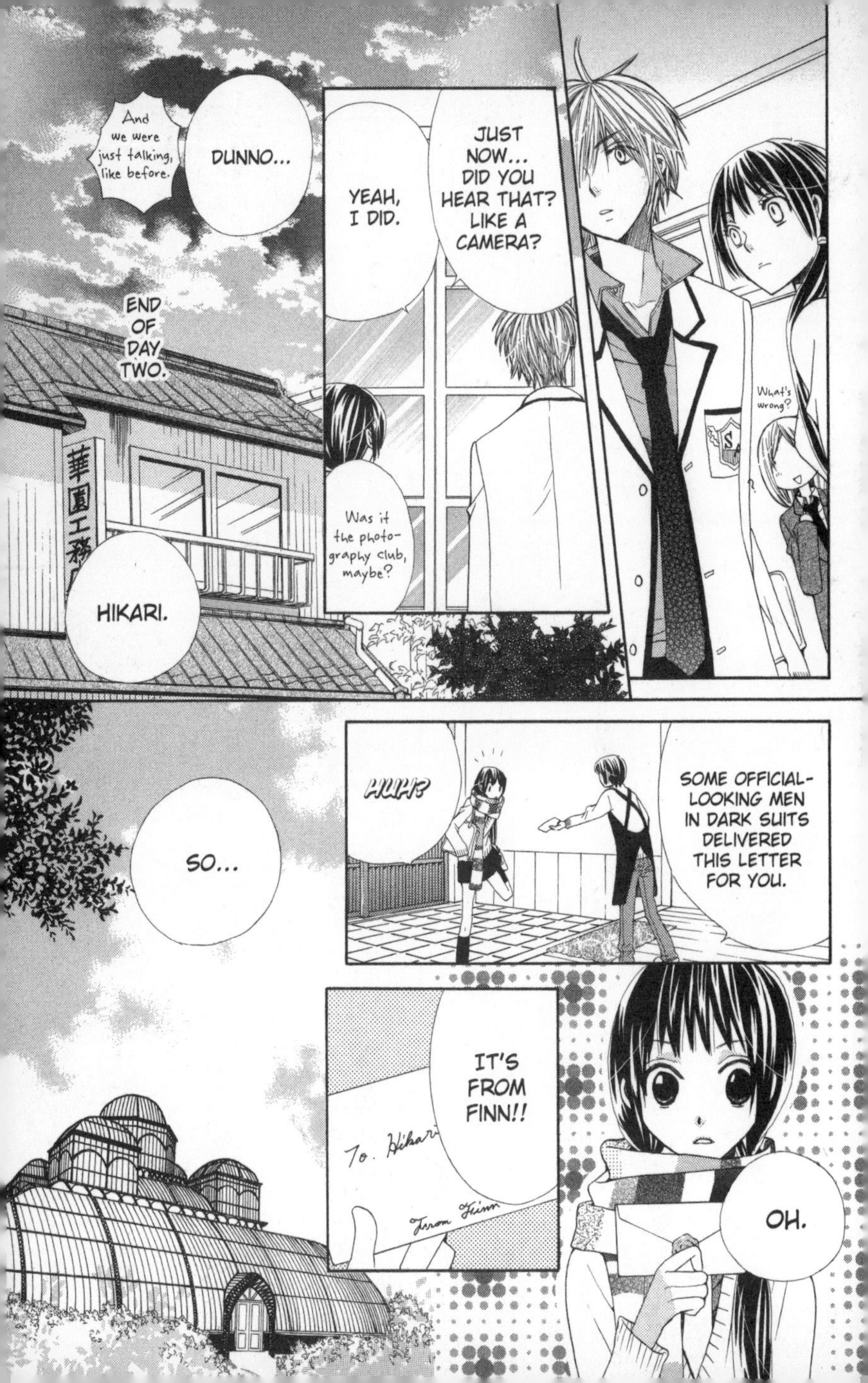

What's wrong?
JUST NOW... DID YOU HEAR THAT? LIKE A CAMERA?
YEAH, I DID.
Was it the photography club, maybe?
DUNNO...
And we were just talking, like before.
END OF DAY TWO.
HIKARI.
SOME OFFICIAL-LOOKING MEN IN DARK SUITS DELIVERED THIS LETTER FOR YOU.
HUH?
OH.
IT'S FROM FINN!!
To. Hikari
From Finn
SO...

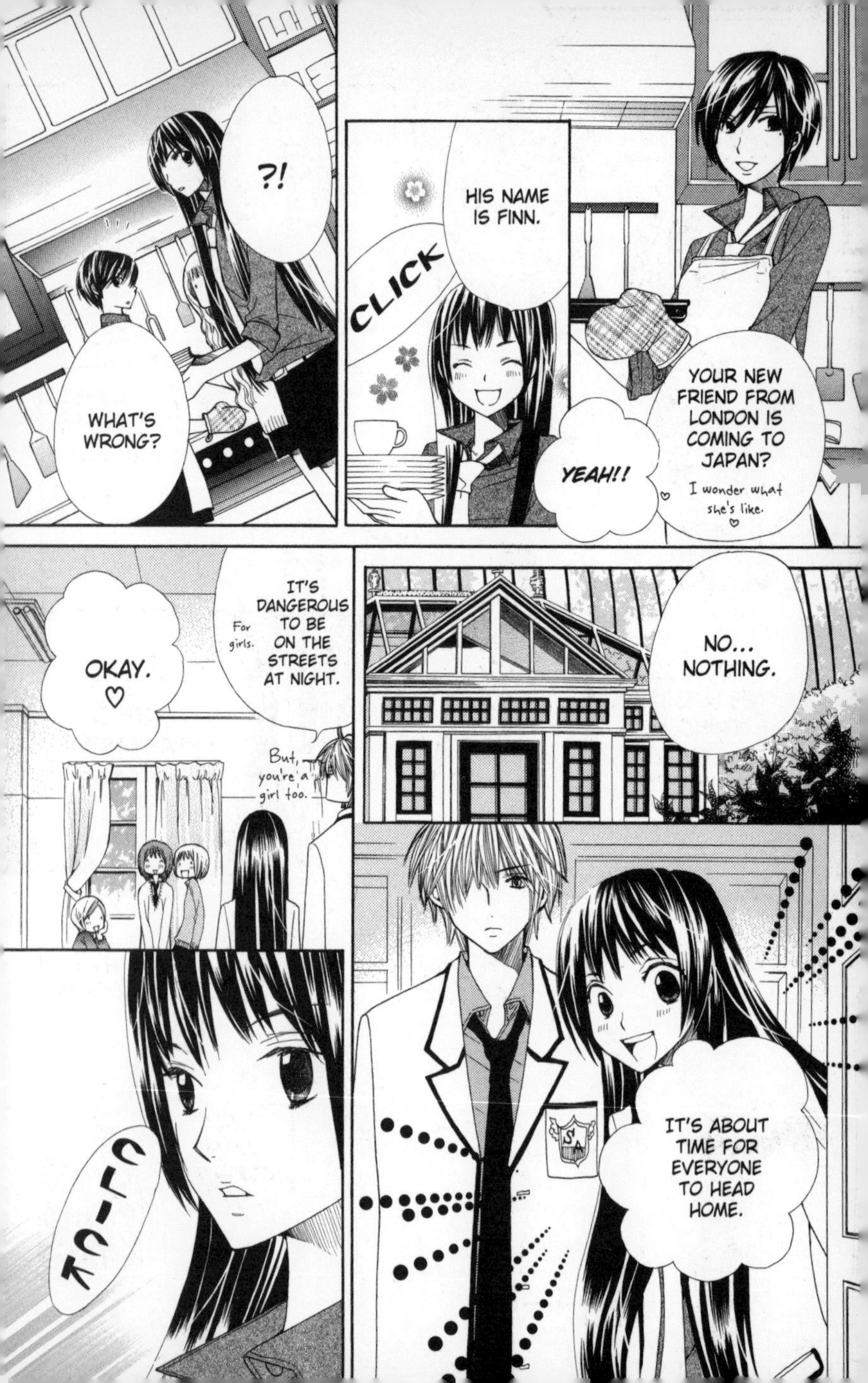
YOUR NEW FRIEND FROM LONDON IS COMING TO JAPAN?
I wonder what she's like. ♡
YEAH!! ♡
HIS NAME IS FINN.
CLICK
?!
WHAT'S WRONG?
NO... NOTHING.
IT'S ABOUT TIME FOR EVERYONE TO HEAD HOME.
IT'S DANGEROUS TO BE ON THE STREETS AT NIGHT.
For girls.
OKAY. ♡
But, you're a girl too.
CLICK

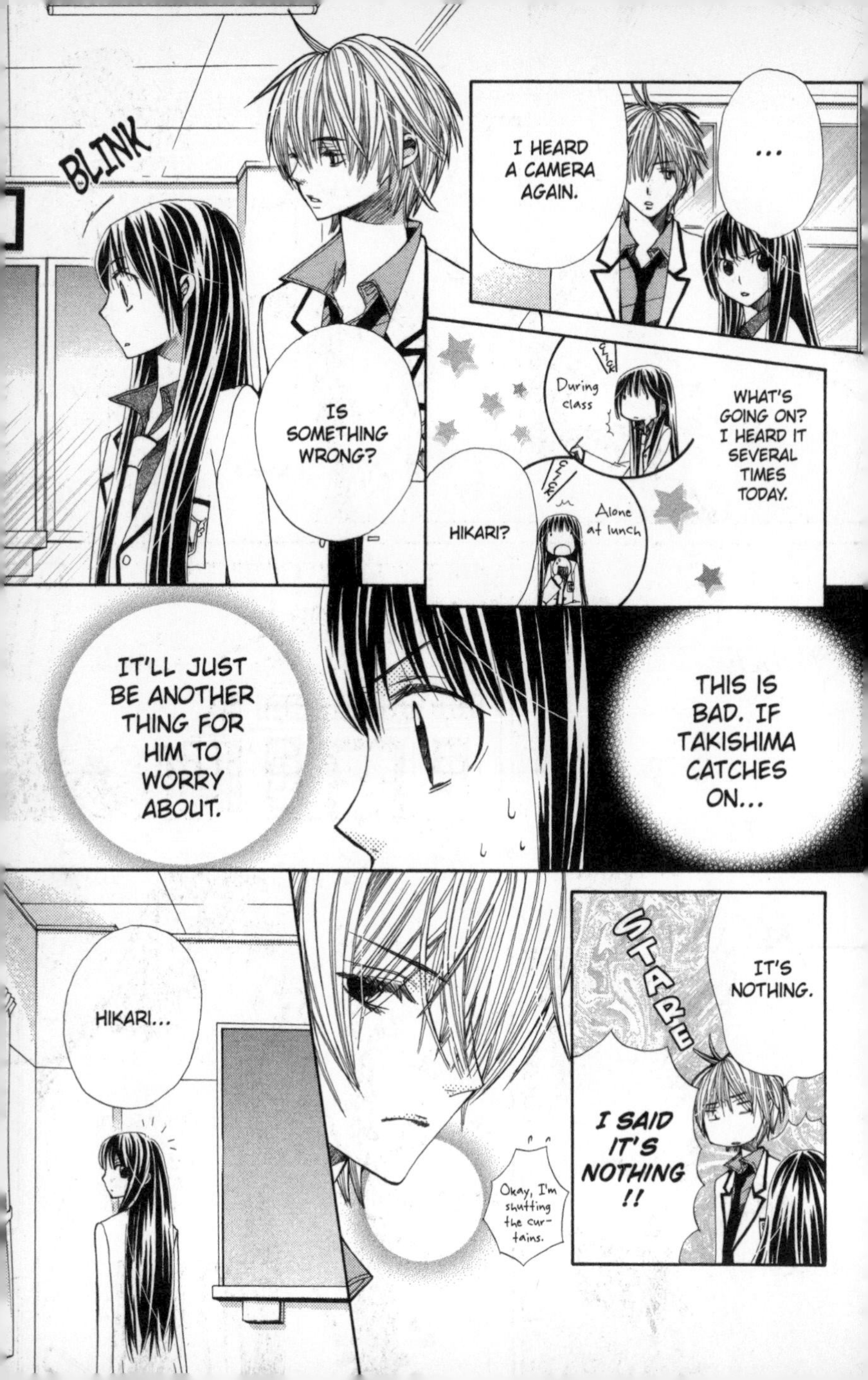
...
I HEARD A CAMERA AGAIN.
WHAT'S GOING ON? I HEARD IT SEVERAL TIMES TODAY.
CLICK
During class
CLICK
Alone at lunch
HIKARI?
IS SOMETHING WRONG?
BLINK
THIS IS BAD. IF TAKISHIMA CATCHES ON...
IT'LL JUST BE ANOTHER THING FOR HIM TO WORRY ABOUT.
IT'S NOTHING.
STARE
I SAID IT'S NOTHING!!
Okay, I'm shutting the cur-tains.
HIKARI...

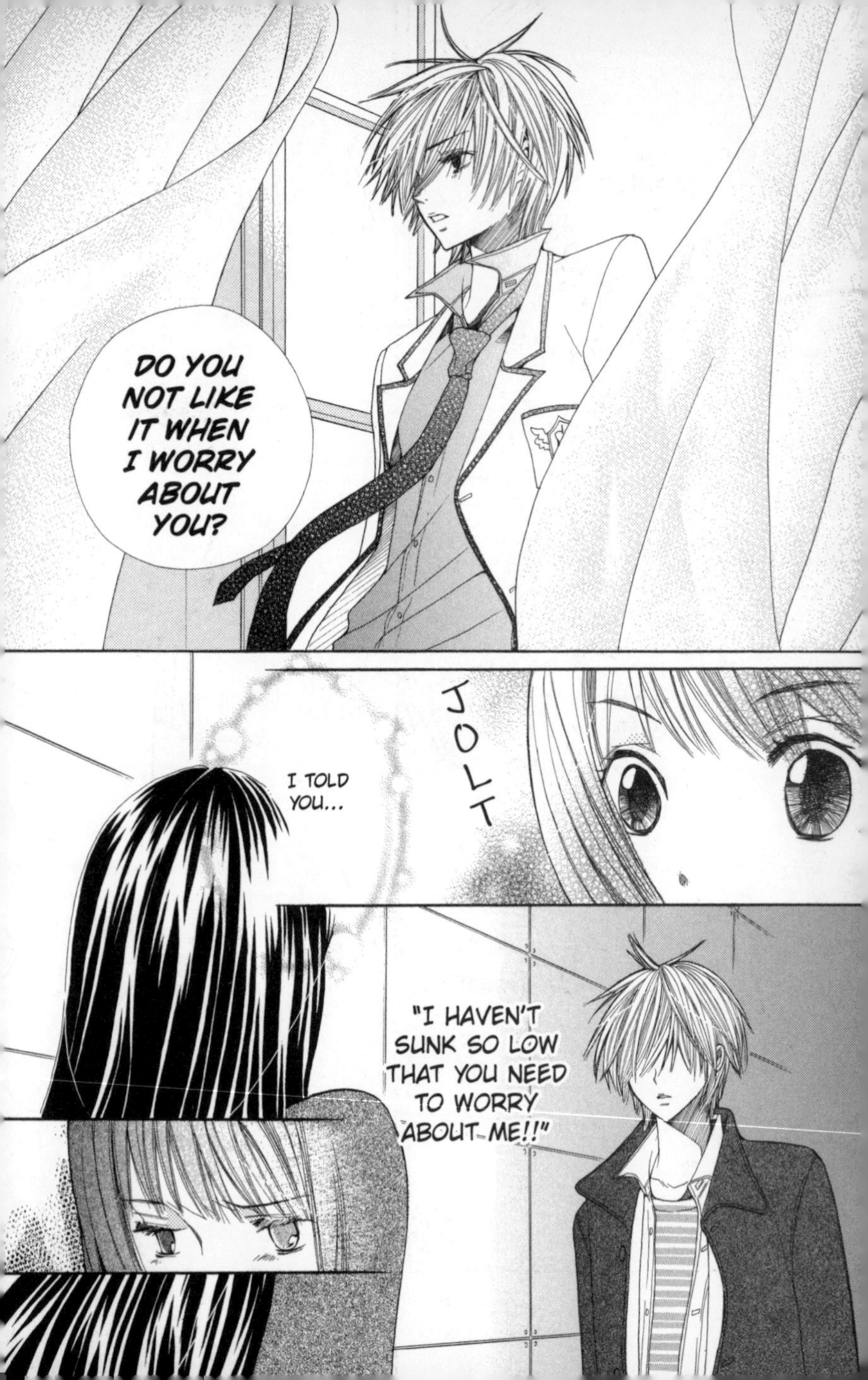
DO YOU NOT LIKE IT WHEN I WORRY ABOUT YOU?
JOLT
I TOLD YOU...
"I HAVEN'T SUNK SO LOW THAT YOU NEED TO WORRY ABOUT ME!!"

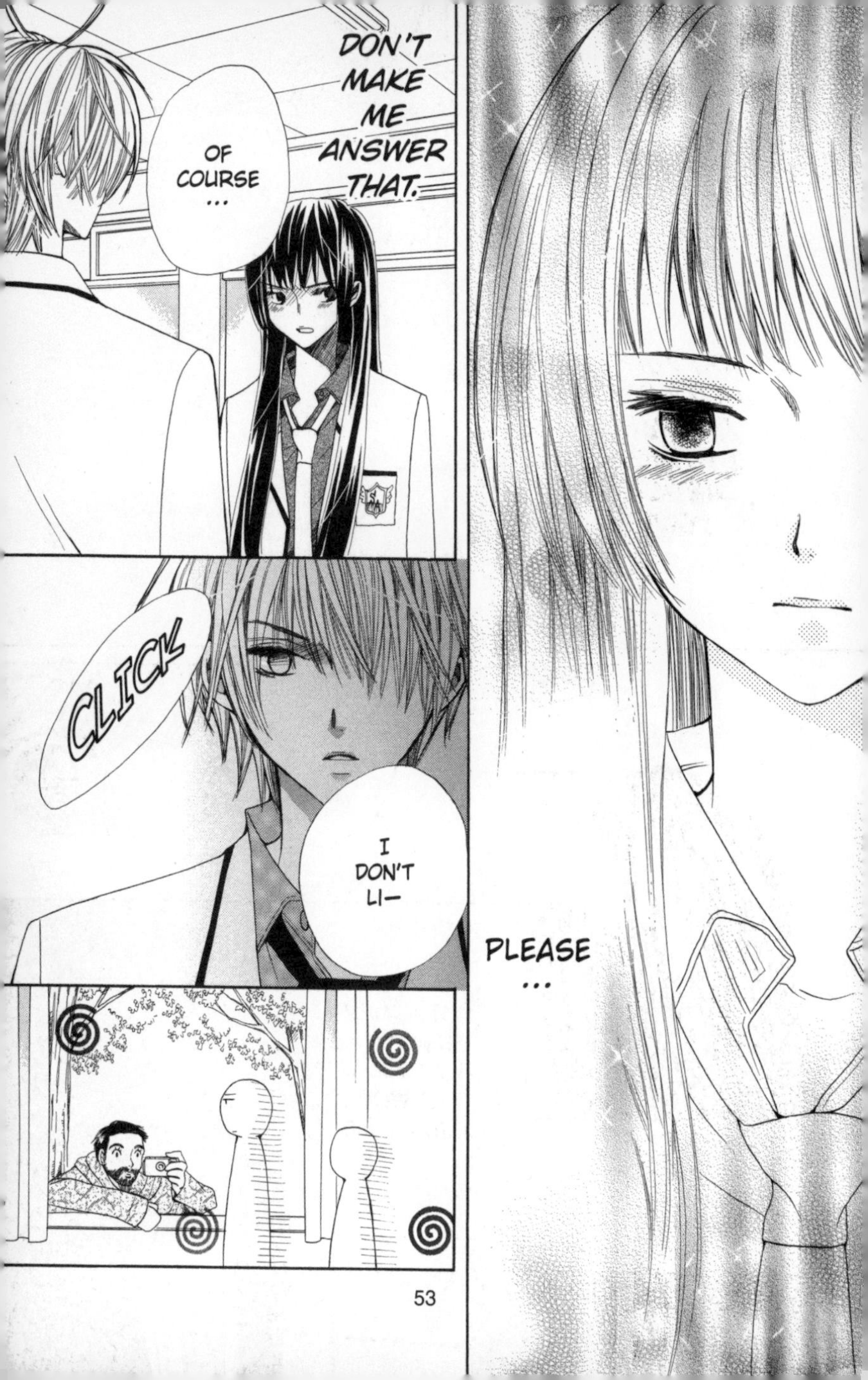
PLEASE ...
DON'T MAKE ME ANSWER THAT.
OF COURSE ...
I DON'T LI—
CLICK

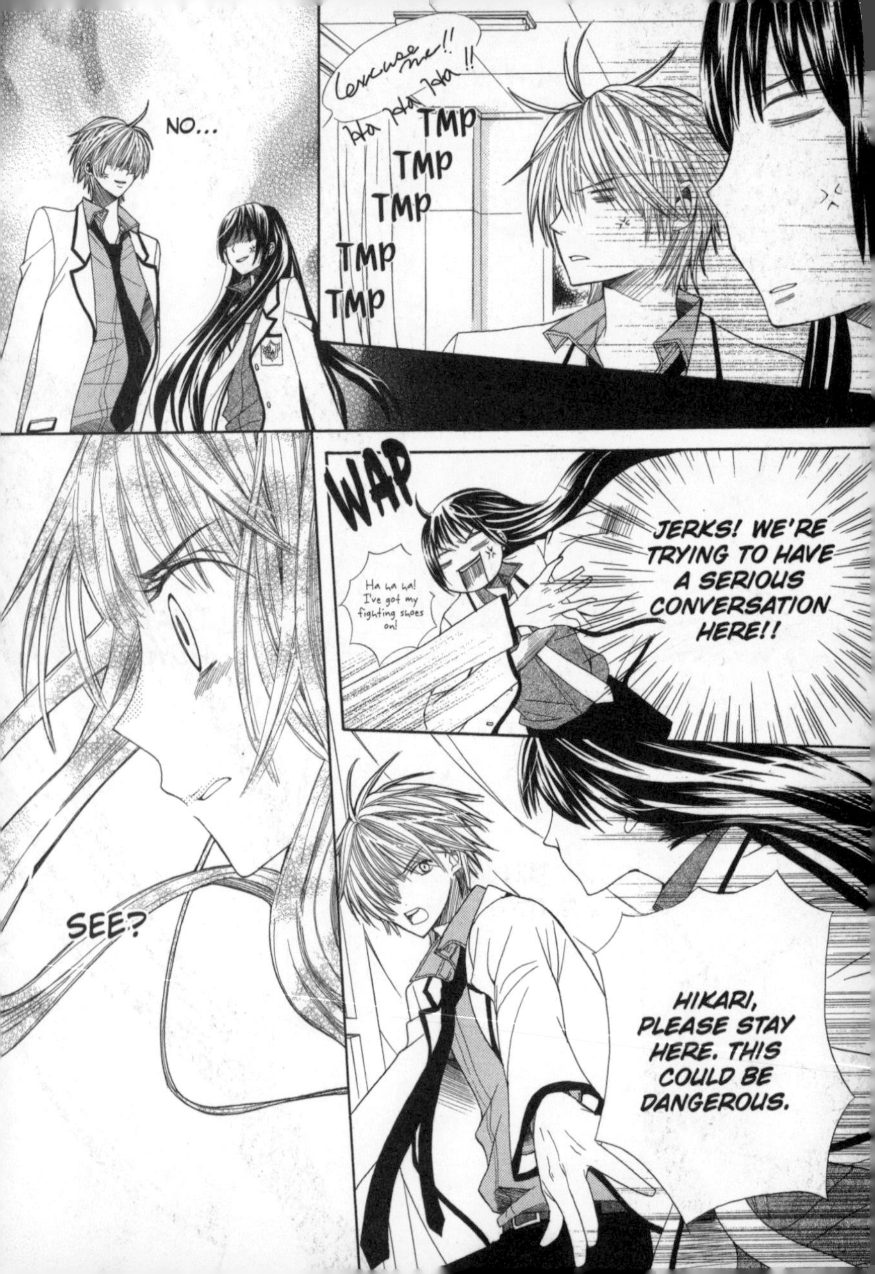
Excuse me!!
TMP
TMP
TMP
TMP
TMP
NO...
WAP
JERKS! WE'RE TRYING TO HAVE A SERIOUS CONVERSATION HERE!!
Ha ha ha! I've got my fighting shoes on!
HIKARI, PLEASE STAY HERE. THIS COULD BE DANGEROUS.
SEE?

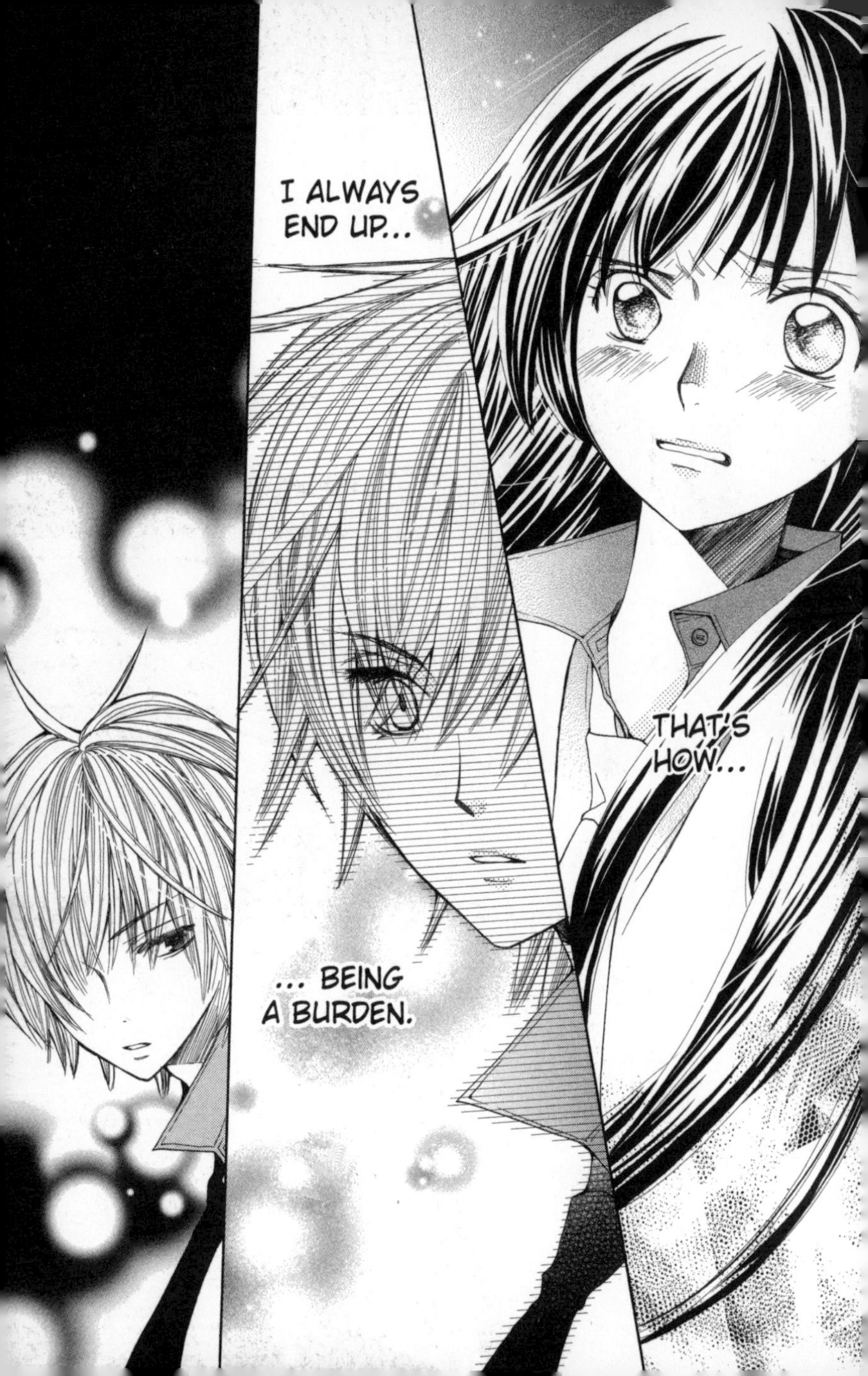
THAT'S HOW...
I ALWAYS END UP...
... BEING A BURDEN.

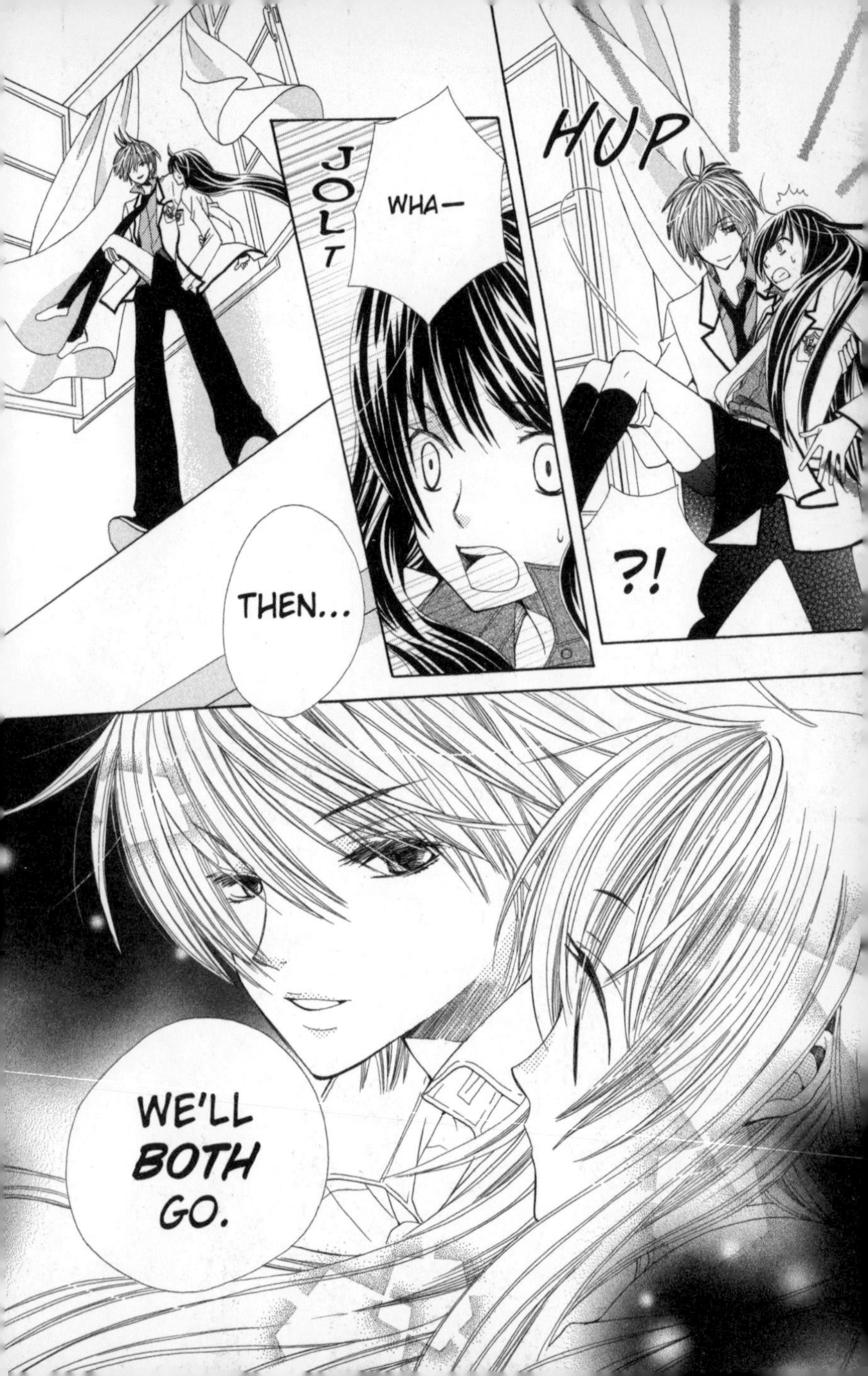
HUP
?!
JOLT
WHA—
THEN...
WE'LL BOTH GO.

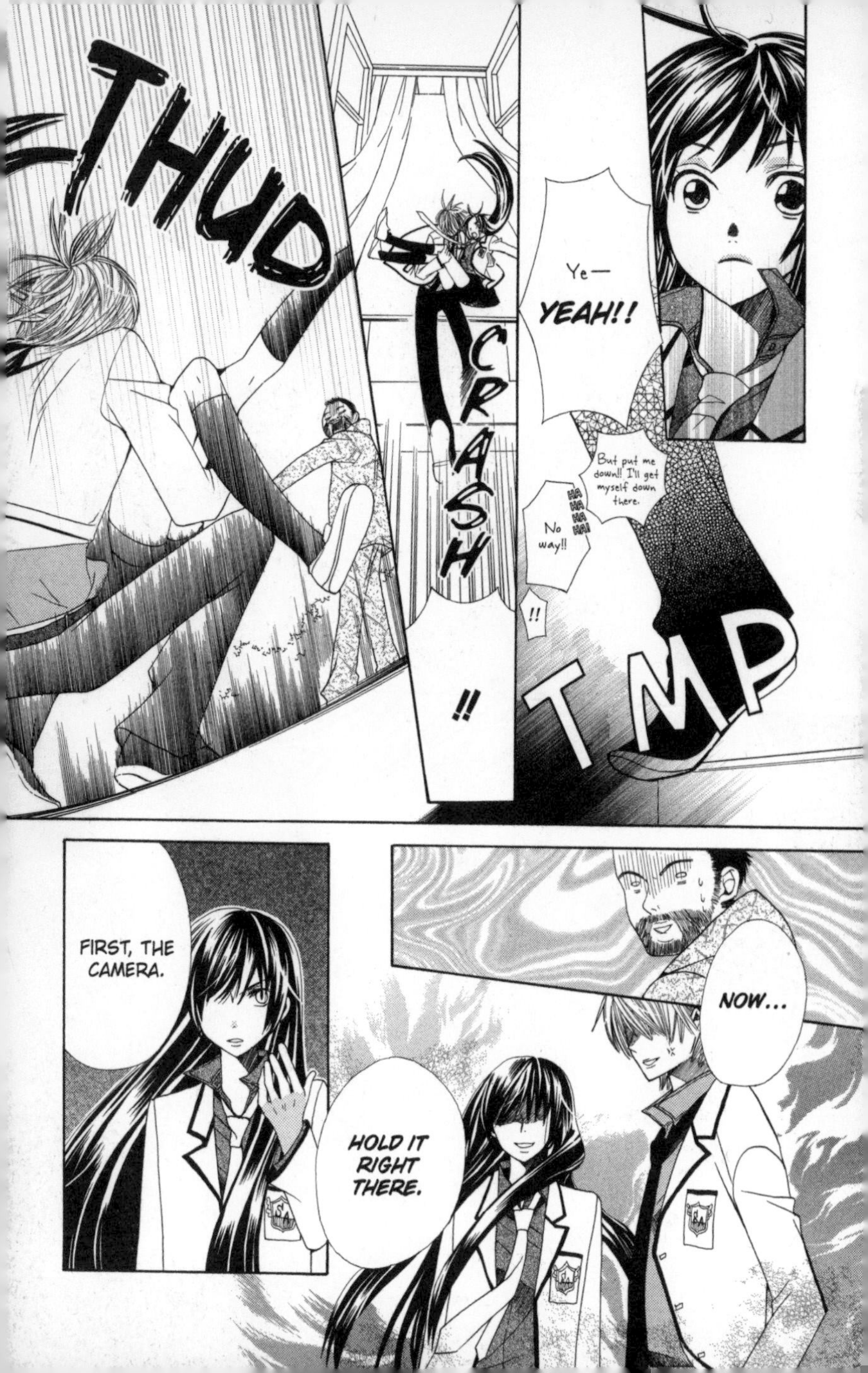
Ye—
YEAH!!
But put me down!! I'll get myself down there.
HA HA HA HA!
No way!!
!!
TMP
CRASH
!!
THUD
NOW...
HOLD IT RIGHT THERE.
FIRST, THE CAMERA.

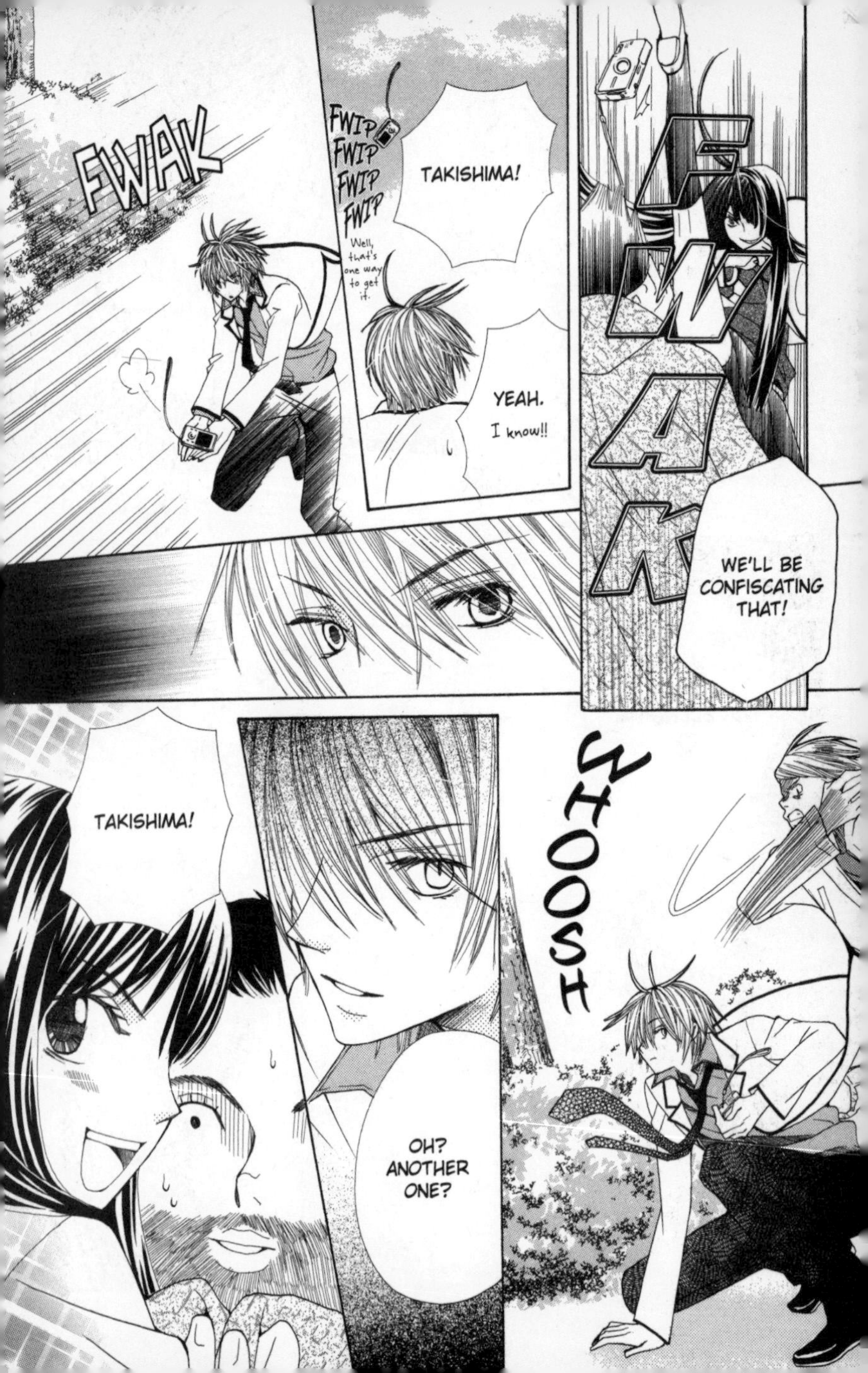
FWAK
WE'LL BE CONFISCATING THAT!
TAKISHIMA!
FWIP FWIP FWIP FWIP
Well, that's one way to get it.
YEAH.
I know!!
FWAK
WHOOSH
OH? ANOTHER ONE?
TAKISHIMA!

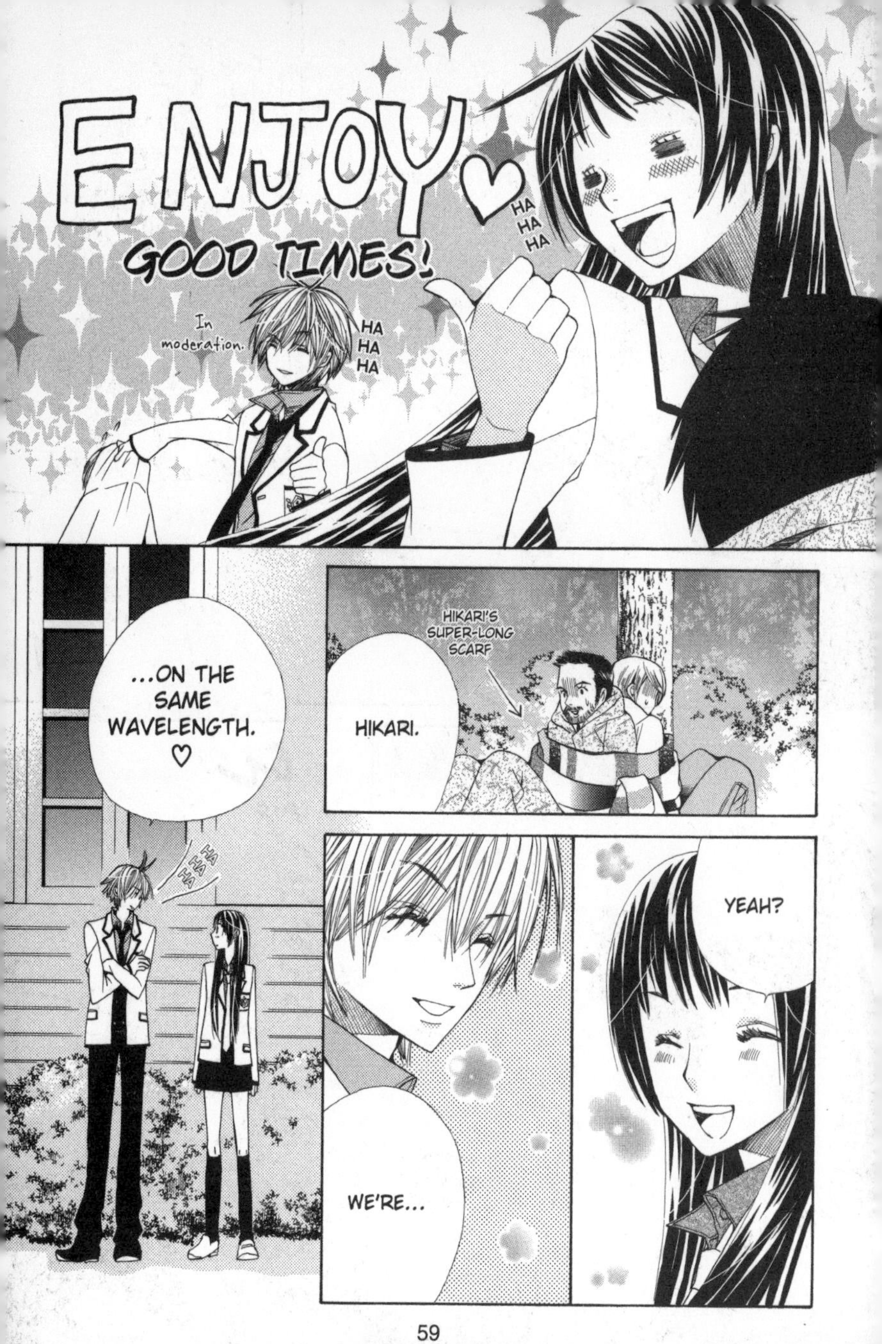

HA HA HA
ENJOY♡
GOOD TIMES!
HA HA HA
In moderation.
HIKARI.
HIKARI'S SUPER-LONG SCARF
YEAH?
WE'RE...
...ON THE SAME WAVELENGTH. ♡
HA HA HA

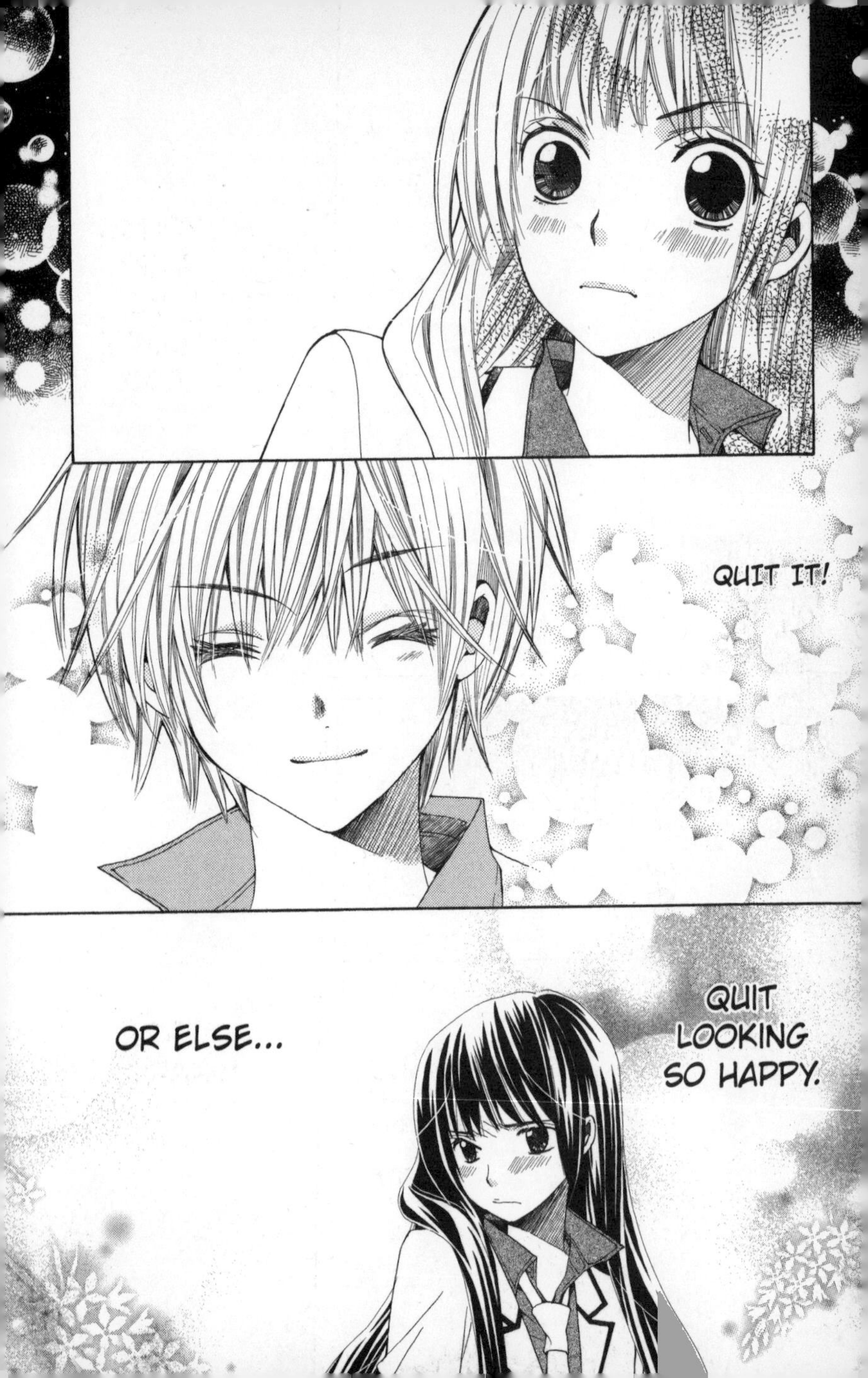
QUIT IT!
QUIT LOOKING SO HAPPY.
OR ELSE...

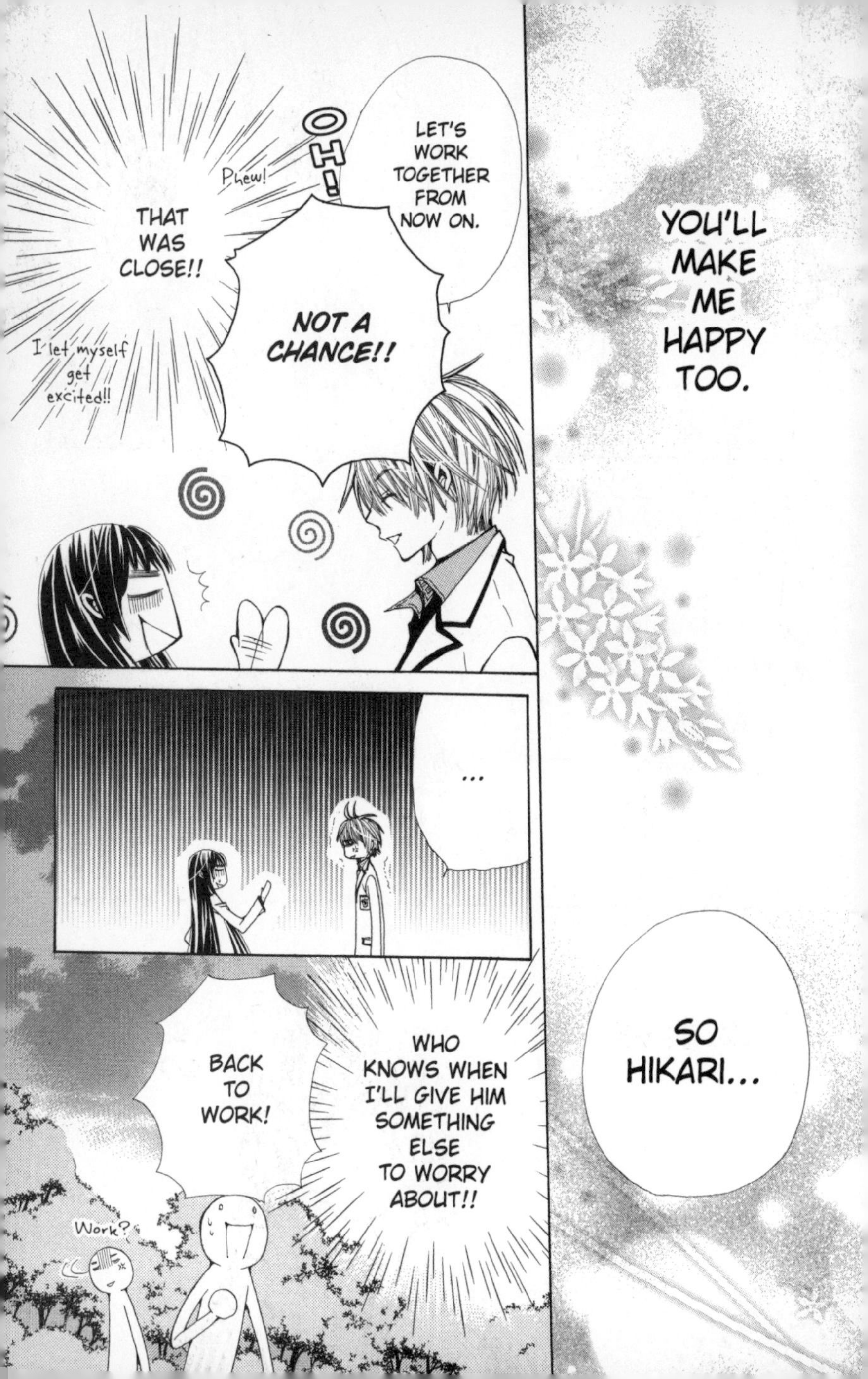
YOU'LL MAKE ME HAPPY TOO.
SO HIKARI...
LET'S WORK TOGETHER FROM NOW ON.
OH!
NOT A CHANCE!!
Phew!
THAT WAS CLOSE!!
I let myself get excited!!
...
WHO KNOWS WHEN I'LL GIVE HIM SOMETHING ELSE TO WORRY ABOUT!!
BACK TO WORK!
Work?

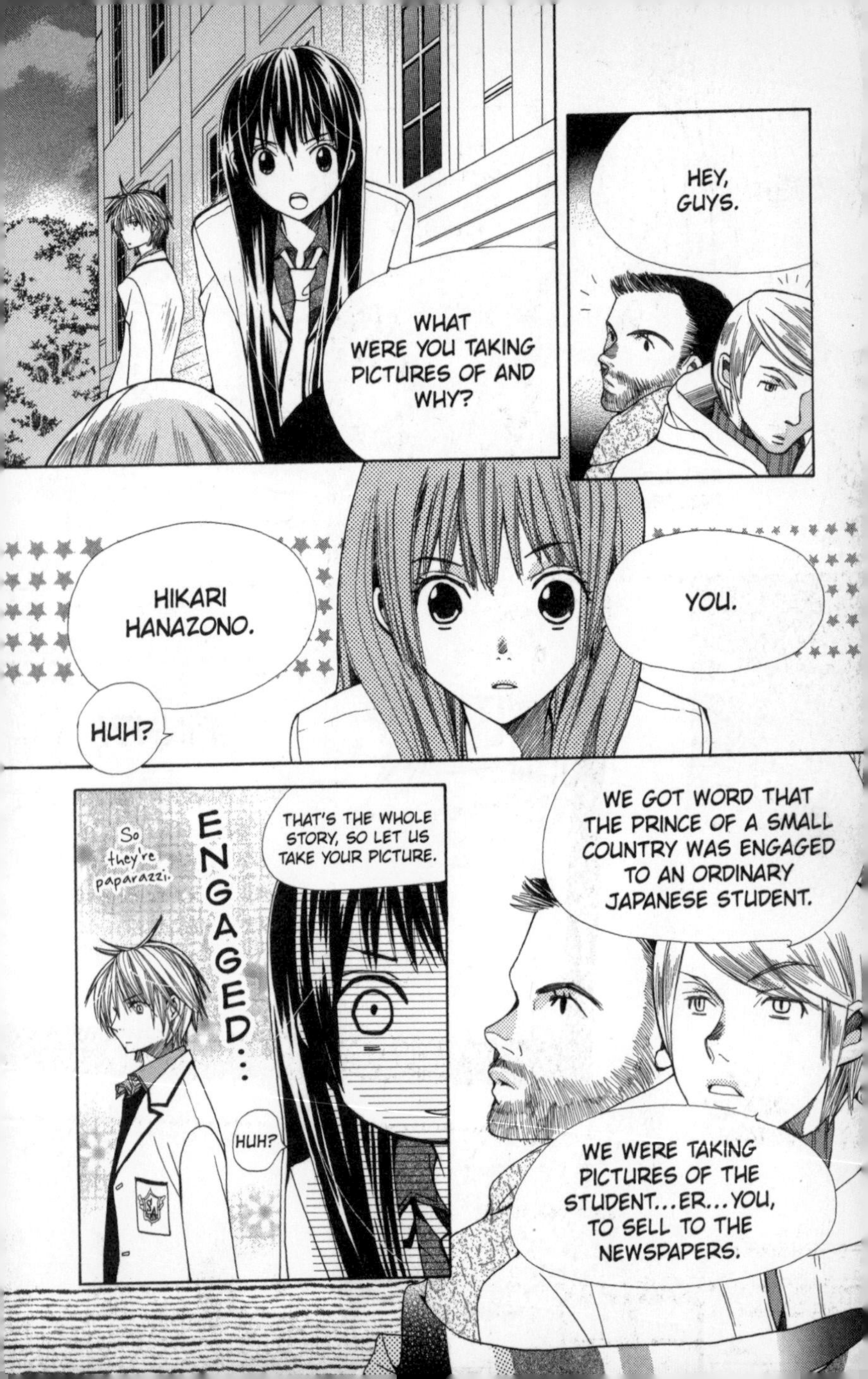
HEY, GUYS.
WHAT WERE YOU TAKING PICTURES OF AND WHY?
YOU.
HIKARI HANAZONO.
HUH?
WE GOT WORD THAT THE PRINCE OF A SMALL COUNTRY WAS ENGAGED TO AN ORDINARY JAPANESE STUDENT.
WE WERE TAKING PICTURES OF THE STUDENT...ER...YOU, TO SELL TO THE NEWSPAPERS.
THAT'S THE WHOLE STORY, SO LET US TAKE YOUR PICTURE.
ENGAGED...
HUH?
So they're paparazzi.

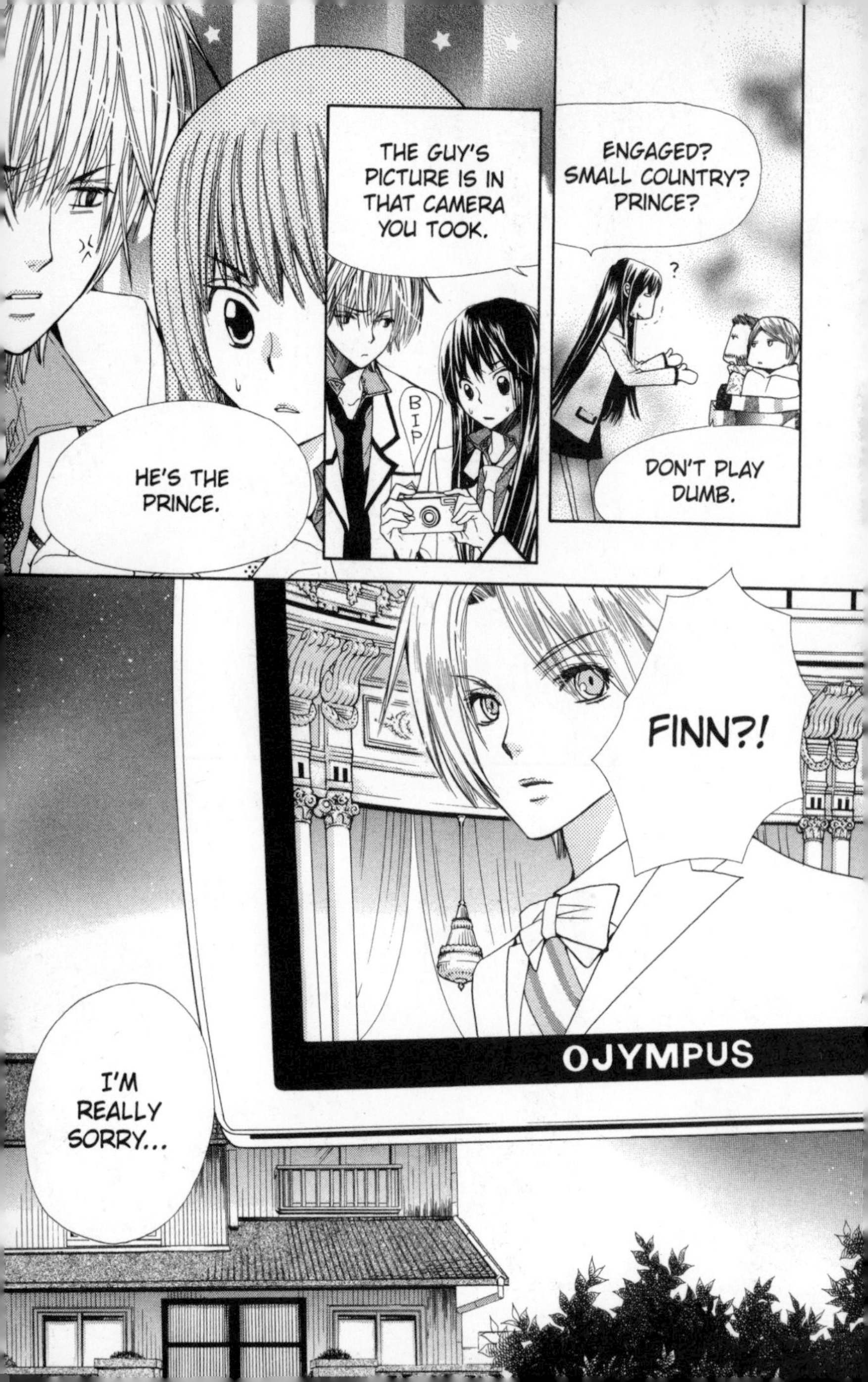
ENGAGED? SMALL COUNTRY? PRINCE?
?
DON'T PLAY DUMB.
THE GUY'S PICTURE IS IN THAT CAMERA YOU TOOK.
BIP
HE'S THE PRINCE.
FINN?!
OJYMPUS
I'M REALLY SORRY...

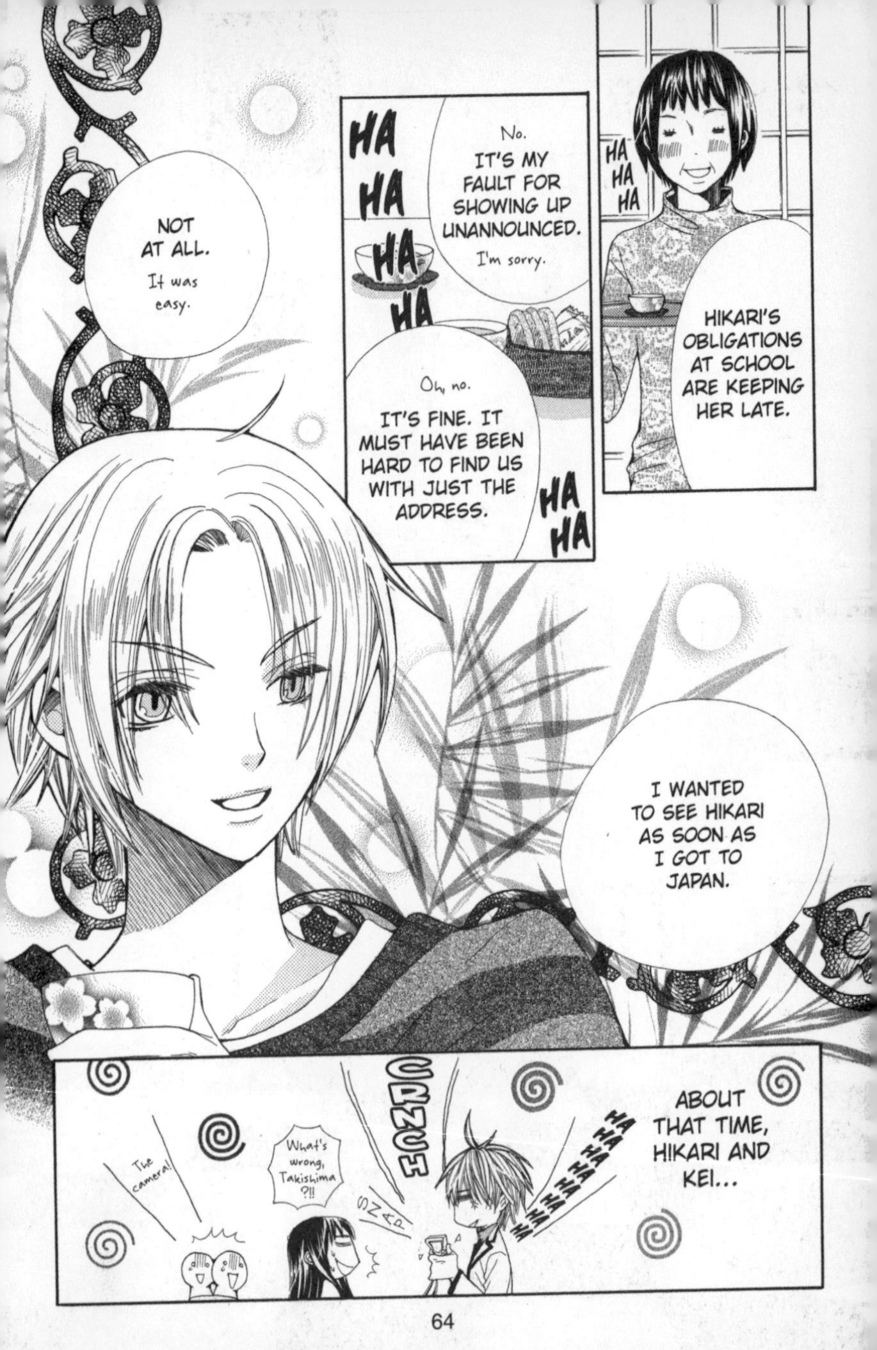
HA HA HA
HIKARI'S OBLIGATIONS AT SCHOOL ARE KEEPING HER LATE.
HA HA HA HA
No. IT'S MY FAULT FOR SHOWING UP UNANNOUNCED. I'm sorry.
Oh, no. IT'S FINE. IT MUST HAVE BEEN HARD TO FIND US WITH JUST THE ADDRESS.
HA HA
NOT AT ALL. It was easy.
I WANTED TO SEE HIKARI AS SOON AS I GOT TO JAPAN.
ABOUT THAT TIME, HIKARI AND KEI...
HAHAHAHAHAHAHAHA
CRNCH
SNAP
What's wrong, Takishima?!!
The camera!

Chapter 49

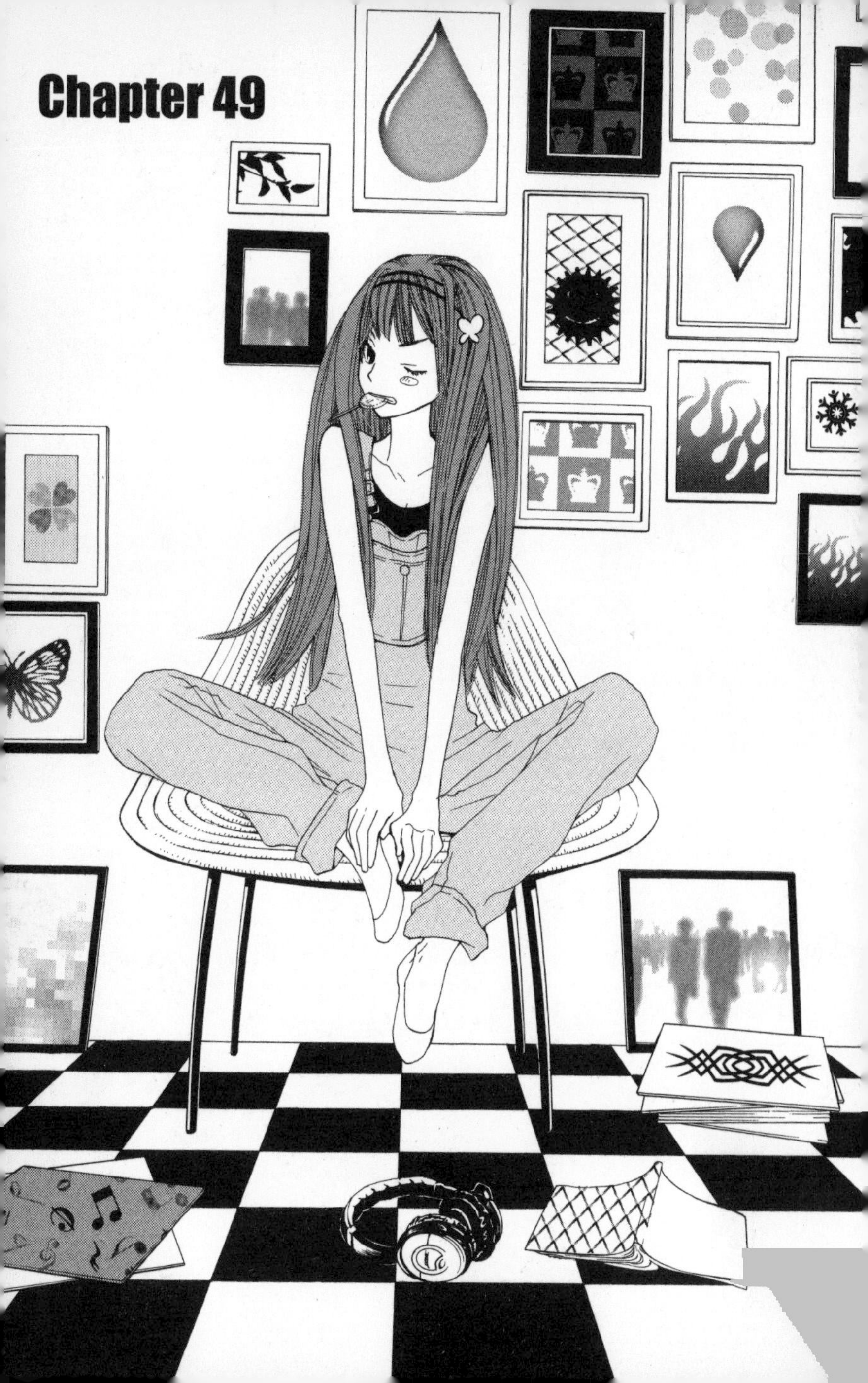

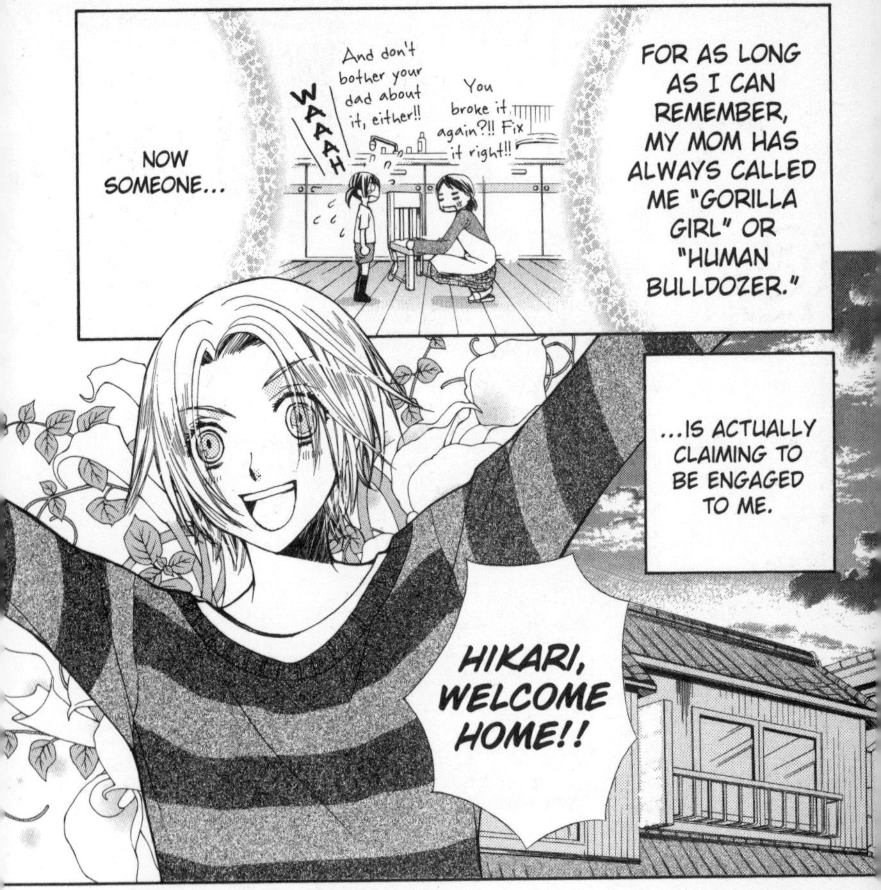
FOR AS LONG AS I CAN REMEMBER, MY MOM HAS ALWAYS CALLED ME "GORILLA GIRL" OR "HUMAN BULLDOZER."
You broke it again?!! Fix it right!!
And don't bother your dad about it, either!!
WAAAH
NOW SOMEONE...
...IS ACTUALLY CLAIMING TO BE ENGAGED TO ME.
HIKARI, WELCOME HOME!!

•BOOKS ON CD, PART 2•

THE VOICE ACTORS AND STAFF WERE ALL WONDERFUL. FIRST THERE WAS A TEST TO MATCH THE CHARACTER WITH THE VOICE. THEN THE DIRECTOR AND STAFF DESCRIBED THE CHARACTERS' TRAITS BETTER THAN EVEN I, THE AUTHOR, COULD. NOT A SURPRISE. I JUST WATCHED WITH MY MOUTH OPEN. FOR THE CHOCOLATE-EATING SCENE, THE VOICE ACTORS ACTUALLY BROUGHT CHOCOLATE. AND TO DO THE KANSAI DIALECT, THEY LISTENED TO A LECTURE BY SOMEONE FROM KANSAI. THEY WERE ALL SO WONDERFUL!! IT REALLY TURNED OUT TO BE A FANTASTIC CD! THANK YOU VERY MUCH!

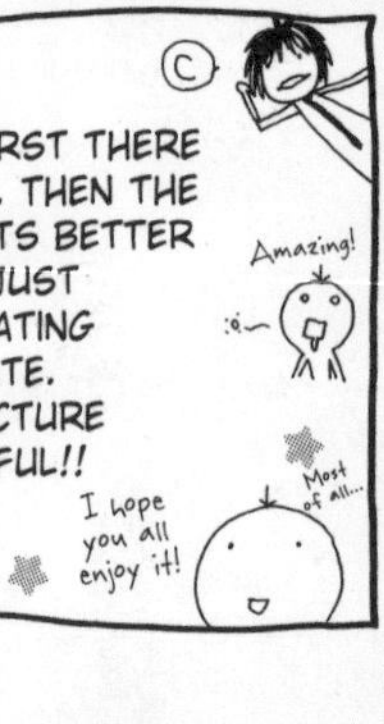
Amazing!
Most of all...
I hope you all enjoy it!

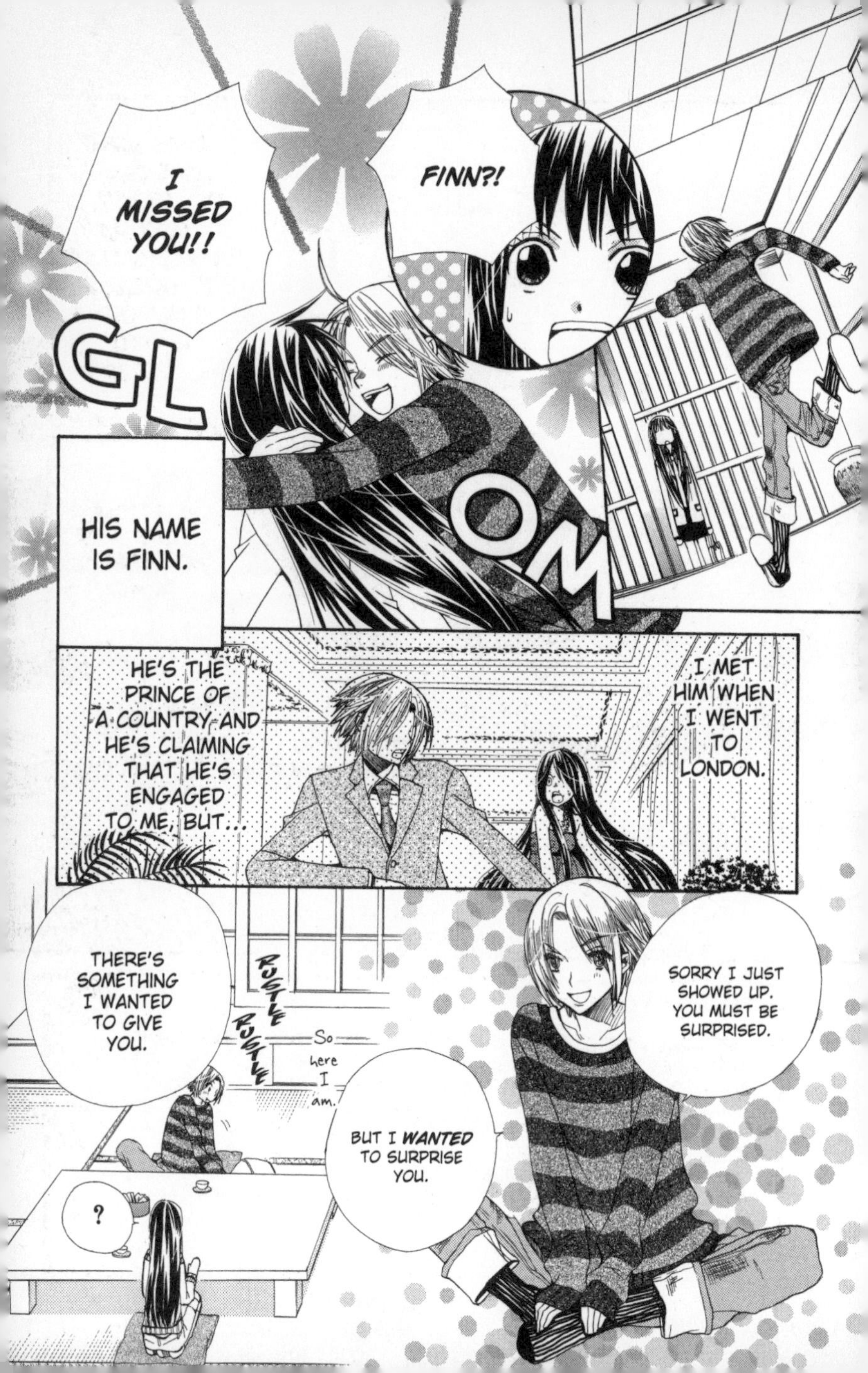

FINN?!
I MISSED YOU!!
GLOMP
HIS NAME IS FINN.
I MET HIM WHEN I WENT TO LONDON.
HE'S THE PRINCE OF A COUNTRY AND HE'S CLAIMING THAT HE'S ENGAGED TO ME, BUT...
SORRY I JUST SHOWED UP. YOU MUST BE SURPRISED.
BUT I *WANTED* TO SURPRISE YOU.
So here I am.
RUSTLE RUSTLE
THERE'S SOMETHING I WANTED TO GIVE YOU.
?

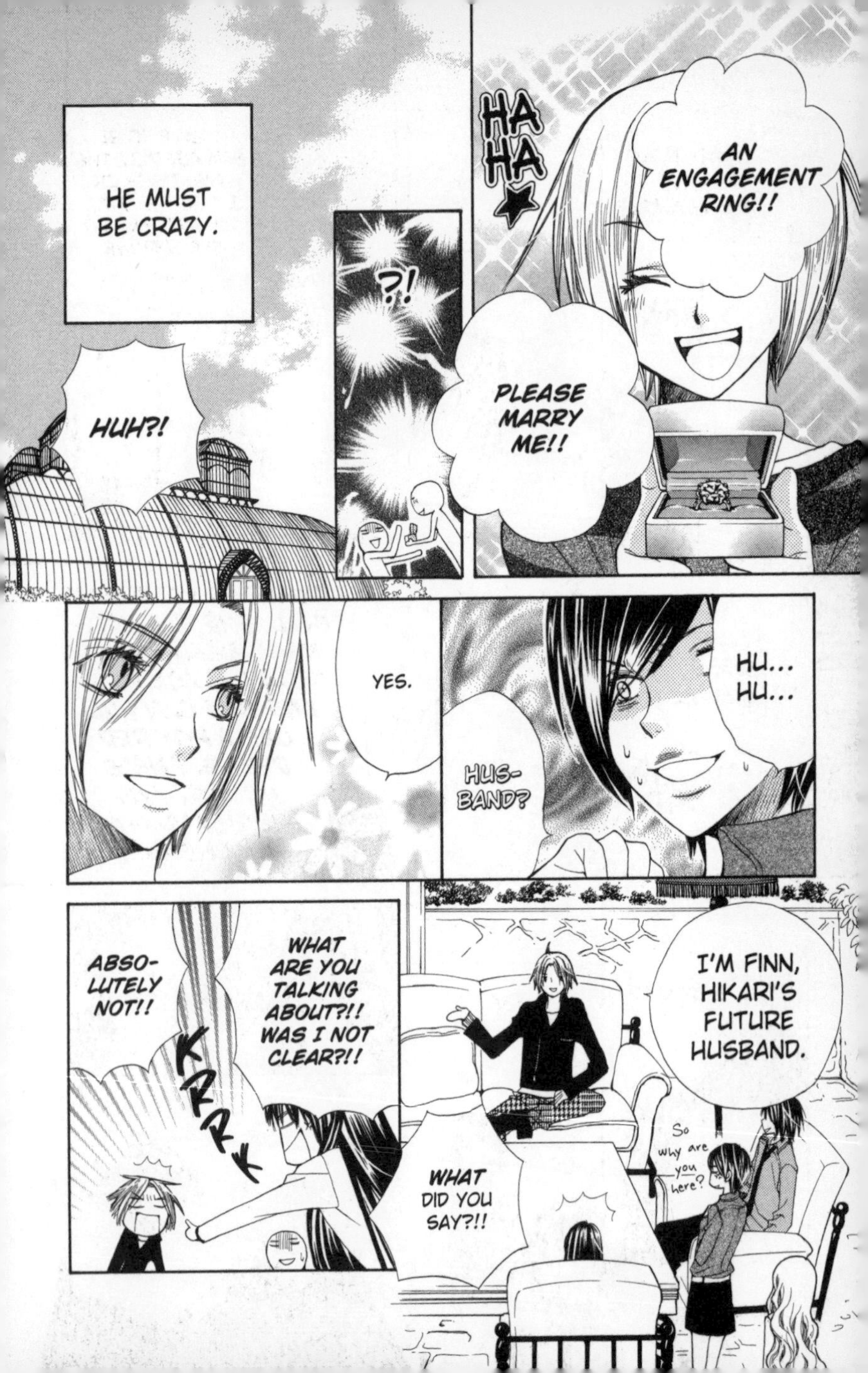
HA HA ★
AN ENGAGEMENT RING!!
PLEASE MARRY ME!!
?!
HE MUST BE CRAZY.
HUH?!
HU... HU...
HUS-BAND?
YES.
I'M FINN, HIKARI'S FUTURE HUSBAND.
So why are you here?
WHAT DID YOU SAY?!!
WHAT ARE YOU TALKING ABOUT?!! WAS I NOT CLEAR?!!
ABSO-LUTELY NOT!!

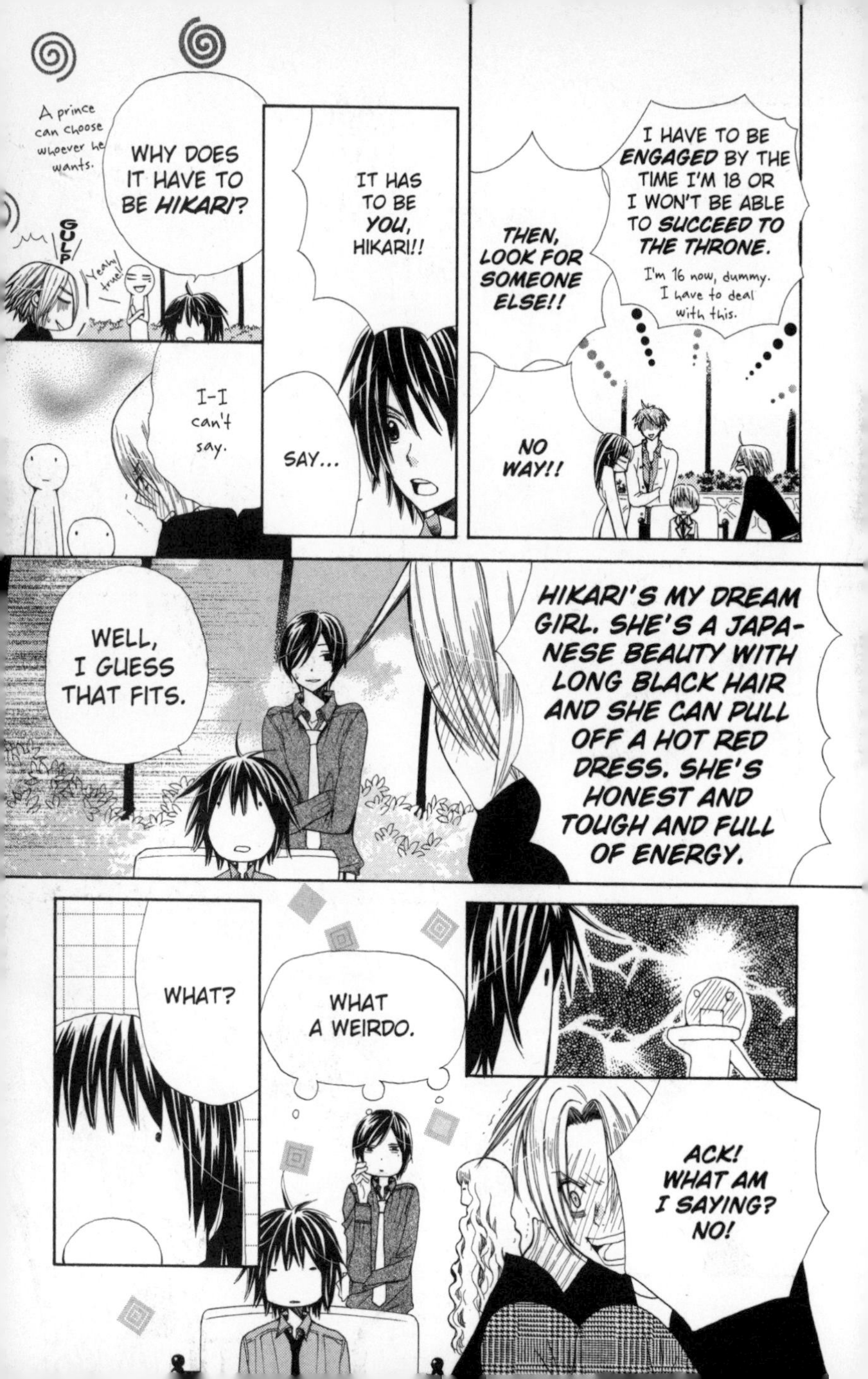
I HAVE TO BE ENGAGED BY THE TIME I'M 18 OR I WON'T BE ABLE TO SUCCEED TO THE THRONE.
I'm 16 now, dummy. I have to deal with this.
THEN, LOOK FOR SOMEONE ELSE!!
NO WAY!!
IT HAS TO BE YOU, HIKARI!!
SAY...
WHY DOES IT HAVE TO BE HIKARI?
A prince can choose whoever he wants.
GULP
Yeah! true!
I-I can't say.
HIKARI'S MY DREAM GIRL. SHE'S A JAPANESE BEAUTY WITH LONG BLACK HAIR AND SHE CAN PULL OFF A HOT RED DRESS. SHE'S HONEST AND TOUGH AND FULL OF ENERGY.
WELL, I GUESS THAT FITS.
ACK! WHAT AM I SAYING? NO!
WHAT A WEIRDO.
WHAT?

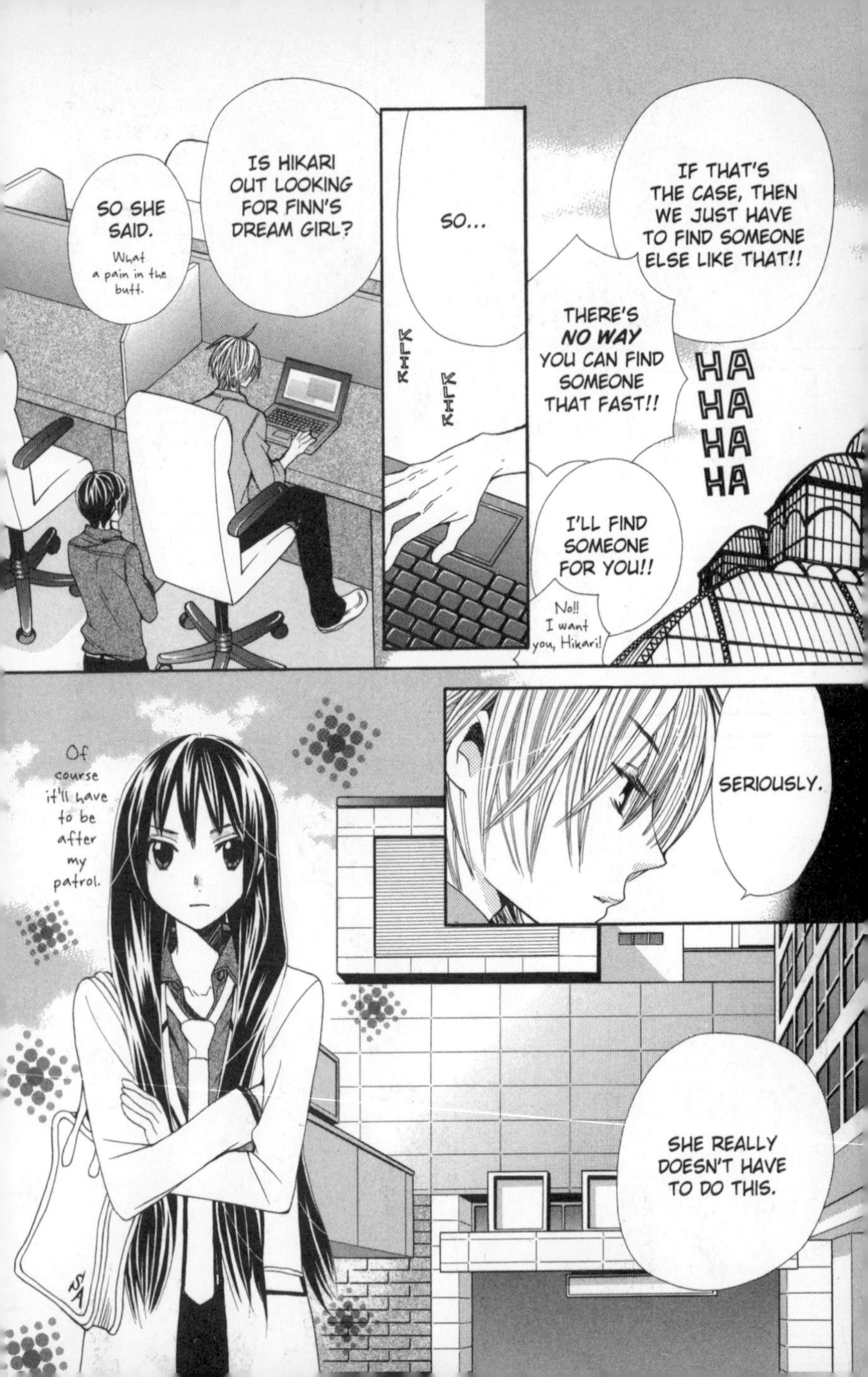
IF THAT'S THE CASE, THEN WE JUST HAVE TO FIND SOMEONE ELSE LIKE THAT!!
THERE'S **NO WAY** YOU CAN FIND SOMEONE THAT FAST!!
HA HA HA HA
I'LL FIND SOMEONE FOR YOU!!
No!! I want you, Hikari!
SO...
KLIK
KLIK
IS HIKARI OUT LOOKING FOR FINN'S DREAM GIRL?
SO SHE SAID.
What a pain in the butt.
SERIOUSLY.
SHE REALLY DOESN'T HAVE TO DO THIS.
Of course it'll have to be after my patrol.

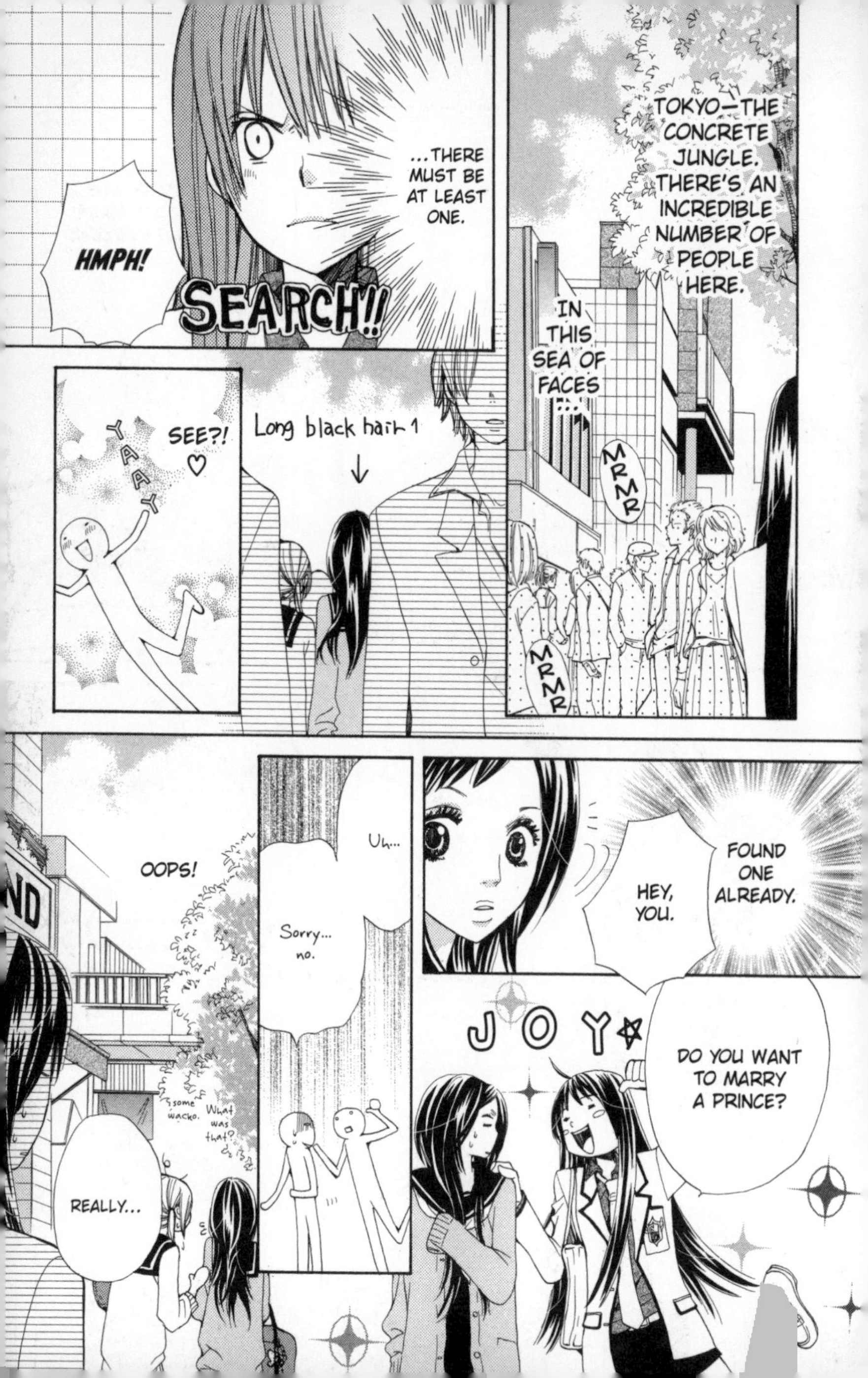
TOKYO—THE CONCRETE JUNGLE. THERE'S AN INCREDIBLE NUMBER OF PEOPLE HERE.
IN THIS SEA OF FACES ...
MRMR
MRMR
...THERE MUST BE AT LEAST ONE.
HMPH!
SEARCH!!
Long black hair 1
SEE?! ♡
YAAAY
FOUND ONE ALREADY.
HEY, YOU.
DO YOU WANT TO MARRY A PRINCE?
JOY
Uh...
Sorry... no.
What was that?
some wacko.
OOPS!
REALLY...

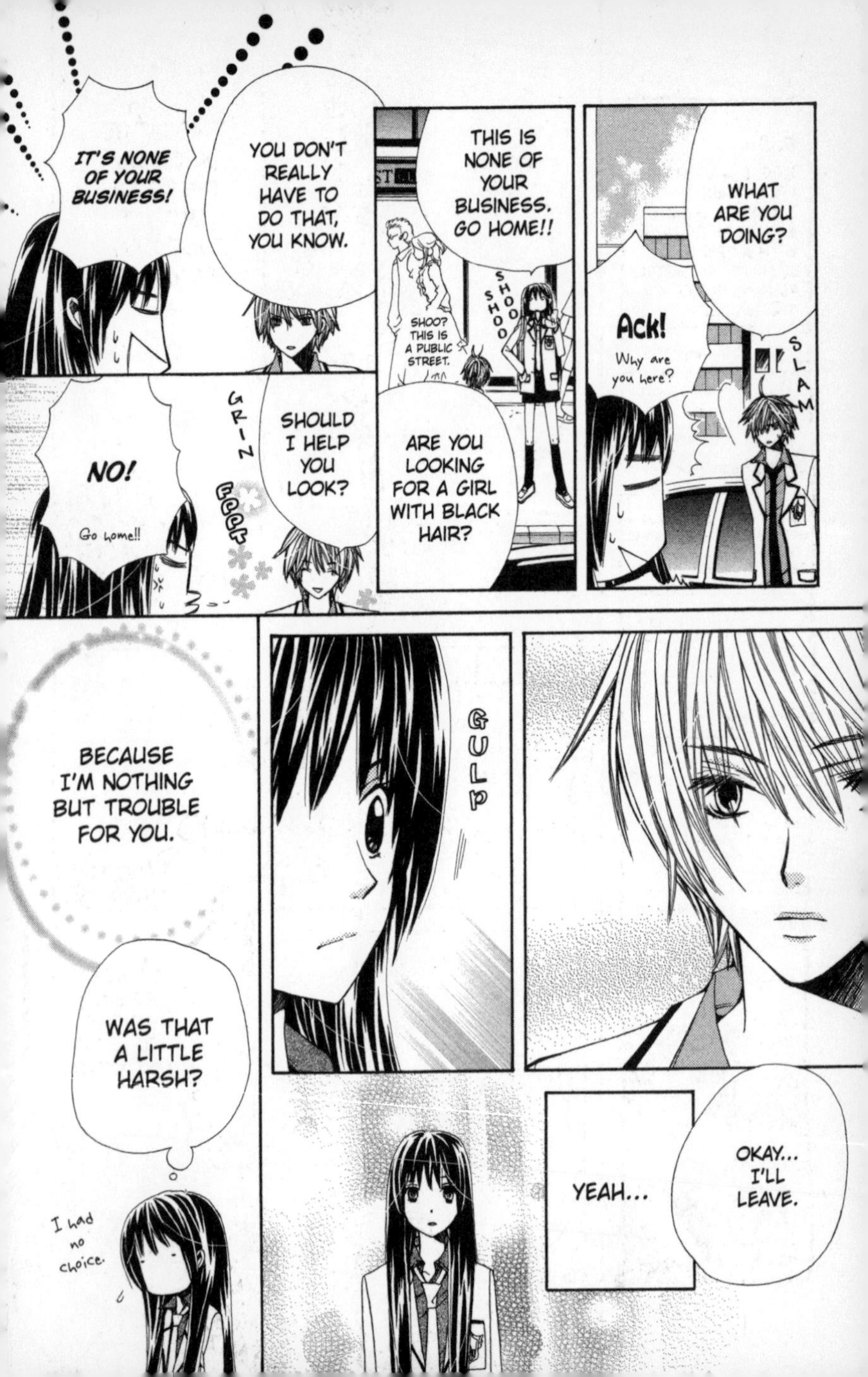
WHAT ARE YOU DOING?
SLAM
Ack!
Why are you here?
THIS IS NONE OF YOUR BUSINESS. GO HOME!!
SHOO SHOO
SHOO? THIS IS A PUBLIC STREET.
ARE YOU LOOKING FOR A GIRL WITH BLACK HAIR?
YOU DON'T REALLY HAVE TO DO THAT, YOU KNOW.
IT'S NONE OF YOUR BUSINESS!
SHOULD I HELP YOU LOOK?
GRIN
NO!
Go home!!
GULP
OKAY... I'LL LEAVE.
YEAH...
BECAUSE I'M NOTHING BUT TROUBLE FOR YOU.
WAS THAT A LITTLE HARSH?
I had no choice.

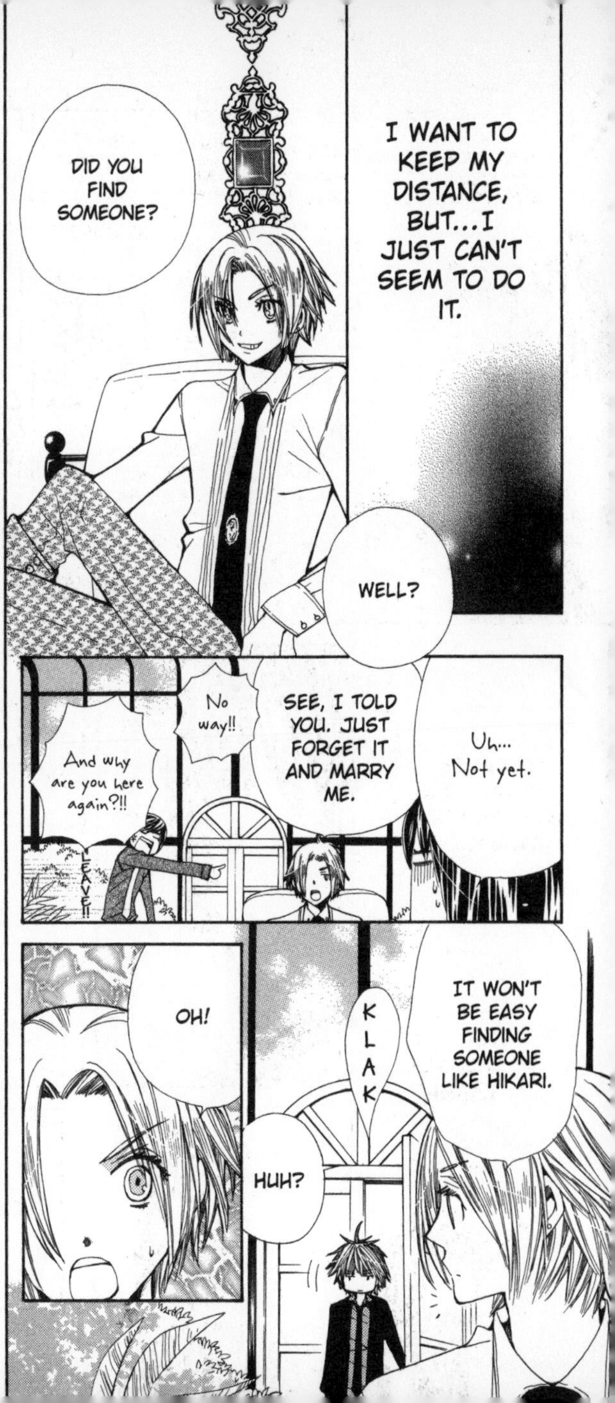
I WANT TO KEEP MY DISTANCE, BUT...I JUST CAN'T SEEM TO DO IT.
DID YOU FIND SOMEONE?
WELL?
Uh... Not yet.
SEE, I TOLD YOU. JUST FORGET IT AND MARRY ME.
No way!!
And why are you here again?!!
LEAVE!!
IT WON'T BE EASY FINDING SOMEONE LIKE HIKARI.
KLAK
HUH?
OH!

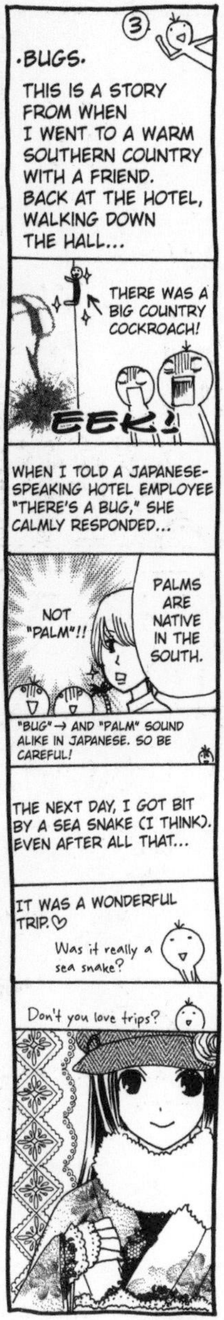
3
·BUGS·
THIS IS A STORY FROM WHEN I WENT TO A WARM SOUTHERN COUNTRY WITH A FRIEND. BACK AT THE HOTEL, WALKING DOWN THE HALL...
THERE WAS A BIG COUNTRY COCKROACH!
EEK!
WHEN I TOLD A JAPANESE-SPEAKING HOTEL EMPLOYEE "THERE'S A BUG," SHE CALMLY RESPONDED...
PALMS ARE NATIVE IN THE SOUTH.
NOT "PALM"!!
"BUG"→ AND "PALM" SOUND ALIKE IN JAPANESE. SO BE CAREFUL!
THE NEXT DAY, I GOT BIT BY A SEA SNAKE (I THINK). EVEN AFTER ALL THAT...
IT WAS A WONDERFUL TRIP.♡
Was it really a sea snake?
Don't you love trips?

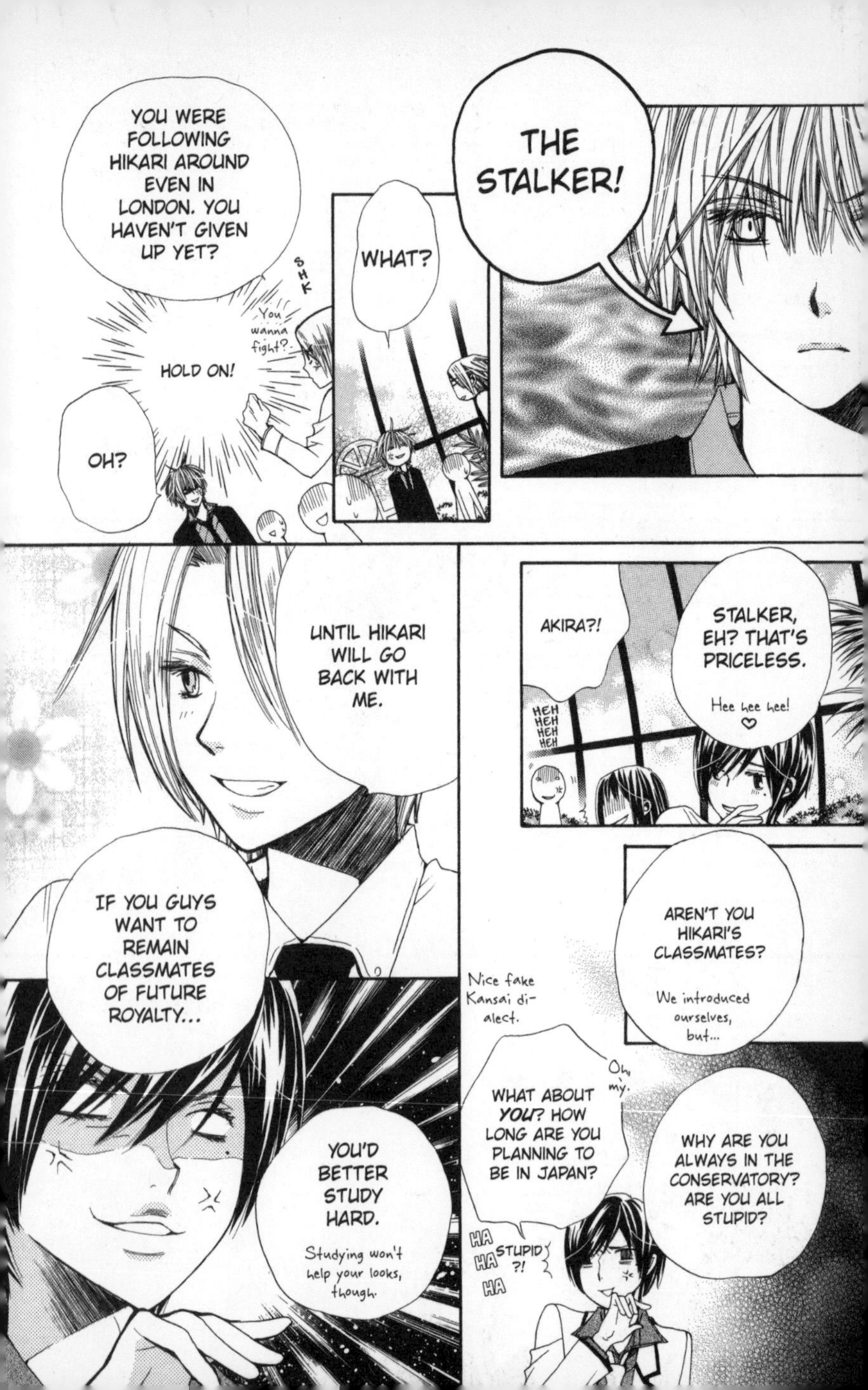
THE STALKER!
WHAT?
YOU WERE FOLLOWING HIKARI AROUND EVEN IN LONDON. YOU HAVEN'T GIVEN UP YET?
SHK
You wanna fight?
HOLD ON!
OH?
STALKER, EH? THAT'S PRICELESS.
Hee hee hee! ♡
AKIRA?!
HEH HEH HEH HEH
AREN'T YOU HIKARI'S CLASSMATES?
We introduced ourselves, but...
WHY ARE YOU ALWAYS IN THE CONSERVATORY? ARE YOU ALL STUPID?
STUPID?!
HA HA HA
Oh, my.
Nice fake Kansai dialect.
WHAT ABOUT *YOU*? HOW LONG ARE YOU PLANNING TO BE IN JAPAN?
UNTIL HIKARI WILL GO BACK WITH ME.
IF YOU GUYS WANT TO REMAIN CLASSMATES OF FUTURE ROYALTY...
YOU'D BETTER STUDY HARD.
Studying won't help your looks, though.

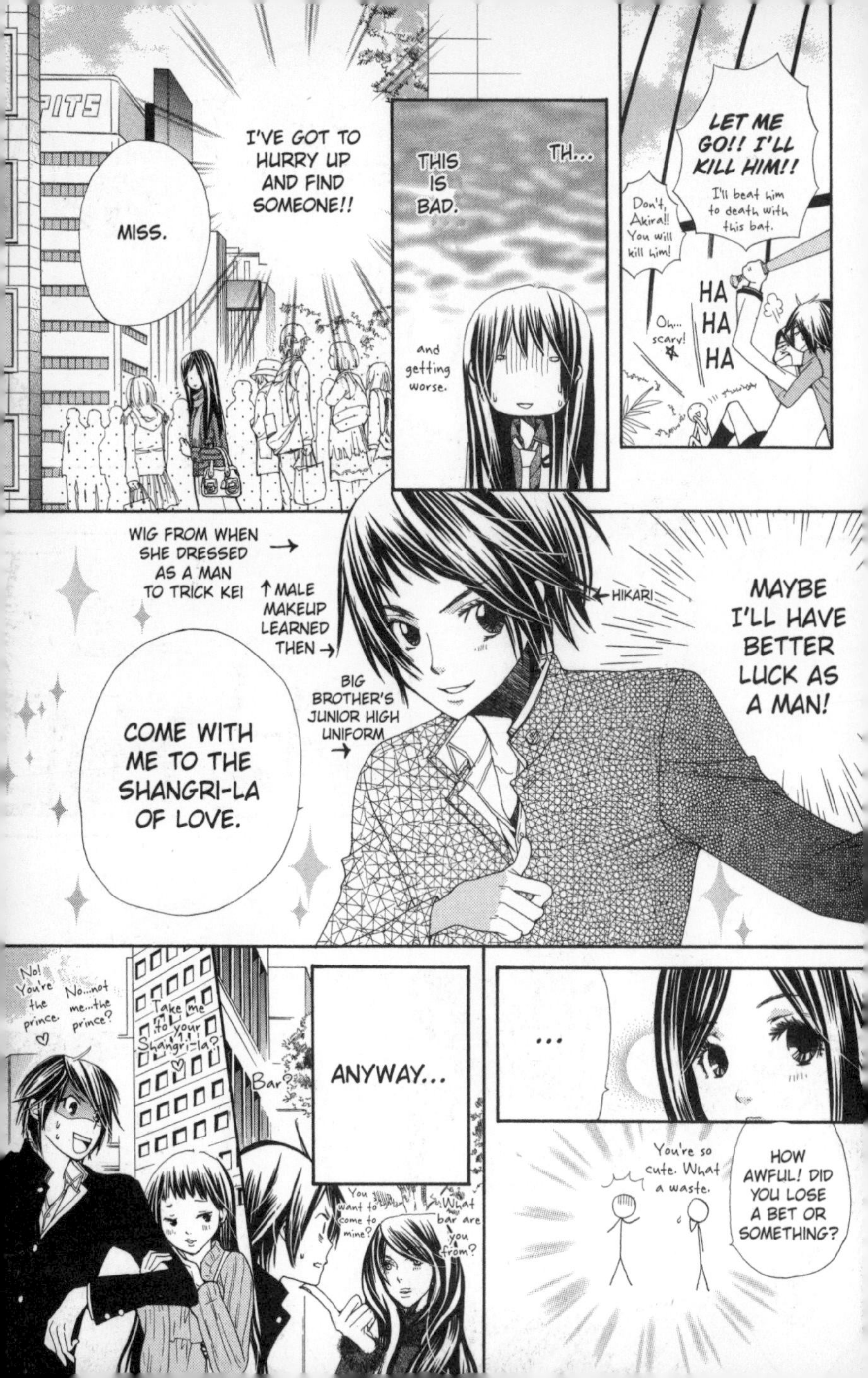
LET ME GO!! I'LL KILL HIM!!
I'll beat him to death with this bat.
Don't, Akira!! You will kill him!
HA HA HA
Oh... scary!
TH...
THIS IS BAD.
and getting worse.
I'VE GOT TO HURRY UP AND FIND SOMEONE!!
MISS.
PITS
MAYBE I'LL HAVE BETTER LUCK AS A MAN!
HIKARI
WIG FROM WHEN SHE DRESSED AS A MAN TO TRICK KEI →
↑ MALE MAKEUP LEARNED THEN →
BIG BROTHER'S JUNIOR HIGH UNIFORM →
COME WITH ME TO THE SHANGRI-LA OF LOVE.
...
HOW AWFUL! DID YOU LOSE A BET OR SOMETHING?
You're so cute. What a waste.
ANYWAY...
What bar are you from?
You want to come to mine?
Bar?
Take me to your Shangri-la?
No...not me...the prince?
No! You're the prince.

WHERE DID FINN'S IDEAL COME FROM?

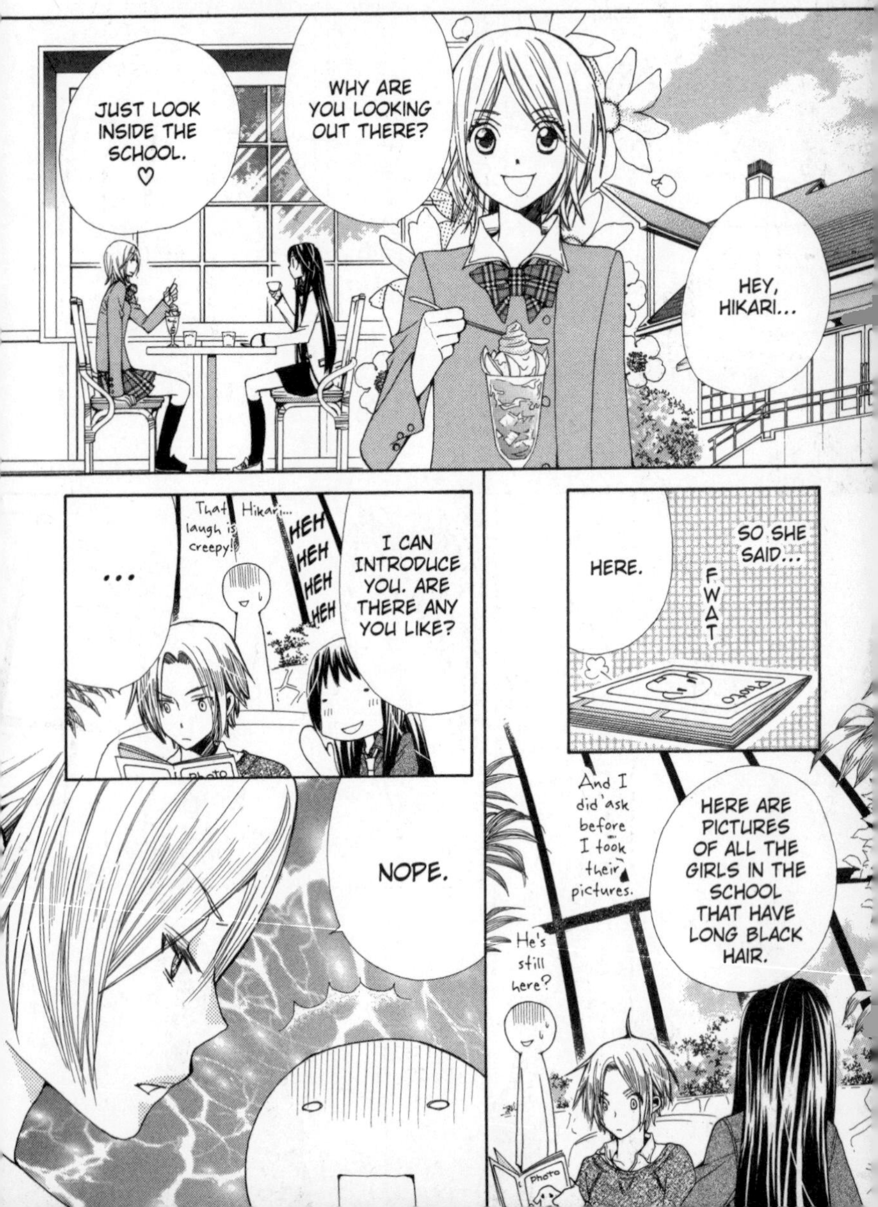
HEY, HIKARI...
WHY ARE YOU LOOKING OUT THERE?
JUST LOOK INSIDE THE SCHOOL. ♡
SO SHE SAID...
HERE.
FWAT
HERE ARE PICTURES OF ALL THE GIRLS IN THE SCHOOL THAT HAVE LONG BLACK HAIR.
And I did ask before I took their pictures.
He's still here?
I CAN INTRODUCE YOU. ARE THERE ANY YOU LIKE?
HEH HEH HEH HEH
That Hikari... laugh is creepy!
...
NOPE.

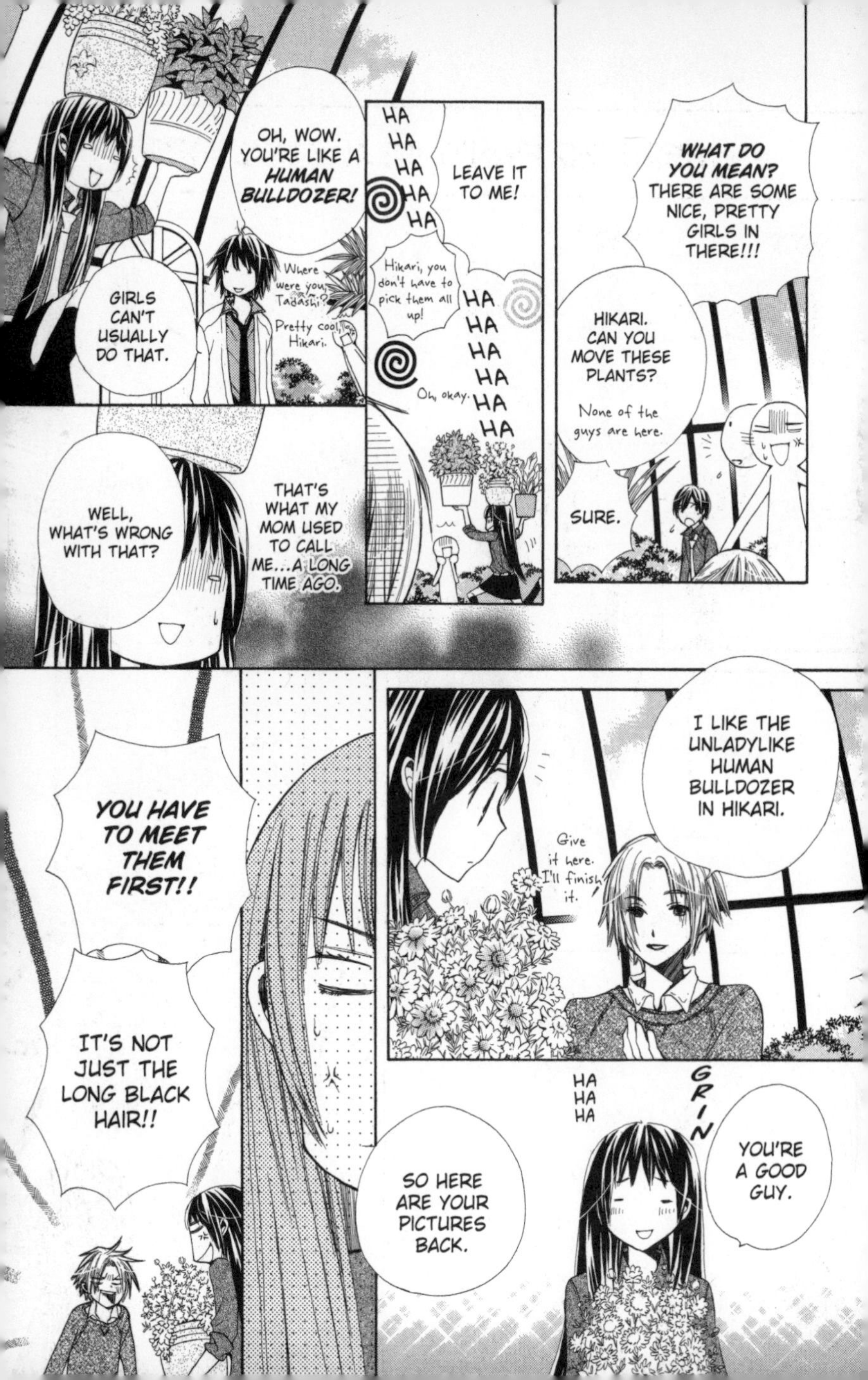
WHAT DO YOU MEAN? THERE ARE SOME NICE, PRETTY GIRLS IN THERE!!!
HIKARI. CAN YOU MOVE THESE PLANTS?
None of the guys are here.
SURE.
HA HA HA HA HA
LEAVE IT TO ME!
Hikari, you don't have to pick them all up!
HA HA HA HA HA HA
Oh, okay.
OH, WOW. YOU'RE LIKE A HUMAN BULLDOZER!
Where were you, Tadashi?
Pretty cool, Hikari.
GIRLS CAN'T USUALLY DO THAT.
THAT'S WHAT MY MOM USED TO CALL ME...A LONG TIME AGO.
WELL, WHAT'S WRONG WITH THAT?
I LIKE THE UNLADYLIKE HUMAN BULLDOZER IN HIKARI.
Give it here. I'll finish it.
YOU HAVE TO MEET THEM FIRST!!
IT'S NOT JUST THE LONG BLACK HAIR!!
GRIN
YOU'RE A GOOD GUY.
HA HA HA
SO HERE ARE YOUR PICTURES BACK.

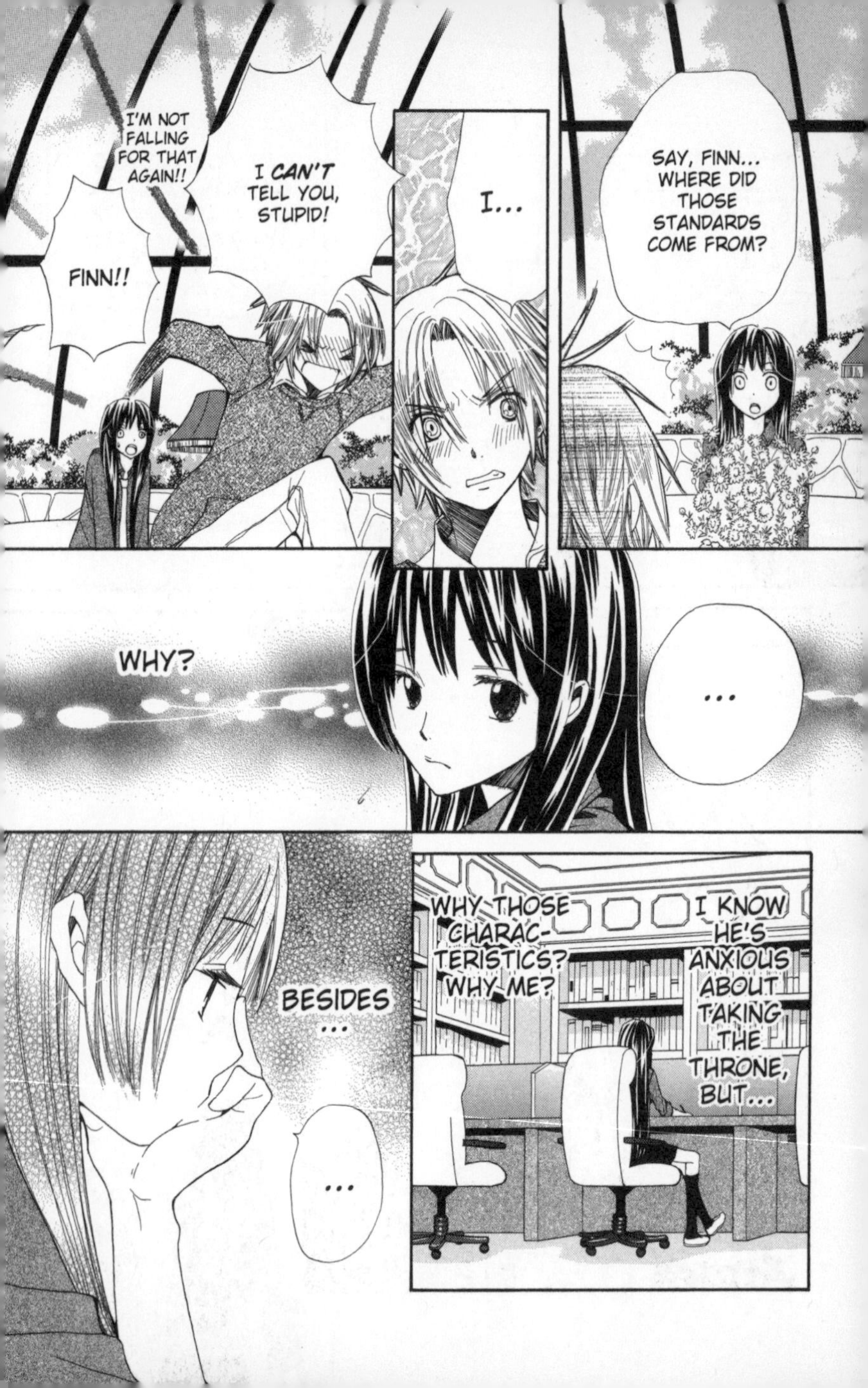
SAY, FINN... WHERE DID THOSE STANDARDS COME FROM?
I...
I *CAN'T* TELL YOU, STUPID!
I'M NOT FALLING FOR THAT AGAIN!!
FINN!!
...
WHY?
I KNOW HE'S ANXIOUS ABOUT TAKING THE THRONE, BUT...
WHY THOSE CHARAC-TERISTICS? WHY ME?
BESIDES...
...

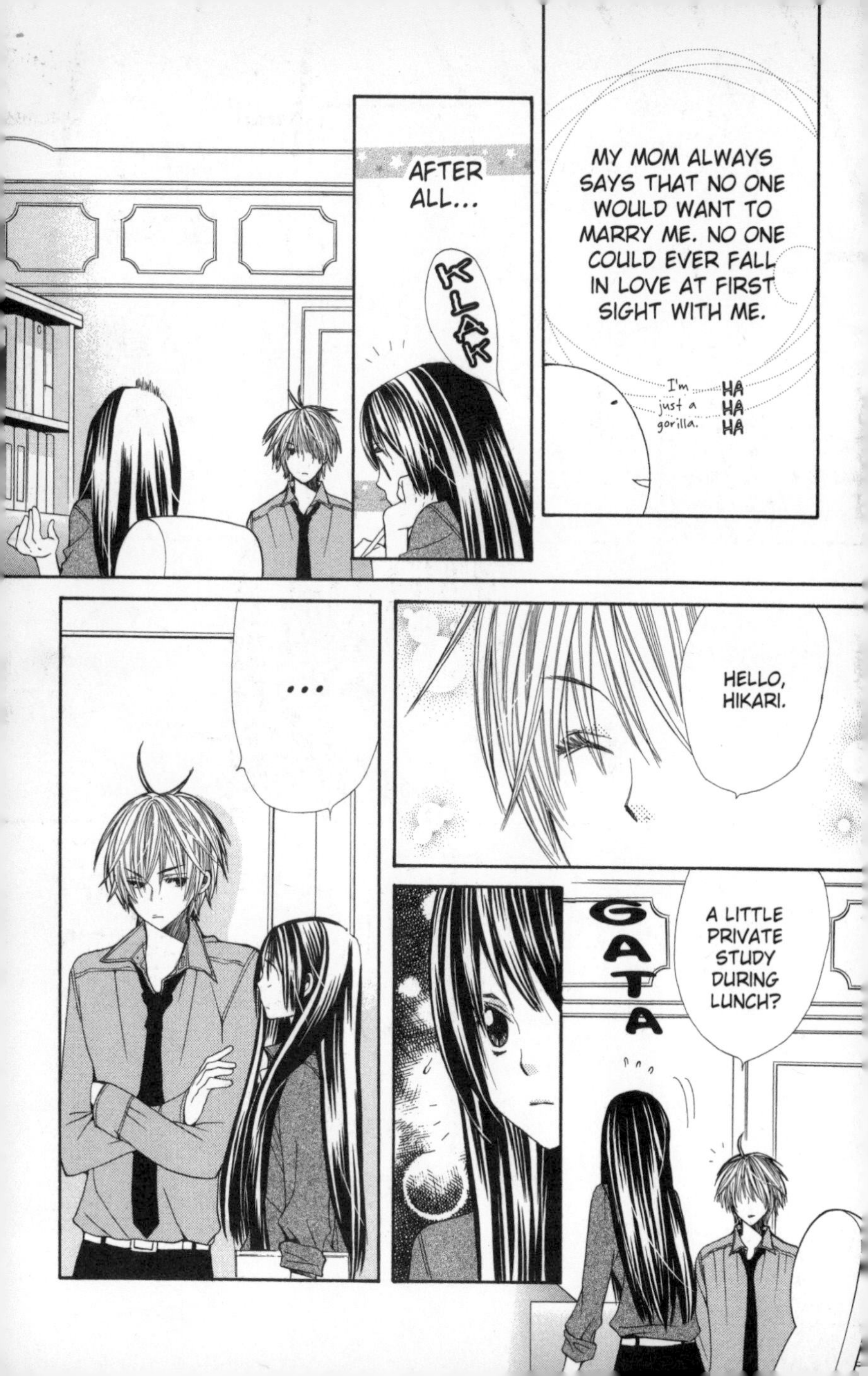
MY MOM ALWAYS SAYS THAT NO ONE WOULD WANT TO MARRY ME. NO ONE COULD EVER FALL IN LOVE AT FIRST SIGHT WITH ME.
I'm just a gorilla.
HA HA HA
AFTER ALL...
KLAK
HELLO, HIKARI.
GATA
A LITTLE PRIVATE STUDY DURING LUNCH?
...

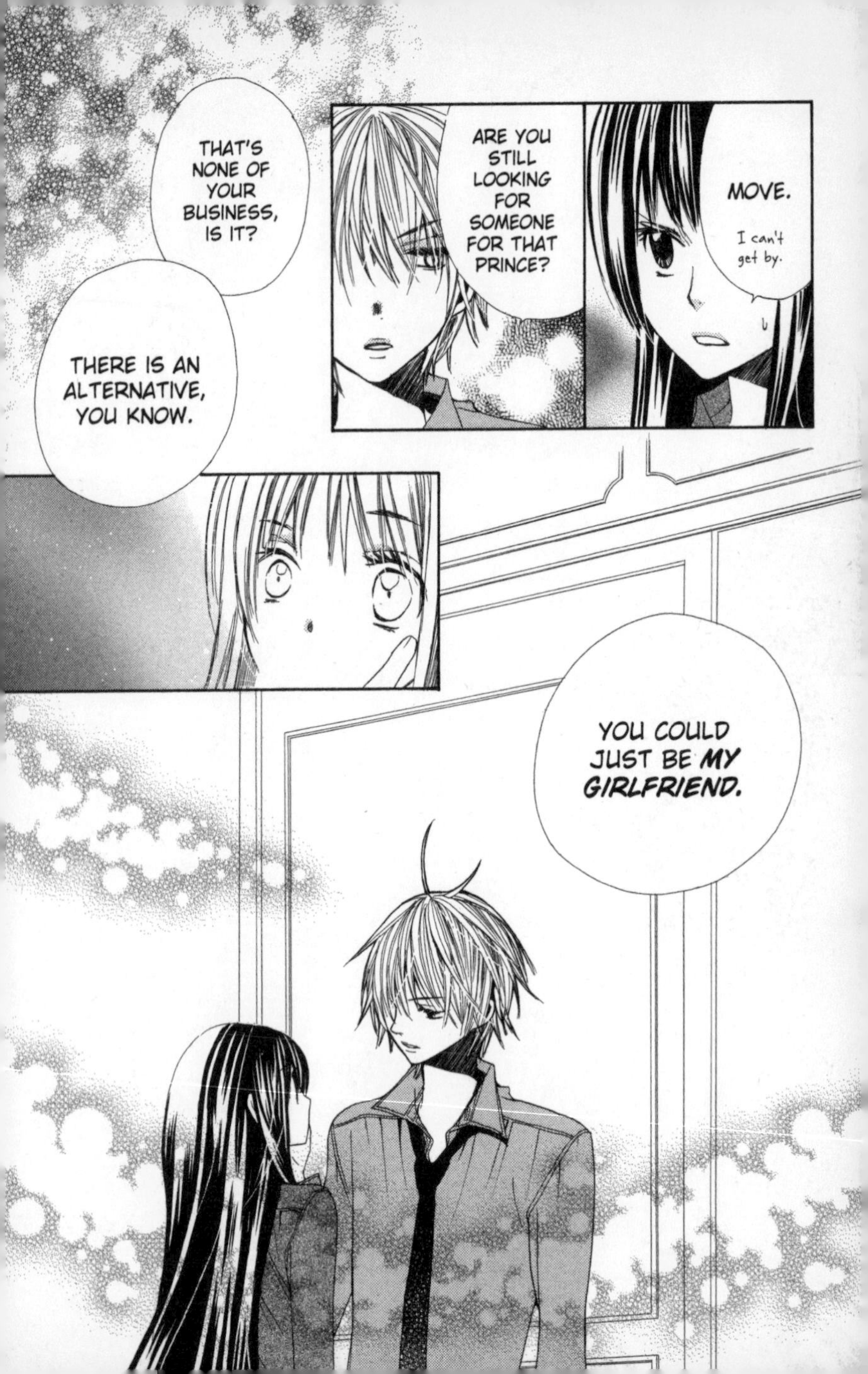
MOVE.
I can't get by.
ARE YOU STILL LOOKING FOR SOMEONE FOR THAT PRINCE?
THAT'S NONE OF YOUR BUSINESS, IS IT?
THERE IS AN ALTERNATIVE, YOU KNOW.
YOU COULD JUST BE MY GIRLFRIEND.

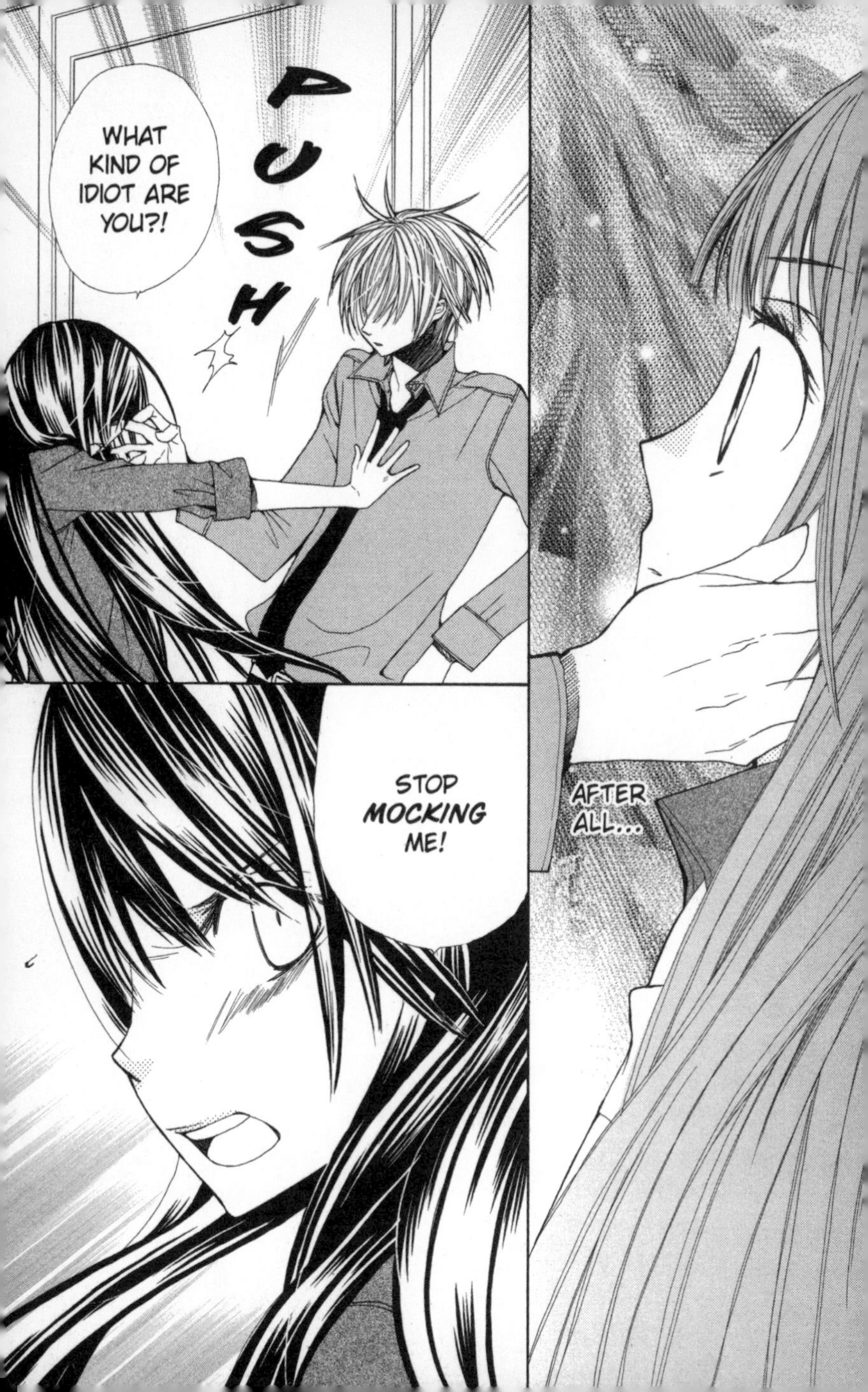
AFTER ALL...
WHAT KIND OF IDIOT ARE YOU?!
PUSH
STOP MOCKING ME!

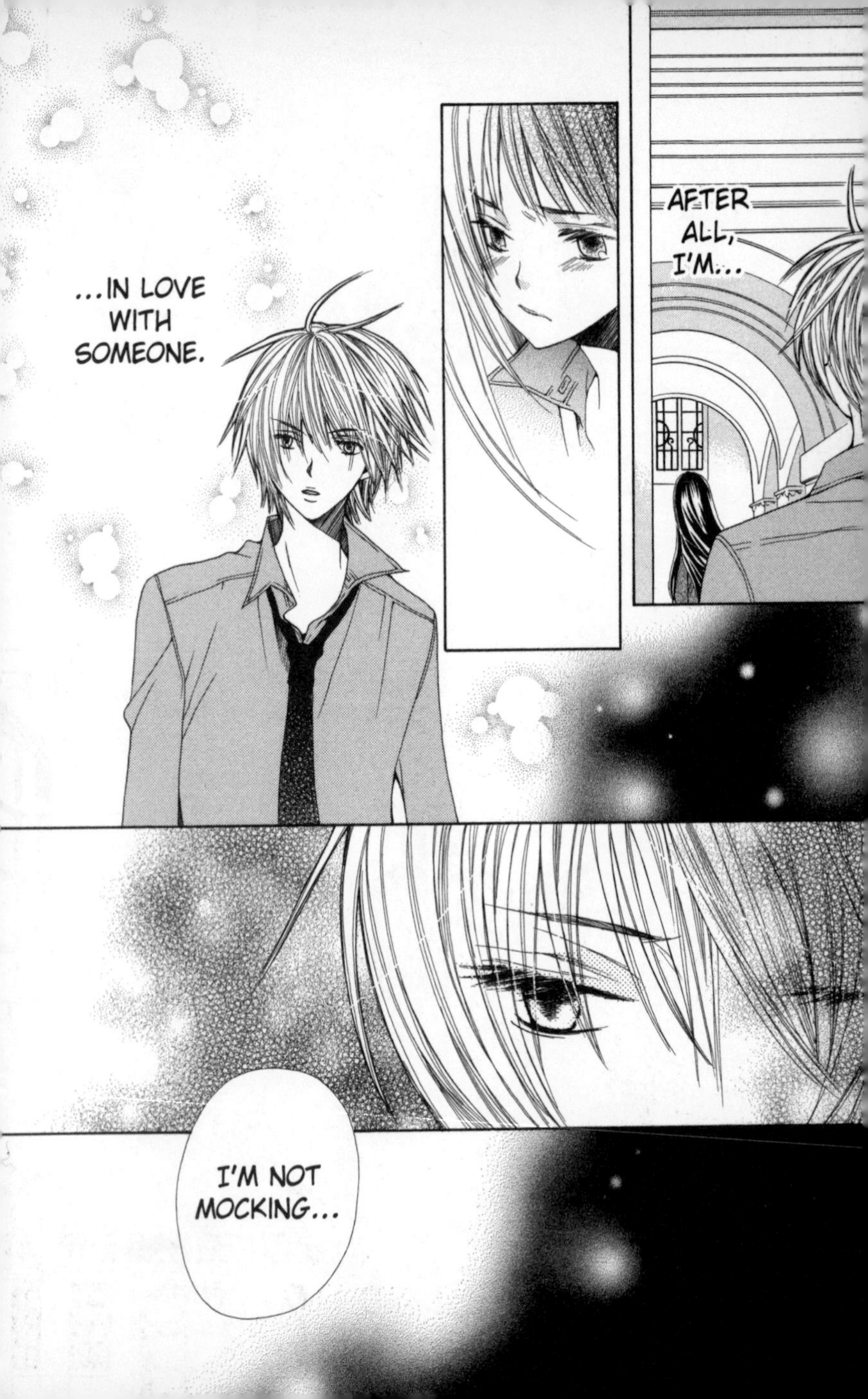
AFTER ALL, I'M...
...IN LOVE WITH SOMEONE.
I'M NOT MOCKING...

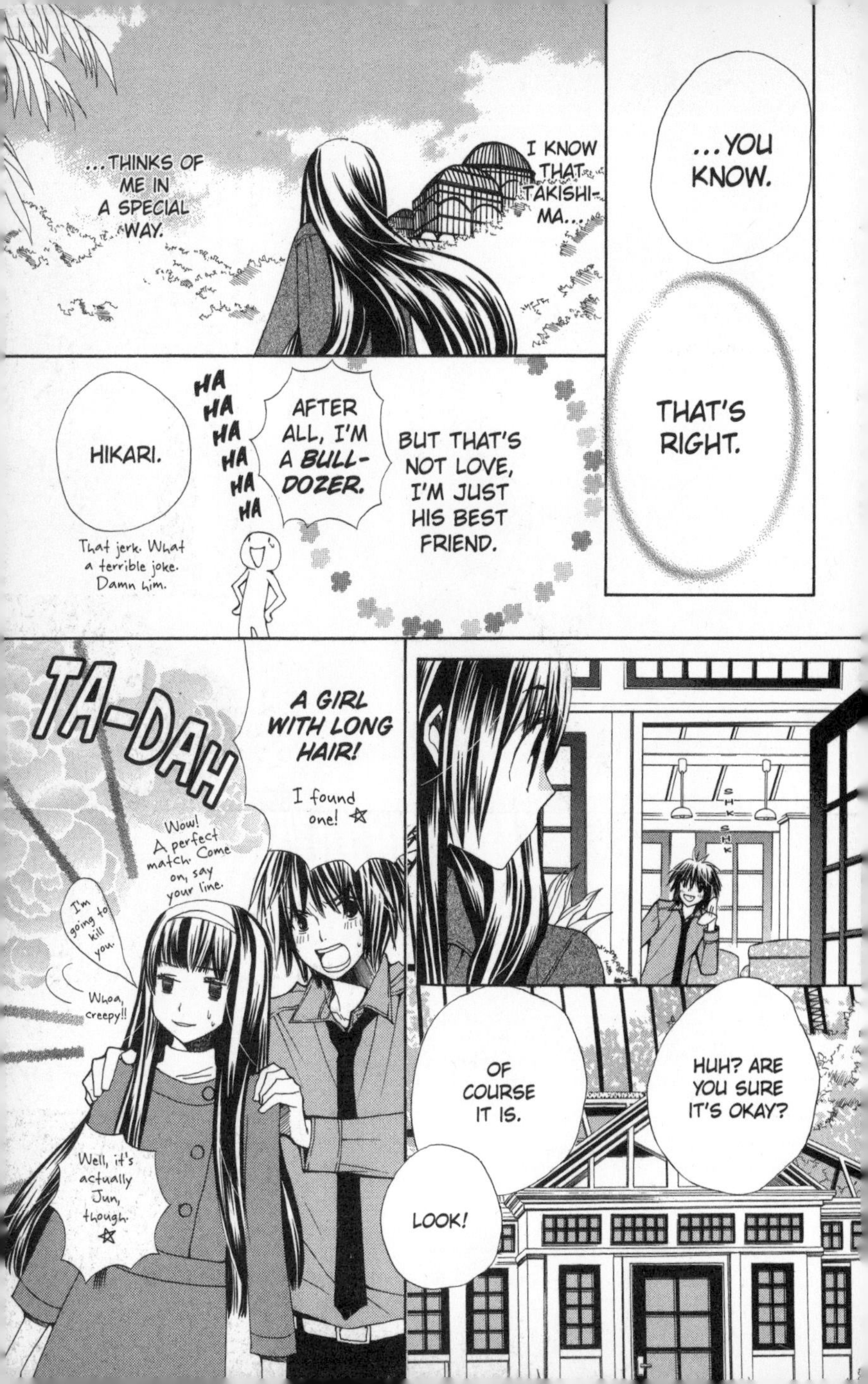
...YOU KNOW.
THAT'S RIGHT.
I KNOW THAT TAKISHIMA...
...THINKS OF ME IN A SPECIAL WAY.
BUT THAT'S NOT LOVE, I'M JUST HIS BEST FRIEND.
AFTER ALL, I'M A *BULLDOZER.*
HA HA HA HA HA HA
HIKARI.
That jerk. What a terrible joke. Damn him.
SHK SHK
HUH? ARE YOU SURE IT'S OKAY?
OF COURSE IT IS.
LOOK!
A GIRL WITH LONG HAIR!
I found one! ☆
TA-DAH
Wow! A perfect match. Come on, say your line.
I'm going to kill you.
Whoa, creepy!!
Well, it's actually Jun, though. ☆

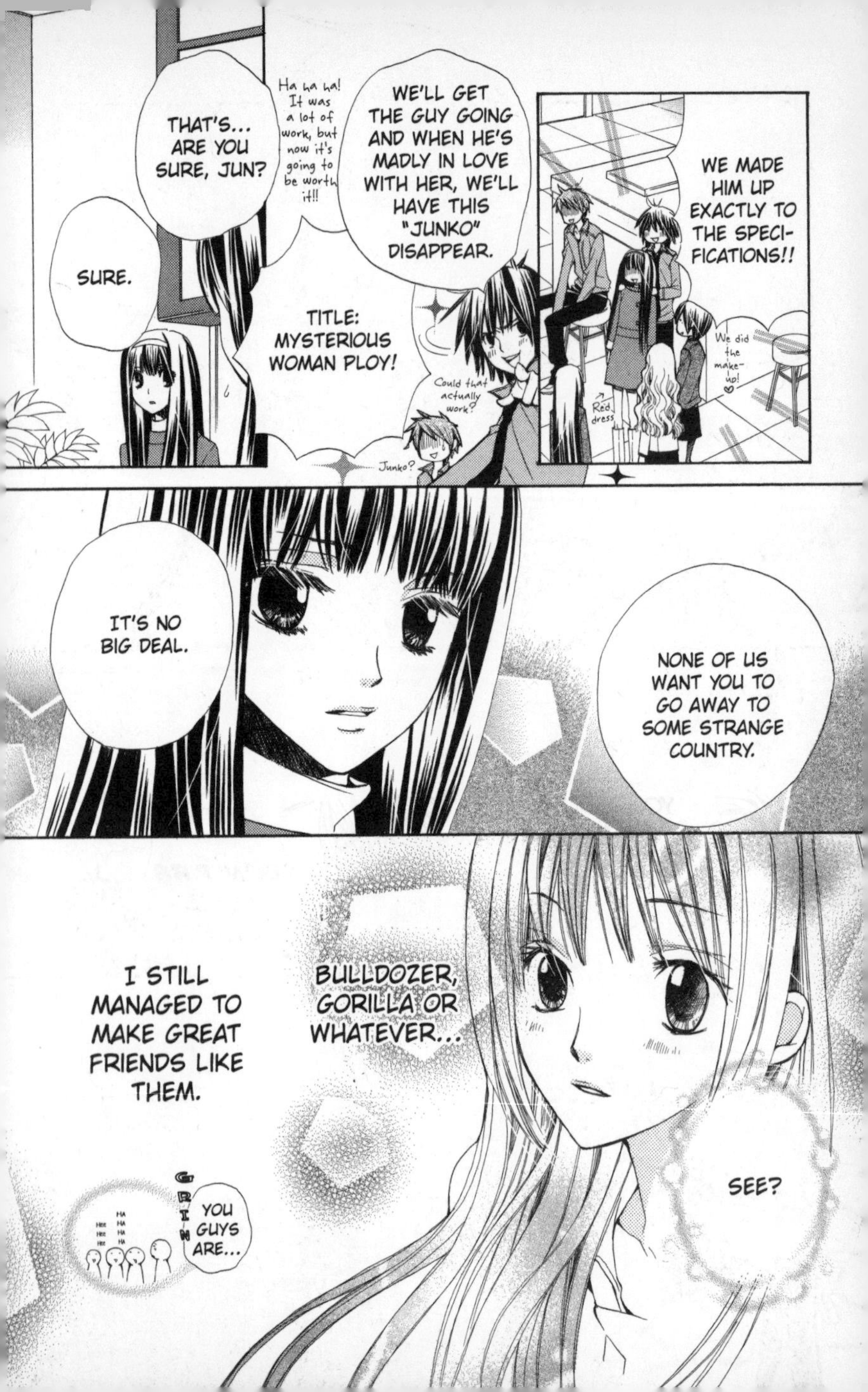
WE MADE HIM UP EXACTLY TO THE SPECIFICATIONS!!
We did the make-up!
Red dress
WE'LL GET THE GUY GOING AND WHEN HE'S MADLY IN LOVE WITH HER, WE'LL HAVE THIS "JUNKO" DISAPPEAR.
Ha ha ha! It was a lot of work, but now it's going to be worth it!!
TITLE: MYSTERIOUS WOMAN PLOY!
Could that actually work?
Junko?
THAT'S... ARE YOU SURE, JUN?
SURE.
NONE OF US WANT YOU TO GO AWAY TO SOME STRANGE COUNTRY.
IT'S NO BIG DEAL.
SEE?
BULLDOZER, GORILLA OR WHATEVER...
I STILL MANAGED TO MAKE GREAT FRIENDS LIKE THEM.
GRIN
YOU GUYS ARE...
HA HA HA
HEE HEE HEE

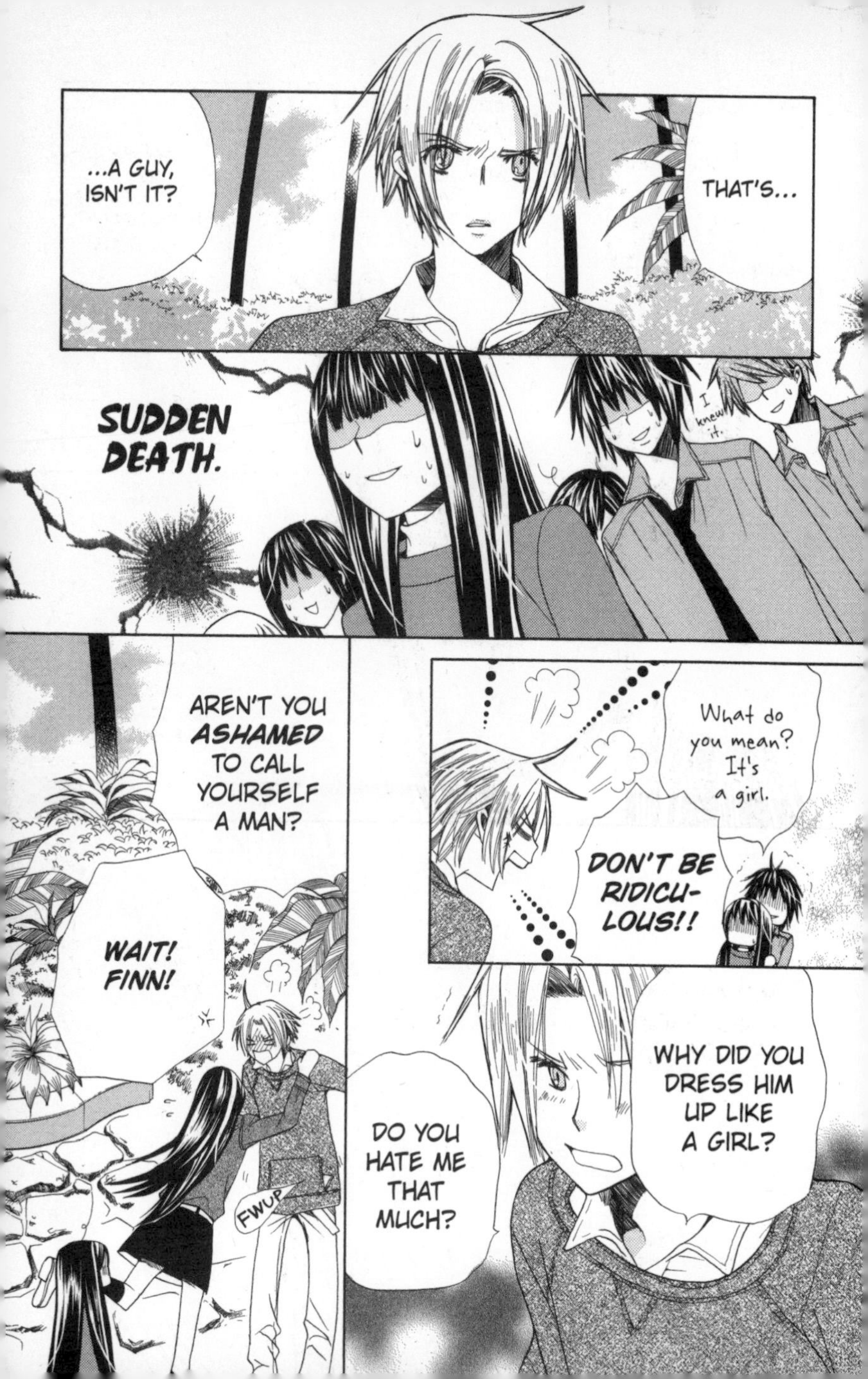
THAT'S...
...A GUY, ISN'T IT?
I knew it.
SUDDEN DEATH.
What do you mean? It's a girl.
DON'T BE RIDICU-LOUS!!
WHY DID YOU DRESS HIM UP LIKE A GIRL?
DO YOU HATE ME THAT MUCH?
AREN'T YOU ASHAMED TO CALL YOURSELF A MAN?
WAIT! FINN!
FWUP

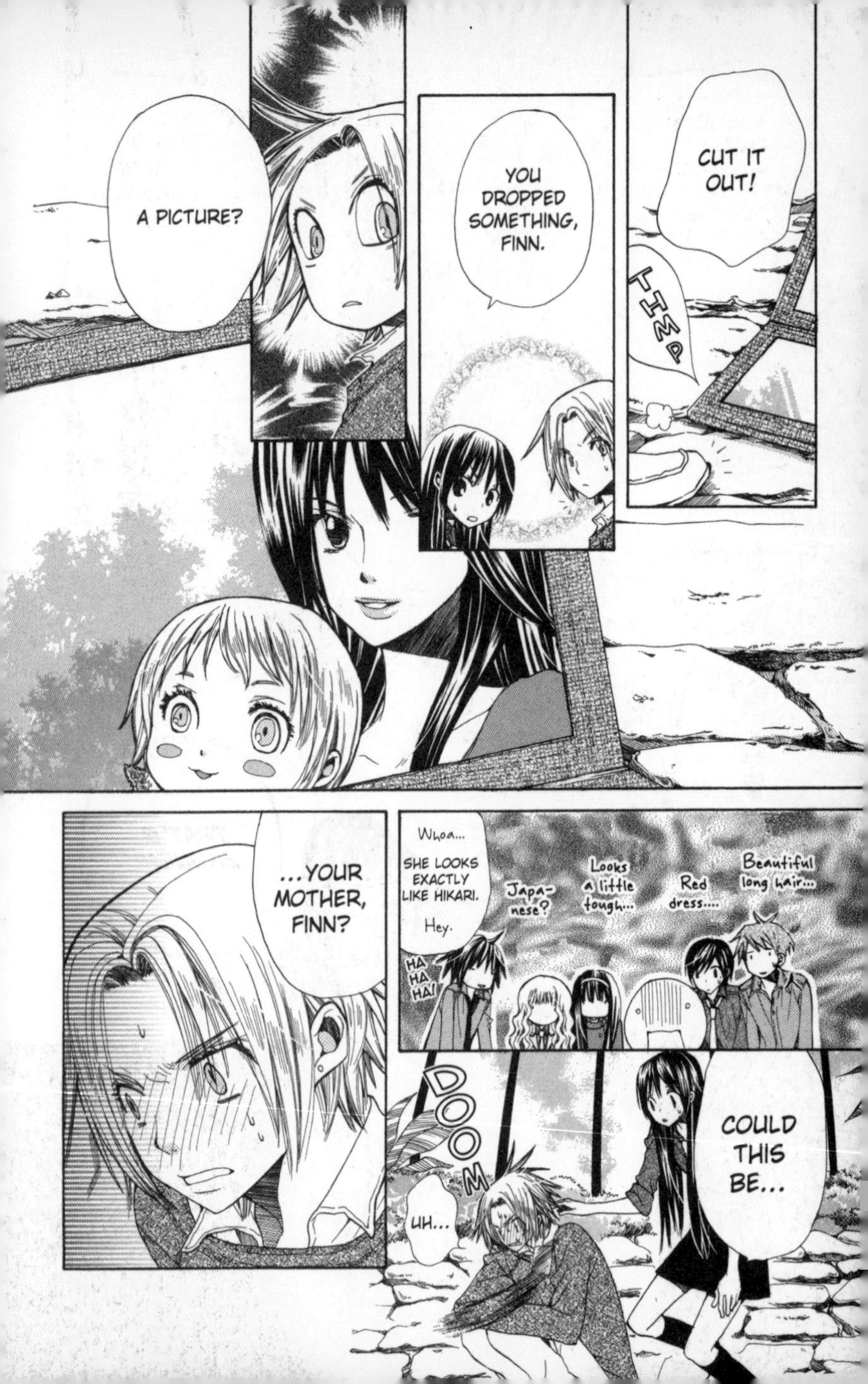
CUT IT OUT!
THMP
YOU DROPPED SOMETHING, FINN.
A PICTURE?
Beautiful long hair...
Red dress....
Looks a little tough...
Japa-nese?
Whoa... SHE LOOKS EXACTLY LIKE HIKARI.
Hey.
HA HA HA!
COULD THIS BE...
DOOOM
UH...
...YOUR MOTHER, FINN?

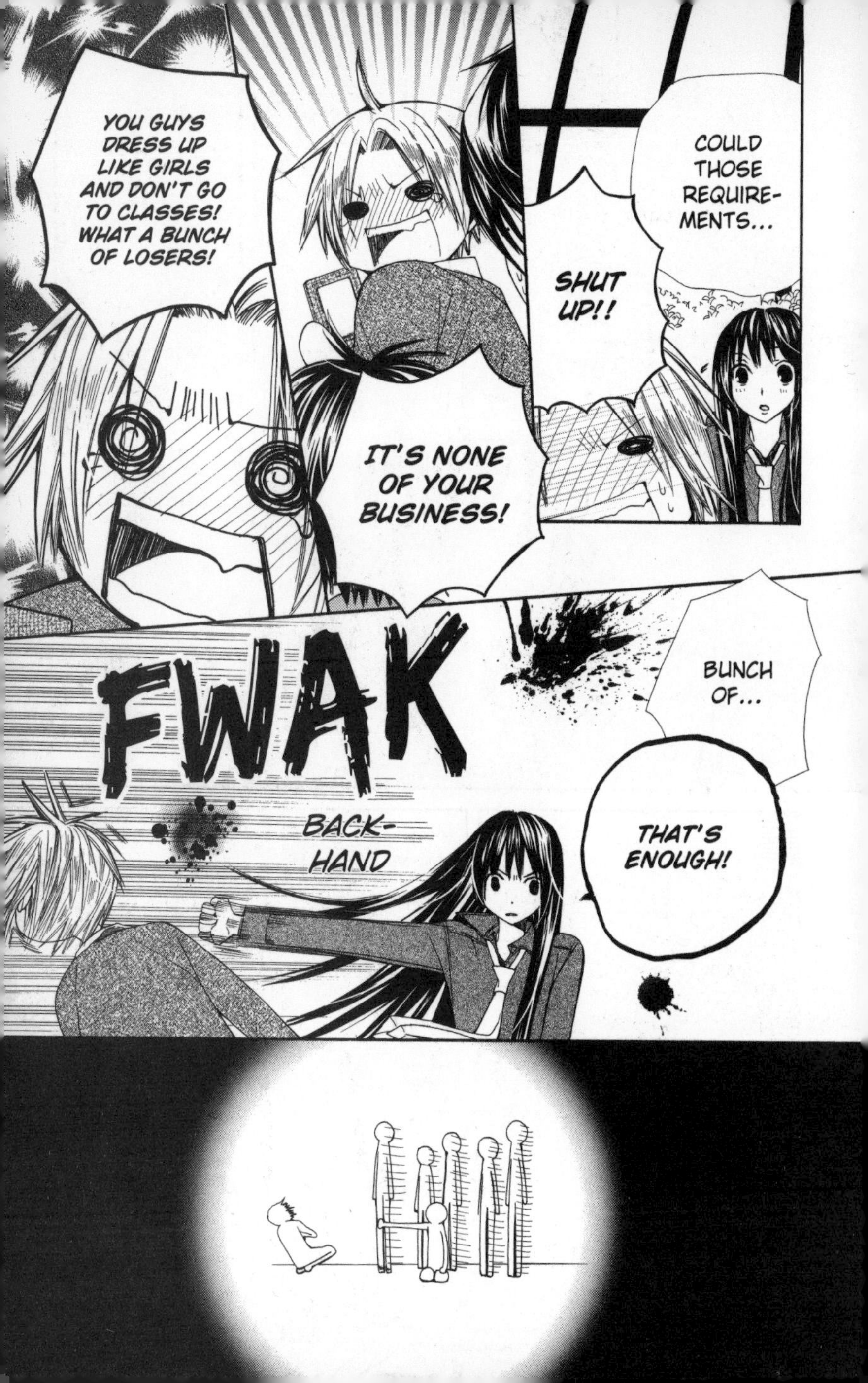
COULD THOSE REQUIRE-MENTS...
SHUT UP!!
YOU GUYS DRESS UP LIKE GIRLS AND DON'T GO TO CLASSES! WHAT A BUNCH OF LOSERS!
IT'S NONE OF YOUR BUSINESS!
BUNCH OF...
FWAK
THAT'S ENOUGH!
BACK-HAND

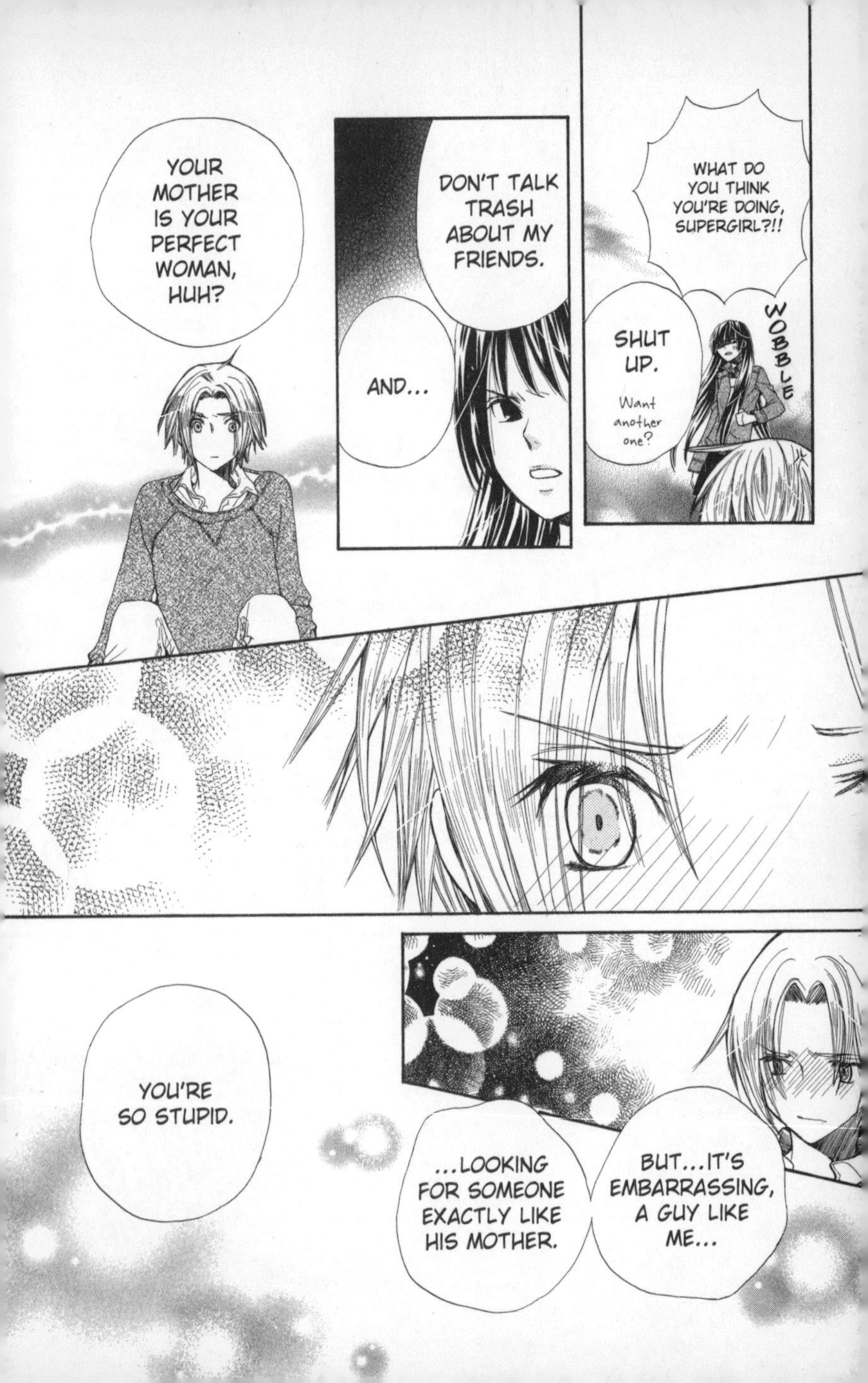
WHAT DO YOU THINK YOU'RE DOING, SUPERGIRL?!!
WOBBLE
SHUT UP.
Want another one?
DON'T TALK TRASH ABOUT MY FRIENDS.
AND...
YOUR MOTHER IS YOUR PERFECT WOMAN, HUH?
BUT...IT'S EMBARRASSING, A GUY LIKE ME...
...LOOKING FOR SOMEONE EXACTLY LIKE HIS MOTHER.
YOU'RE SO STUPID.

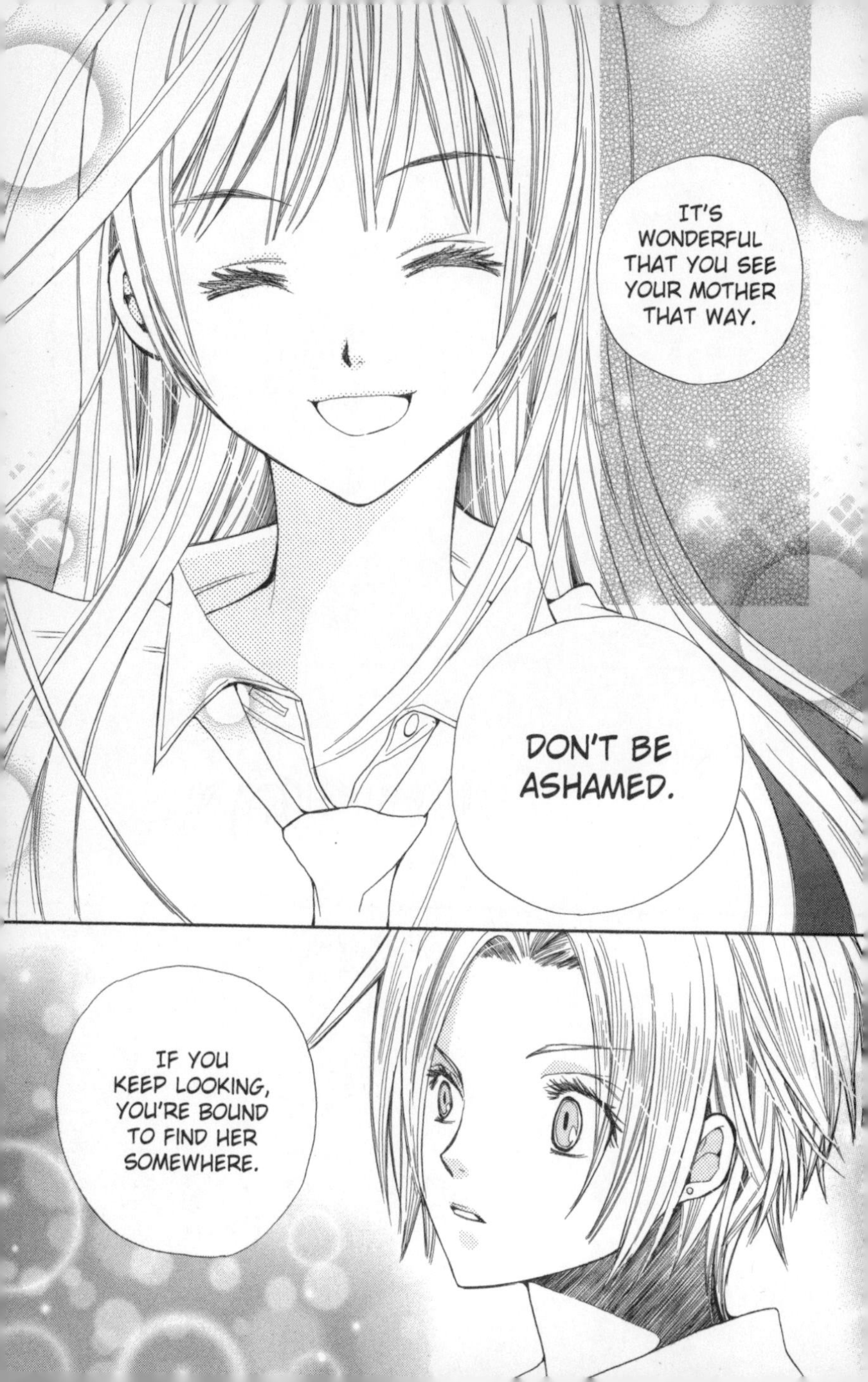
IT'S WONDERFUL THAT YOU SEE YOUR MOTHER THAT WAY.
DON'T BE ASHAMED.
IF YOU KEEP LOOKING, YOU'RE BOUND TO FIND HER SOMEWHERE.

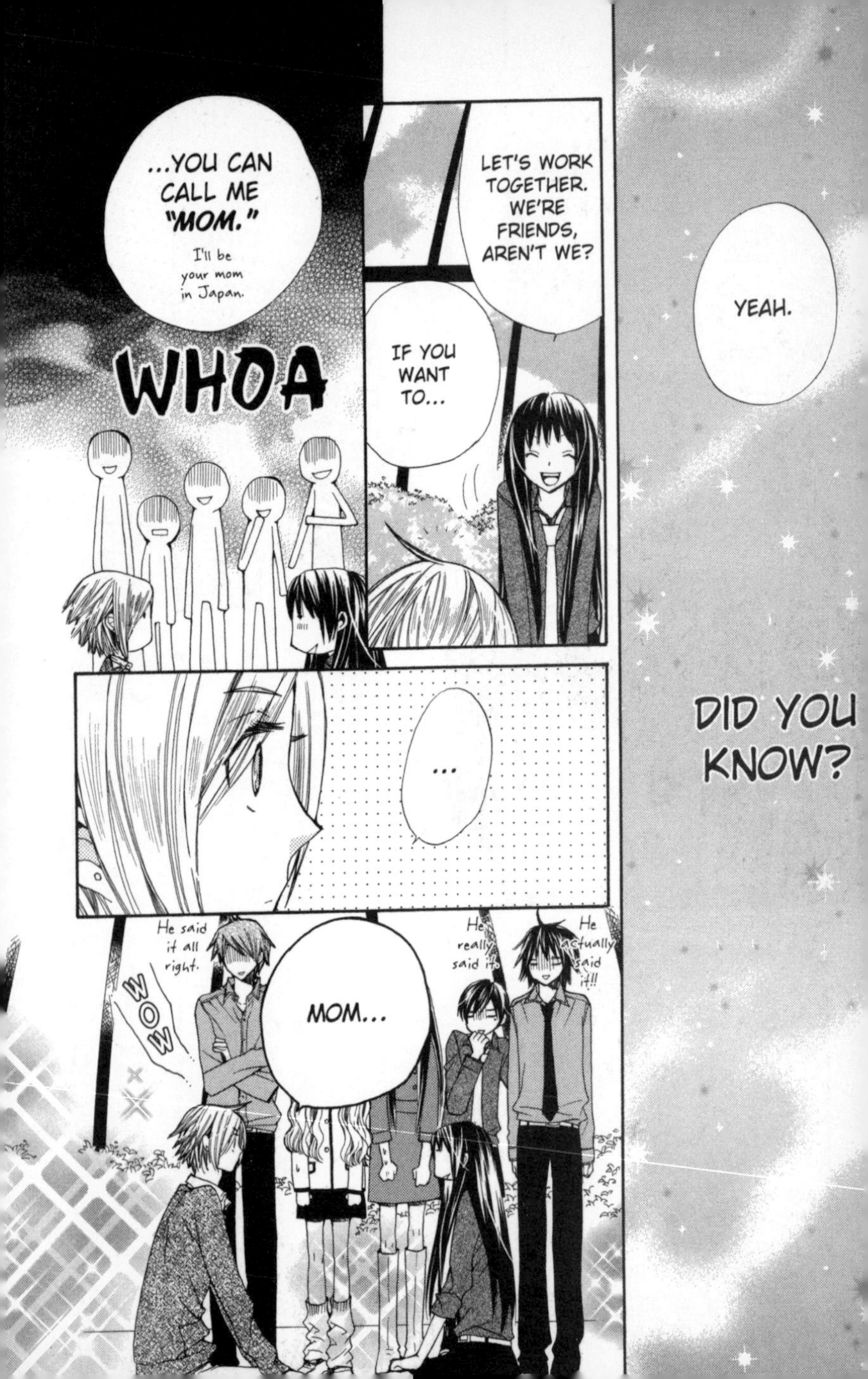
YEAH.
DID YOU KNOW?
LET'S WORK TOGETHER. WE'RE FRIENDS, AREN'T WE?
IF YOU WANT TO...
...YOU CAN CALL ME "MOM."
I'll be your mom in Japan.
WHOA
...
He actually said it!!
He really said it.
He said it all right.
MOM...
WOW

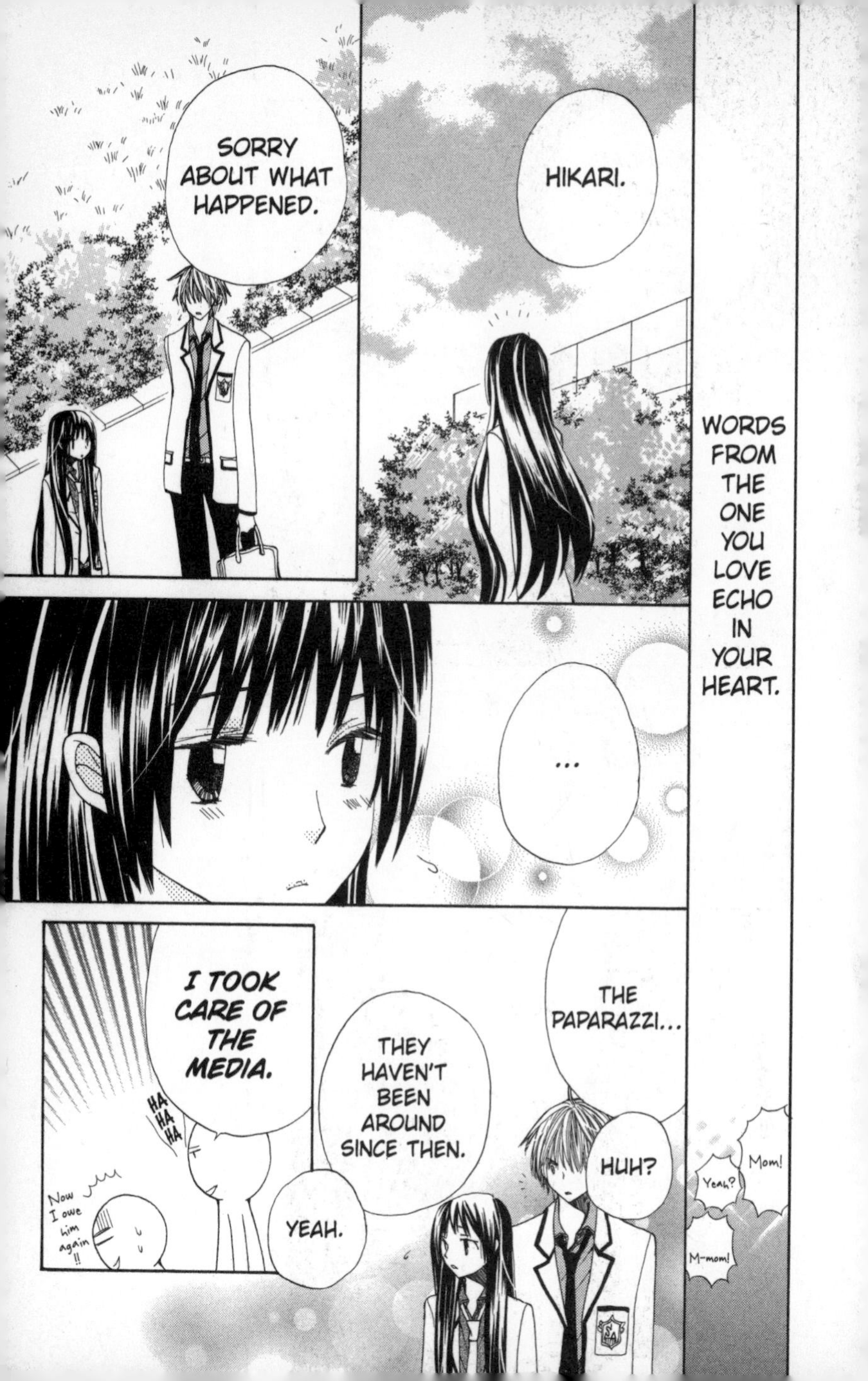
WORDS FROM THE ONE YOU LOVE ECHO IN YOUR HEART.
HIKARI.
SORRY ABOUT WHAT HAPPENED.
...
Mom!
Yeah?
M-mom!
THE PAPARAZZI...
HUH?
THEY HAVEN'T BEEN AROUND SINCE THEN.
YEAH.
I TOOK CARE OF THE MEDIA.
HA HA HA
Now I owe him again!!

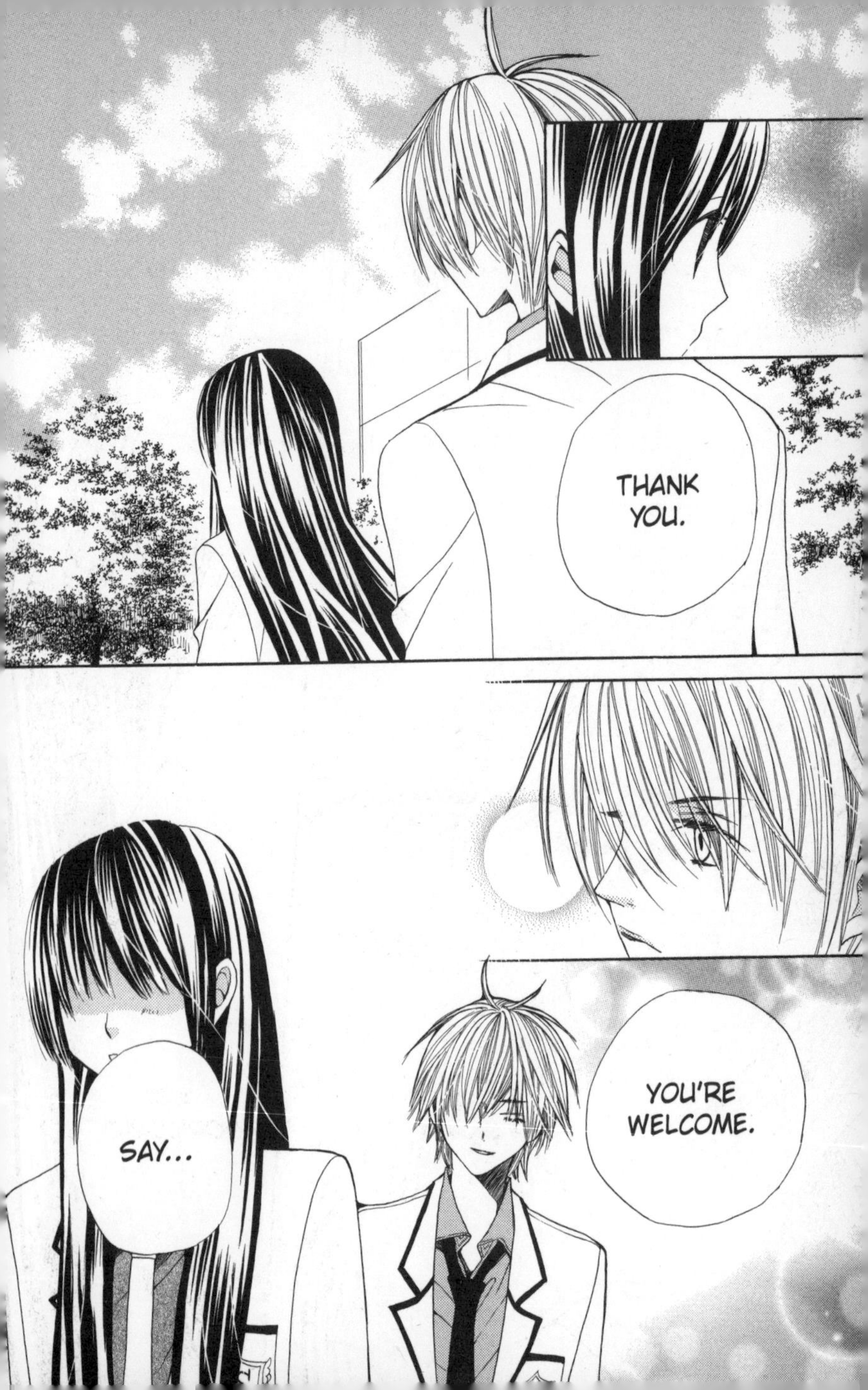
THANK YOU.
YOU'RE WELCOME.
SAY...

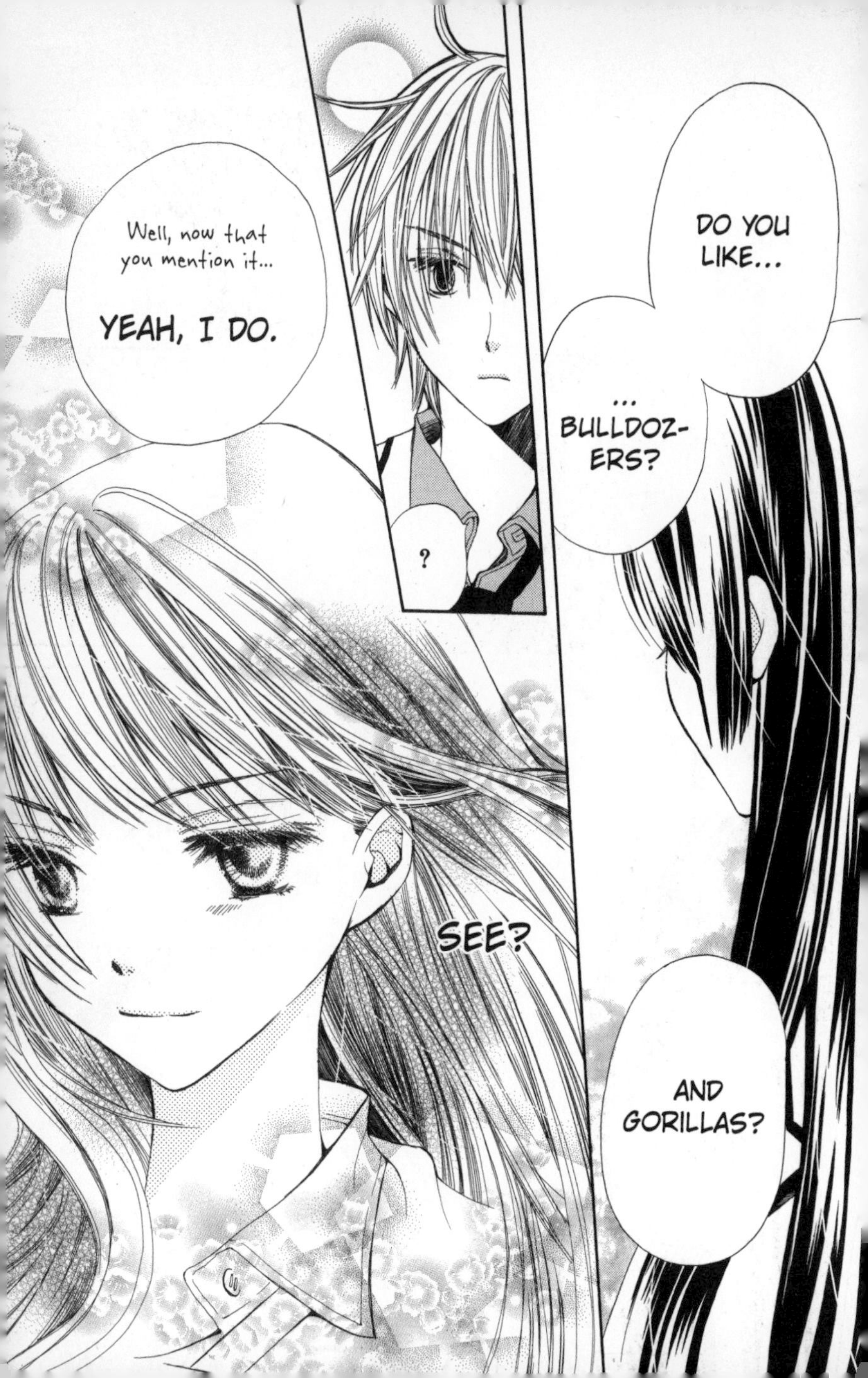
DO YOU LIKE...
... BULLDOZ-ERS?
?
Well, now that you mention it...
YEAH, I DO.
SEE?
AND GORILLAS?

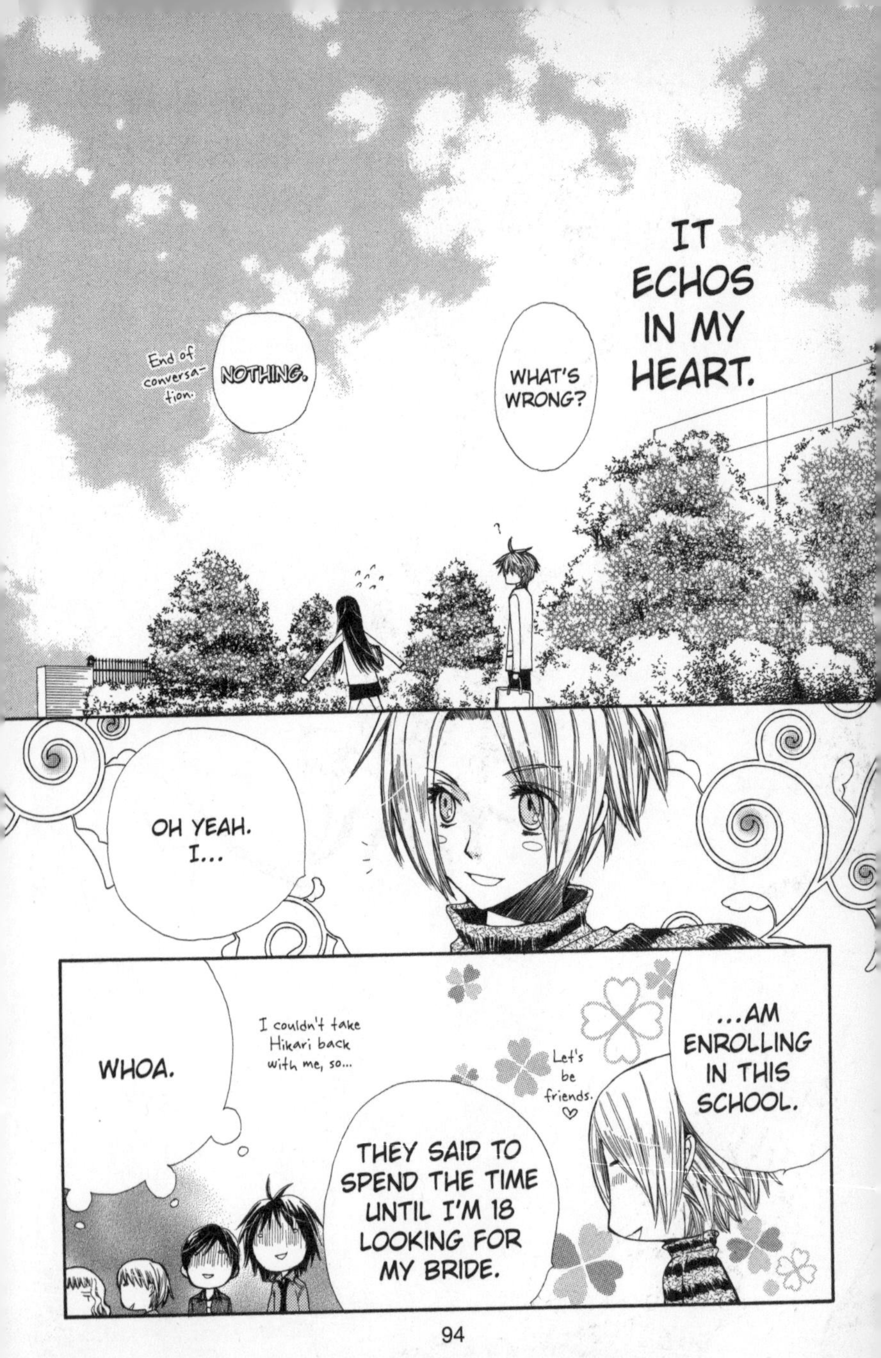
IT ECHOS IN MY HEART.
WHAT'S WRONG?
NOTHING.
End of conversa-tion.
OH YEAH. I...
...AM ENROLLING IN THIS SCHOOL.
Let's be friends. ♡
THEY SAID TO SPEND THE TIME UNTIL I'M 18 LOOKING FOR MY BRIDE.
I couldn't take Hikari back with me, so...
WHOA.

Chapter 50

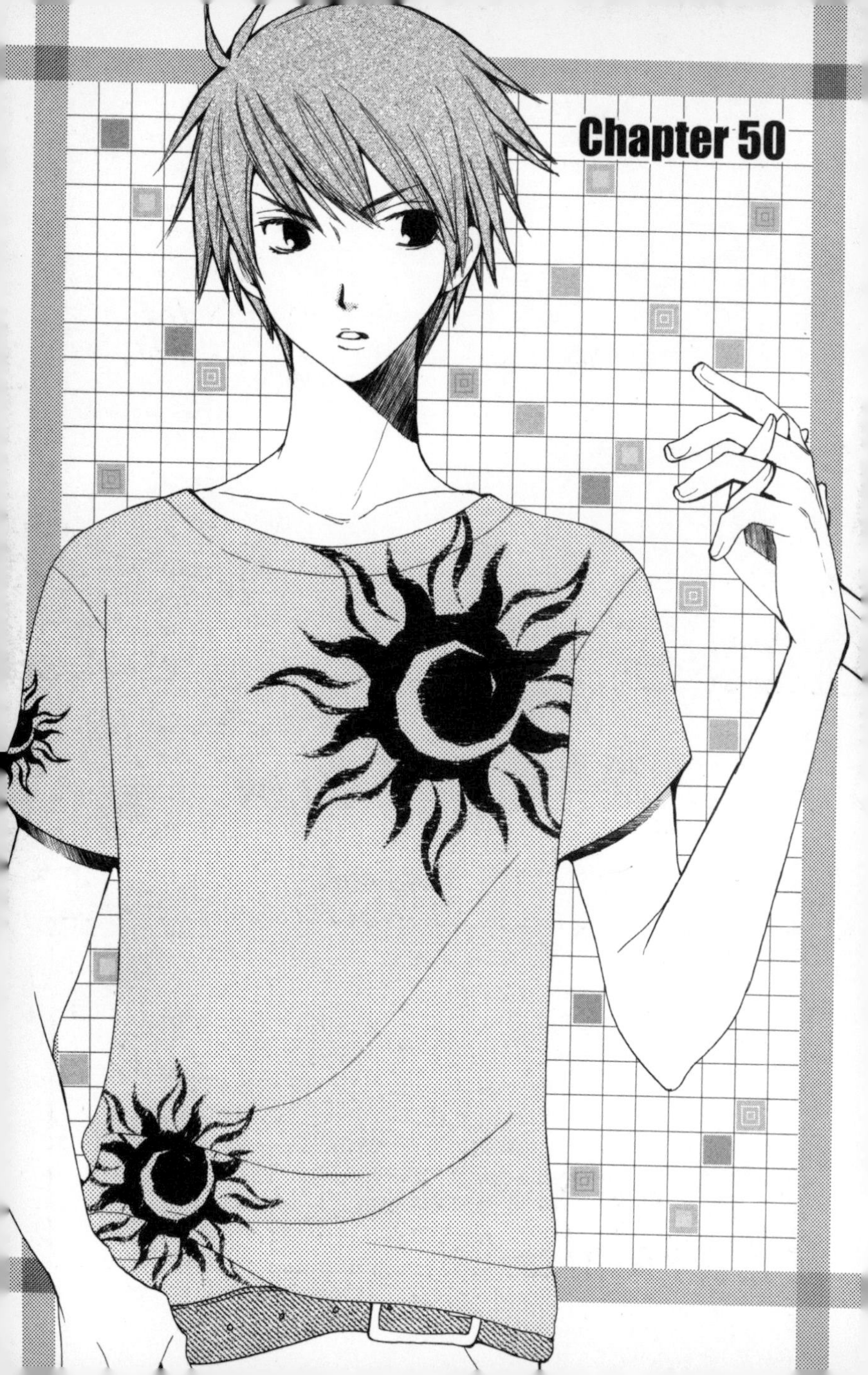

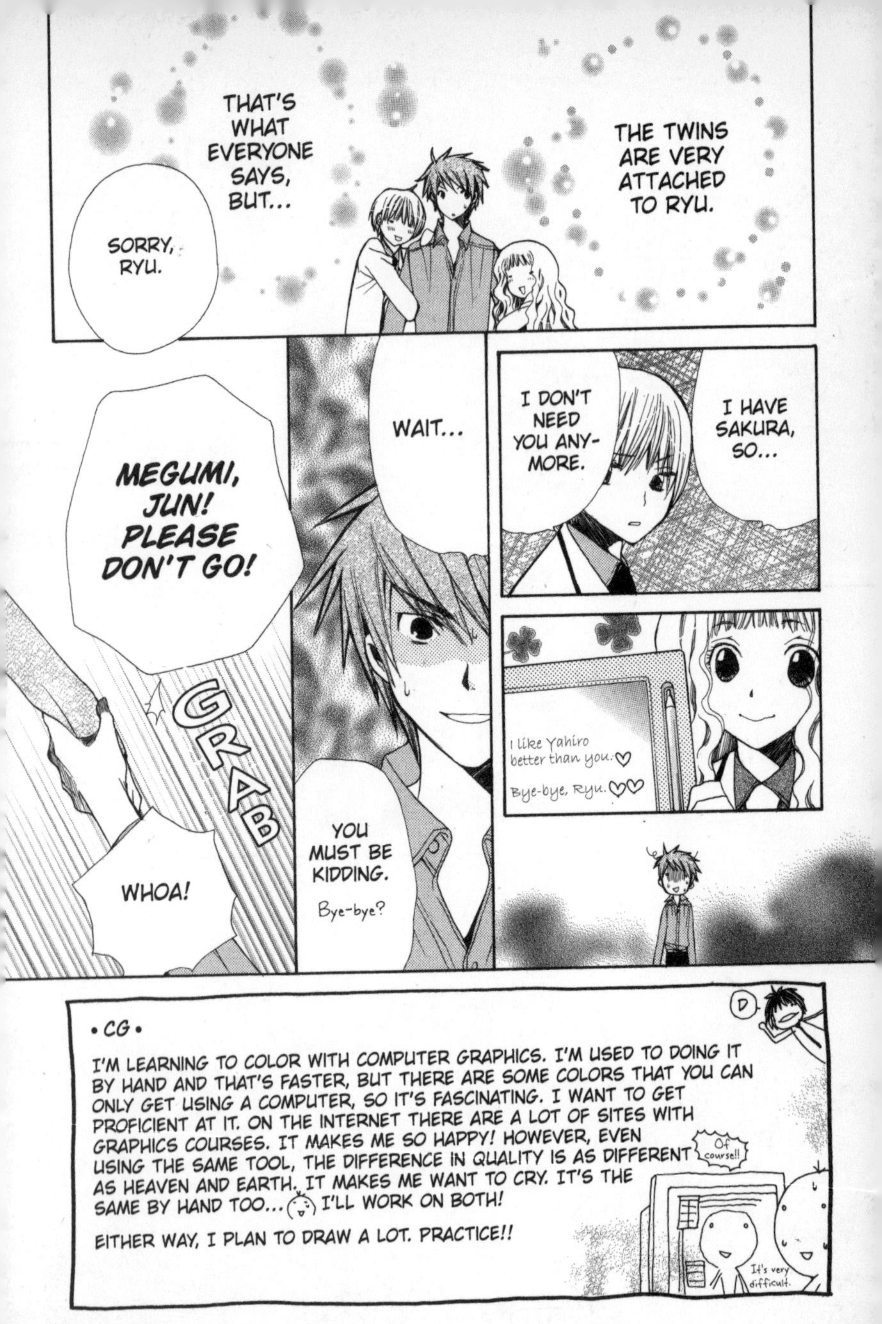
THE TWINS ARE VERY ATTACHED TO RYU.
THAT'S WHAT EVERYONE SAYS, BUT...
SORRY, RYU.
I HAVE SAKURA, SO...
I DON'T NEED YOU ANYMORE.
I like Yahiro better than you. ♡
Bye-bye, Ryu. ♡♡
WAIT...
YOU MUST BE KIDDING.
Bye-bye?
MEGUMI, JUN! PLEASE DON'T GO!
GRAB
WHOA!

• CG •

I'M LEARNING TO COLOR WITH COMPUTER GRAPHICS. I'M USED TO DOING IT BY HAND AND THAT'S FASTER, BUT THERE ARE SOME COLORS THAT YOU CAN ONLY GET USING A COMPUTER, SO IT'S FASCINATING. I WANT TO GET PROFICIENT AT IT. ON THE INTERNET THERE ARE A LOT OF SITES WITH GRAPHICS COURSES. IT MAKES ME SO HAPPY! HOWEVER, EVEN USING THE SAME TOOL, THE DIFFERENCE IN QUALITY IS AS DIFFERENT (Of course!!) AS HEAVEN AND EARTH. IT MAKES ME WANT TO CRY. IT'S THE SAME BY HAND TOO... I'LL WORK ON BOTH!

EITHER WAY, I PLAN TO DRAW A LOT. PRACTICE!!

It's very difficult.

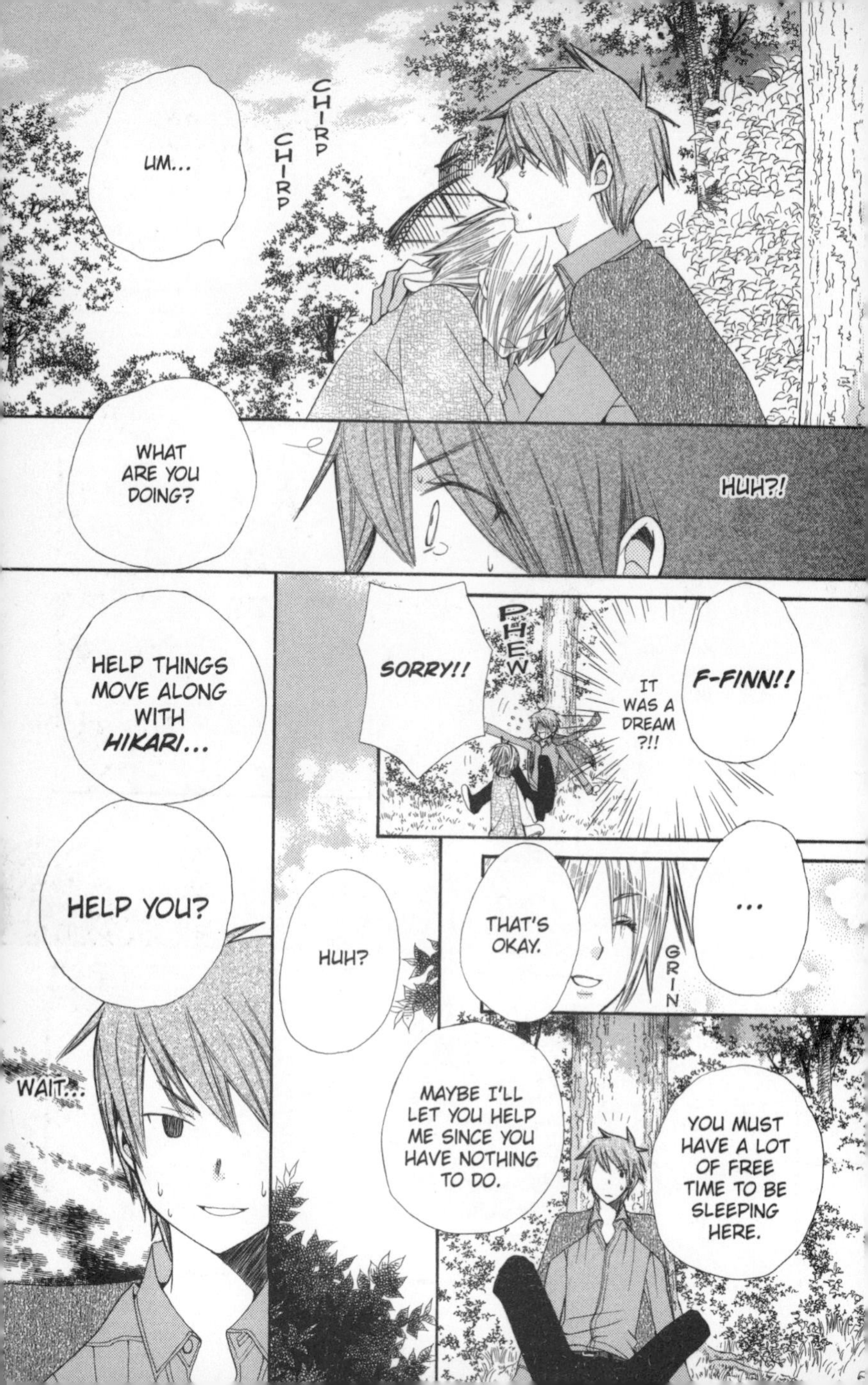
CHIRP
CHIRP
UM...
HUH?!
WHAT ARE YOU DOING?
F-FINN!!
IT WAS A DREAM?!!
PHEW
SORRY!!
...
GRIN
THAT'S OKAY.
HUH?
YOU MUST HAVE A LOT OF FREE TIME TO BE SLEEPING HERE.
MAYBE I'LL LET YOU HELP ME SINCE YOU HAVE NOTHING TO DO.
HELP THINGS MOVE ALONG WITH HIKARI...
HELP YOU?
WAIT...

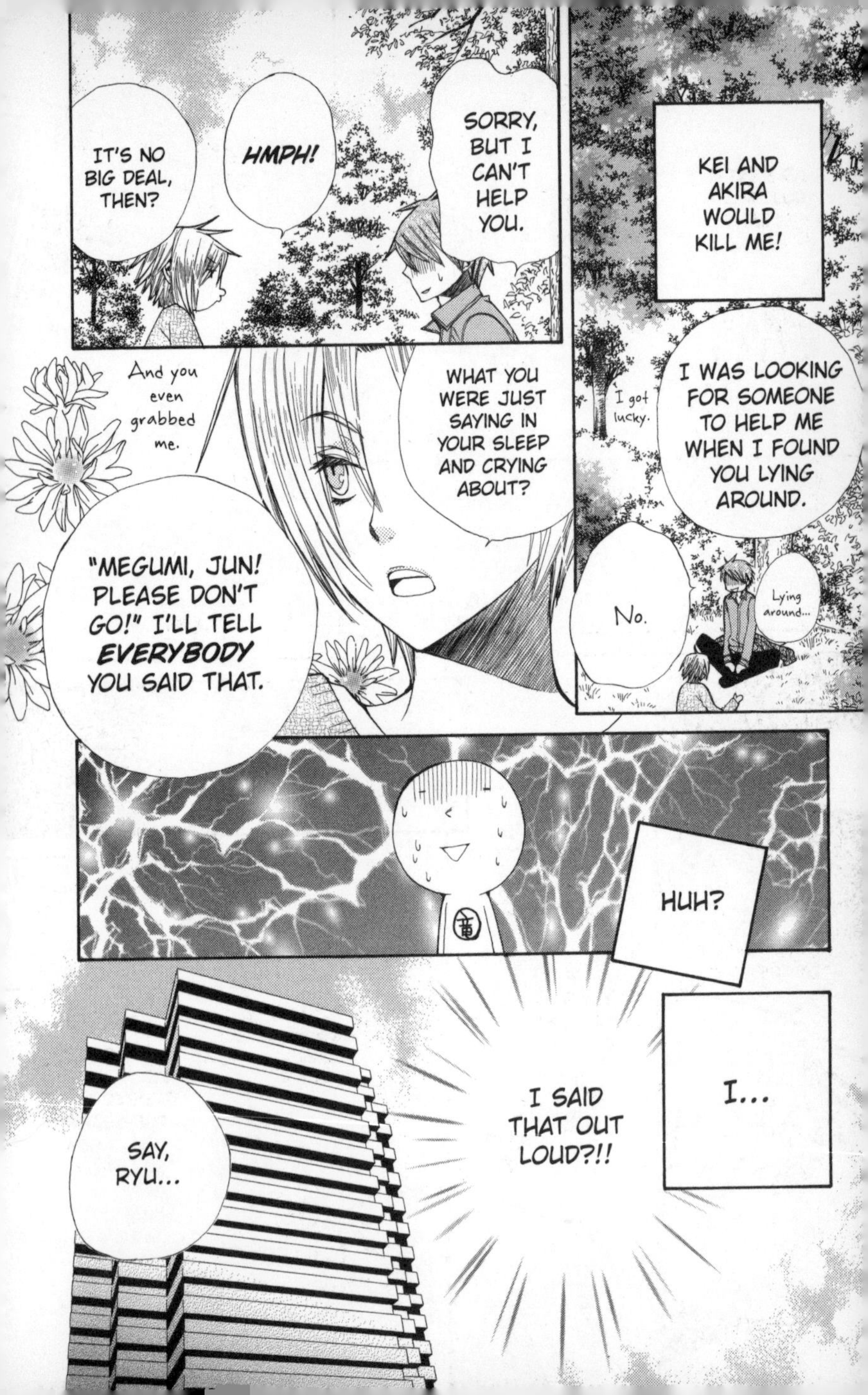
KEI AND AKIRA WOULD KILL ME!
I WAS LOOKING FOR SOMEONE TO HELP ME WHEN I FOUND YOU LYING AROUND.
I got lucky.
Lying around...
No.
SORRY, BUT I CAN'T HELP YOU.
HMPH!
IT'S NO BIG DEAL, THEN?
WHAT YOU WERE JUST SAYING IN YOUR SLEEP AND CRYING ABOUT?
And you even grabbed me.
"MEGUMI, JUN! PLEASE DON'T GO!" I'LL TELL ***EVERYBODY*** YOU SAID THAT.
HUH?
I...
I SAID THAT OUT LOUD?!!
SAY, RYU...

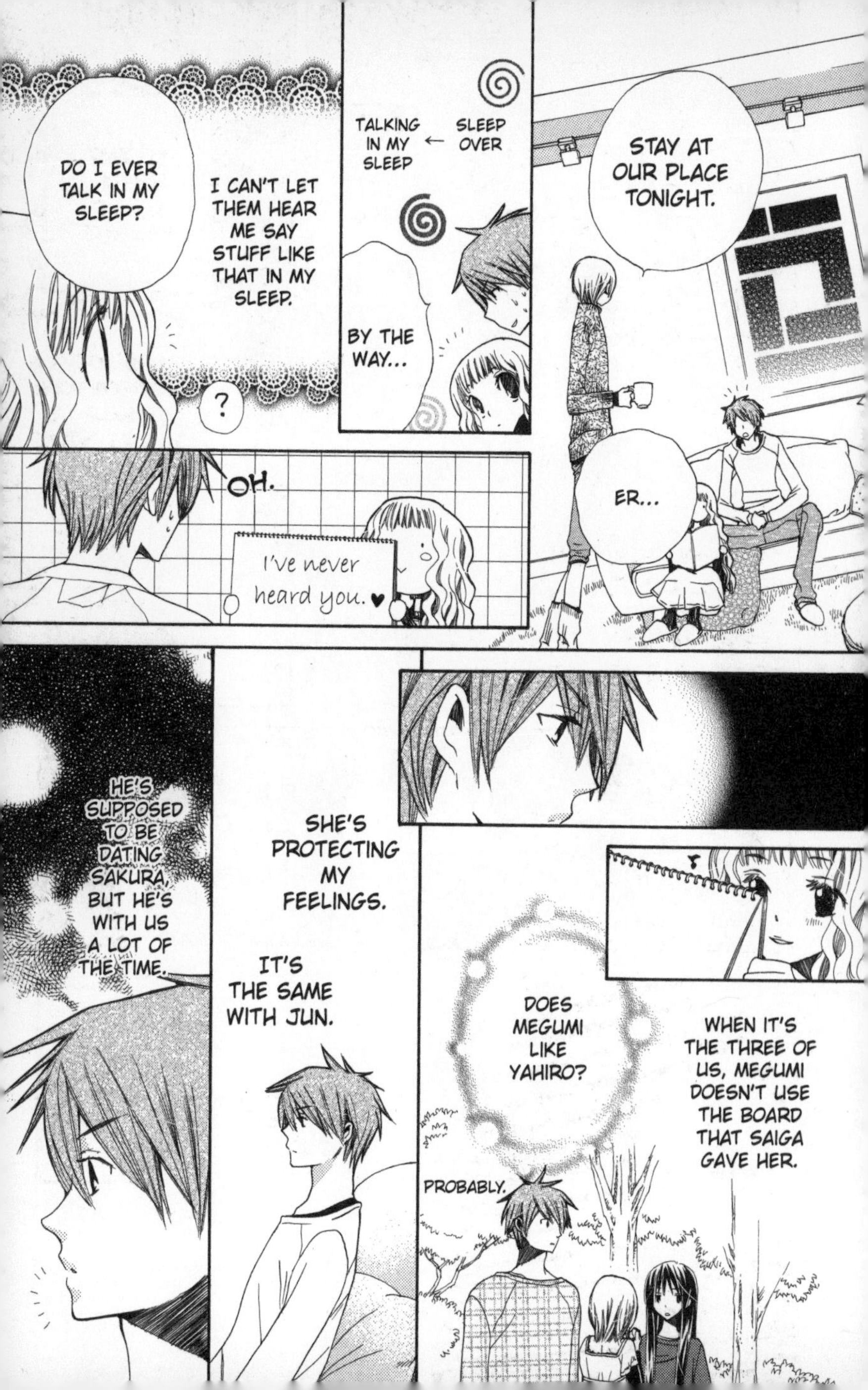
STAY AT OUR PLACE TONIGHT.
ER...
SLEEP OVER ← TALKING IN MY SLEEP
BY THE WAY...
DO I EVER TALK IN MY SLEEP?
I CAN'T LET THEM HEAR ME SAY STUFF LIKE THAT IN MY SLEEP.
?
OH.
I've never heard you. ♥
WHEN IT'S THE THREE OF US, MEGUMI DOESN'T USE THE BOARD THAT SAIGA GAVE HER.
DOES MEGUMI LIKE YAHIRO?
PROBABLY.
SHE'S PROTECTING MY FEELINGS.
IT'S THE SAME WITH JUN.
HE'S SUPPOSED TO BE DATING SAKURA, BUT HE'S WITH US A LOT OF THE TIME.

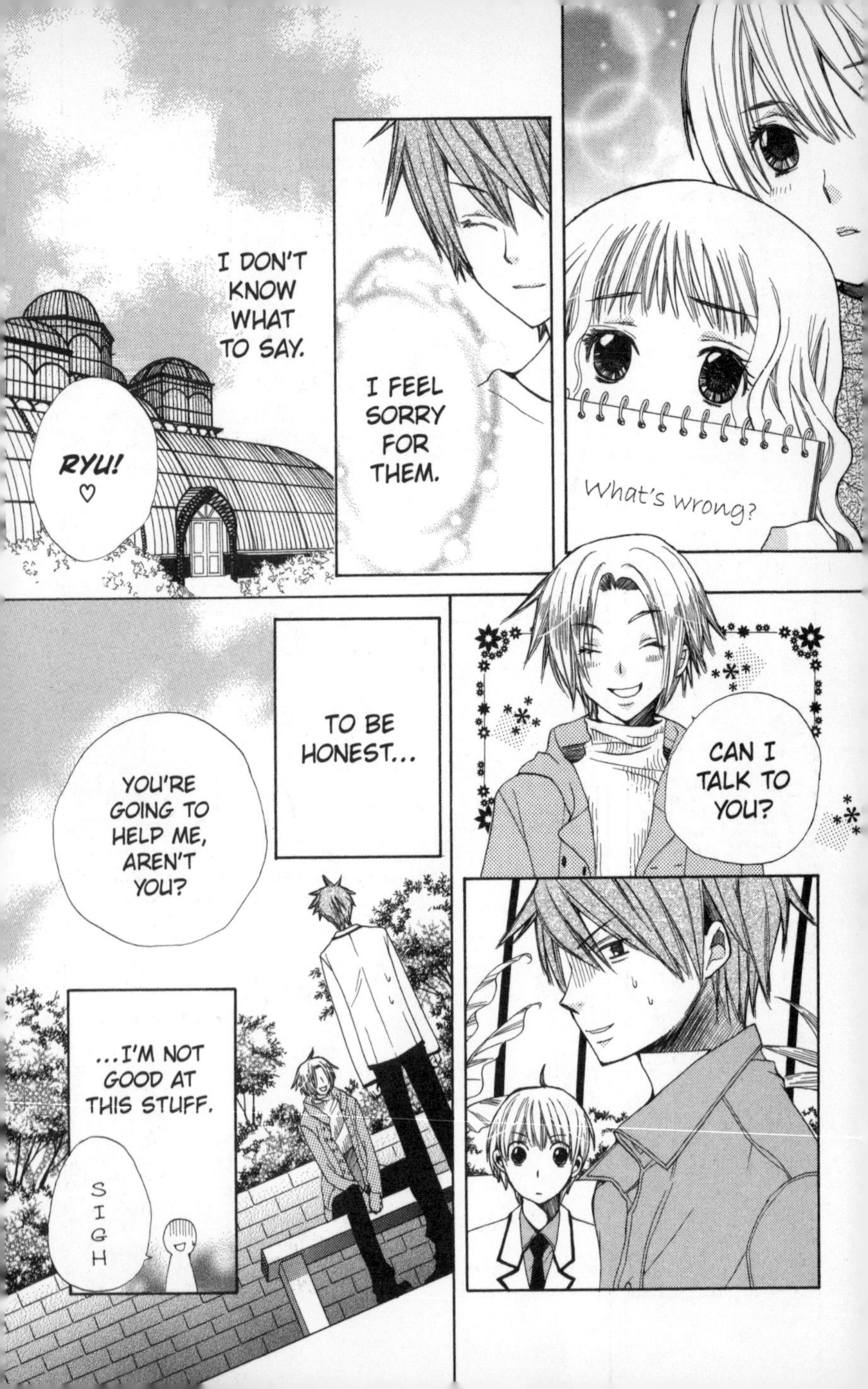
What's wrong?
I FEEL SORRY FOR THEM.
I DON'T KNOW WHAT TO SAY.
RYU! ♡
CAN I TALK TO YOU?
TO BE HONEST...
YOU'RE GOING TO HELP ME, AREN'T YOU?
...I'M NOT GOOD AT THIS STUFF.
SIGH

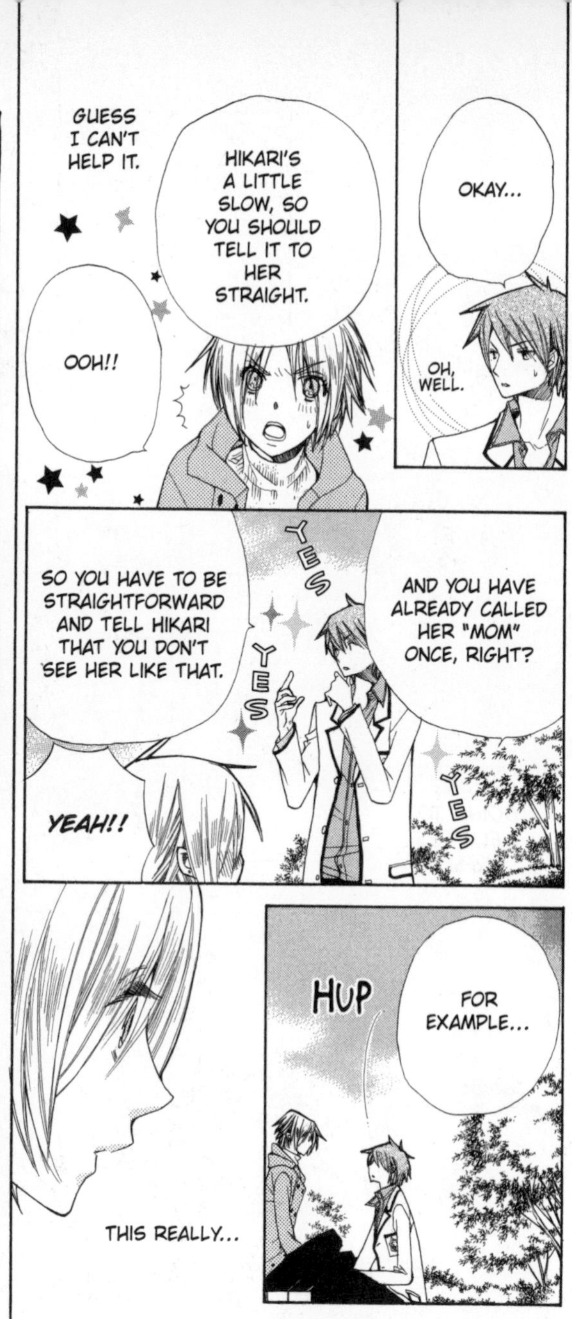
OKAY...
OH, WELL.
HIKARI'S A LITTLE SLOW, SO YOU SHOULD TELL IT TO HER STRAIGHT.
GUESS I CAN'T HELP IT.
OOH!!
AND YOU HAVE ALREADY CALLED HER "MOM" ONCE, RIGHT?
YES
YES
YES
SO YOU HAVE TO BE STRAIGHTFORWARD AND TELL HIKARI THAT YOU DON'T SEE HER LIKE THAT.
YEAH!!
FOR EXAMPLE...
HUP
THIS REALLY...

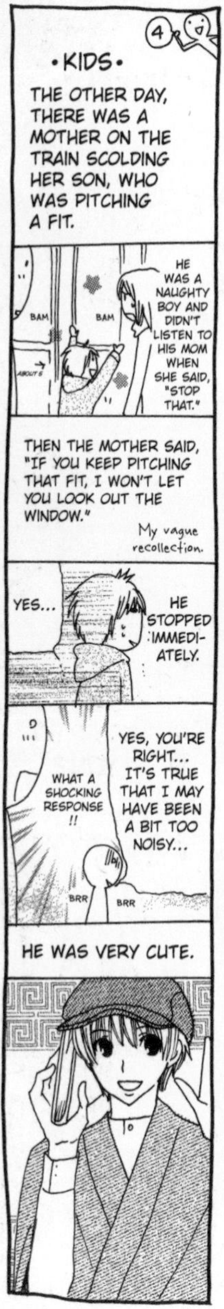
4
•KIDS•
THE OTHER DAY, THERE WAS A MOTHER ON THE TRAIN SCOLDING HER SON, WHO WAS PITCHING A FIT.
HE WAS A NAUGHTY BOY AND DIDN'T LISTEN TO HIS MOM WHEN SHE SAID, "STOP THAT."
BAM
BAM
THEN THE MOTHER SAID, "IF YOU KEEP PITCHING THAT FIT, I WON'T LET YOU LOOK OUT THE WINDOW."
My vague recollection.
HE STOPPED IMMEDI-ATELY.
YES...
YES, YOU'RE RIGHT... IT'S TRUE THAT I MAY HAVE BEEN A BIT TOO NOISY...
WHAT A SHOCKING RESPONSE !!
BRR
BRR
HE WAS VERY CUTE.

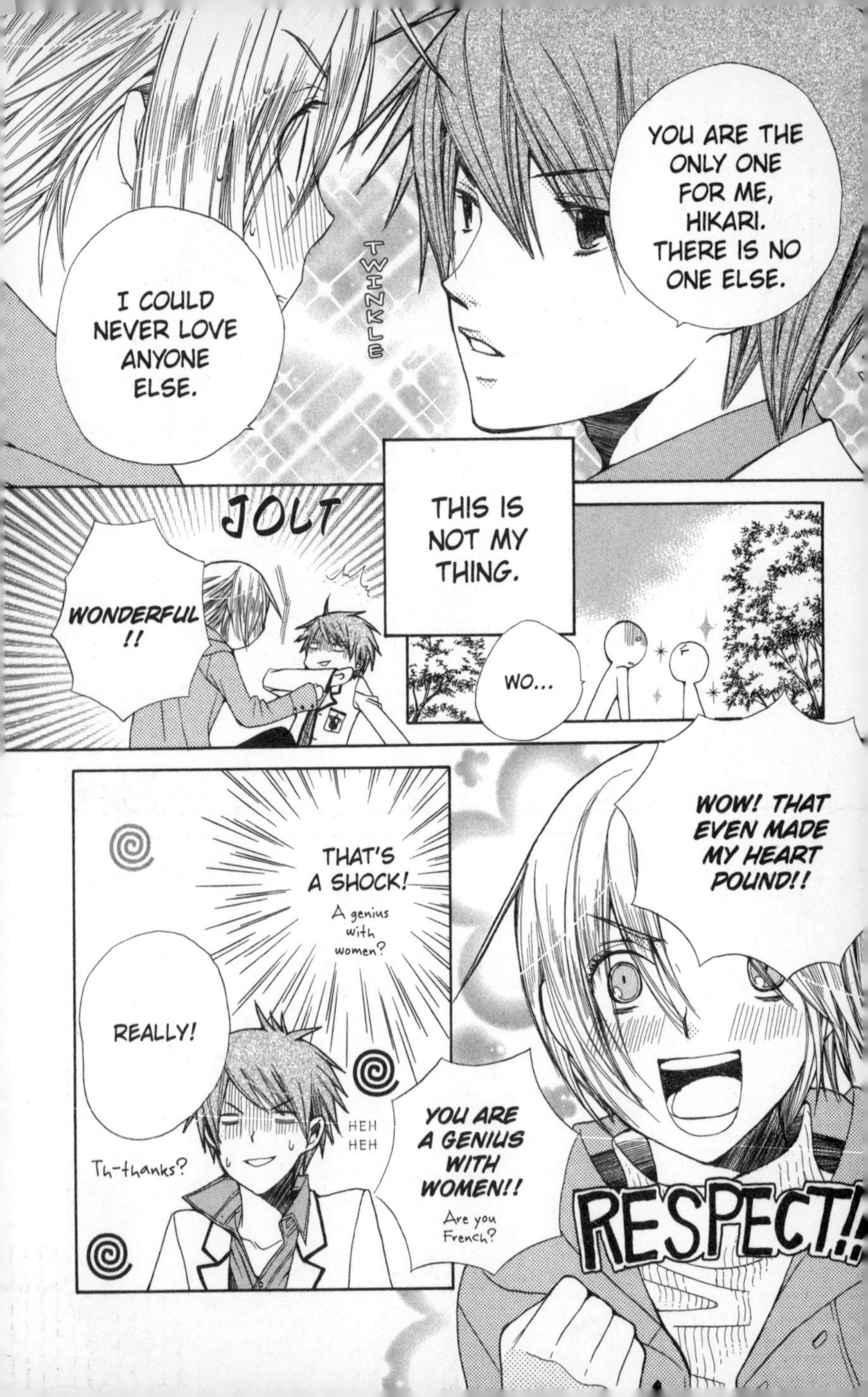
YOU ARE THE ONLY ONE FOR ME, HIKARI. THERE IS NO ONE ELSE.
TWINKLE
I COULD NEVER LOVE ANYONE ELSE.
THIS IS NOT MY THING.
WO...
JOLT
WONDERFUL!!
WOW! THAT EVEN MADE MY HEART POUND!!
YOU ARE A GENIUS WITH WOMEN!!
Are you French?
RESPECT!!
THAT'S A SHOCK!
A genius with women?
REALLY!
HEH HEH
Th-thanks?

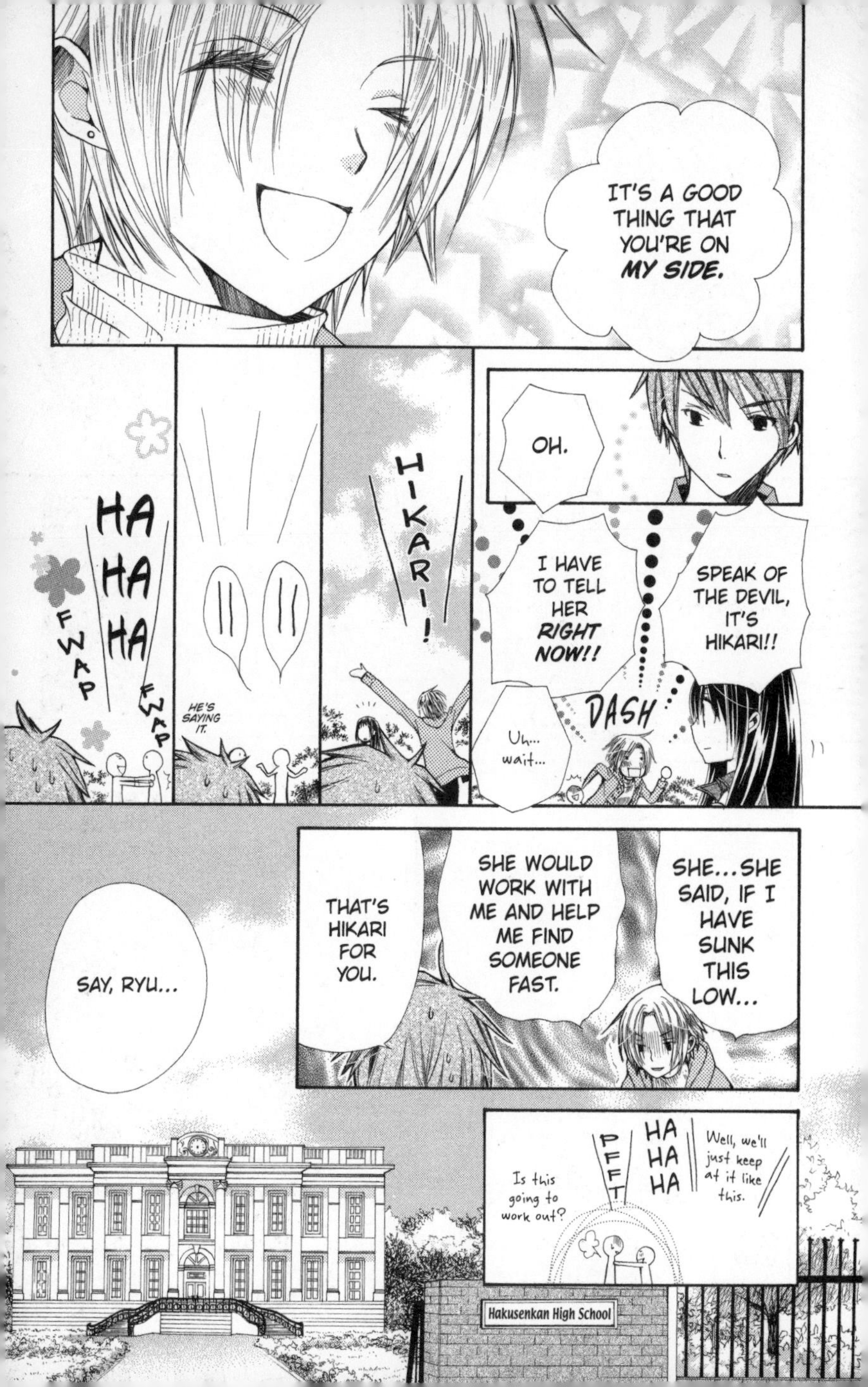
IT'S A GOOD THING THAT YOU'RE ON MY SIDE.
OH.
SPEAK OF THE DEVIL, IT'S HIKARI!!
I HAVE TO TELL HER RIGHT NOW!!
DASH
Uh... wait...
HIKARI!
HE'S SAYING IT.
HA HA HA
FWAP
FWAP
SHE...SHE SAID, IF I HAVE SUNK THIS LOW...
SHE WOULD WORK WITH ME AND HELP ME FIND SOMEONE FAST.
THAT'S HIKARI FOR YOU.
SAY, RYU...
Well, we'll just keep at it like this.
HA HA HA
PFFT
Is this going to work out?
Hakusenkan High School

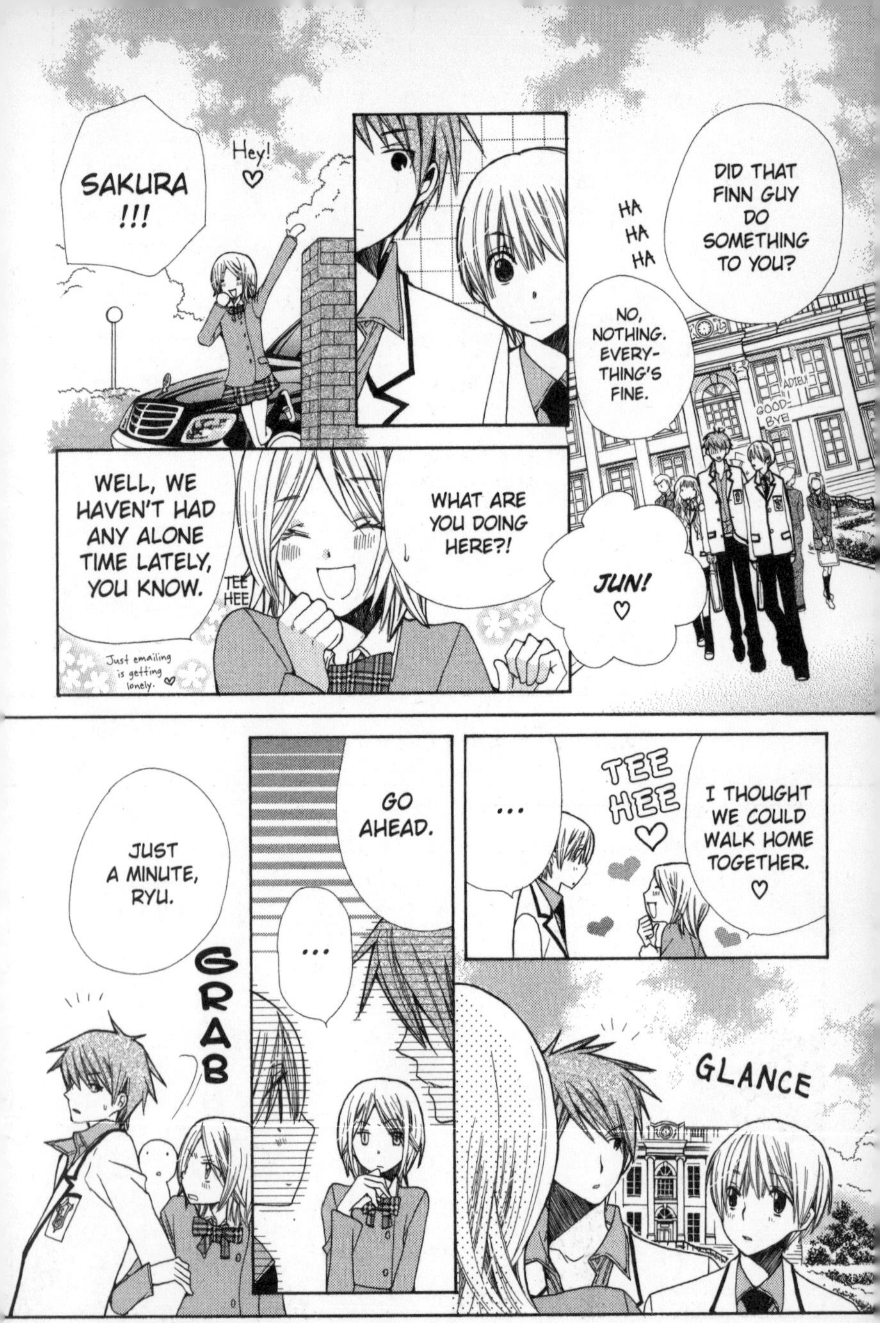
DID THAT FINN GUY DO SOMETHING TO YOU?
HA HA HA
NO, NOTHING. EVERY-THING'S FINE.
ADIEU! GOOD-BYE!
JUN! ♡
SAKURA!!!
Hey! ♡
WHAT ARE YOU DOING HERE?!
WELL, WE HAVEN'T HAD ANY ALONE TIME LATELY, YOU KNOW.
TEE HEE
Just emailing is getting lonely. ♡
I THOUGHT WE COULD WALK HOME TOGETHER. ♡
TEE HEE ♡
...
GO AHEAD.
...
JUST A MINUTE, RYU.
GRAB
GLANCE

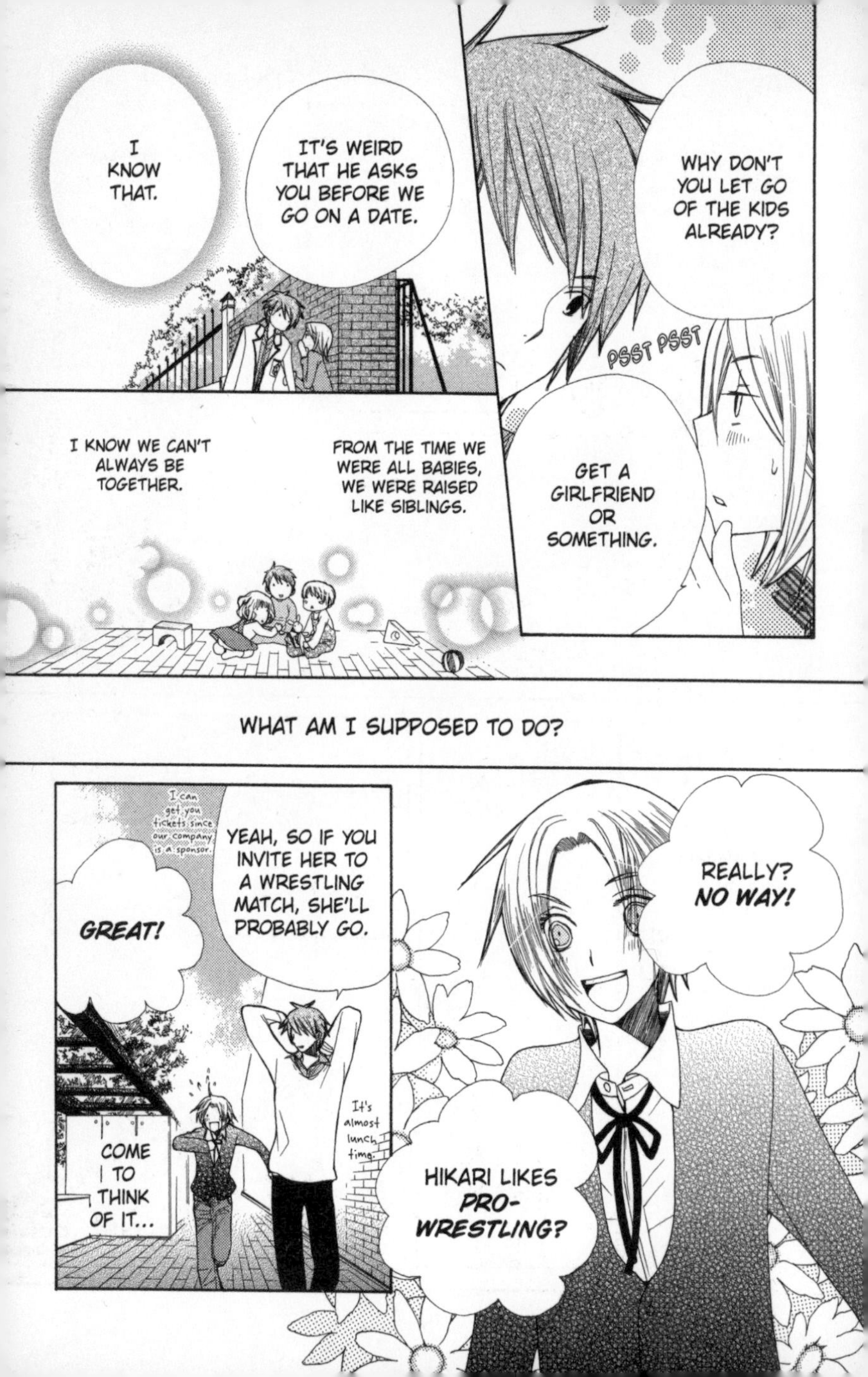
WHY DON'T YOU LET GO OF THE KIDS ALREADY?
PSST PSST
GET A GIRLFRIEND OR SOMETHING.
IT'S WEIRD THAT HE ASKS YOU BEFORE WE GO ON A DATE.
I KNOW THAT.
FROM THE TIME WE WERE ALL BABIES, WE WERE RAISED LIKE SIBLINGS.
I KNOW WE CAN'T ALWAYS BE TOGETHER.
WHAT AM I SUPPOSED TO DO?
REALLY? *NO WAY!*
HIKARI LIKES *PRO-WRESTLING?*
YEAH, SO IF YOU INVITE HER TO A WRESTLING MATCH, SHE'LL PROBABLY GO.
I can get you tickets since our company is a sponsor.
GREAT!
It's almost lunch time.
COME TO THINK OF IT...

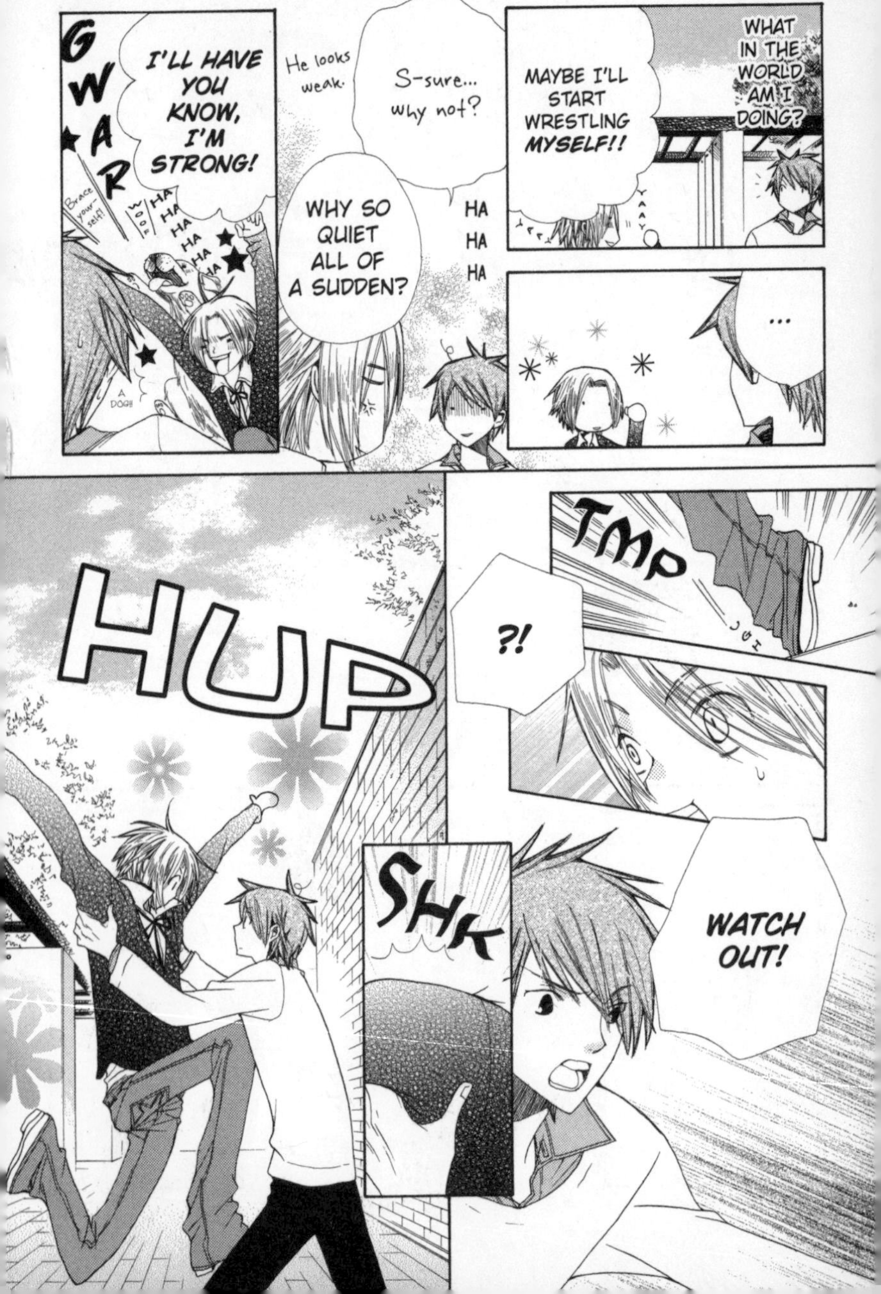
WHAT IN THE WORLD AM I DOING?
MAYBE I'LL START WRESTLING MYSELF!!
He looks weak.
S-sure... why not?
WHY SO QUIET ALL OF A SUDDEN?
HA HA HA
GWAR
I'LL HAVE YOU KNOW, I'M STRONG!
Brace yourself!
WOOF
HA HA HA HA HA HA
A DOG!!
...
TMP
?!
WATCH OUT!
SHK
HUP

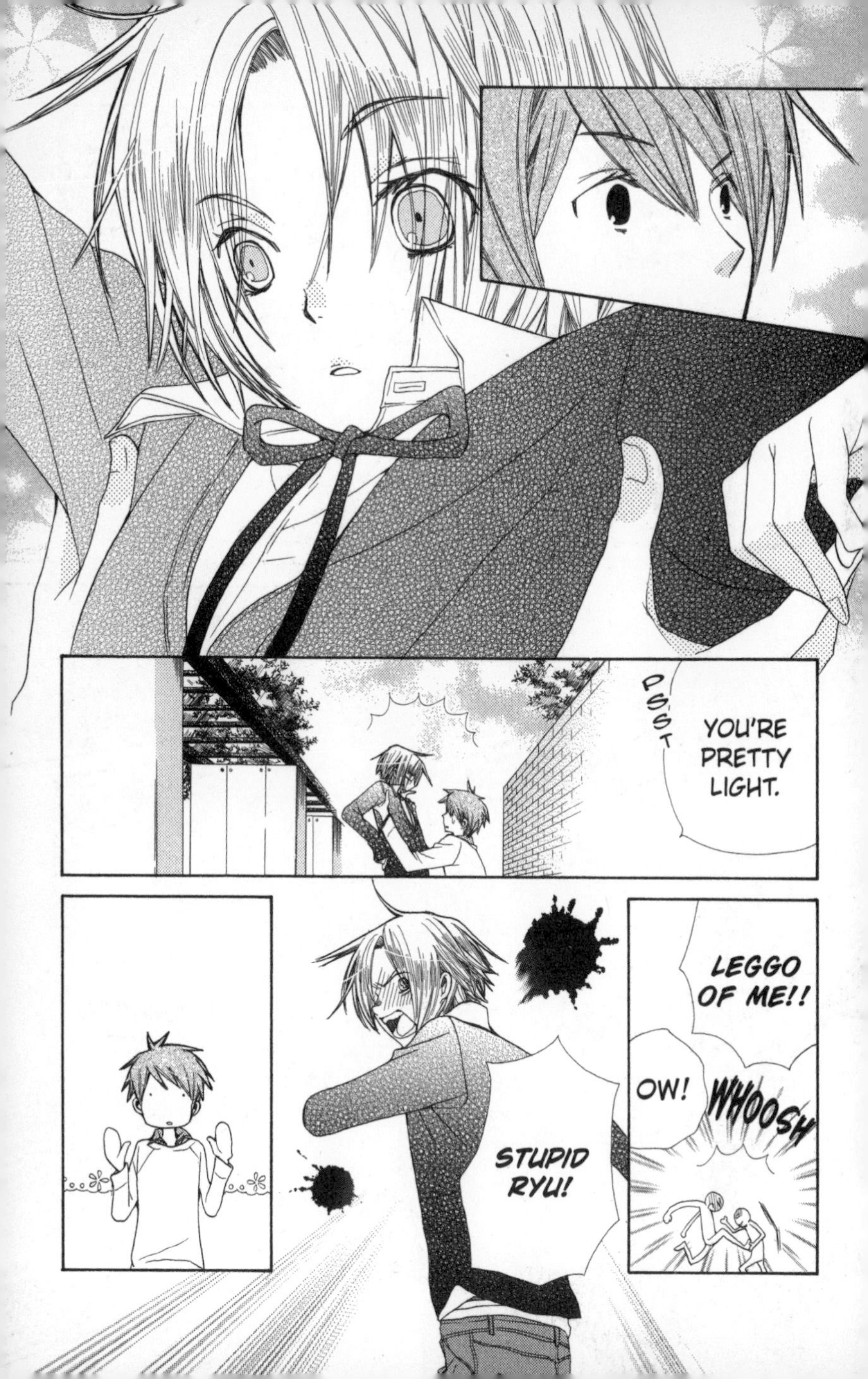
PSST
YOU'RE PRETTY LIGHT.
LEGGO OF ME!!
OW!
WHOOSH
STUPID RYU!

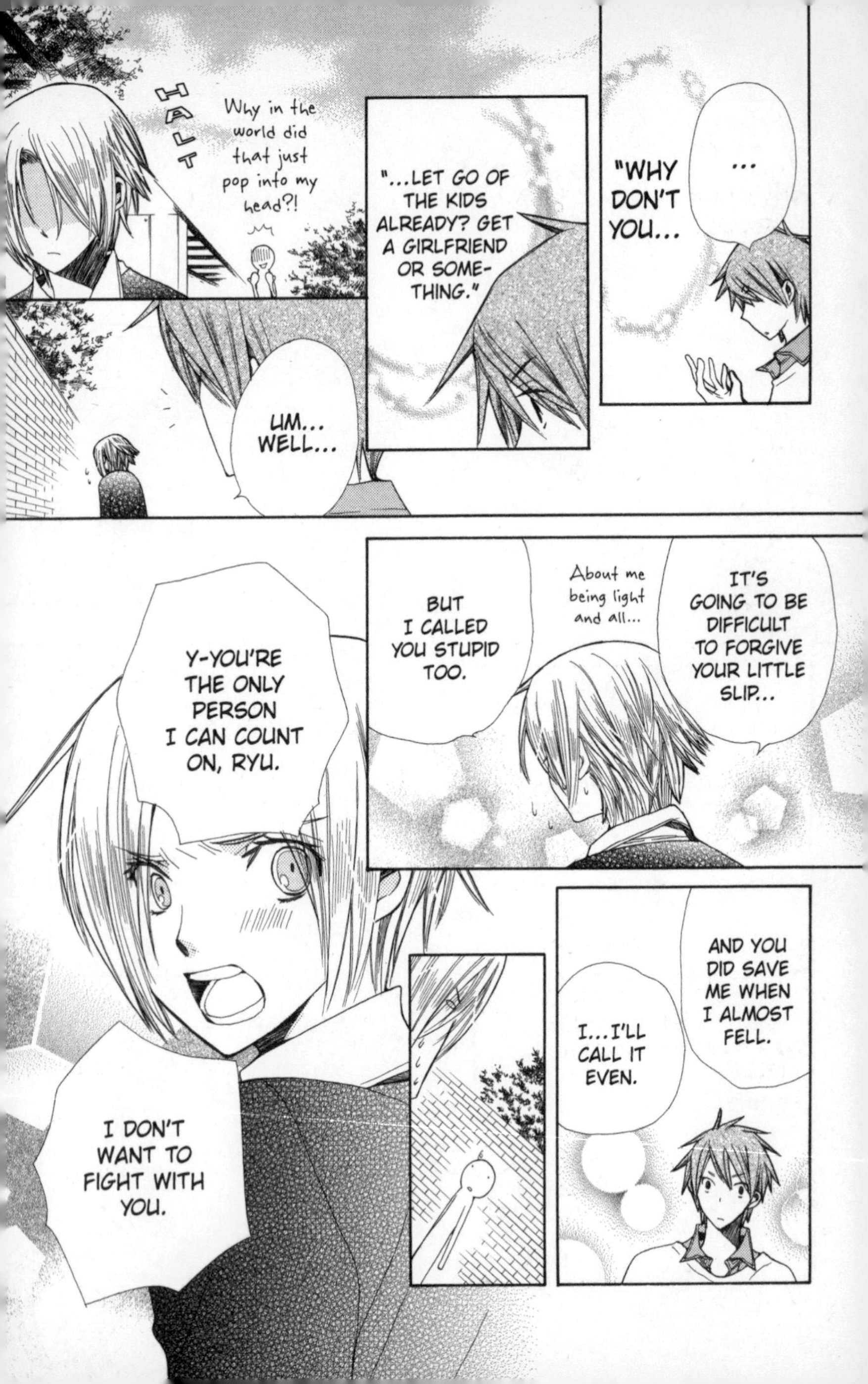
...
"WHY DON'T YOU...
"...LET GO OF THE KIDS ALREADY? GET A GIRLFRIEND OR SOME-THING."
HALT
Why in the world did that just pop into my head?!
UM... WELL...
IT'S GOING TO BE DIFFICULT TO FORGIVE YOUR LITTLE SLIP...
About me being light and all...
BUT I CALLED YOU STUPID TOO.
AND YOU DID SAVE ME WHEN I ALMOST FELL.
I...I'LL CALL IT EVEN.
Y-YOU'RE THE ONLY PERSON I CAN COUNT ON, RYU.
I DON'T WANT TO FIGHT WITH YOU.

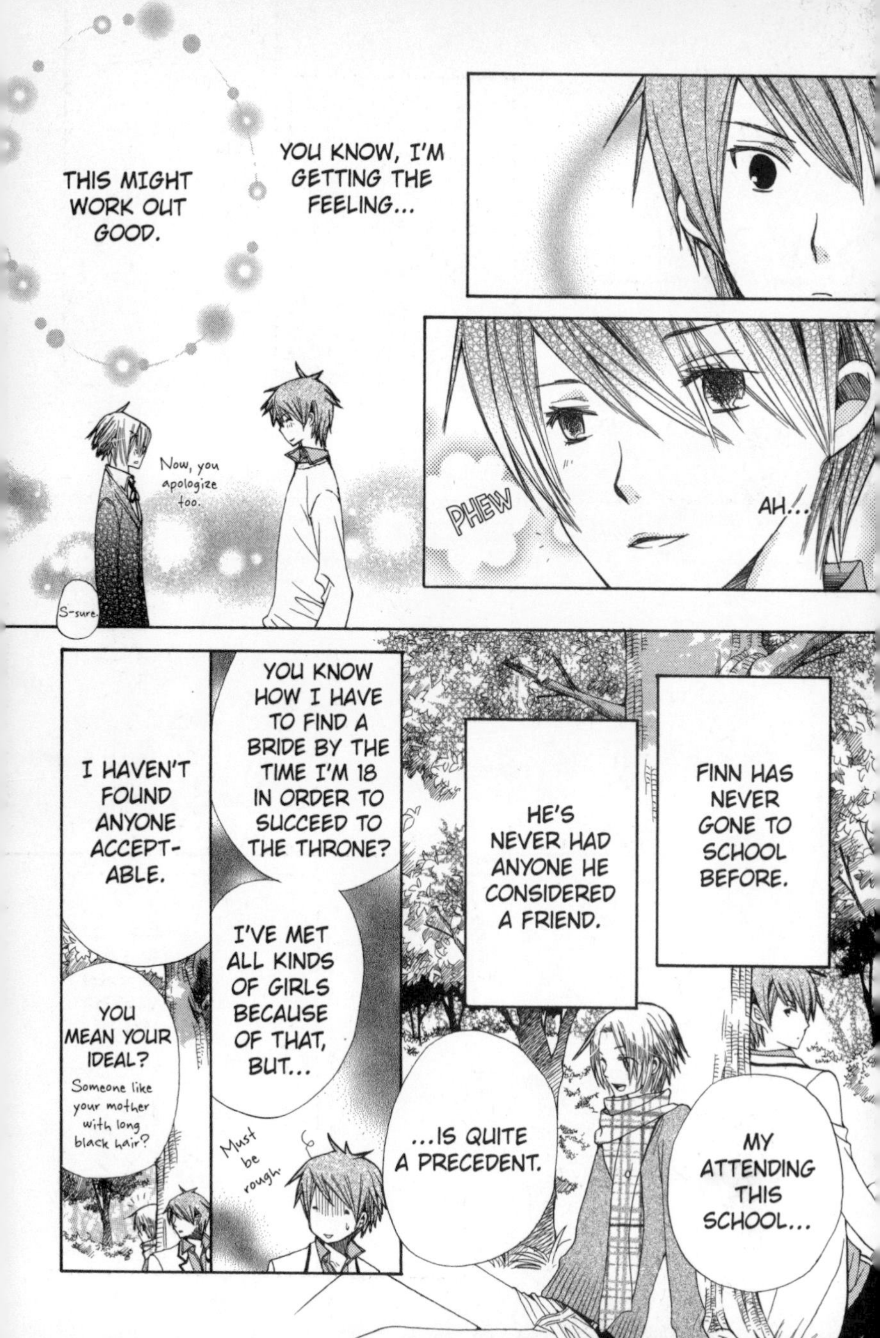
AH...
PHEW
YOU KNOW, I'M GETTING THE FEELING...
THIS MIGHT WORK OUT GOOD.
Now, you apologize too.
S-sure.
FINN HAS NEVER GONE TO SCHOOL BEFORE.
HE'S NEVER HAD ANYONE HE CONSIDERED A FRIEND.
MY ATTENDING THIS SCHOOL...
...IS QUITE A PRECEDENT.
YOU KNOW HOW I HAVE TO FIND A BRIDE BY THE TIME I'M 18 IN ORDER TO SUCCEED TO THE THRONE?
I'VE MET ALL KINDS OF GIRLS BECAUSE OF THAT, BUT...
Must be rough.
I HAVEN'T FOUND ANYONE ACCEPT-ABLE.
YOU MEAN YOUR IDEAL?
Someone like your mother with long black hair?

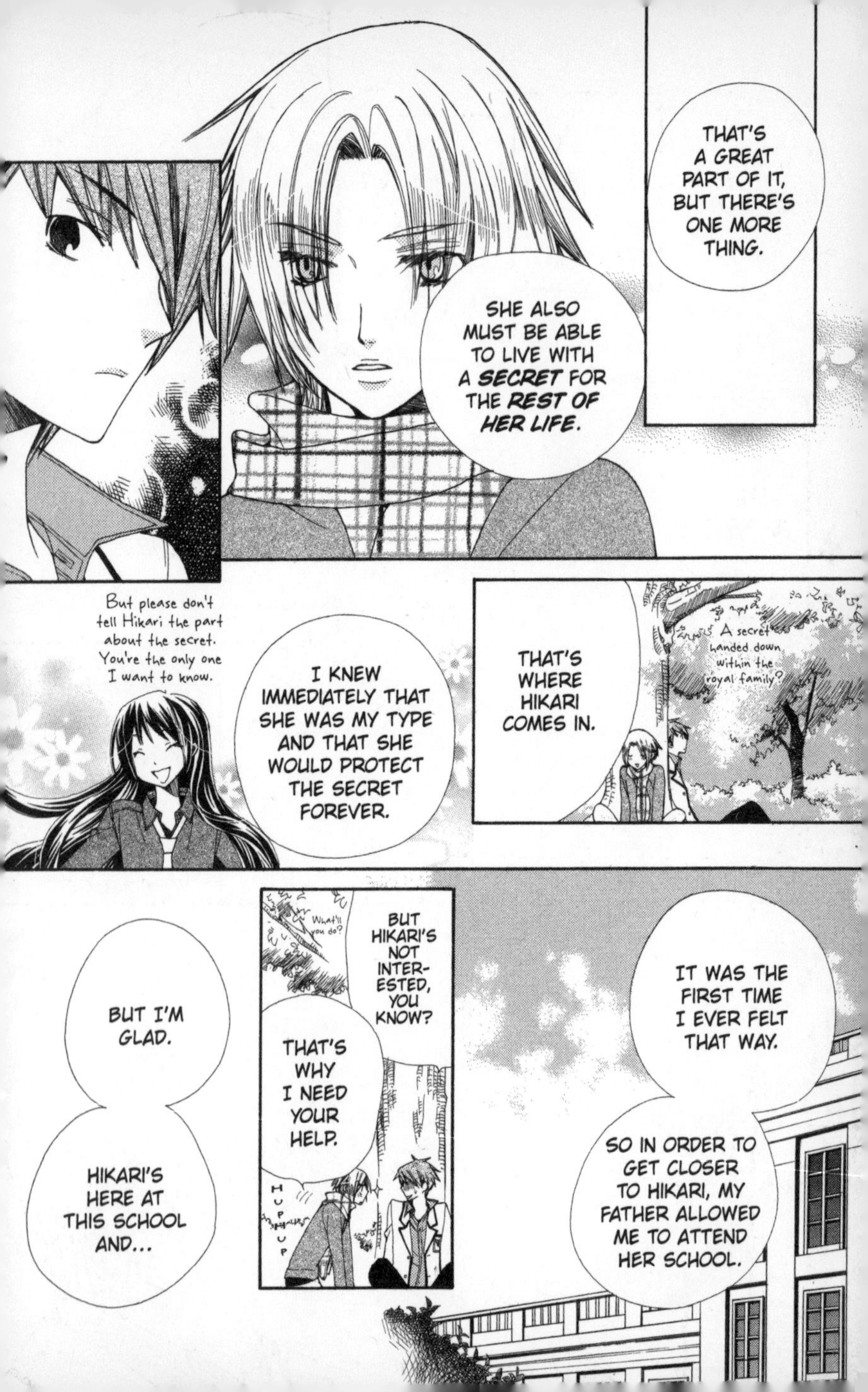
THAT'S A GREAT PART OF IT, BUT THERE'S ONE MORE THING.
SHE ALSO MUST BE ABLE TO LIVE WITH A ***SECRET*** FOR THE ***REST OF HER LIFE***.
A secret handed down within the royal family?
THAT'S WHERE HIKARI COMES IN.
I KNEW IMMEDIATELY THAT SHE WAS MY TYPE AND THAT SHE WOULD PROTECT THE SECRET FOREVER.
But please don't tell Hikari the part about the secret. You're the only one I want to know.
IT WAS THE FIRST TIME I EVER FELT THAT WAY.
SO IN ORDER TO GET CLOSER TO HIKARI, MY FATHER ALLOWED ME TO ATTEND HER SCHOOL.
What'll you do?
BUT HIKARI'S NOT INTER-ESTED, YOU KNOW?
THAT'S WHY I NEED YOUR HELP.
HUP HUP
BUT I'M GLAD.
HIKARI'S HERE AT THIS SCHOOL AND...

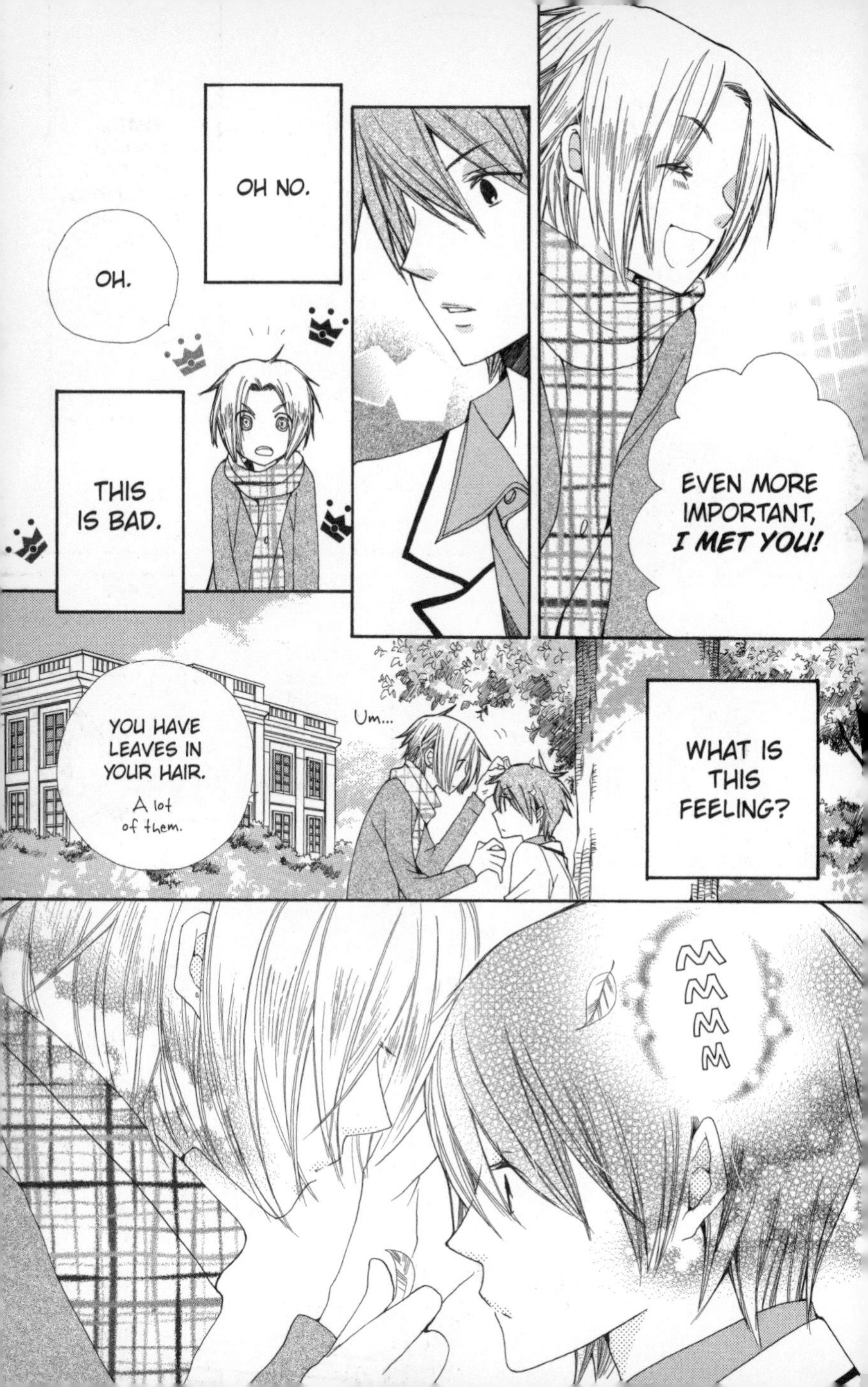
EVEN MORE IMPORTANT, I MET YOU!
OH NO.
OH.
THIS IS BAD.
WHAT IS THIS FEELING?
Um...
YOU HAVE LEAVES IN YOUR HAIR.
A lot of them.
MMMM

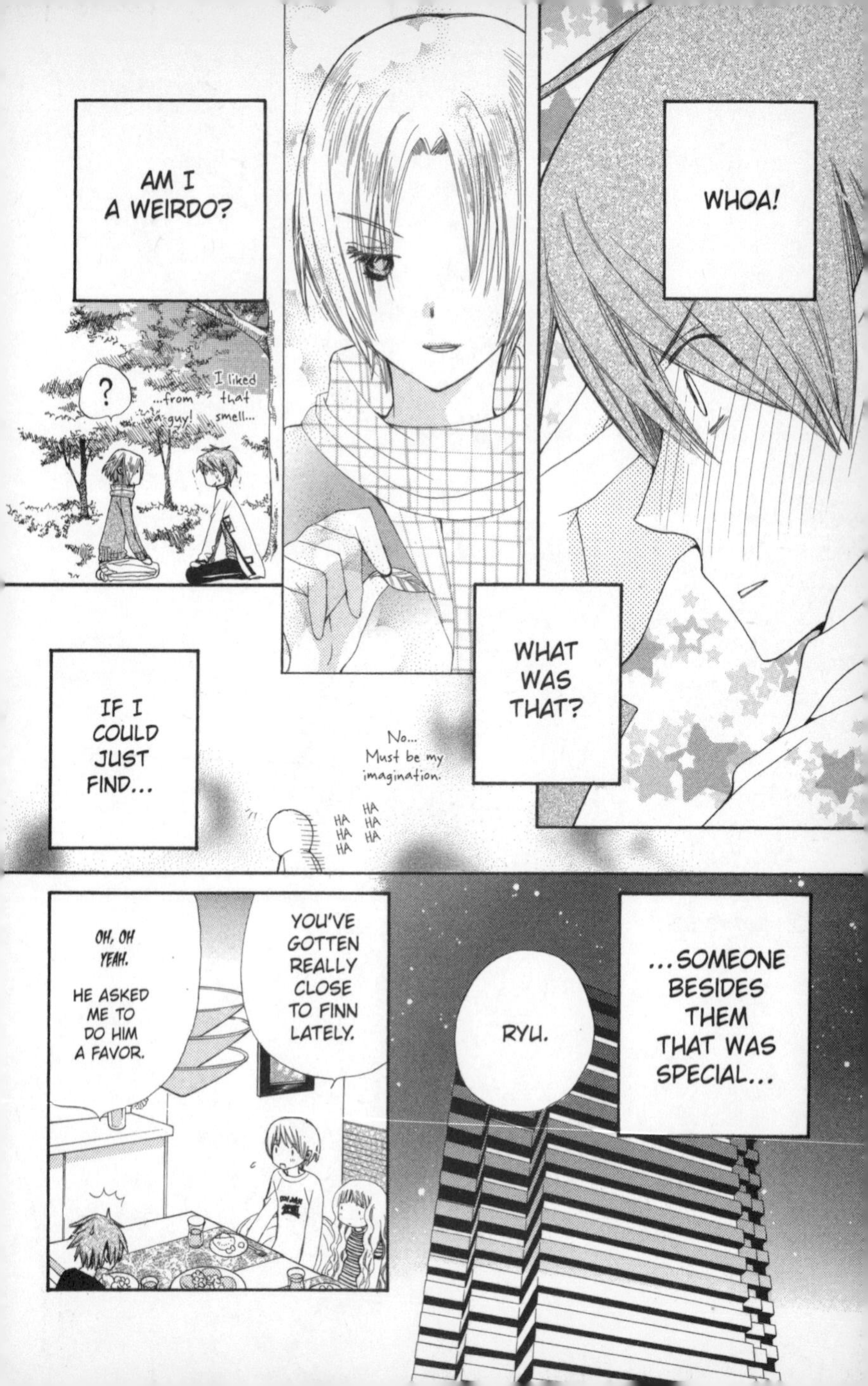
WHOA!
WHAT WAS THAT?
AM I A WEIRDO?
?
I liked that smell...
...from a guy!
No... Must be my imagination.
HA HA HA HA HA HA HA
IF I COULD JUST FIND...
...SOMEONE BESIDES THEM THAT WAS SPECIAL...
RYU.
YOU'VE GOTTEN REALLY CLOSE TO FINN LATELY.
OH, OH YEAH.
HE ASKED ME TO DO HIM A FAVOR.

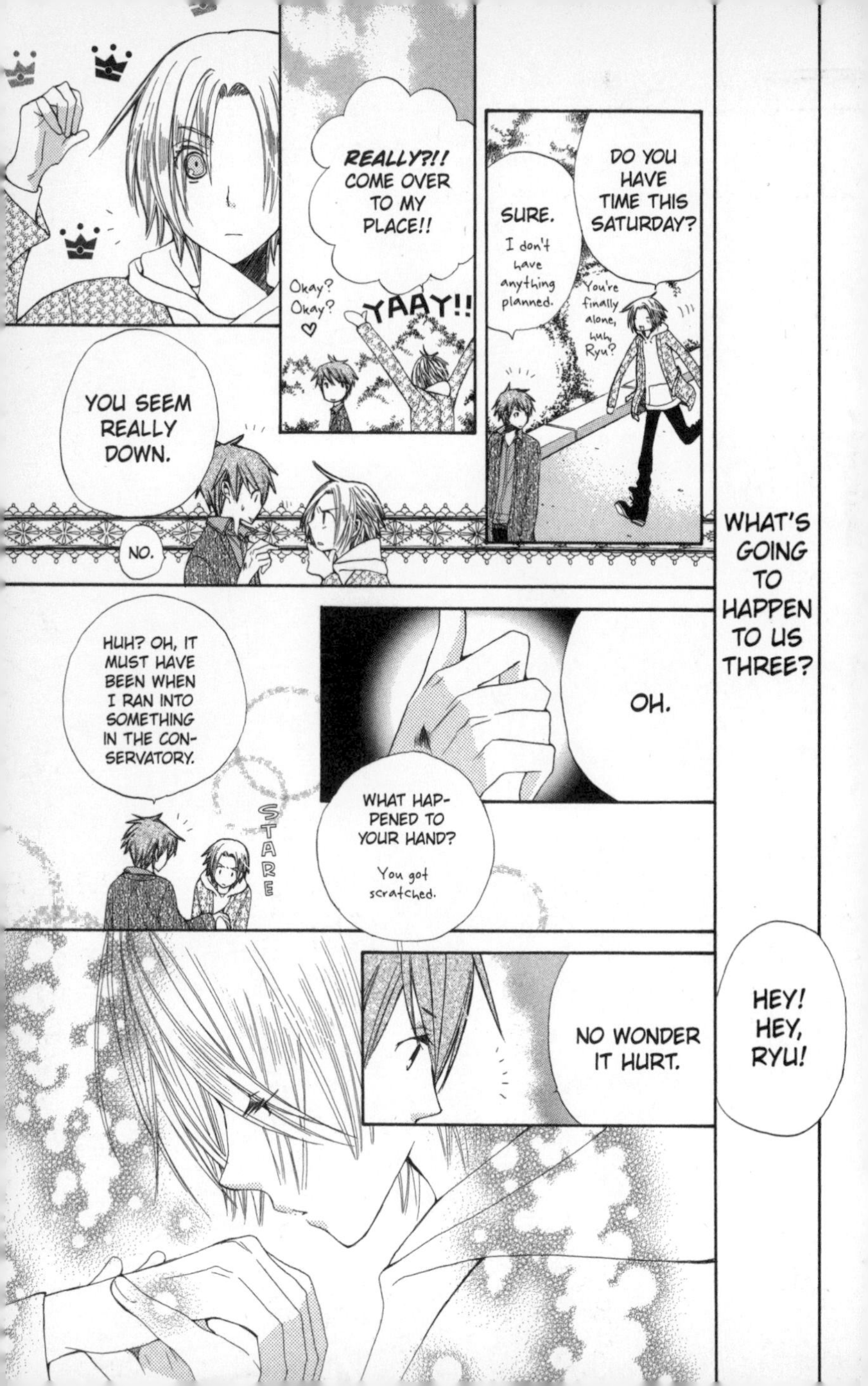
WHAT'S GOING TO HAPPEN TO US THREE?
HEY! HEY, RYU!
DO YOU HAVE TIME THIS SATURDAY?
You're finally alone, huh, Ryu?
SURE.
I don't have anything planned.
REALLY?!! COME OVER TO MY PLACE!!
Okay? Okay?
YAAY!!
YOU SEEM REALLY DOWN.
NO.
OH.
WHAT HAPPENED TO YOUR HAND?
You got scratched.
HUH? OH, IT MUST HAVE BEEN WHEN I RAN INTO SOMETHING IN THE CONSERVATORY.
STARE
NO WONDER IT HURT.

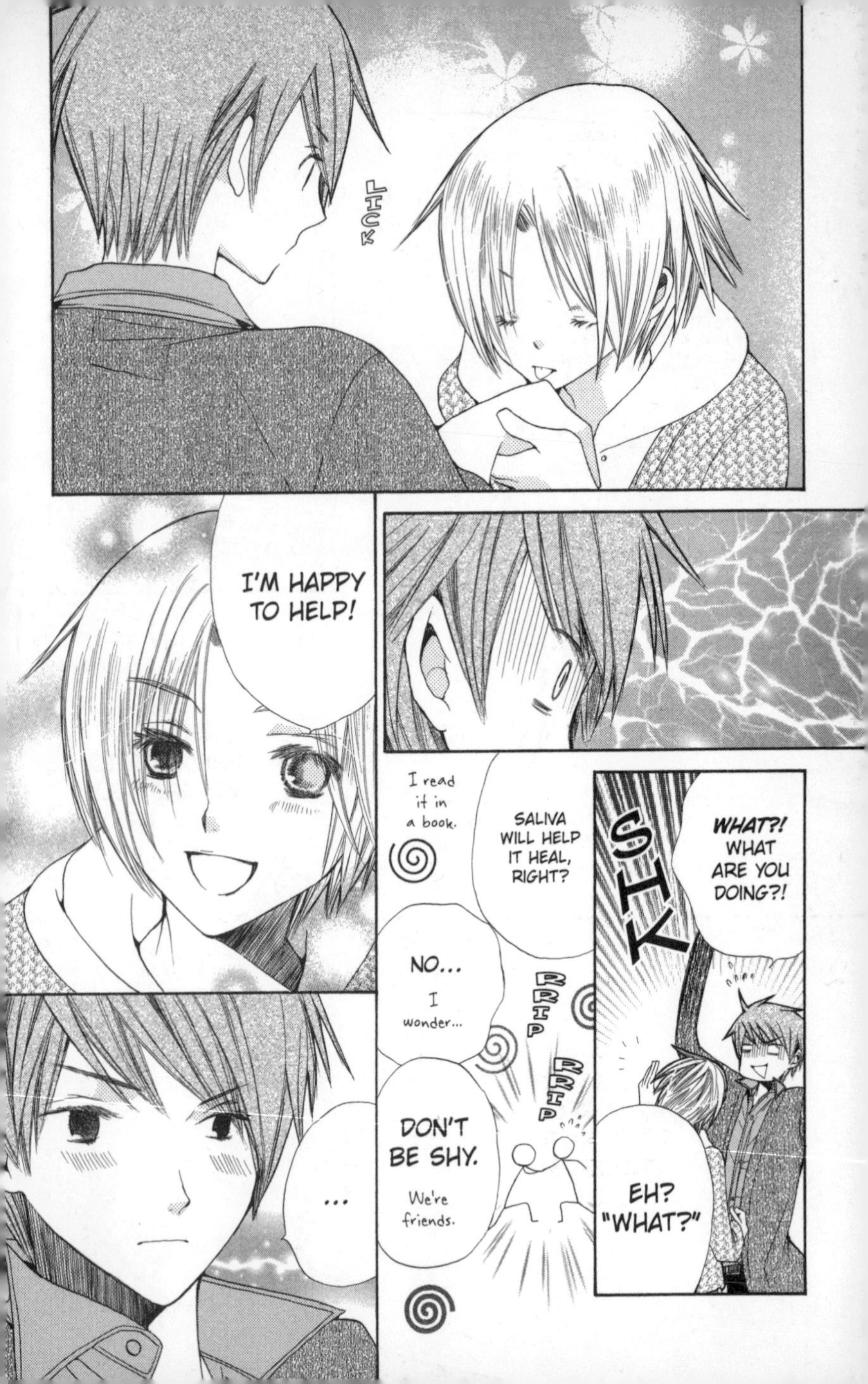
LICK
I'M HAPPY TO HELP!
WHAT?! WHAT ARE YOU DOING?!
SHK
EH? "WHAT?"
SALIVA WILL HELP IT HEAL, RIGHT?
I read it in a book.
NO... I wonder...
RRIP RRIP
DON'T BE SHY. We're friends.
...

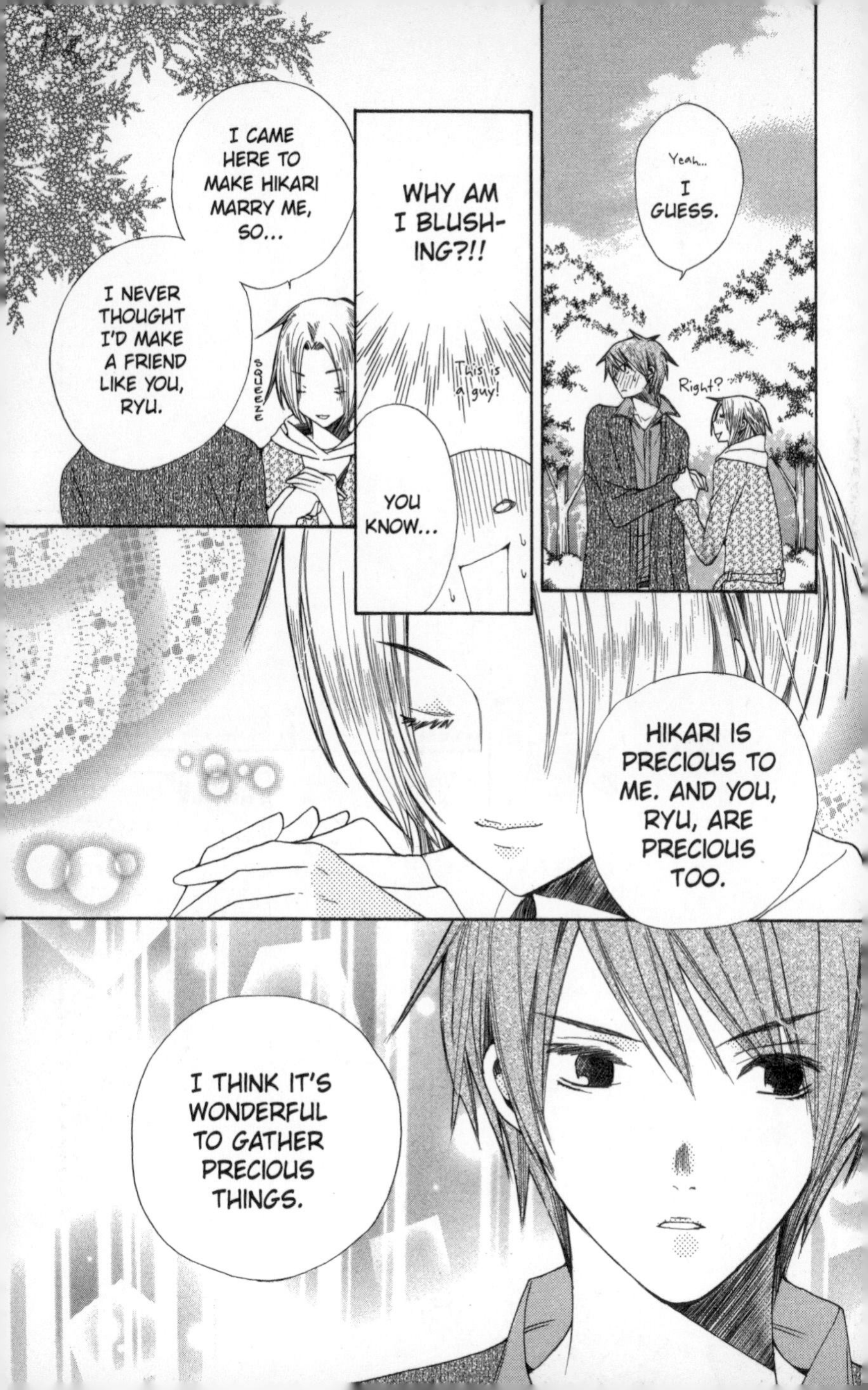

Yeah... I GUESS.
Right?
WHY AM I BLUSH-ING?!!
This is a guy!
YOU KNOW...
I CAME HERE TO MAKE HIKARI MARRY ME, SO...
I NEVER THOUGHT I'D MAKE A FRIEND LIKE YOU, RYU.
SQUEEZE
HIKARI IS PRECIOUS TO ME. AND YOU, RYU, ARE PRECIOUS TOO.
I THINK IT'S WONDERFUL TO GATHER PRECIOUS THINGS.

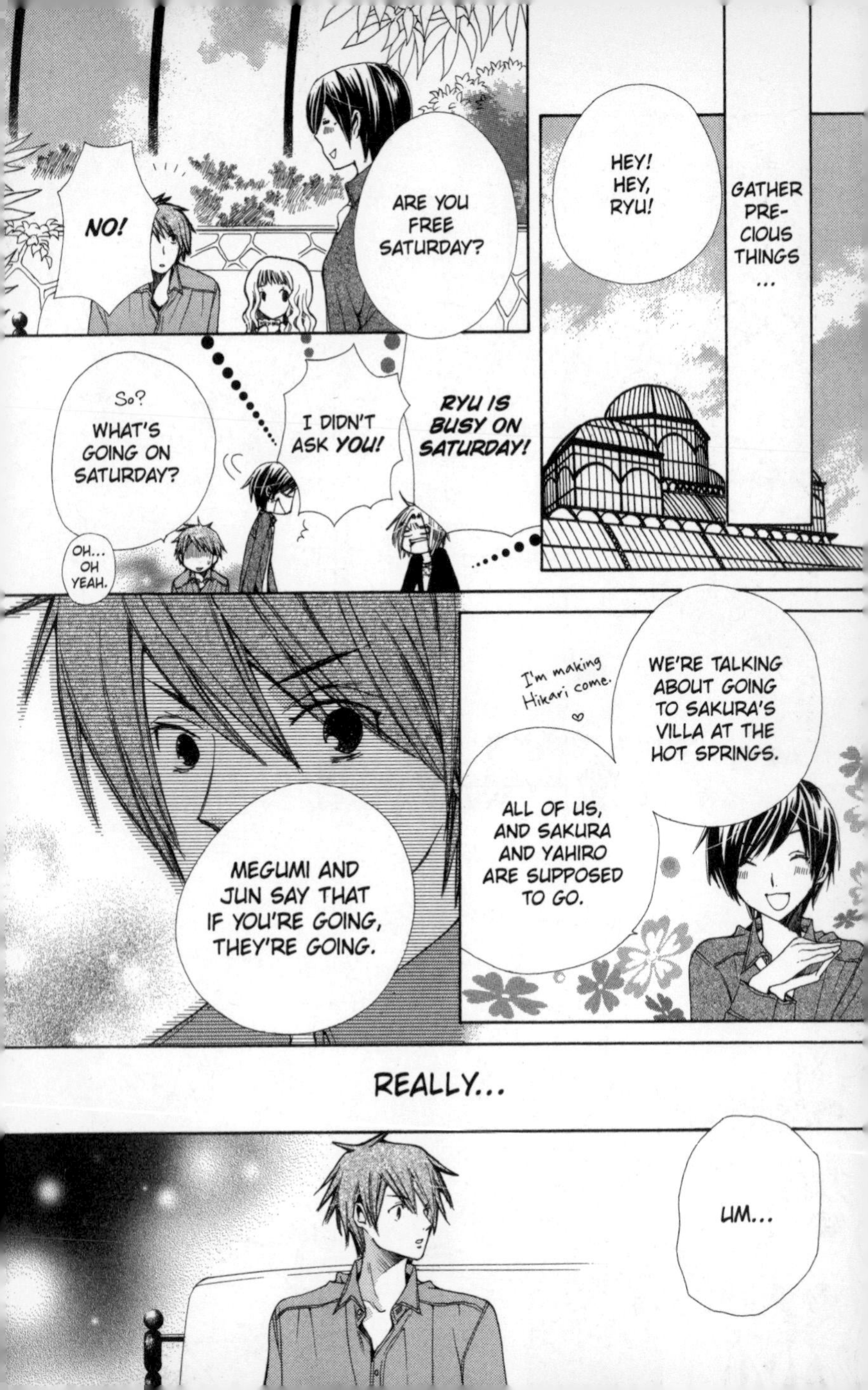
GATHER PRECIOUS THINGS...
HEY! HEY, RYU!
ARE YOU FREE SATURDAY?
NO!
RYU IS BUSY ON SATURDAY!
I DIDN'T ASK YOU!
So? WHAT'S GOING ON SATURDAY?
OH... OH YEAH.
WE'RE TALKING ABOUT GOING TO SAKURA'S VILLA AT THE HOT SPRINGS.
I'm making Hikari come.
ALL OF US, AND SAKURA AND YAHIRO ARE SUPPOSED TO GO.
MEGUMI AND JUN SAY THAT IF YOU'RE GOING, THEY'RE GOING.
REALLY...
UM...

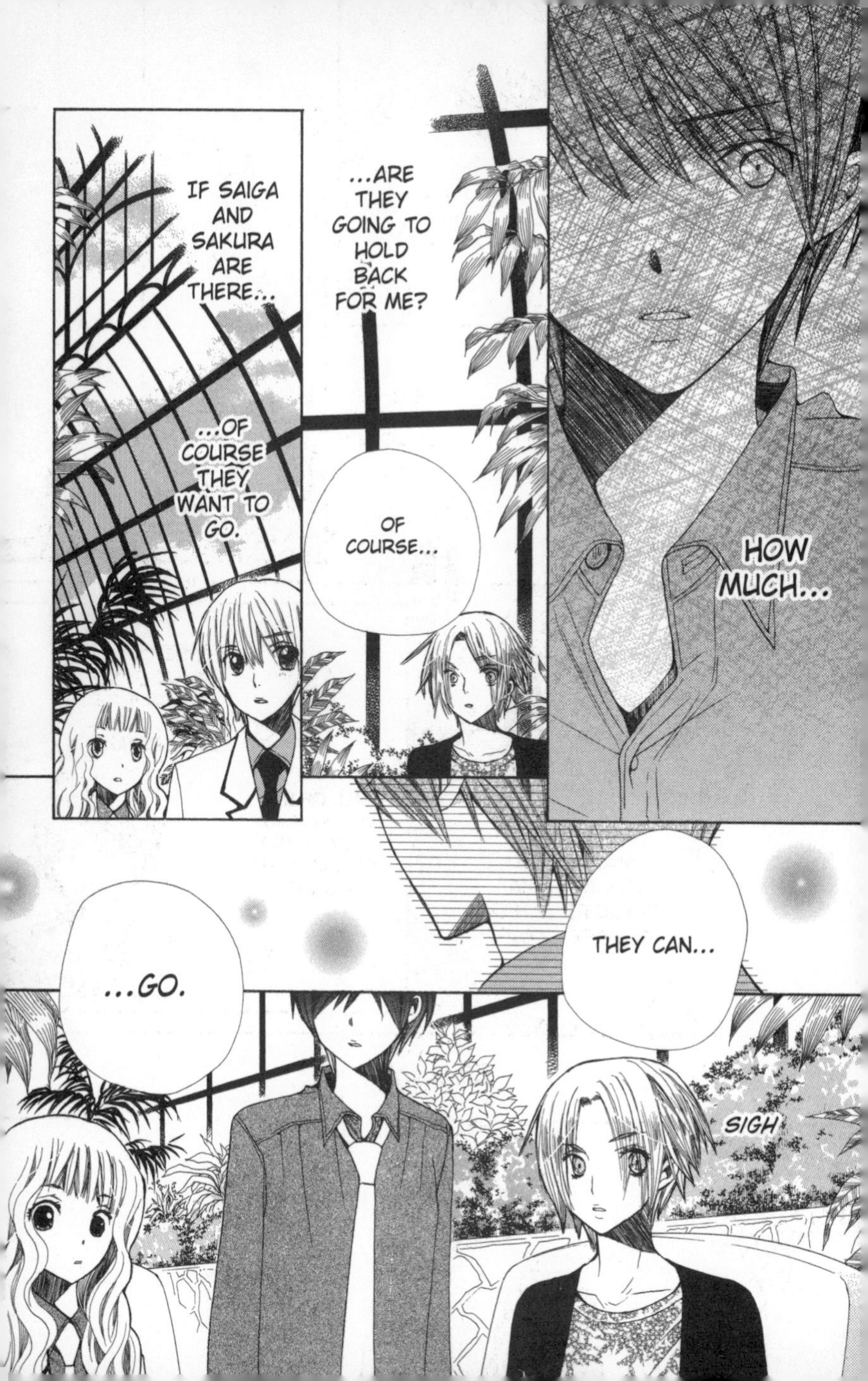
HOW MUCH...
...ARE THEY GOING TO HOLD BACK FOR ME?
OF COURSE...
IF SAIGA AND SAKURA ARE THERE...
...OF COURSE THEY WANT TO GO.
THEY CAN...
...GO.
SIGH

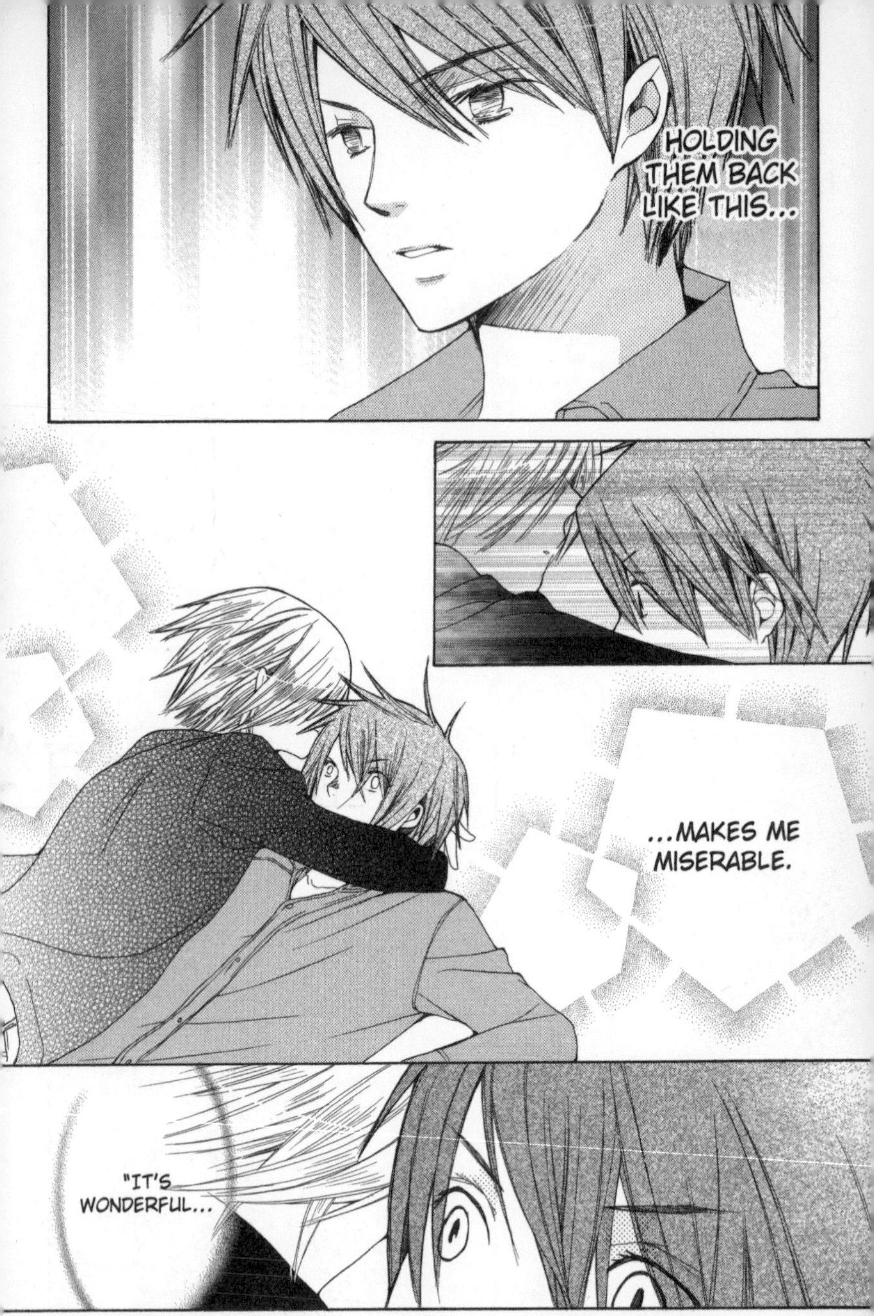
HOLDING THEM BACK LIKE THIS...
...MAKES ME MISERABLE.
"IT'S WONDERFUL...

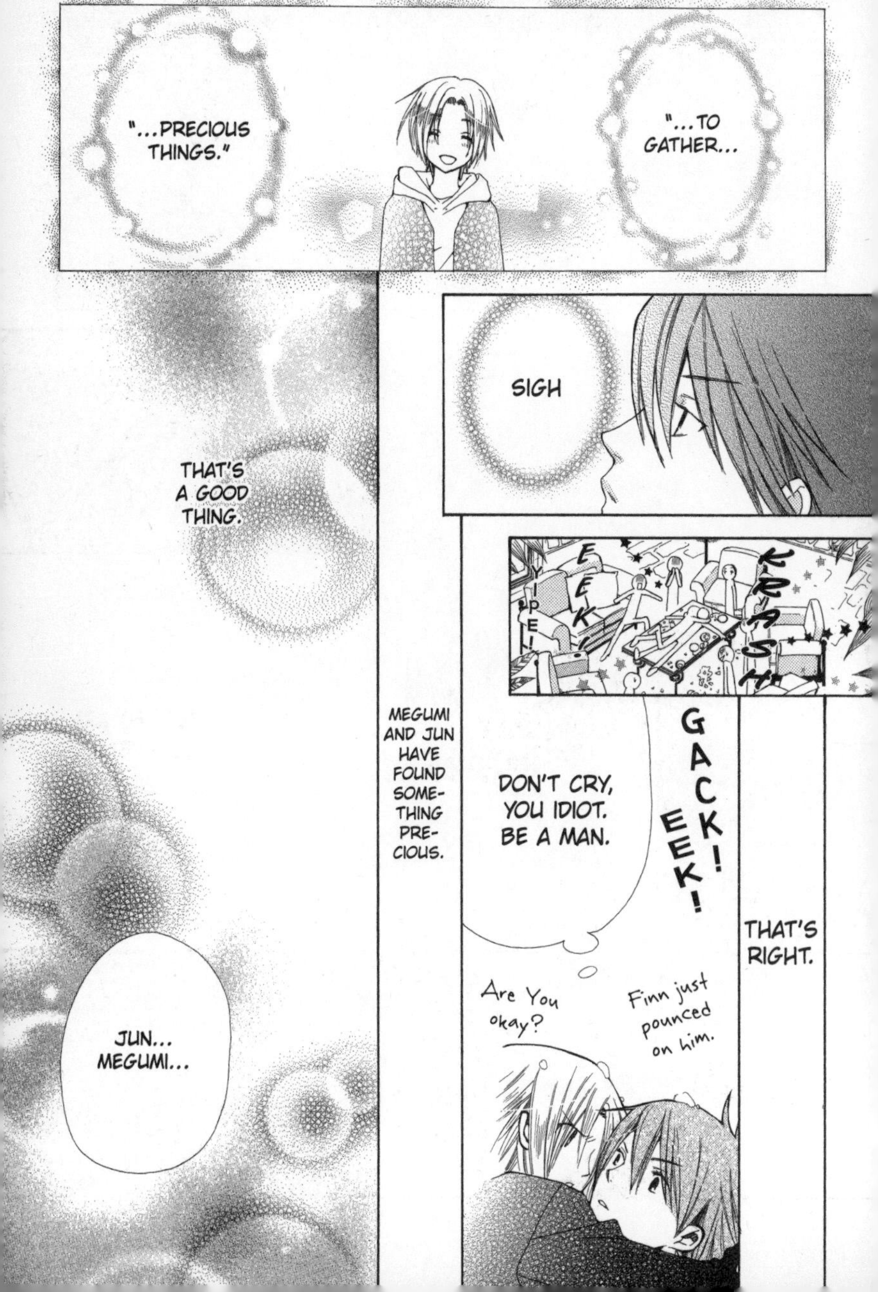
"...TO GATHER...
"...PRECIOUS THINGS."
SIGH
KRASH
EEK!
YIPE!
THAT'S RIGHT.
GACK!
EEK!
DON'T CRY, YOU IDIOT. BE A MAN.
Finn just pounced on him.
Are You okay?
MEGUMI AND JUN HAVE FOUND SOME-THING PRE-CIOUS.
THAT'S A GOOD THING.
JUN... MEGUMI...

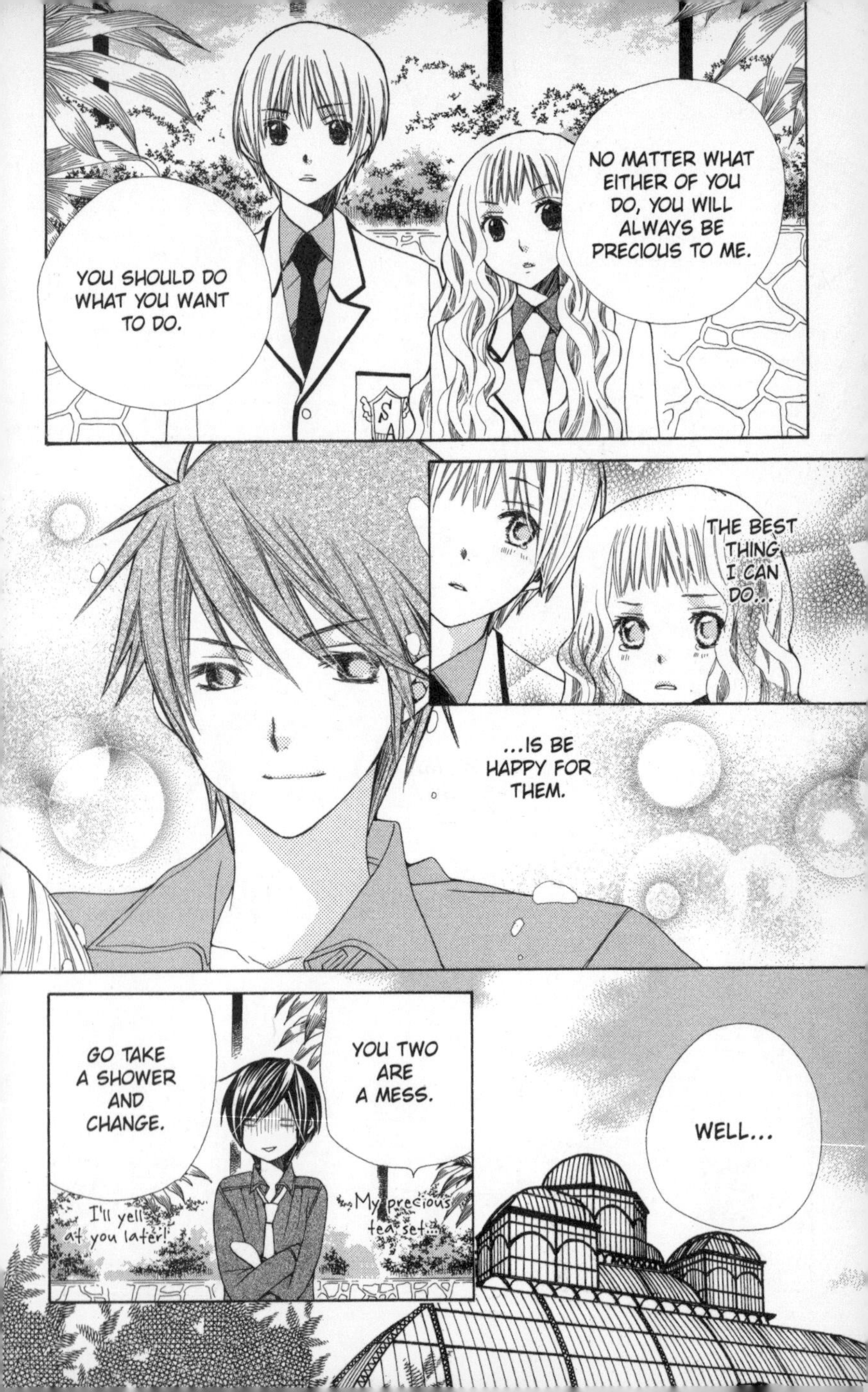
NO MATTER WHAT EITHER OF YOU DO, YOU WILL ALWAYS BE PRECIOUS TO ME.
YOU SHOULD DO WHAT YOU WANT TO DO.
THE BEST THING I CAN DO...
...IS BE HAPPY FOR THEM.
WELL...
YOU TWO ARE A MESS.
GO TAKE A SHOWER AND CHANGE.
My precious tea set...
I'll yell at you later!

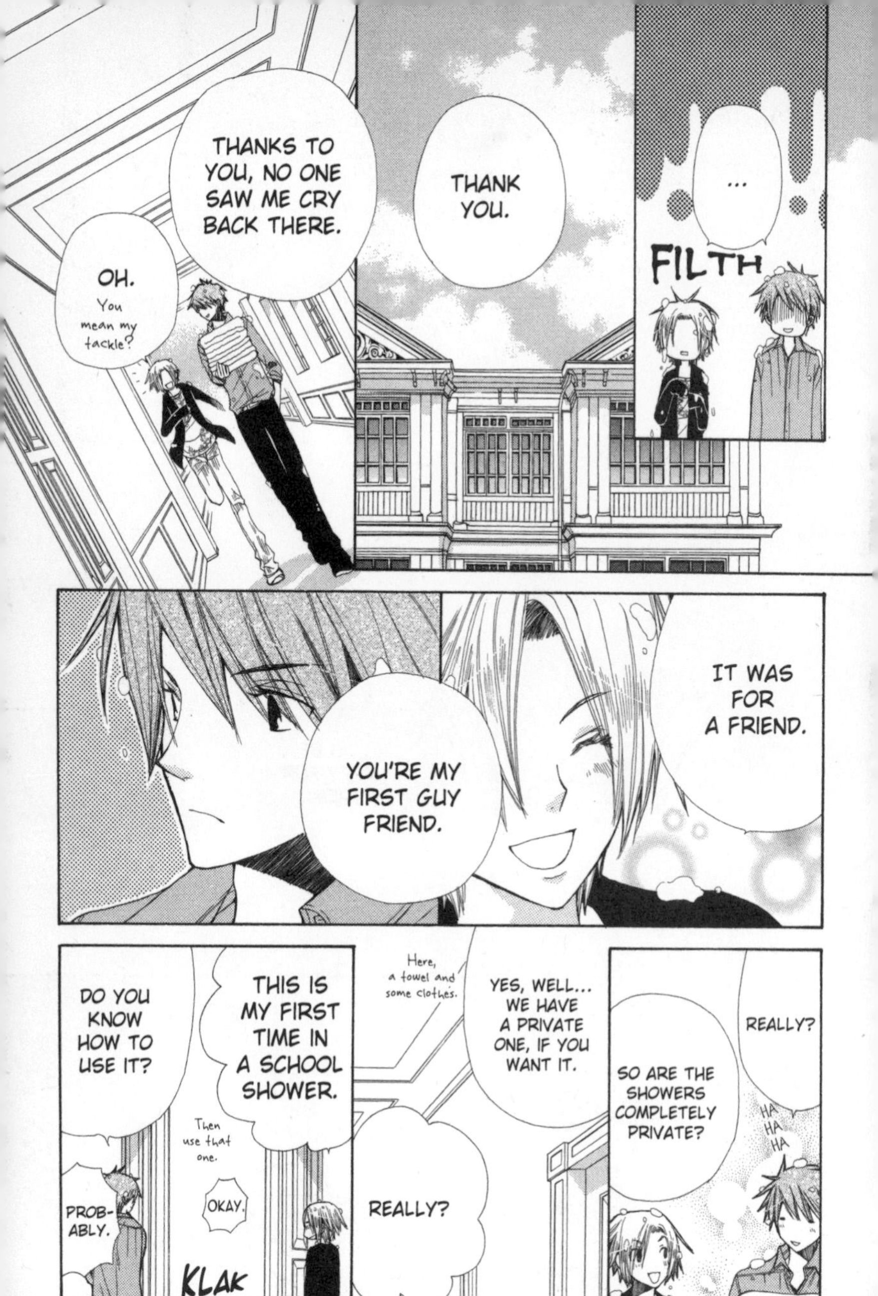
THANK YOU.
THANKS TO YOU, NO ONE SAW ME CRY BACK THERE.
OH. You mean my tackle?
...
FILTH
IT WAS FOR A FRIEND.
YOU'RE MY FIRST GUY FRIEND.
REALLY?
SO ARE THE SHOWERS COMPLETELY PRIVATE?
HA HA HA
YES, WELL... WE HAVE A PRIVATE ONE, IF YOU WANT IT.
REALLY?
Then use that one.
OKAY.
Here, a towel and some clothes.
THIS IS MY FIRST TIME IN A SCHOOL SHOWER.
DO YOU KNOW HOW TO USE IT?
PROBABLY.
KLAK

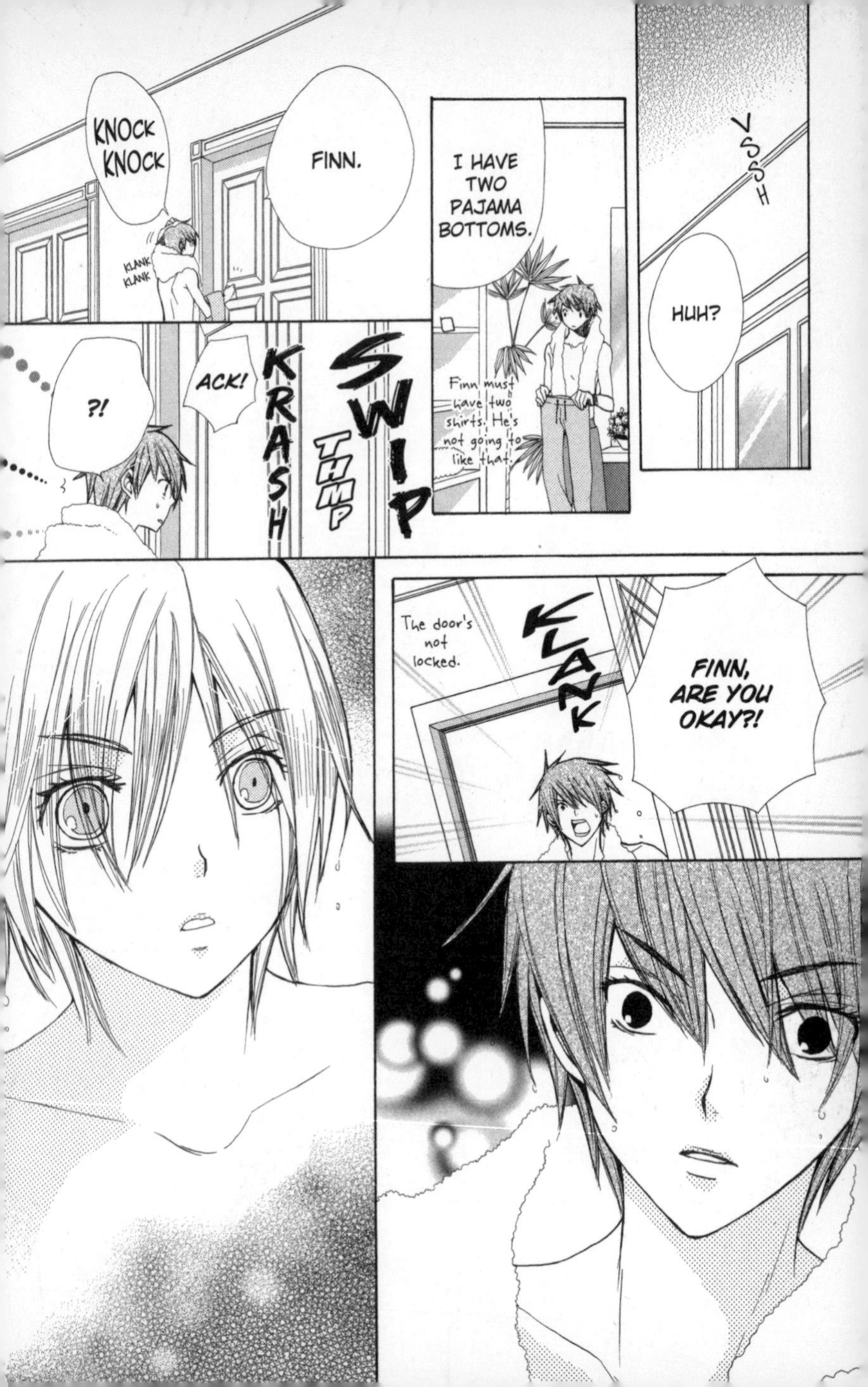
VSSH
HUH?
I HAVE TWO PAJAMA BOTTOMS.
Finn must have two shirts. He's not going to like that.
FINN.
KNOCK KNOCK
KLANK KLANK
SWIP
THMP
KRASH
ACK!
?!
FINN, ARE YOU OKAY?!
KLANK
The door's not locked.

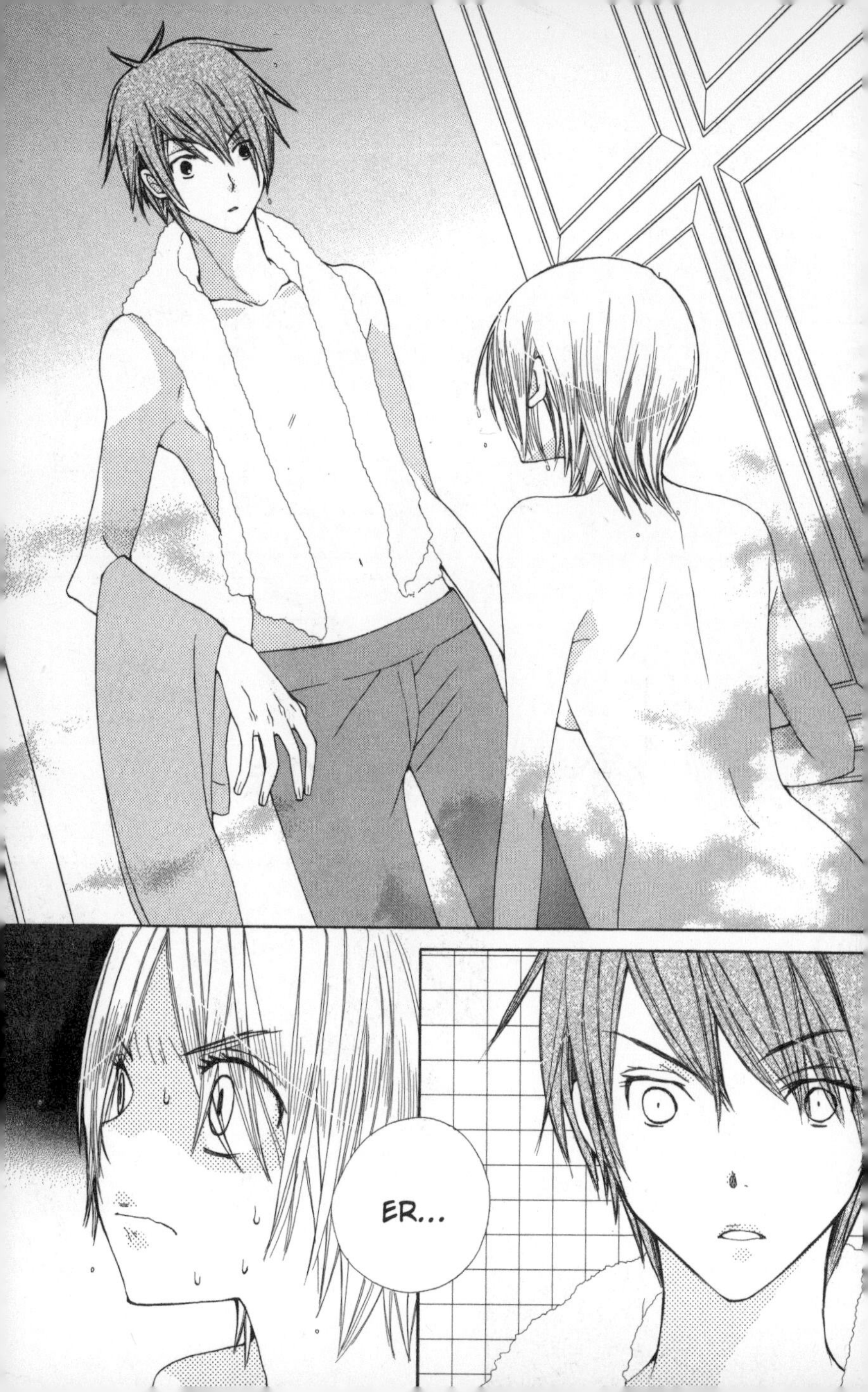
ER...

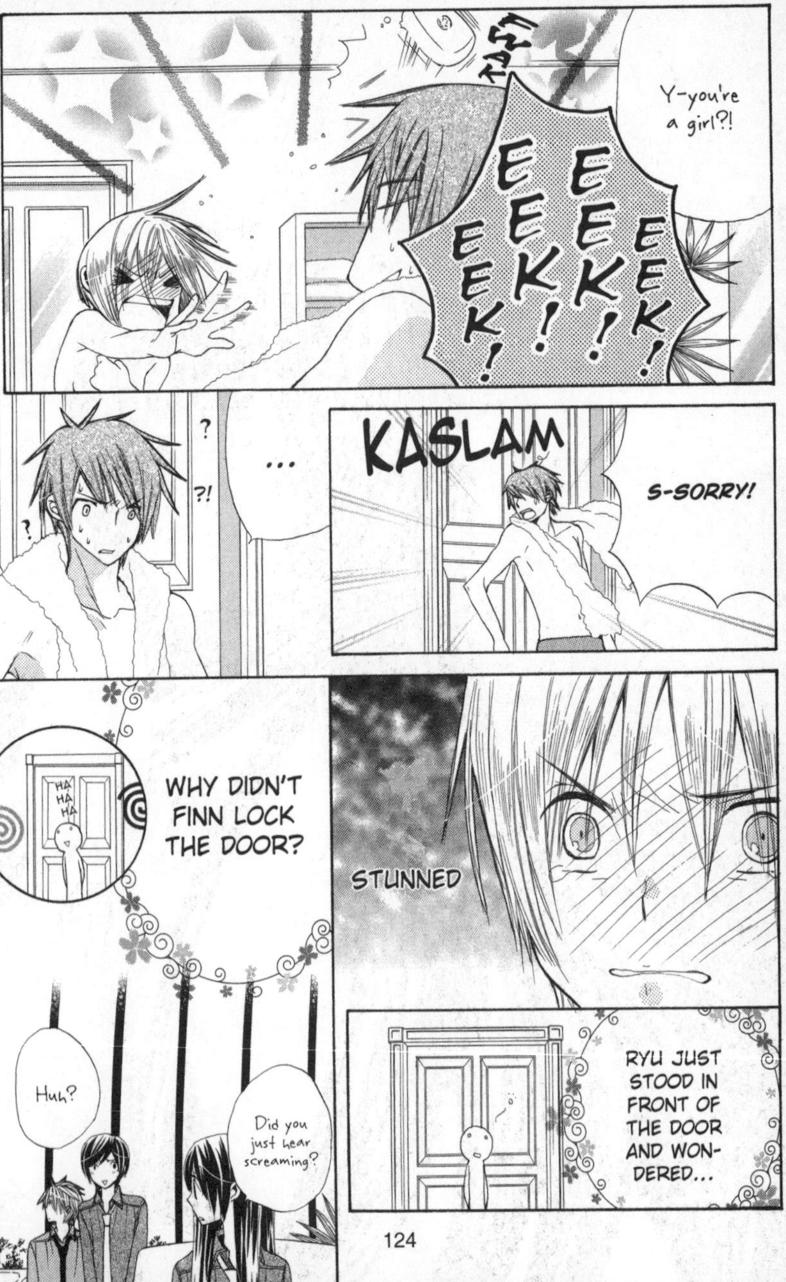
Y-you're a girl?!
EEK! EEK! EEK! EEK!
S-SORRY!
KASLAM
...
?
?!
?
STUNNED
WHY DIDN'T FINN LOCK THE DOOR?
HA HA HA
RYU JUST STOOD IN FRONT OF THE DOOR AND WONDERED...
Did you just hear screaming?
Huh?

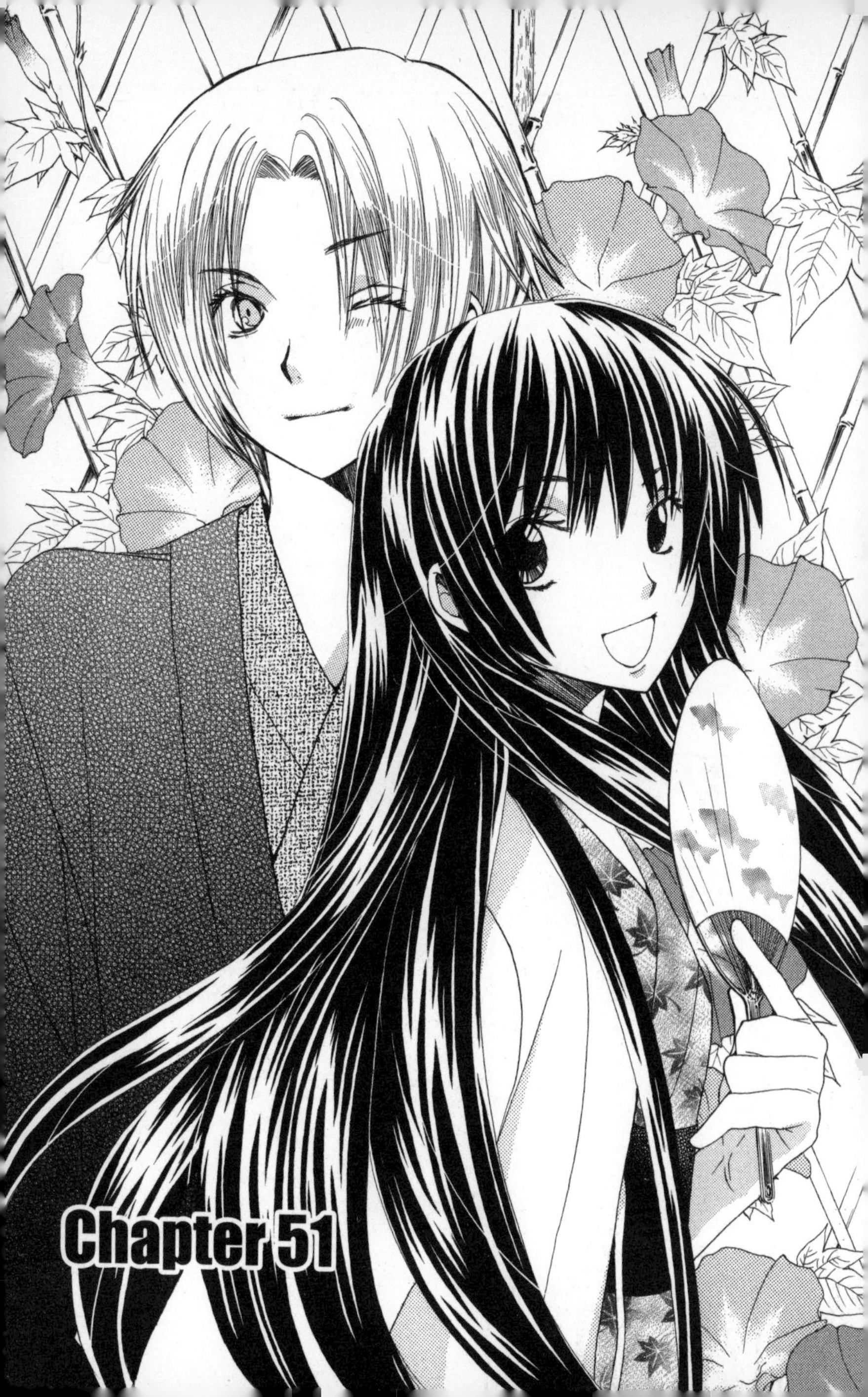
Chapter 51

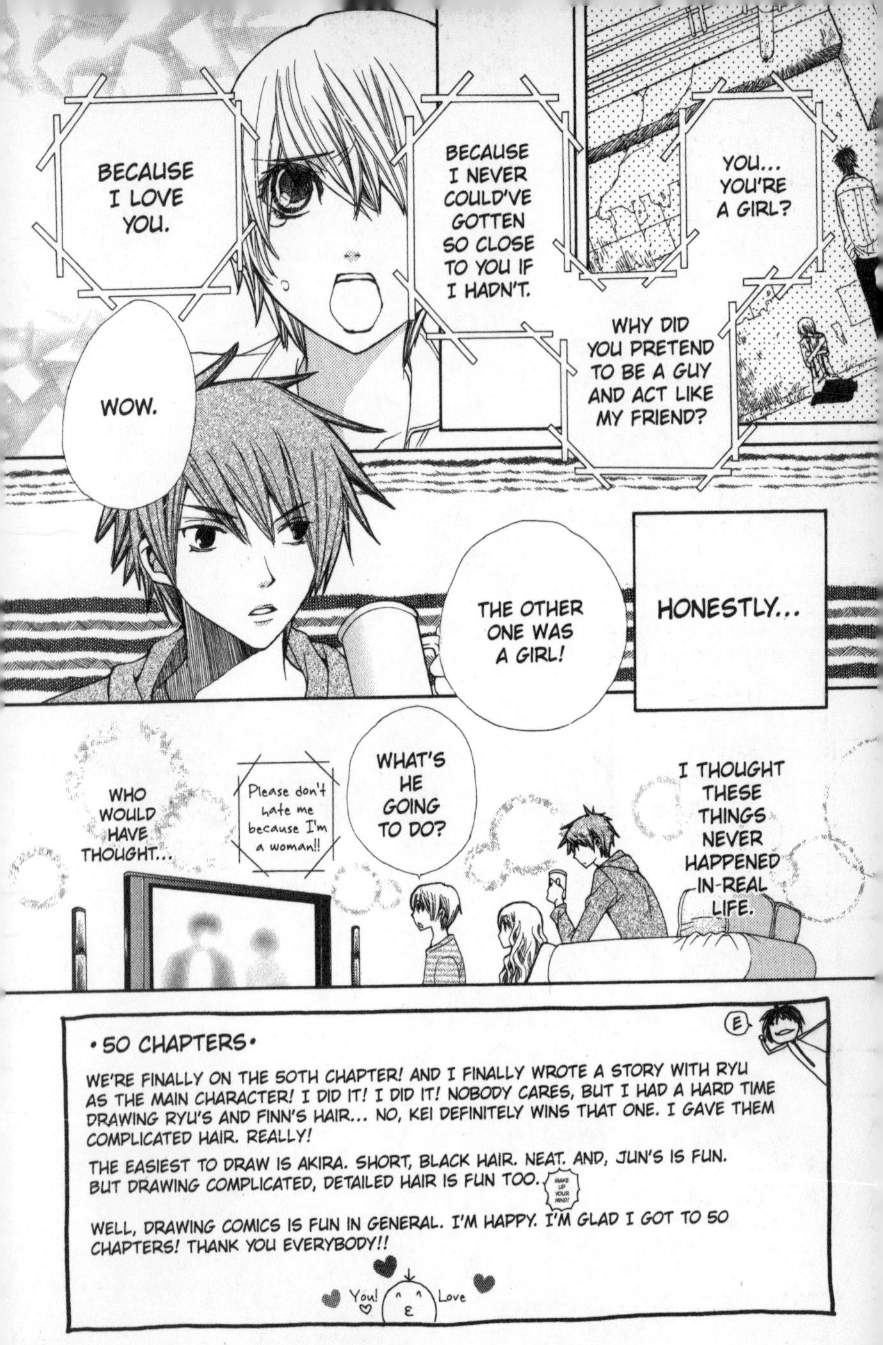
YOU... YOU'RE A GIRL?
WHY DID YOU PRETEND TO BE A GUY AND ACT LIKE MY FRIEND?
BECAUSE I NEVER COULD'VE GOTTEN SO CLOSE TO YOU IF I HADN'T.
BECAUSE I LOVE YOU.
WOW.
HONESTLY...
THE OTHER ONE WAS A GIRL!
I THOUGHT THESE THINGS NEVER HAPPENED IN REAL LIFE.
WHAT'S HE GOING TO DO?
Please don't hate me because I'm a woman!!
WHO WOULD HAVE THOUGHT...

• 50 CHAPTERS •

WE'RE FINALLY ON THE 50TH CHAPTER! AND I FINALLY WROTE A STORY WITH RYU AS THE MAIN CHARACTER! I DID IT! I DID IT! NOBODY CARES, BUT I HAD A HARD TIME DRAWING RYU'S AND FINN'S HAIR... NO, KEI DEFINITELY WINS THAT ONE. I GAVE THEM COMPLICATED HAIR. REALLY!

THE EASIEST TO DRAW IS AKIRA. SHORT, BLACK HAIR. NEAT. AND, JUN'S IS FUN. BUT DRAWING COMPLICATED, DETAILED HAIR IS FUN TOO. (MAKE UP YOUR MIND!)

WELL, DRAWING COMICS IS FUN IN GENERAL. I'M HAPPY. I'M GLAD I GOT TO 50 CHAPTERS! THANK YOU EVERYBODY!!

You! Love

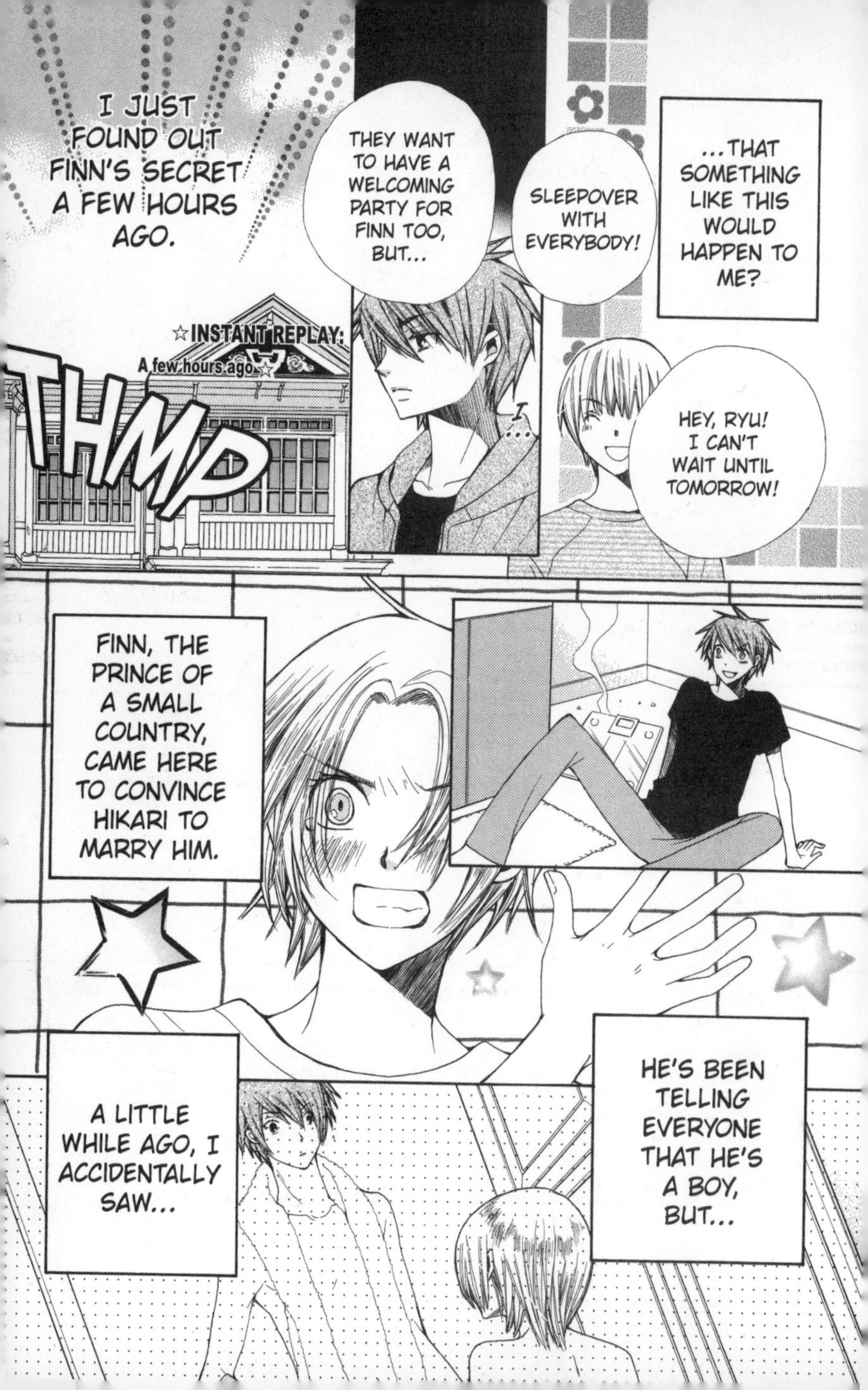
...THAT SOMETHING LIKE THIS WOULD HAPPEN TO ME?
HEY, RYU! I CAN'T WAIT UNTIL TOMORROW!
I...
SLEEPOVER WITH EVERYBODY!
THEY WANT TO HAVE A WELCOMING PARTY FOR FINN TOO, BUT...
I JUST FOUND OUT FINN'S SECRET A FEW HOURS AGO.
☆INSTANT REPLAY: A few hours ago☆
THMP
FINN, THE PRINCE OF A SMALL COUNTRY, CAME HERE TO CONVINCE HIKARI TO MARRY HIM.
HE'S BEEN TELLING EVERYONE THAT HE'S A BOY, BUT...
A LITTLE WHILE AGO, I ACCIDENTALLY SAW...

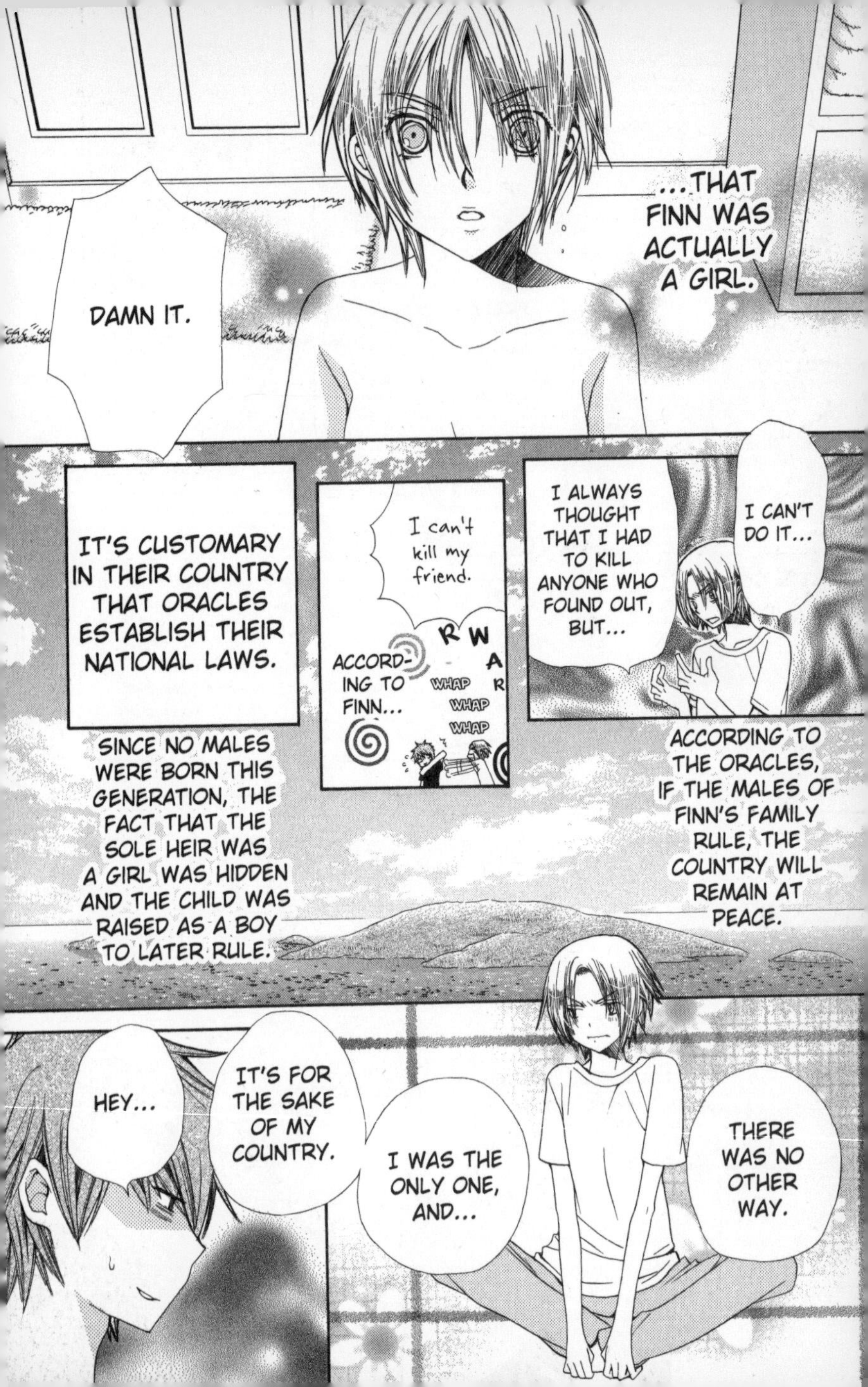
...THAT FINN WAS ACTUALLY A GIRL.
DAMN IT.
I CAN'T DO IT...
I ALWAYS THOUGHT THAT I HAD TO KILL ANYONE WHO FOUND OUT, BUT...
I can't kill my friend.
RWAR
ACCORDING TO FINN...
WHAP WHAP WHAP
IT'S CUSTOMARY IN THEIR COUNTRY THAT ORACLES ESTABLISH THEIR NATIONAL LAWS.
ACCORDING TO THE ORACLES, IF THE MALES OF FINN'S FAMILY RULE, THE COUNTRY WILL REMAIN AT PEACE.
SINCE NO MALES WERE BORN THIS GENERATION, THE FACT THAT THE SOLE HEIR WAS A GIRL WAS HIDDEN AND THE CHILD WAS RAISED AS A BOY TO LATER RULE.
THERE WAS NO OTHER WAY.
I WAS THE ONLY ONE, AND...
IT'S FOR THE SAKE OF MY COUNTRY.
HEY...

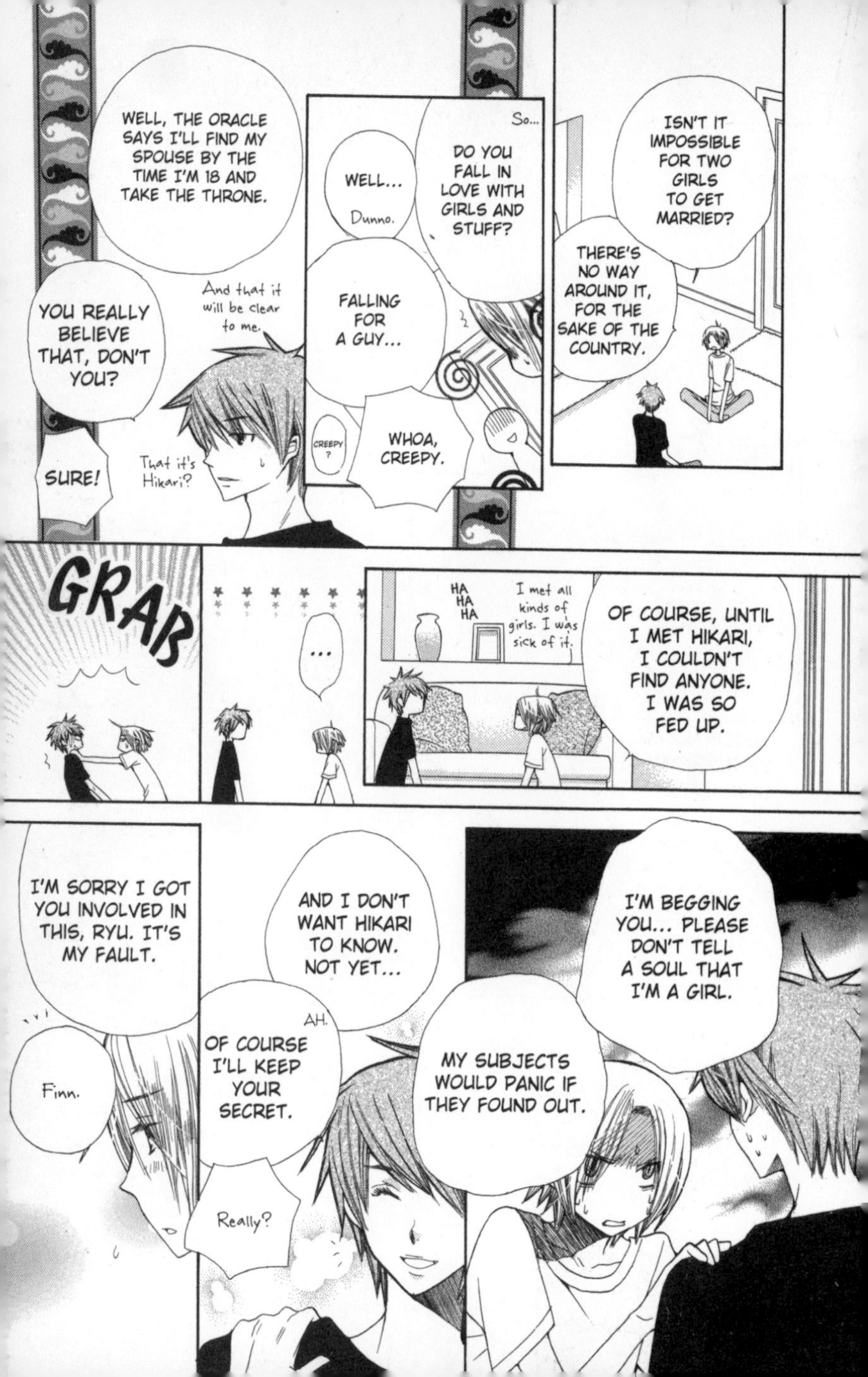
ISN'T IT IMPOSSIBLE FOR TWO GIRLS TO GET MARRIED?
THERE'S NO WAY AROUND IT, FOR THE SAKE OF THE COUNTRY.
So...
DO YOU FALL IN LOVE WITH GIRLS AND STUFF?
WELL...
Dunno.
FALLING FOR A GUY...
WHOA, CREEPY.
CREEPY?
WELL, THE ORACLE SAYS I'LL FIND MY SPOUSE BY THE TIME I'M 18 AND TAKE THE THRONE.
And that it will be clear to me.
YOU REALLY BELIEVE THAT, DON'T YOU?
That it's Hikari?
SURE!
OF COURSE, UNTIL I MET HIKARI, I COULDN'T FIND ANYONE. I WAS SO FED UP.
I met all kinds of girls. I was sick of it.
HA HA HA
...
GRAB
I'M BEGGING YOU... PLEASE DON'T TELL A SOUL THAT I'M A GIRL.
MY SUBJECTS WOULD PANIC IF THEY FOUND OUT.
AND I DON'T WANT HIKARI TO KNOW. NOT YET...
AH.
OF COURSE I'LL KEEP YOUR SECRET.
Really?
I'M SORRY I GOT YOU INVOLVED IN THIS, RYU. IT'S MY FAULT.
Finn.

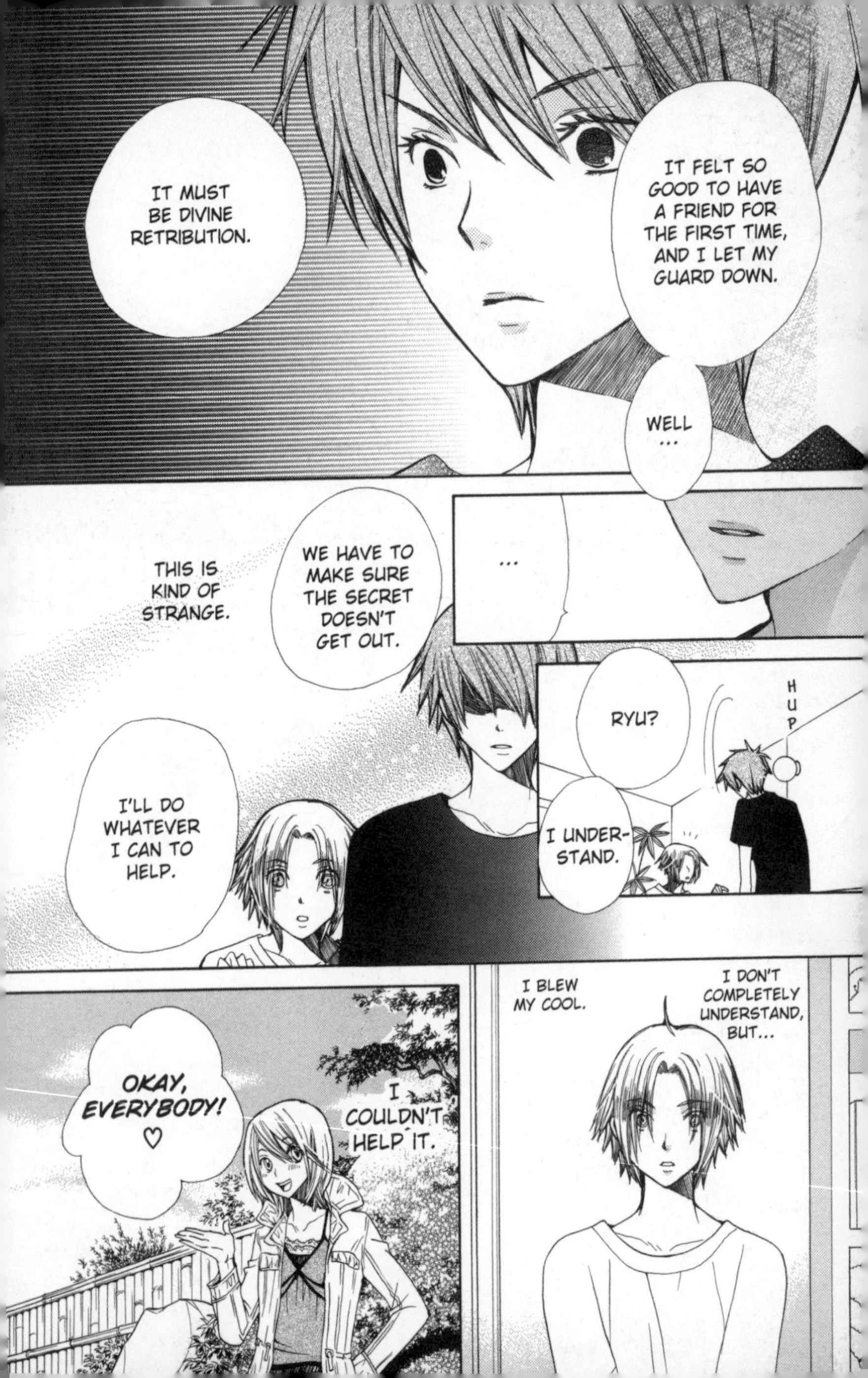
IT FELT SO GOOD TO HAVE A FRIEND FOR THE FIRST TIME, AND I LET MY GUARD DOWN.
IT MUST BE DIVINE RETRIBUTION.
WELL ...
...
WE HAVE TO MAKE SURE THE SECRET DOESN'T GET OUT.
THIS IS KIND OF STRANGE.
HUP
RYU?
I UNDER-STAND.
I'LL DO WHATEVER I CAN TO HELP.
I DON'T COMPLETELY UNDERSTAND, BUT...
I BLEW MY COOL.
I COULDN'T HELP IT.
OKAY, EVERYBODY! ♡

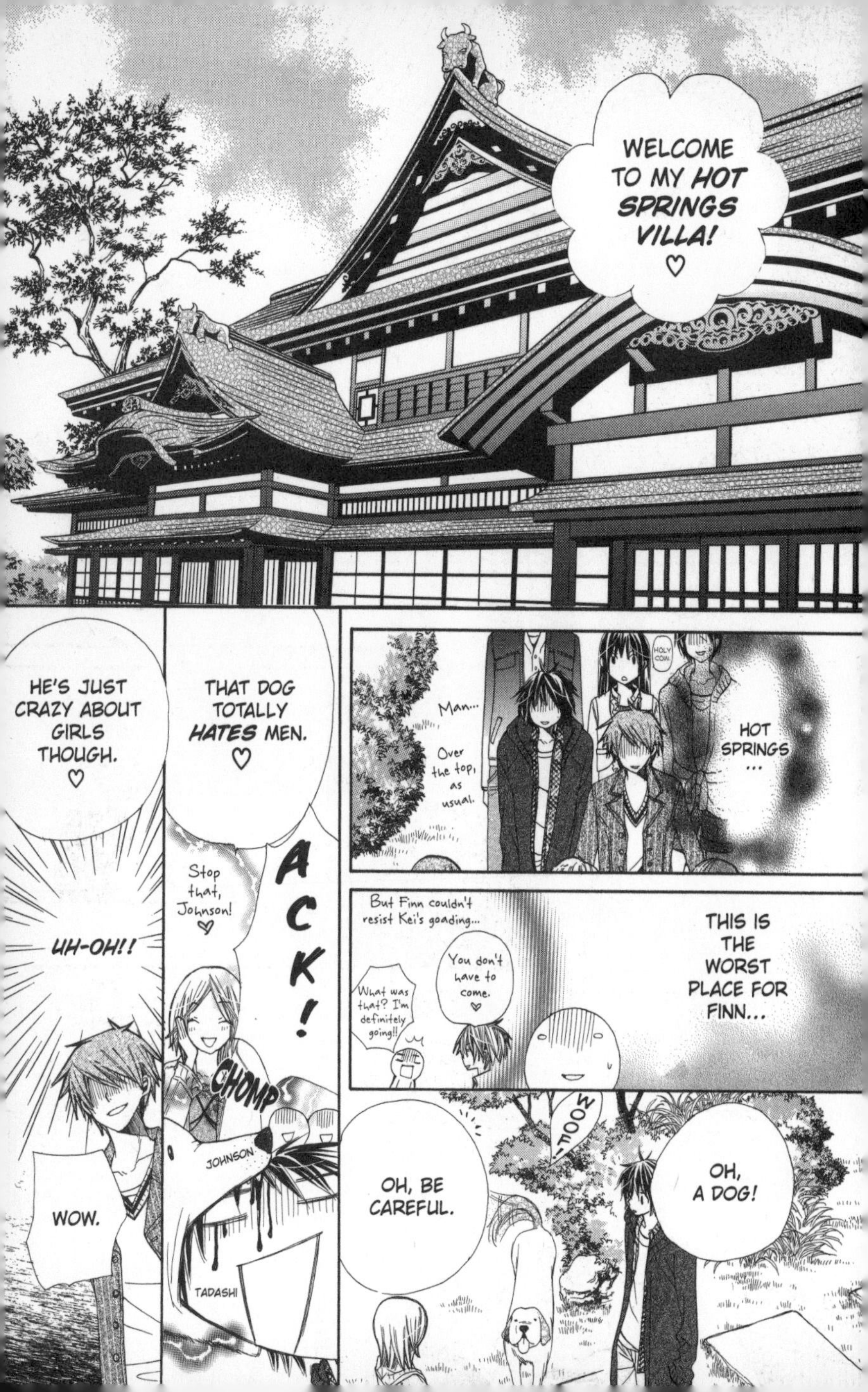
WELCOME TO MY HOT SPRINGS VILLA! ♡
HOLY COW.
HOT SPRINGS...
Man...
Over the top, as usual.
THIS IS THE WORST PLACE FOR FINN...
But Finn couldn't resist Kei's goading...
You don't have to come. ♡
What was that? I'm definitely going!!
OH, A DOG!
WOOF!
OH, BE CAREFUL.
THAT DOG TOTALLY HATES MEN. ♡
ACK!
Stop that, Johnson! ♡
CHOMP
JOHNSON
TADASHI
HE'S JUST CRAZY ABOUT GIRLS THOUGH. ♡
UH-OH!!
WOW.

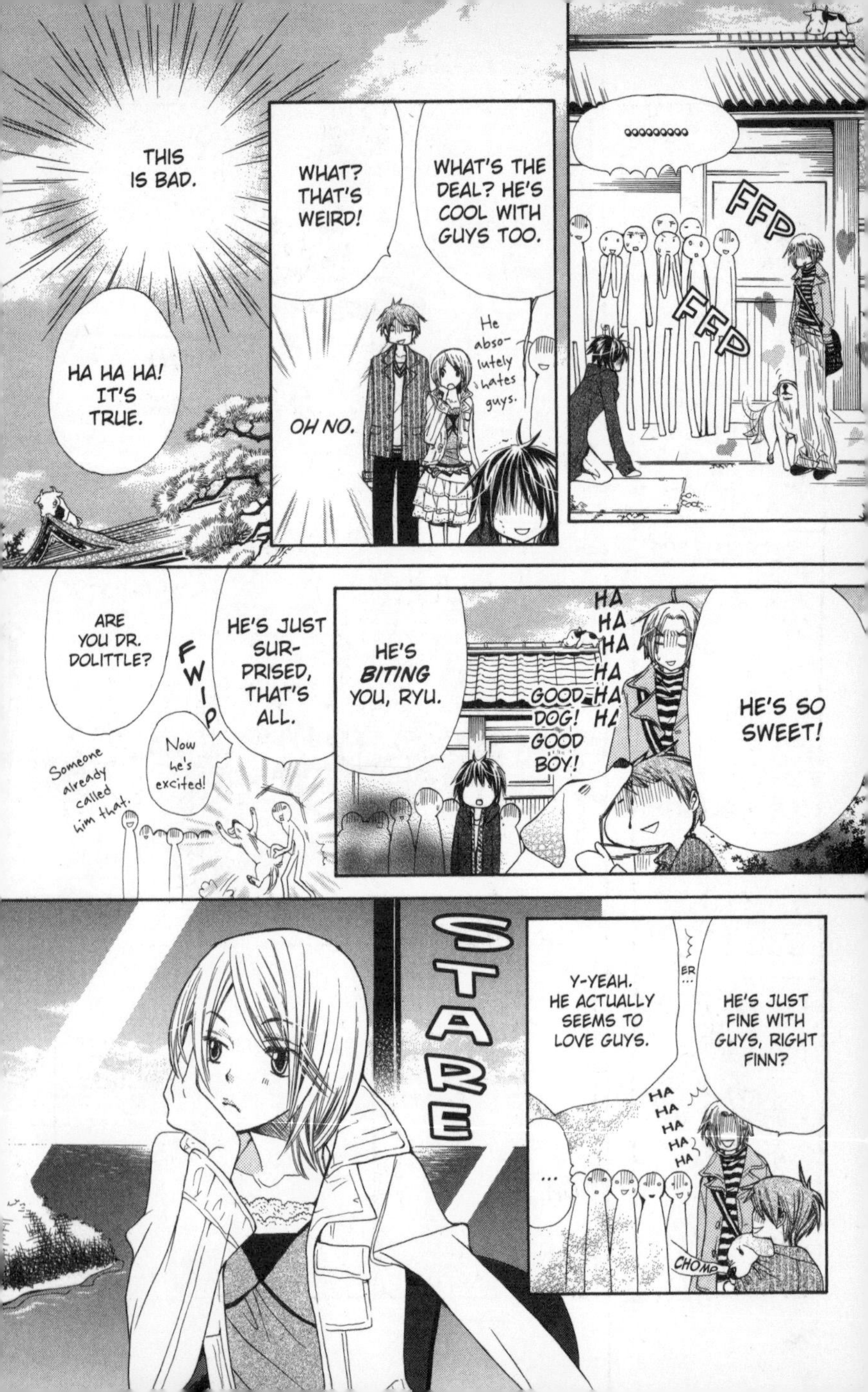
FFP
FFP
WHAT'S THE DEAL? HE'S COOL WITH GUYS TOO.
WHAT? THAT'S WEIRD!
He absolutely hates guys.
OH NO.
THIS IS BAD.
HA HA HA! IT'S TRUE.
HE'S SO SWEET!
HA HA HA HA HA HA
GOOD DOG! GOOD BOY!
HE'S *BITING* YOU, RYU.
HE'S JUST SURPRISED, THAT'S ALL.
FWIP
Now he's excited!
ARE YOU DR. DOLITTLE?
Someone already called him that.
HE'S JUST FINE WITH GUYS, RIGHT FINN?
ER...
Y-YEAH. HE ACTUALLY SEEMS TO LOVE GUYS.
HA HA HA HA HA
...
CHOMP
STARE

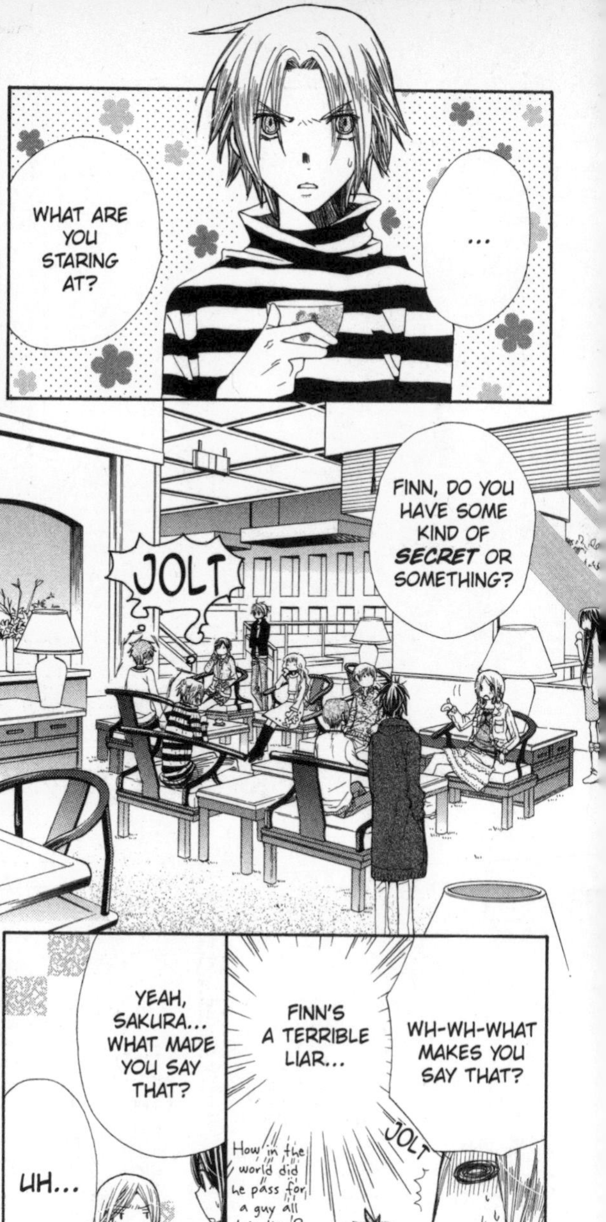
...
WHAT ARE YOU STARING AT?
FINN, DO YOU HAVE SOME KIND OF SECRET OR SOMETHING?
JOLT
WH-WH-WHAT MAKES YOU SAY THAT?
JOLT
FINN'S A TERRIBLE LIAR...
How in the world did he pass for a guy all this time?
Hmmm?
YEAH, SAKURA... WHAT MADE YOU SAY THAT?
UH...

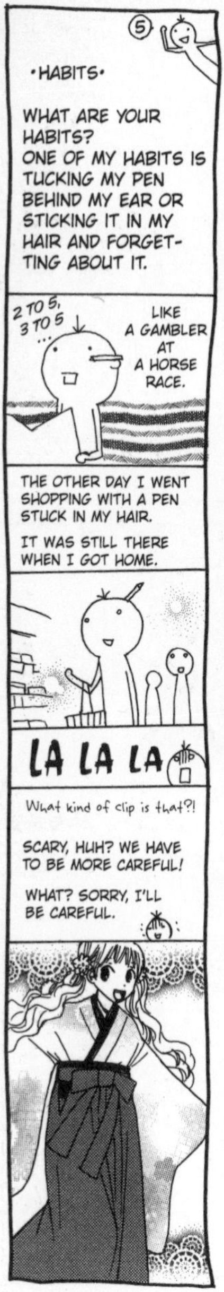
5
•HABITS•
WHAT ARE YOUR HABITS?
ONE OF MY HABITS IS TUCKING MY PEN BEHIND MY EAR OR STICKING IT IN MY HAIR AND FORGET-TING ABOUT IT.
2 TO 5, 3 TO 5 ...
LIKE A GAMBLER AT A HORSE RACE.
THE OTHER DAY I WENT SHOPPING WITH A PEN STUCK IN MY HAIR.
IT WAS STILL THERE WHEN I GOT HOME.
LA LA LA
What kind of clip is that?!
SCARY, HUH? WE HAVE TO BE MORE CAREFUL!
WHAT? SORRY, I'LL BE CAREFUL.

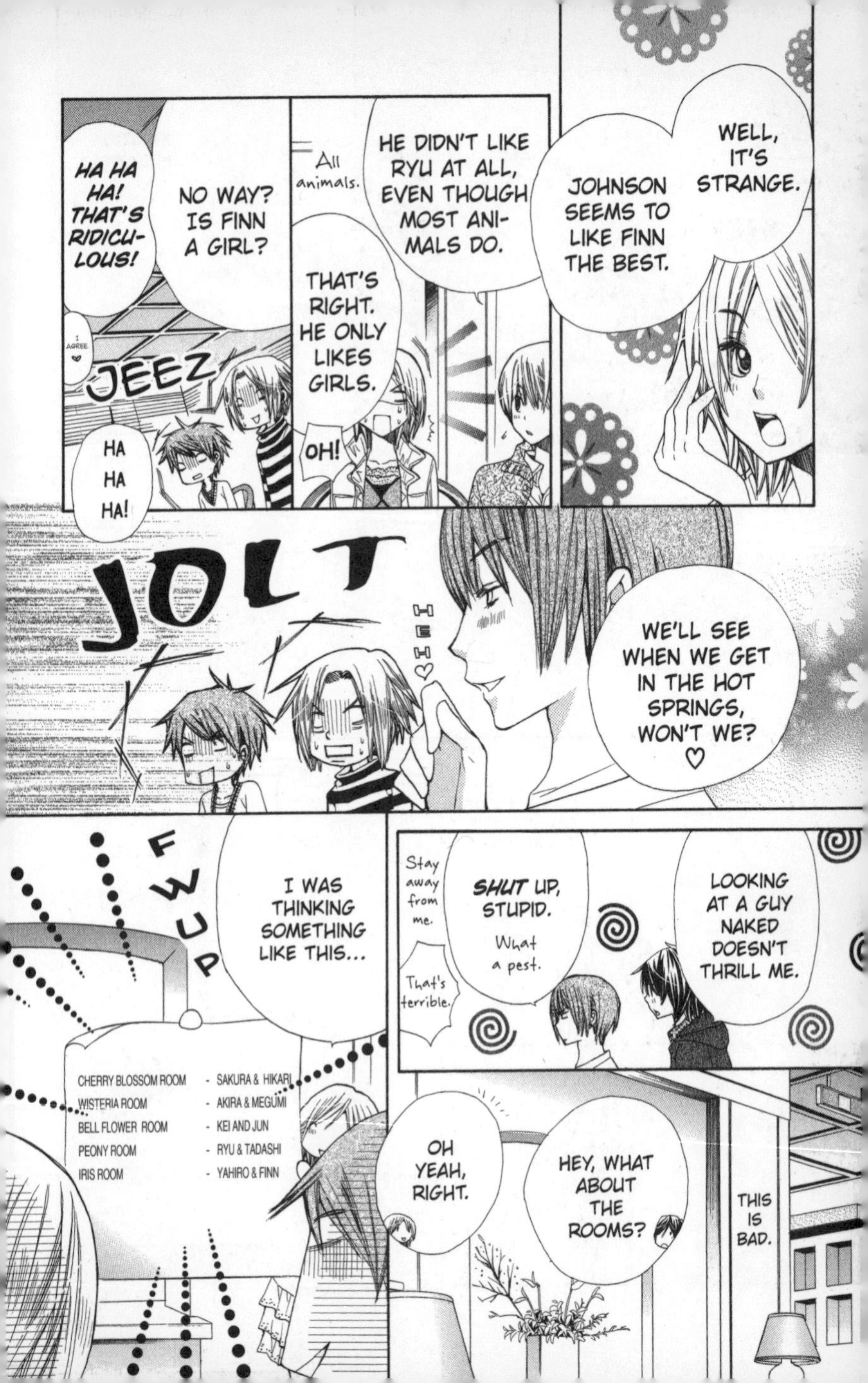
WELL, IT'S STRANGE.
JOHNSON SEEMS TO LIKE FINN THE BEST.
HE DIDN'T LIKE RYU AT ALL, EVEN THOUGH MOST ANIMALS DO.
All animals.
THAT'S RIGHT. HE ONLY LIKES GIRLS.
OH!
NO WAY? IS FINN A GIRL?
HA HA HA! THAT'S RIDICULOUS!
I AGREE ♡
JEEZ
HA HA HA!
WE'LL SEE WHEN WE GET IN THE HOT SPRINGS, WON'T WE? ♡
HEH ♡
JOLT
LOOKING AT A GUY NAKED DOESN'T THRILL ME.
SHUT UP, STUPID.
What a pest.
Stay away from me.
That's terrible.
THIS IS BAD.
HEY, WHAT ABOUT THE ROOMS?
OH YEAH, RIGHT.
I WAS THINKING SOMETHING LIKE THIS...
FWUP
CHERRY BLOSSOM ROOM - SAKURA & HIKARI
WISTERIA ROOM - AKIRA & MEGUMI
BELL FLOWER ROOM - KEI AND JUN
PEONY ROOM - RYU & TADASHI
IRIS ROOM - YAHIRO & FINN

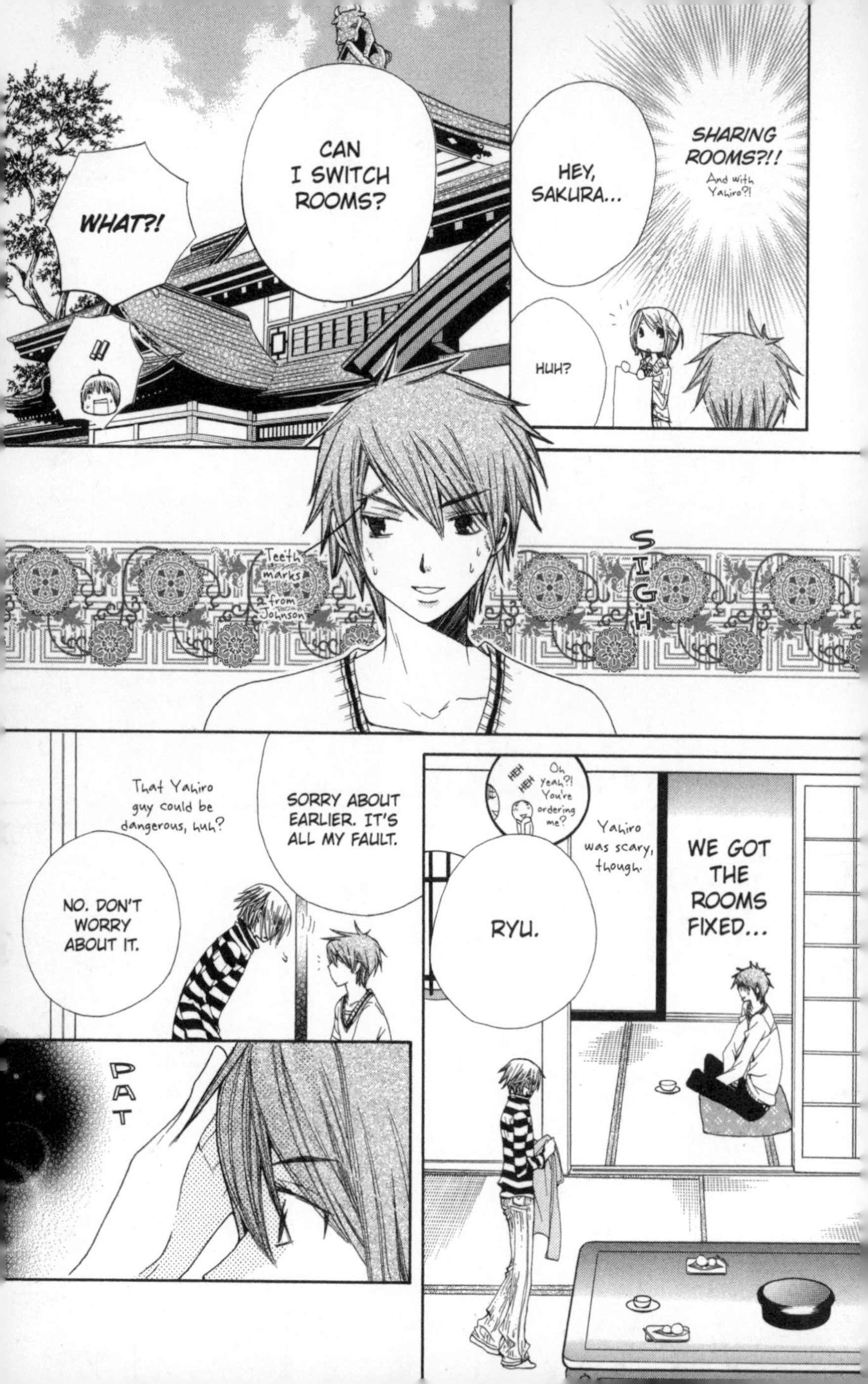
SHARING ROOMS?!!
And with Yahiro?!
HEY, SAKURA...
HUH?
CAN I SWITCH ROOMS?
WHAT?!
!!
SIGH
Teeth marks from Johnson
WE GOT THE ROOMS FIXED...
Yahiro was scary, though.
Oh yeah?! You're ordering me?
HEH HEH
RYU.
SORRY ABOUT EARLIER. IT'S ALL MY FAULT.
That Yahiro guy could be dangerous, huh?
NO. DON'T WORRY ABOUT IT.
PAT

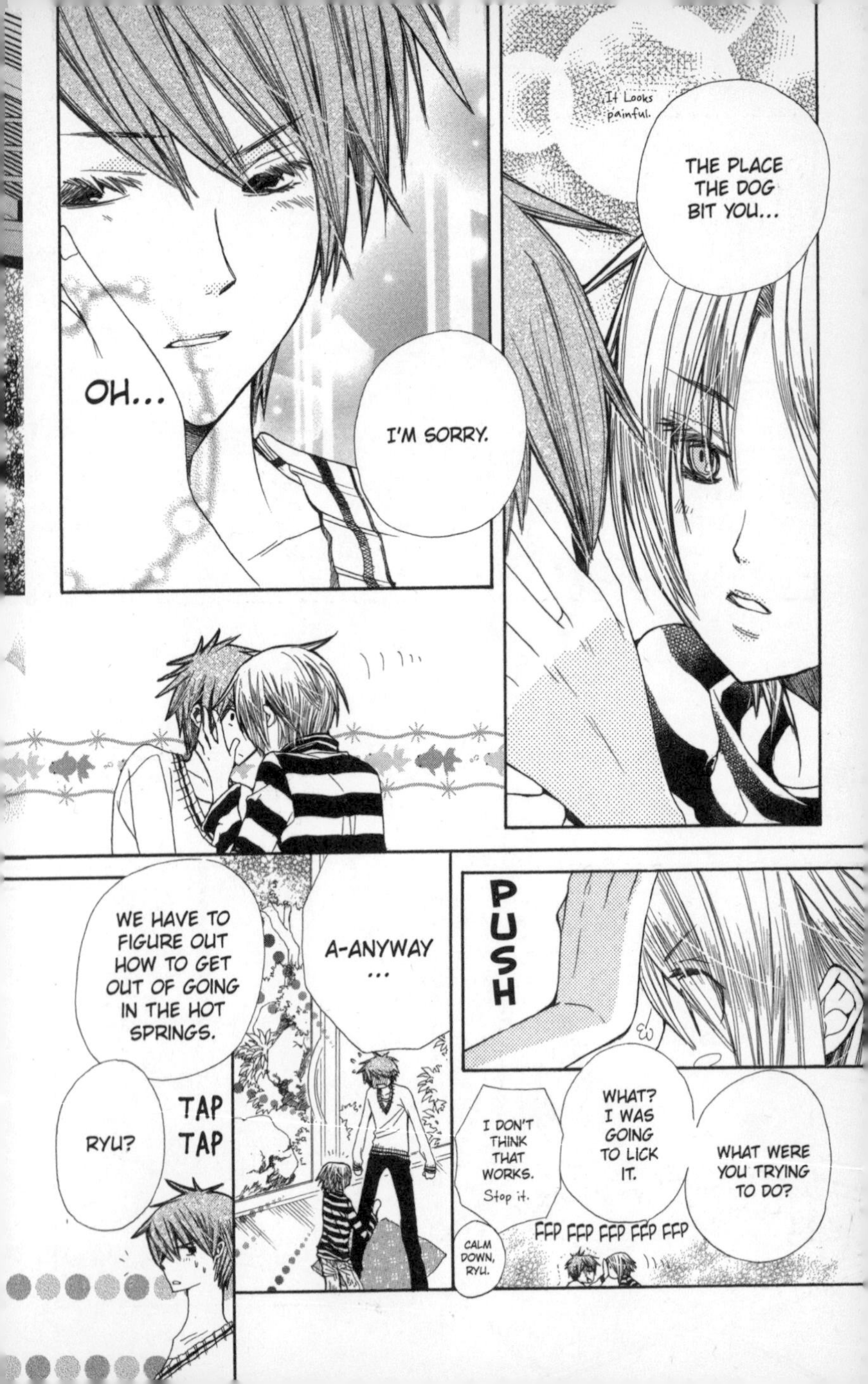
It Looks painful.
THE PLACE THE DOG BIT YOU...
I'M SORRY.
OH...
PUSH
WHAT WERE YOU TRYING TO DO?
WHAT? I WAS GOING TO LICK IT.
I DON'T THINK THAT WORKS.
Stop it.
FFP FFP FFP FFP FFP
CALM DOWN, RYU.
A-ANYWAY...
WE HAVE TO FIGURE OUT HOW TO GET OUT OF GOING IN THE HOT SPRINGS.
TAP TAP
RYU?

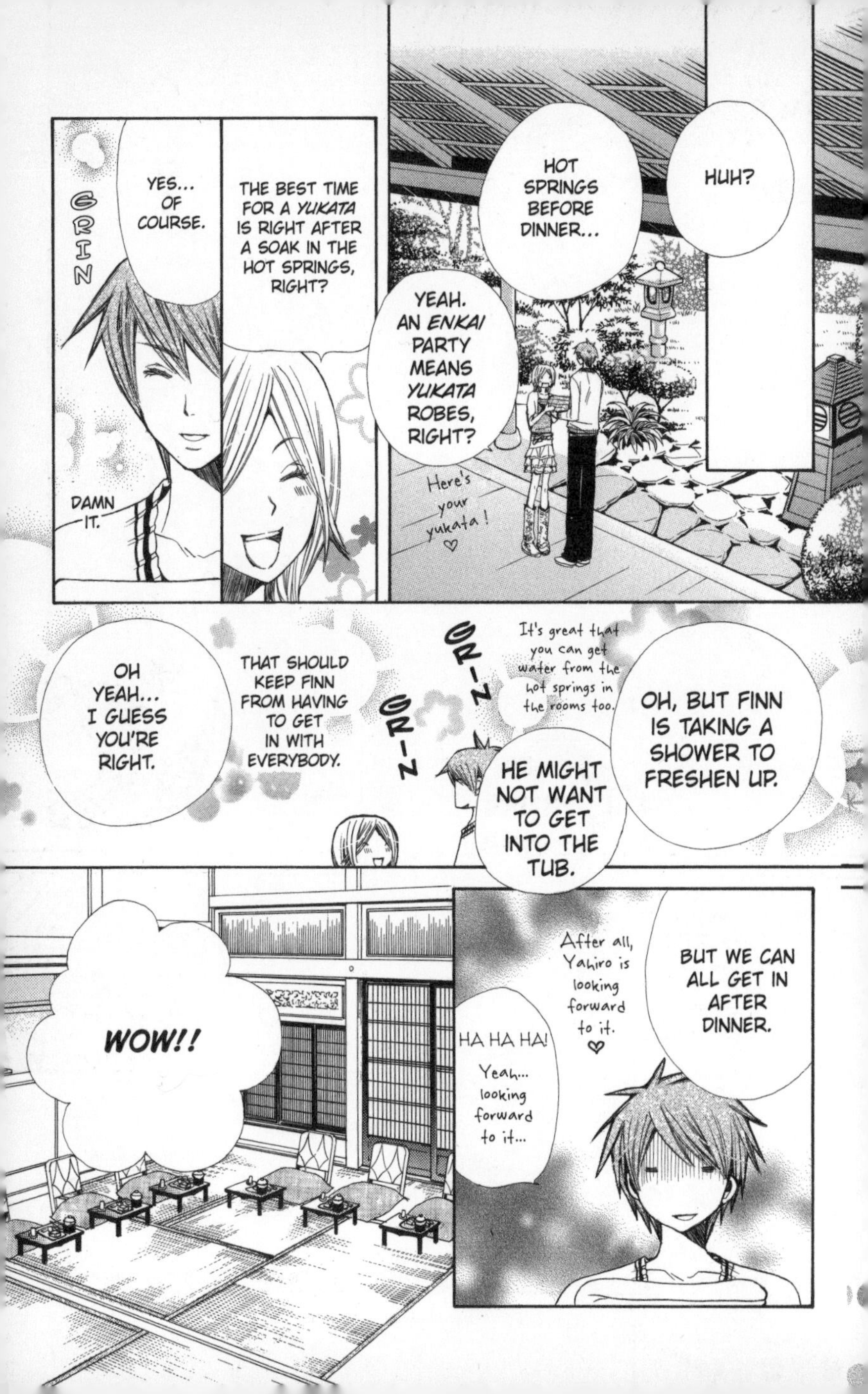
HUH?
HOT SPRINGS BEFORE DINNER...
YEAH. AN ENKAI PARTY MEANS YUKATA ROBES, RIGHT?
Here's your yukata! ♡
THE BEST TIME FOR A YUKATA IS RIGHT AFTER A SOAK IN THE HOT SPRINGS, RIGHT?
GRIN
YES... OF COURSE.
DAMN IT.
OH, BUT FINN IS TAKING A SHOWER TO FRESHEN UP.
HE MIGHT NOT WANT TO GET INTO THE TUB.
It's great that you can get water from the hot springs in the rooms too.
GRIN
GRIN
THAT SHOULD KEEP FINN FROM HAVING TO GET IN WITH EVERYBODY.
OH YEAH... I GUESS YOU'RE RIGHT.
BUT WE CAN ALL GET IN AFTER DINNER.
After all, Yahiro is looking forward to it. ♡
HA HA HA!
Yeah... looking forward to it...
WOW!!

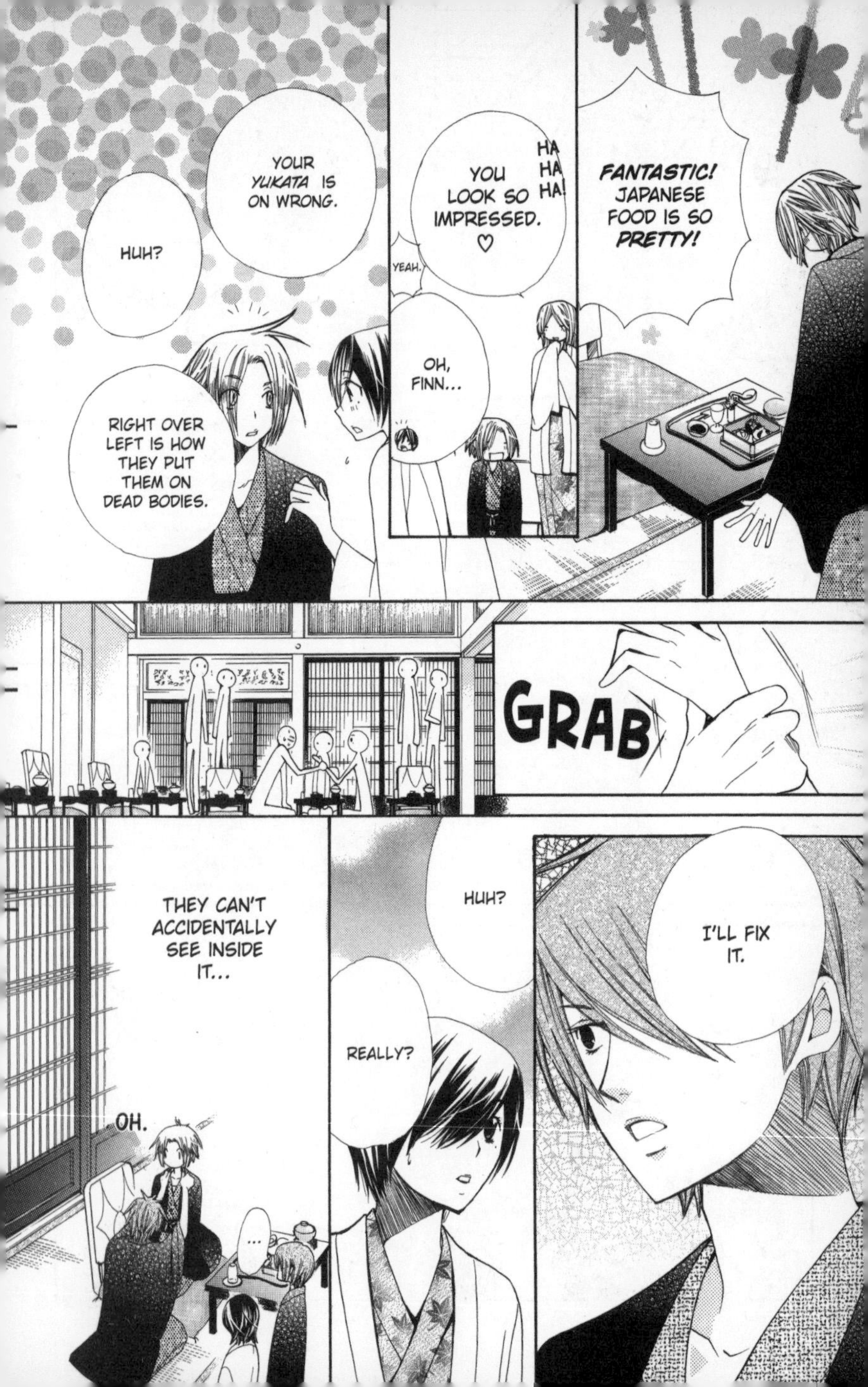
FANTASTIC! JAPANESE FOOD IS SO PRETTY!
YOU LOOK SO IMPRESSED. ♡
HA HA HA!
YEAH.
OH, FINN...
YOUR YUKATA IS ON WRONG.
HUH?
RIGHT OVER LEFT IS HOW THEY PUT THEM ON DEAD BODIES.
GRAB
I'LL FIX IT.
HUH?
REALLY?
THEY CAN'T ACCIDENTALLY SEE INSIDE IT...
OH.
...

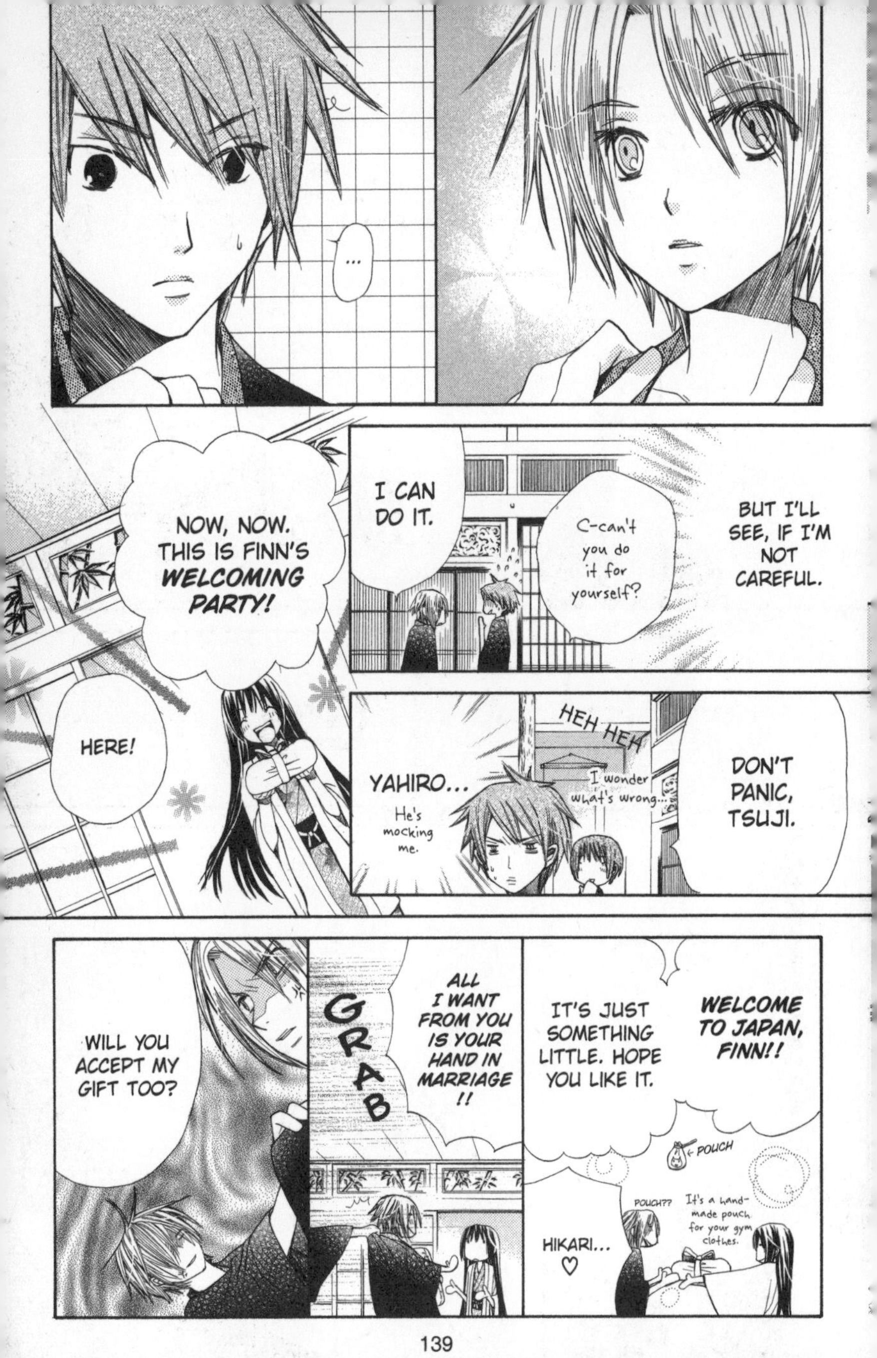
...
BUT I'LL SEE, IF I'M NOT CAREFUL.
C-can't you do it for yourself?
I CAN DO IT.
DON'T PANIC, TSUJI.
HEH HEH
I wonder what's wrong...
YAHIRO...
He's mocking me.
NOW, NOW. THIS IS FINN'S **WELCOMING PARTY!**
HERE!
WELCOME TO JAPAN, FINN!!
IT'S JUST SOMETHING LITTLE. HOPE YOU LIKE IT.
← POUCH
It's a hand-made pouch for your gym clothes.
POUCH??
HIKARI... ♡
ALL I WANT FROM YOU IS YOUR HAND IN MARRIAGE !!
GRAB
WILL YOU ACCEPT MY GIFT TOO?

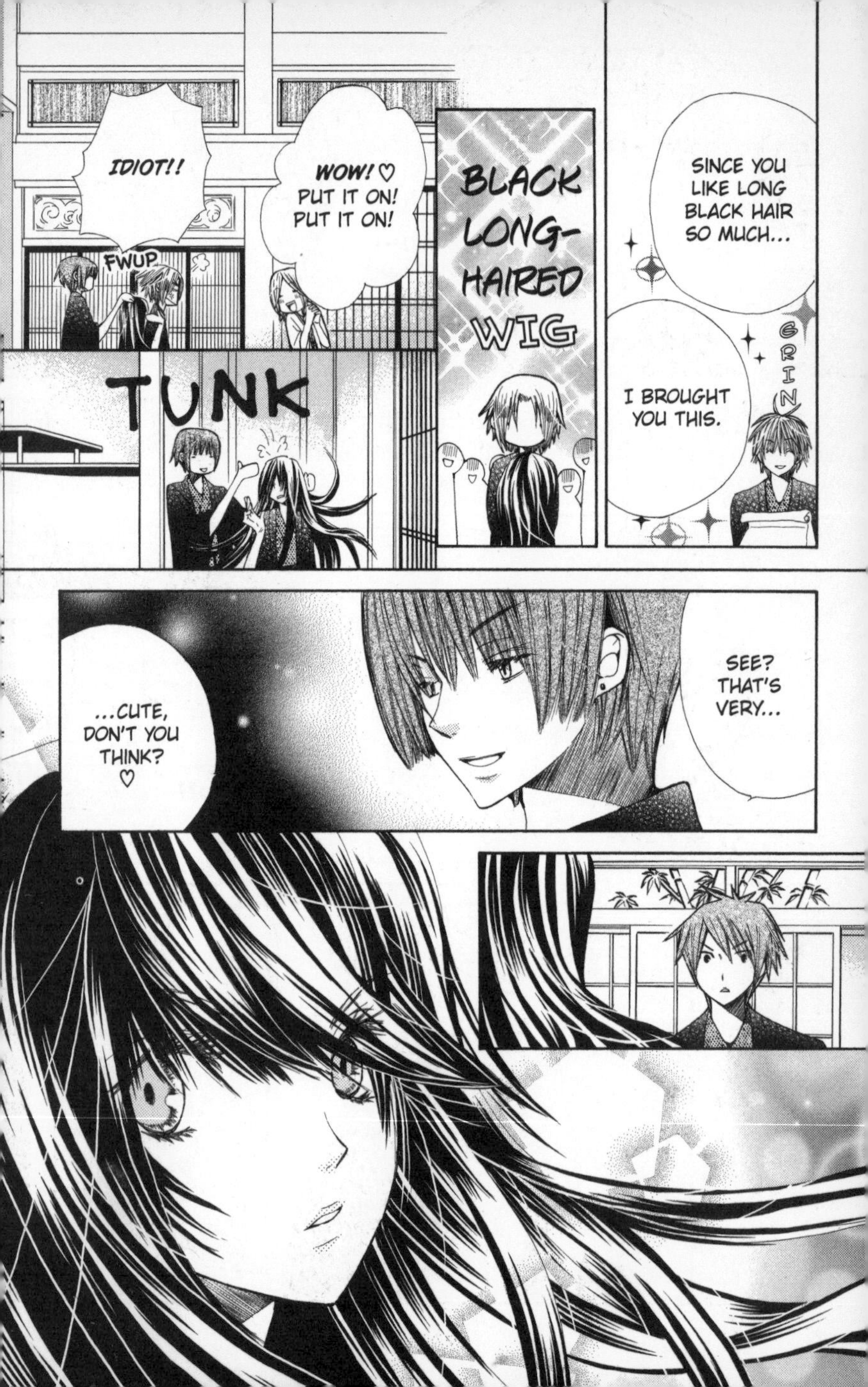
SINCE YOU LIKE LONG BLACK HAIR SO MUCH...
I BROUGHT YOU THIS.
GRIN
BLACK LONG-HAIRED WIG
WOW! ♡ PUT IT ON! PUT IT ON!
IDIOT!!
FWUP
TUNK
SEE? THAT'S VERY...
...CUTE, DON'T YOU THINK? ♡

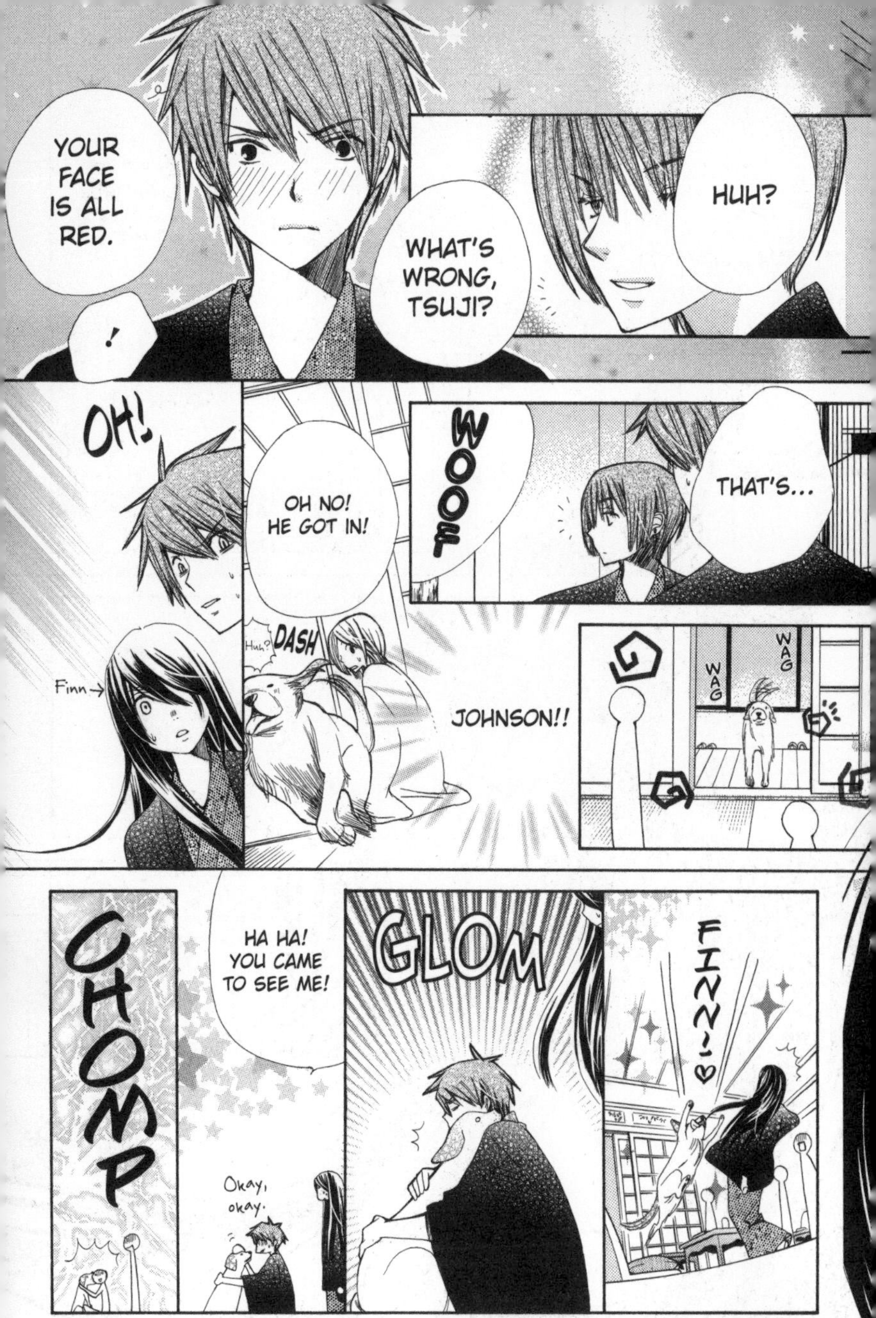
HUH?
WHAT'S WRONG, TSUJI?
YOUR FACE IS ALL RED.
!
THAT'S...
WOOF
WAG
WAG
JOHNSON!!
OH NO! HE GOT IN!
DASH
Huh?
OH!
Finn→
FINN!♡
GLOM
HA HA! YOU CAME TO SEE ME!
Okay, okay.
CHOMP

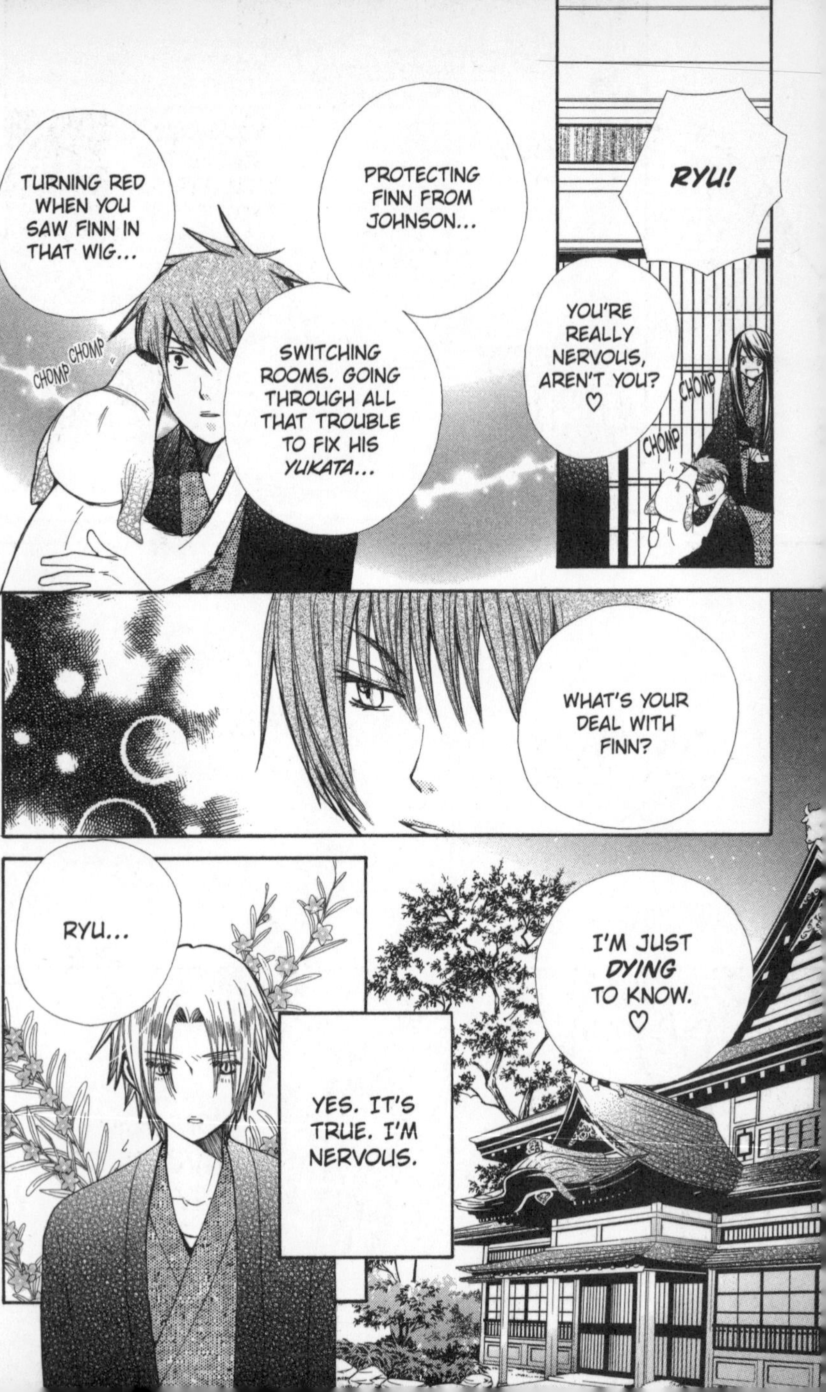
RYU!
YOU'RE REALLY NERVOUS, AREN'T YOU? ♡
CHOMP
CHOMP
PROTECTING FINN FROM JOHNSON...
TURNING RED WHEN YOU SAW FINN IN THAT WIG...
CHOMP CHOMP
SWITCHING ROOMS. GOING THROUGH ALL THAT TROUBLE TO FIX HIS *YUKATA*...
WHAT'S YOUR DEAL WITH FINN?
I'M JUST *DYING* TO KNOW. ♡
RYU...
YES. IT'S TRUE. I'M NERVOUS.

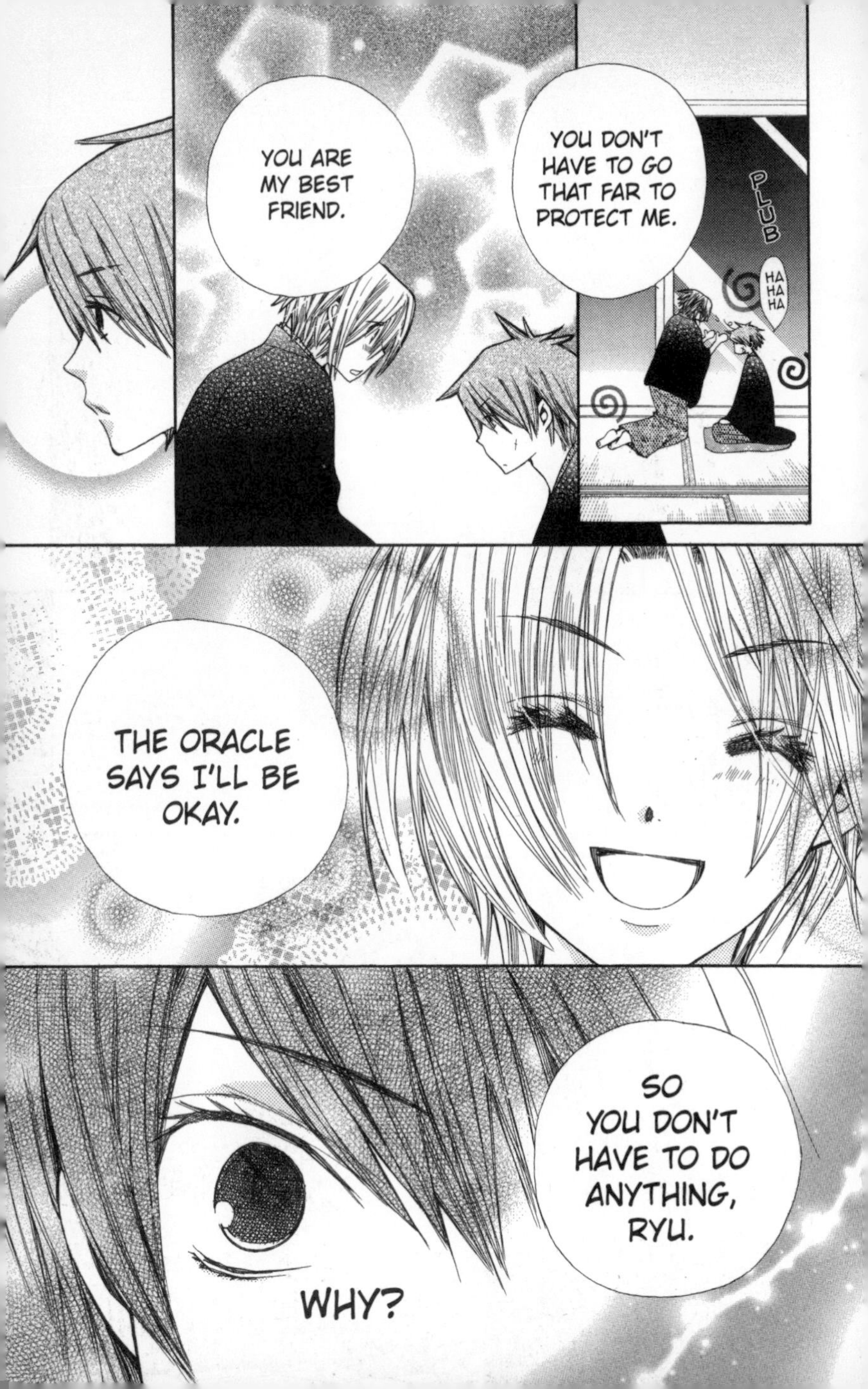
PLUB
HA HA HA
YOU DON'T HAVE TO GO THAT FAR TO PROTECT ME.
YOU ARE MY BEST FRIEND.
THE ORACLE SAYS I'LL BE OKAY.
SO YOU DON'T HAVE TO DO ANYTHING, RYU.
WHY?

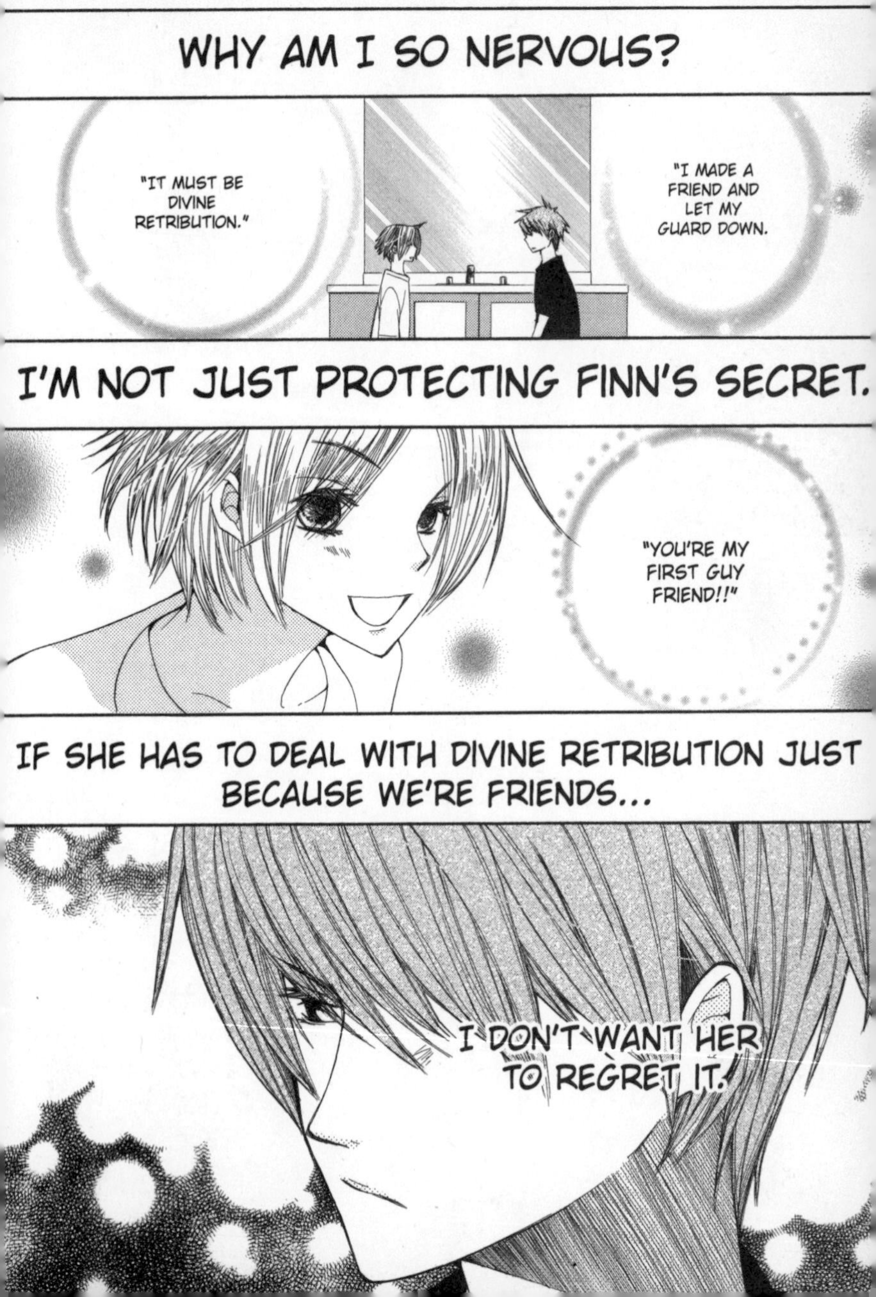
WHY AM I SO NERVOUS?
"I MADE A FRIEND AND LET MY GUARD DOWN.
"IT MUST BE DIVINE RETRIBUTION."
I'M NOT JUST PROTECTING FINN'S SECRET.
"YOU'RE MY FIRST GUY FRIEND!!"
IF SHE HAS TO DEAL WITH DIVINE RETRIBUTION JUST BECAUSE WE'RE FRIENDS...
I DON'T WANT HER TO REGRET IT.

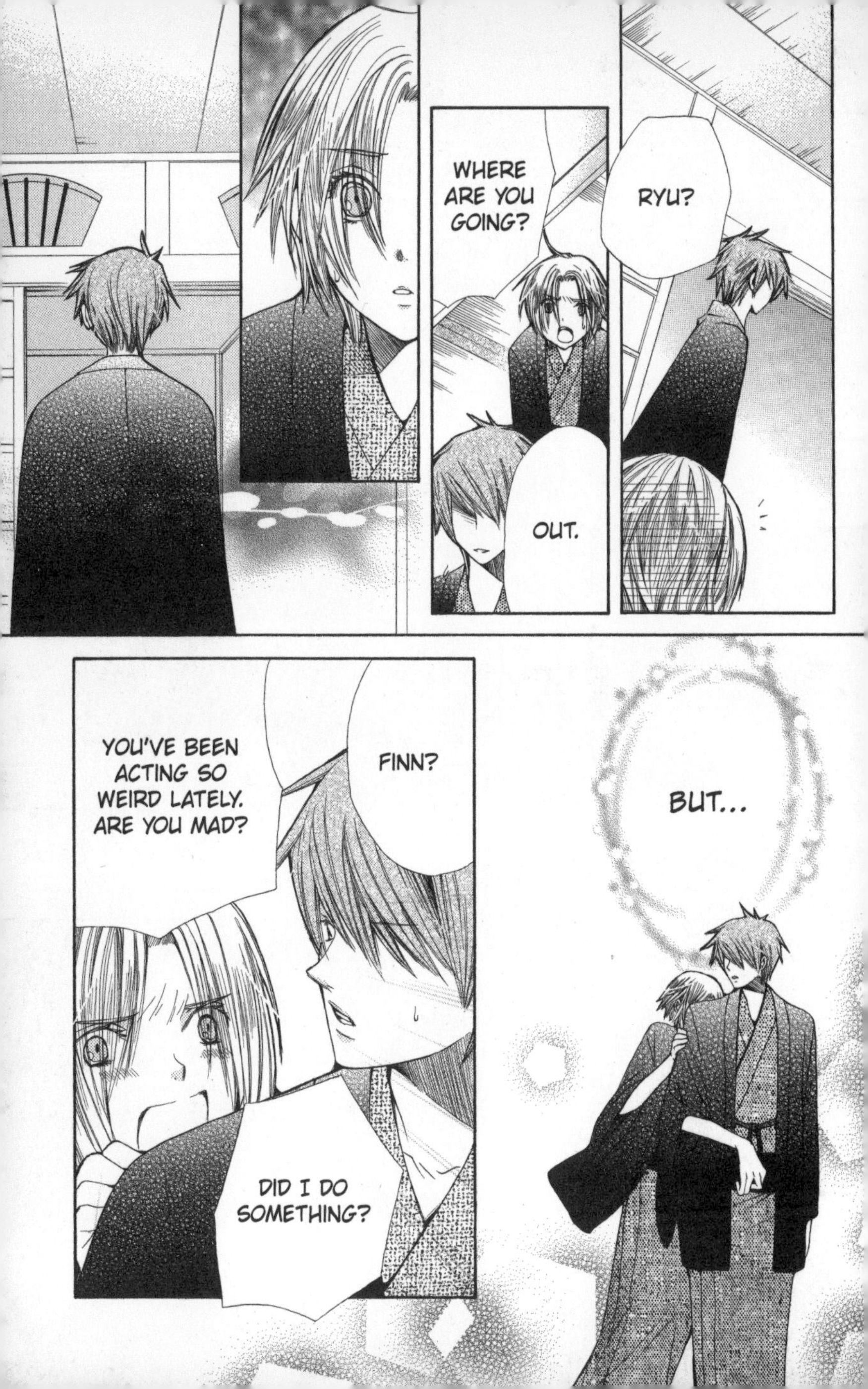
RYU?
WHERE ARE YOU GOING?
OUT.
BUT...
FINN?
YOU'VE BEEN ACTING SO WEIRD LATELY. ARE YOU MAD?
DID I DO SOMETHING?

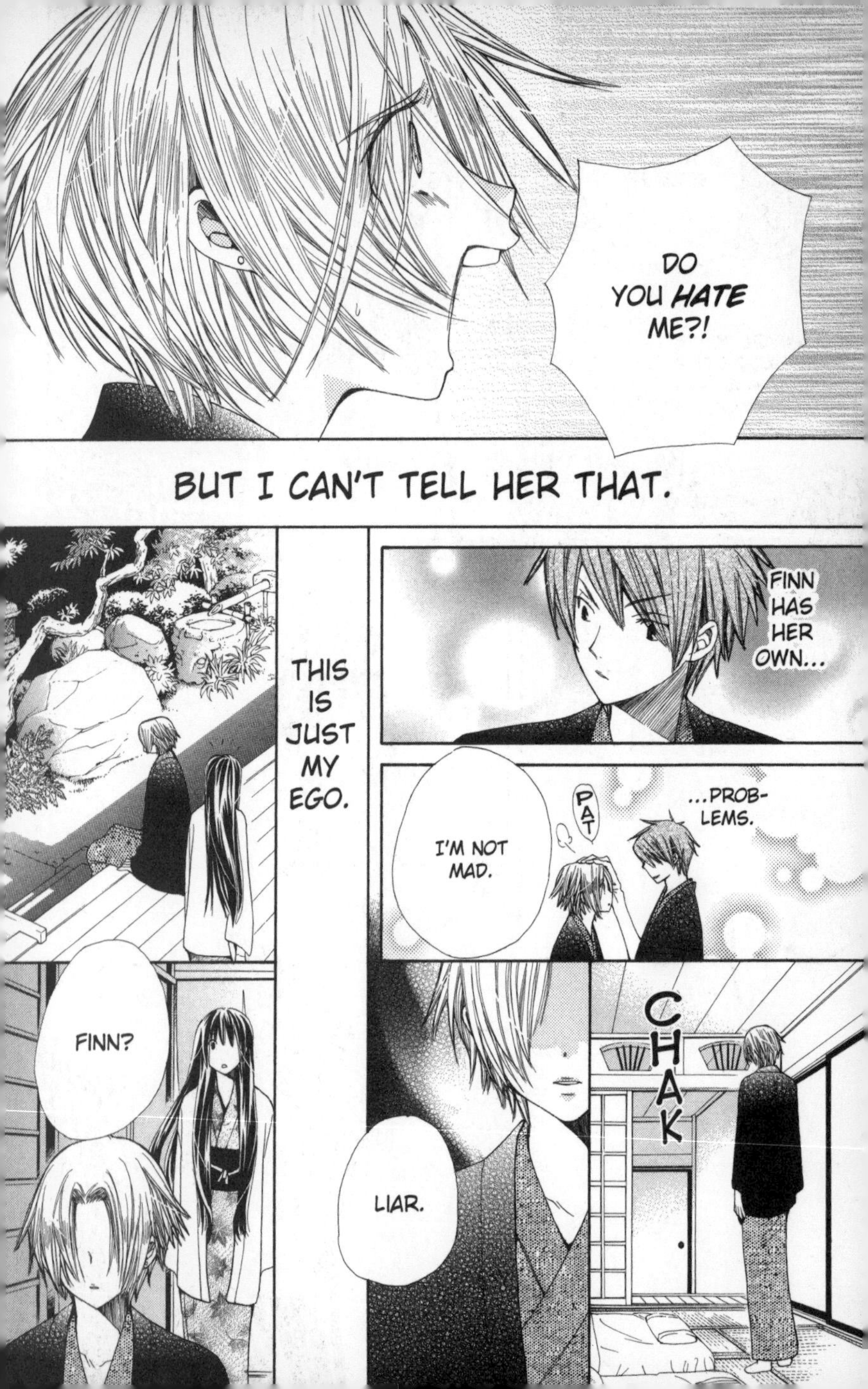
DO YOU HATE ME?!
BUT I CAN'T TELL HER THAT.
FINN HAS HER OWN...
PAT
...PROB-LEMS.
I'M NOT MAD.
THIS IS JUST MY EGO.
CHAK
LIAR.
FINN?

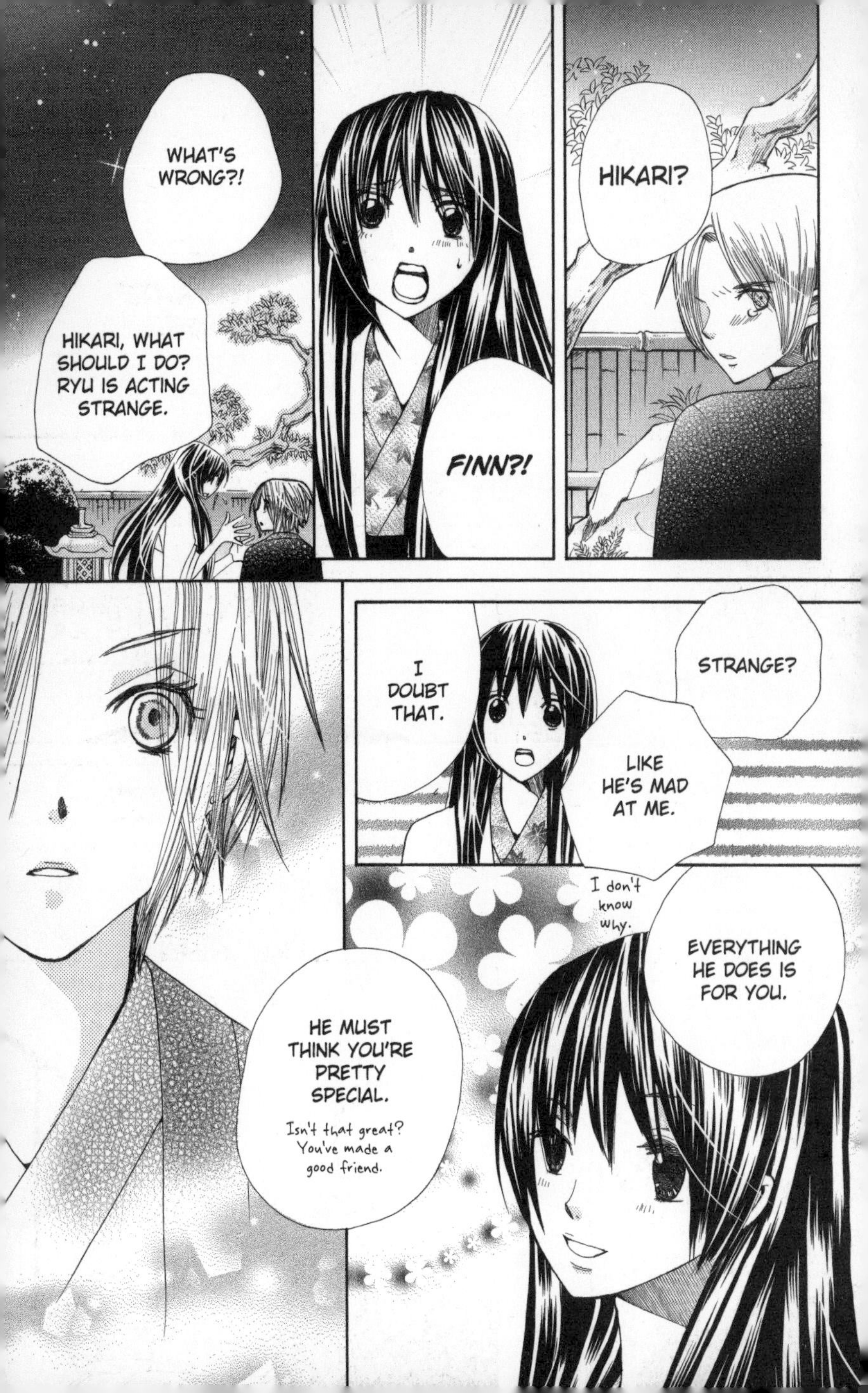
HIKARI?
FINN?!
WHAT'S WRONG?!
HIKARI, WHAT SHOULD I DO? RYU IS ACTING STRANGE.
STRANGE?
LIKE HE'S MAD AT ME.
I don't know why.
I DOUBT THAT.
EVERYTHING HE DOES IS FOR YOU.
HE MUST THINK YOU'RE PRETTY SPECIAL.
Isn't that great? You've made a good friend.

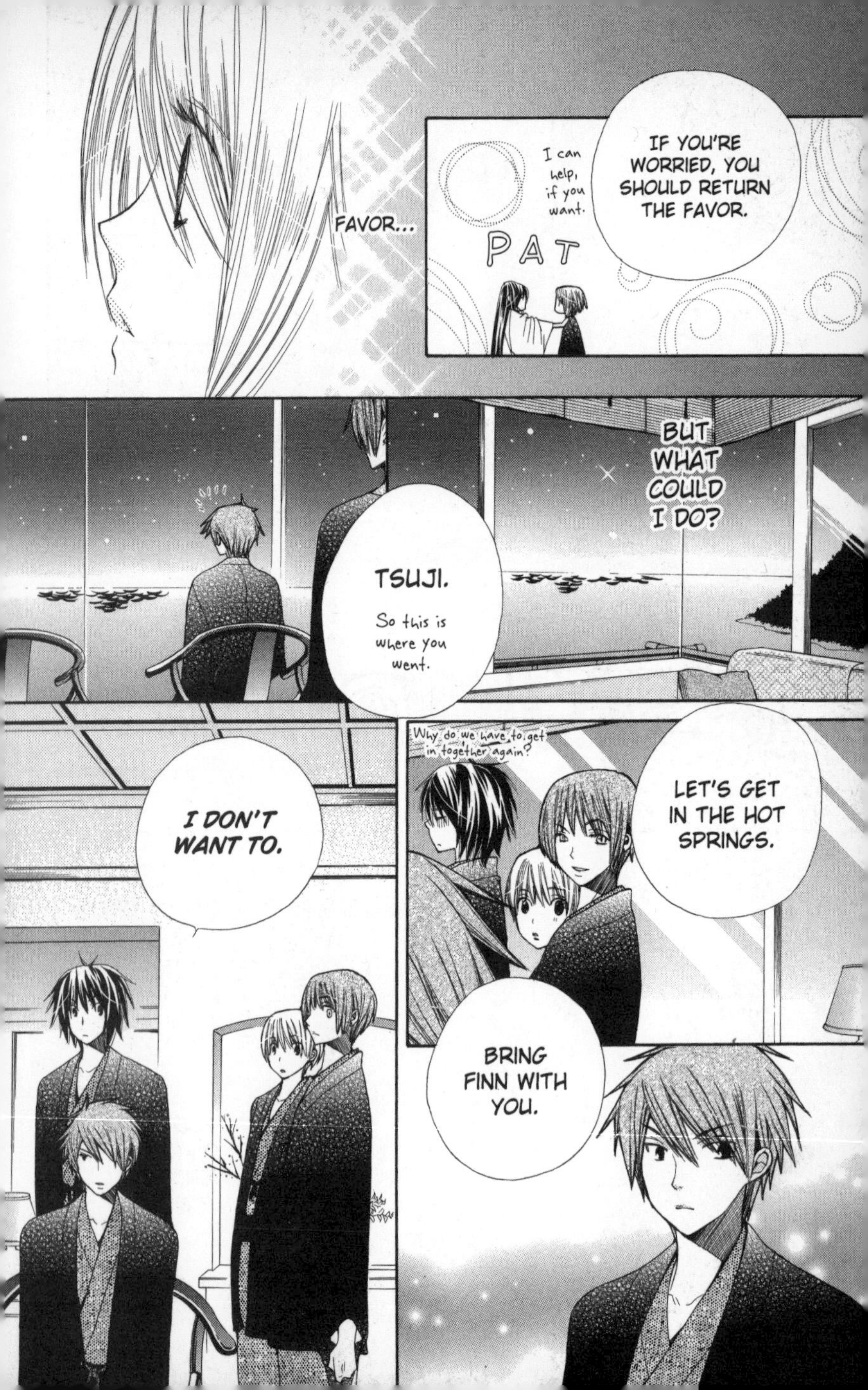
IF YOU'RE WORRIED, YOU SHOULD RETURN THE FAVOR.
I can help, if you want.
PAT
FAVOR...
BUT WHAT COULD I DO?
TSUJI.
So this is where you went.
LET'S GET IN THE HOT SPRINGS.
Why do we have to get in together again?
I DON'T WANT TO.
BRING FINN WITH YOU.

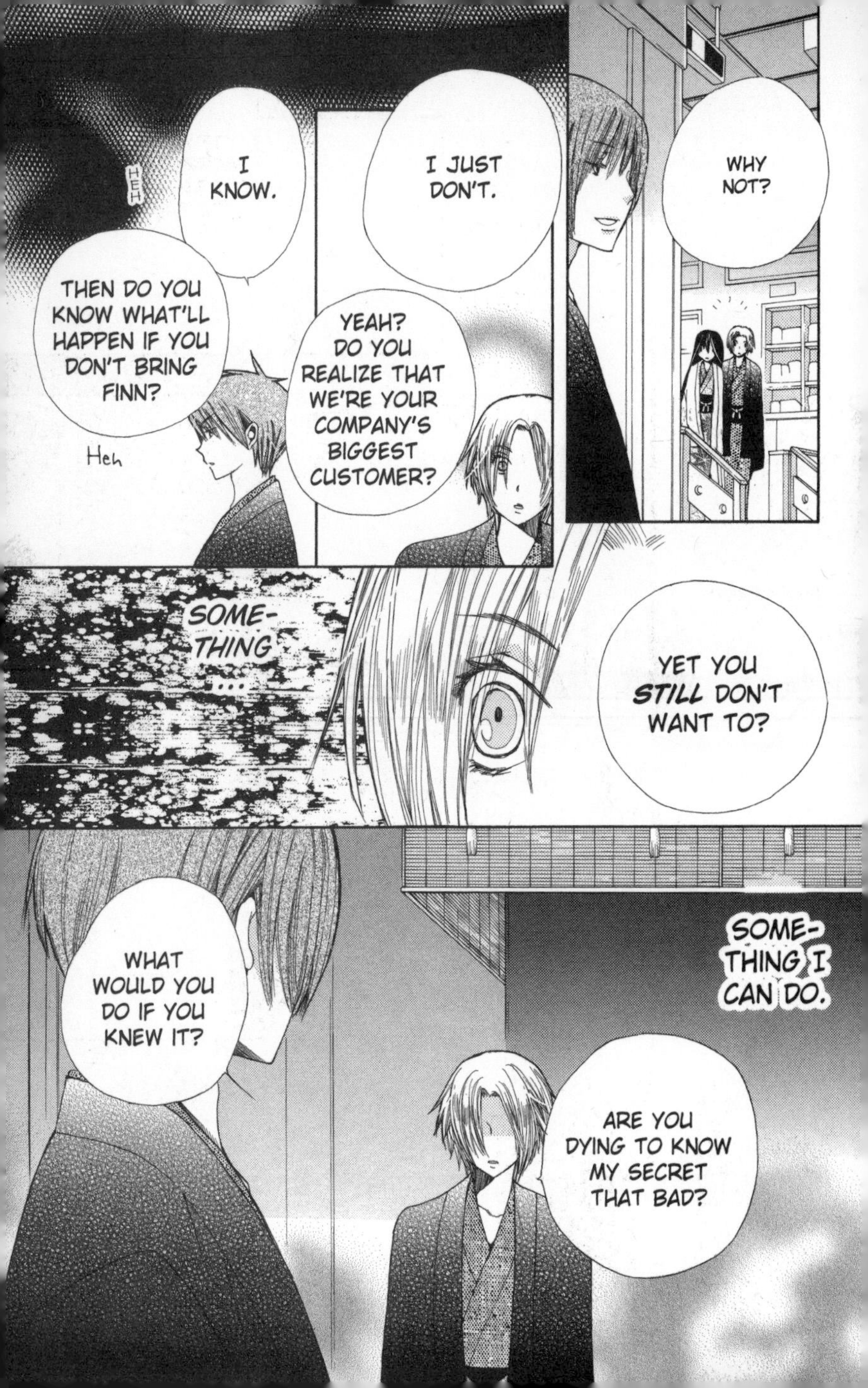
WHY NOT?
I JUST DON'T.
YEAH? DO YOU REALIZE THAT WE'RE YOUR COMPANY'S BIGGEST CUSTOMER?
I KNOW.
HEH
THEN DO YOU KNOW WHAT'LL HAPPEN IF YOU DON'T BRING FINN?
Heh
YET YOU *STILL* DON'T WANT TO?
SOME-THING...
SOME-THING I CAN DO.
ARE YOU DYING TO KNOW MY SECRET THAT BAD?
WHAT WOULD YOU DO IF YOU KNEW IT?

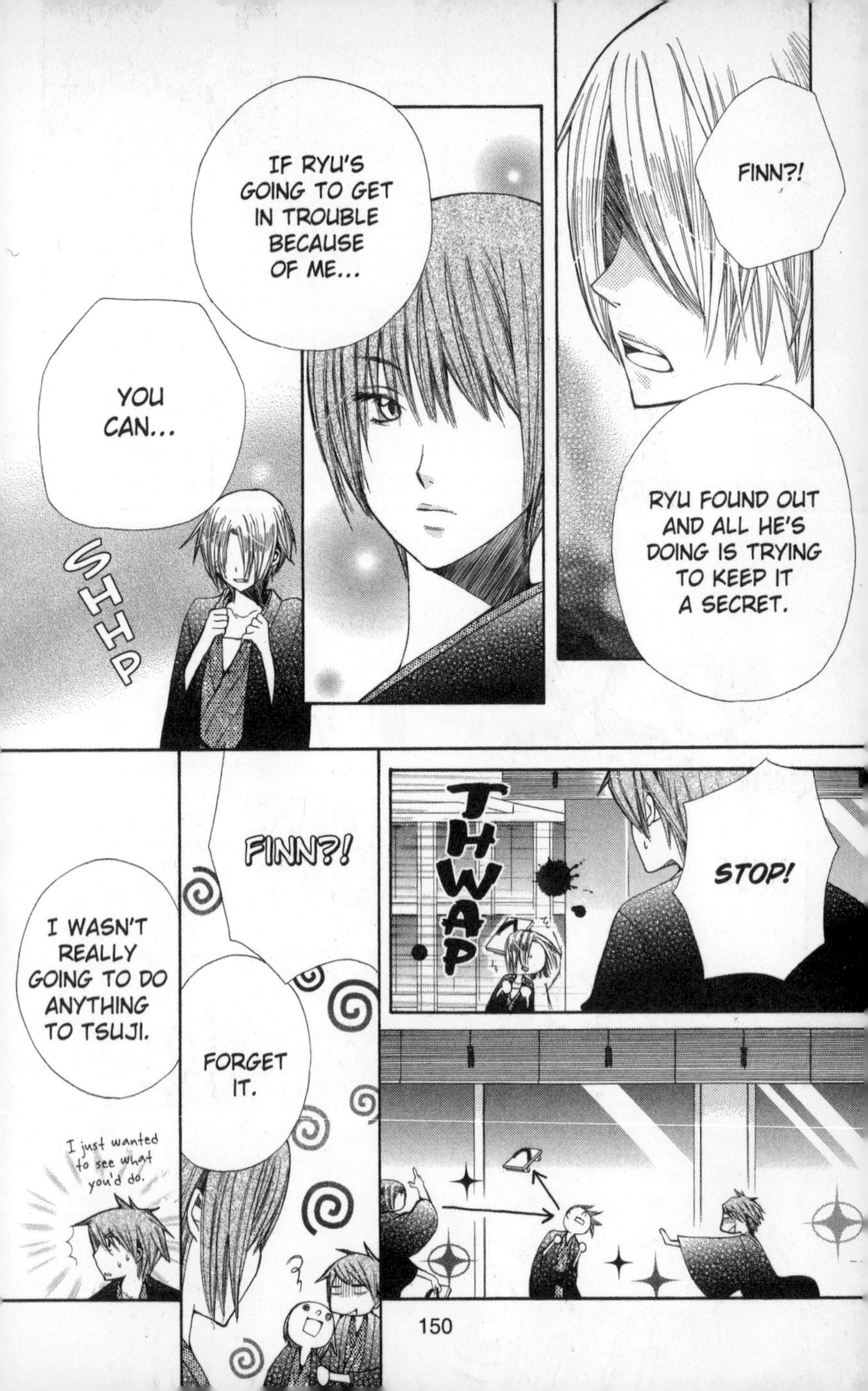
FINN?!
RYU FOUND OUT AND ALL HE'S DOING IS TRYING TO KEEP IT A SECRET.
IF RYU'S GOING TO GET IN TROUBLE BECAUSE OF ME...
YOU CAN...
SHHHP
STOP!
THWAP
FINN?!
FORGET IT.
I WASN'T REALLY GOING TO DO ANYTHING TO TSUJI.
I just wanted to see what you'd do.

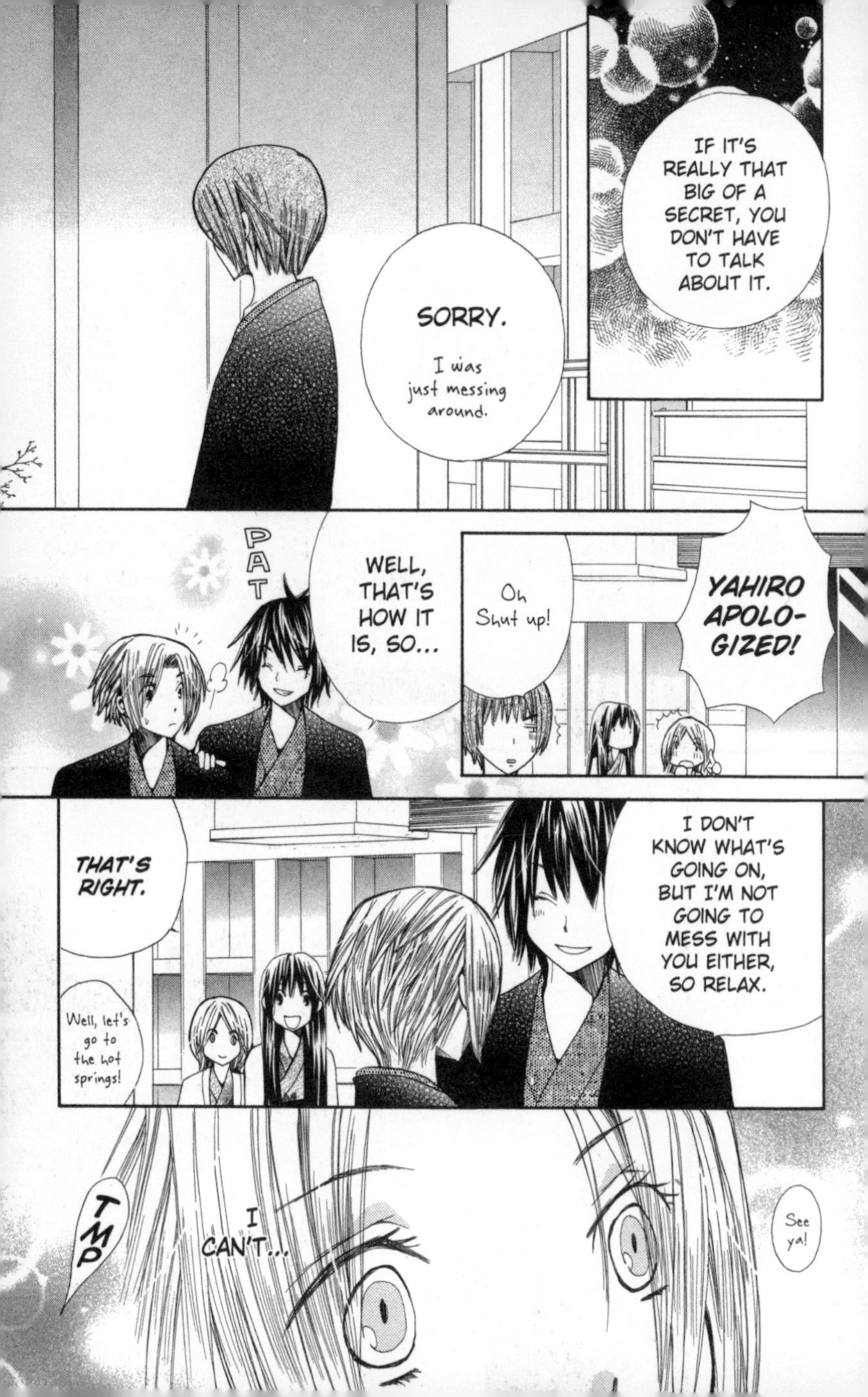
IF IT'S REALLY THAT BIG OF A SECRET, YOU DON'T HAVE TO TALK ABOUT IT.
SORRY.
I was just messing around.
YAHIRO APOLO-GIZED!
Oh Shut up!
PAT
WELL, THAT'S HOW IT IS, SO...
I DON'T KNOW WHAT'S GOING ON, BUT I'M NOT GOING TO MESS WITH YOU EITHER, SO RELAX.
THAT'S RIGHT.
Well, let's go to the hot springs!
See ya!
I CAN'T...
TMP

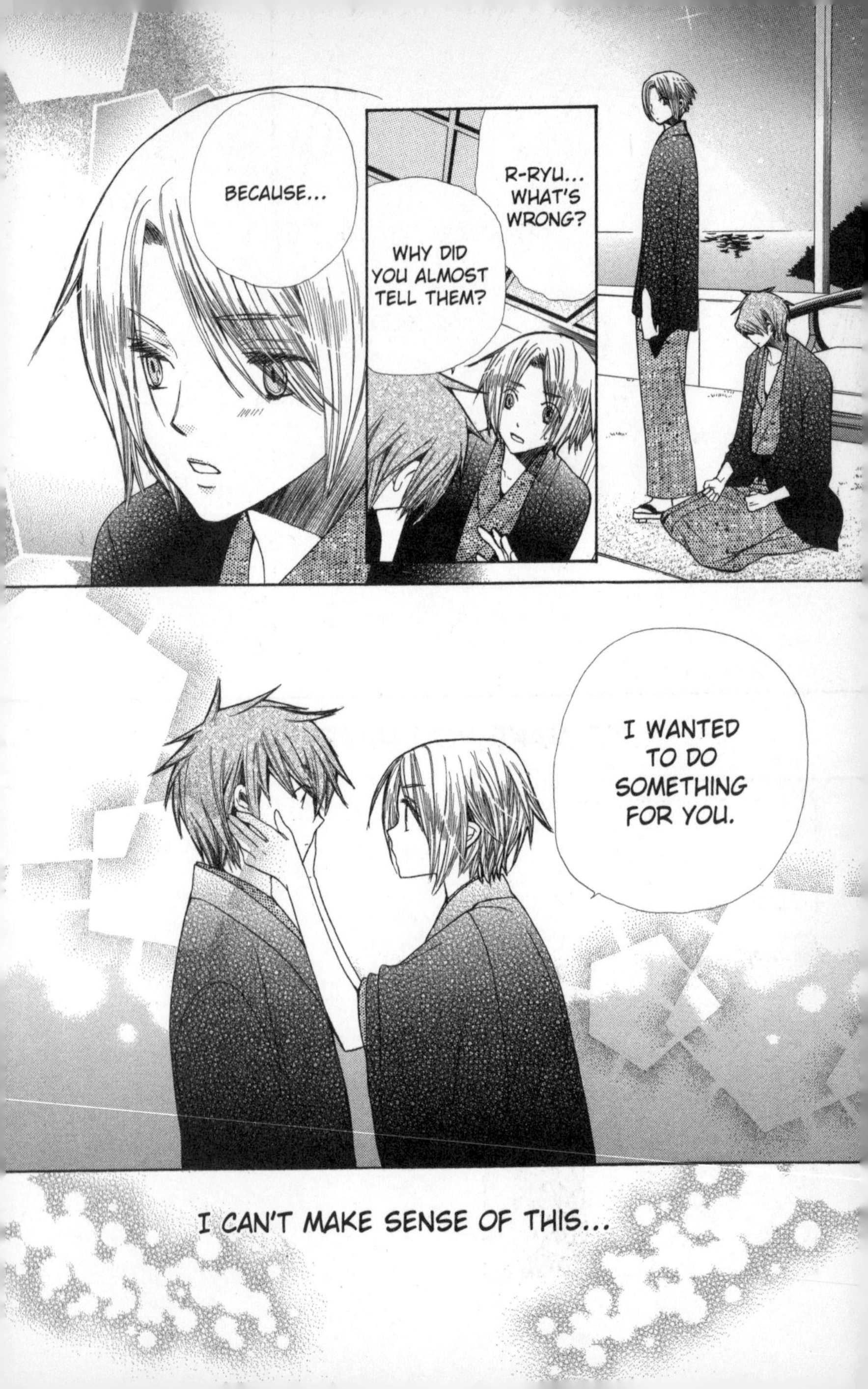
R-RYU... WHAT'S WRONG?
WHY DID YOU ALMOST TELL THEM?
BECAUSE...
I WANTED TO DO SOMETHING FOR YOU.
I CAN'T MAKE SENSE OF THIS...

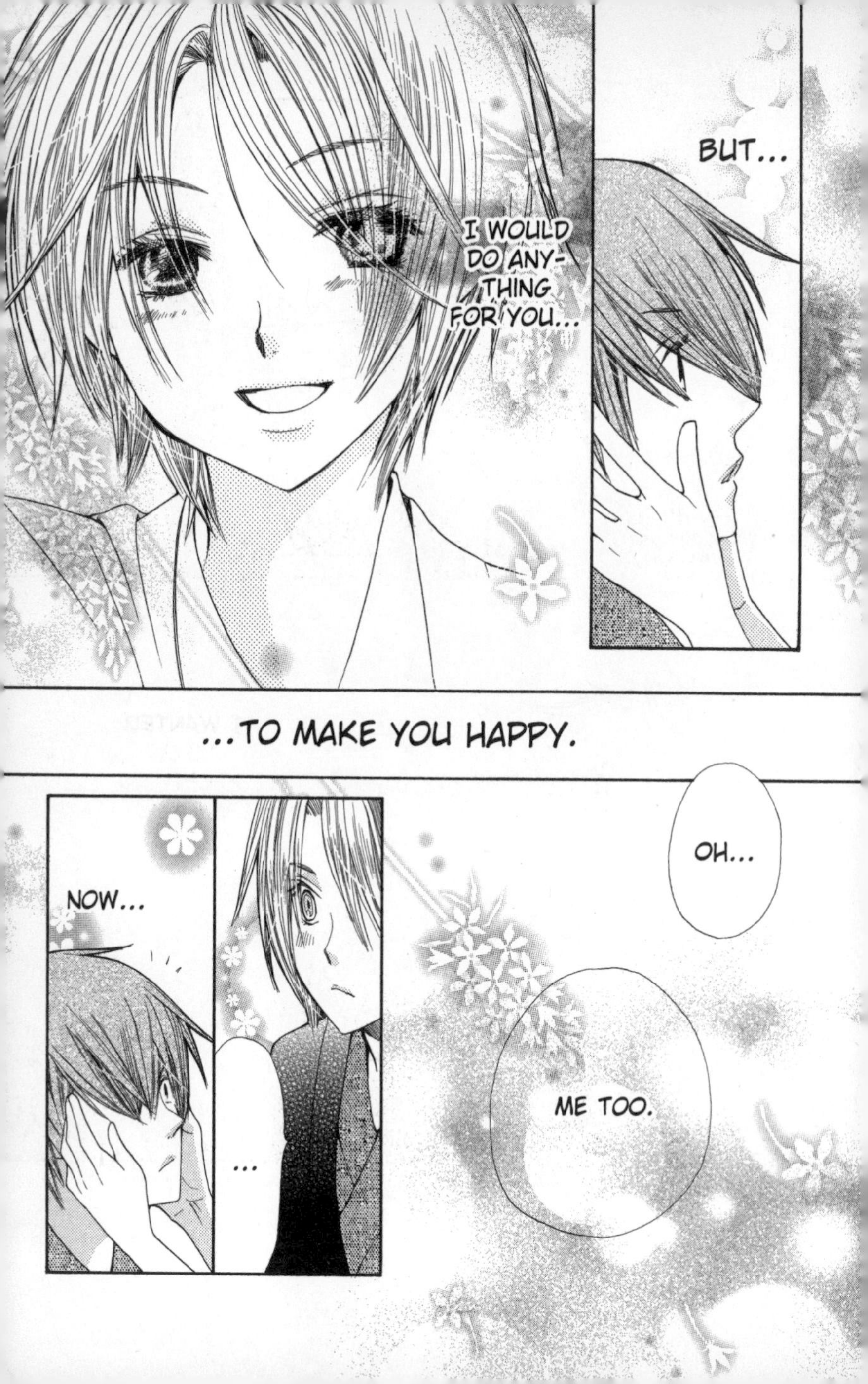

BUT...
I WOULD DO ANYTHING FOR YOU...
...TO MAKE YOU HAPPY.
OH...
ME TOO.
...
NOW...

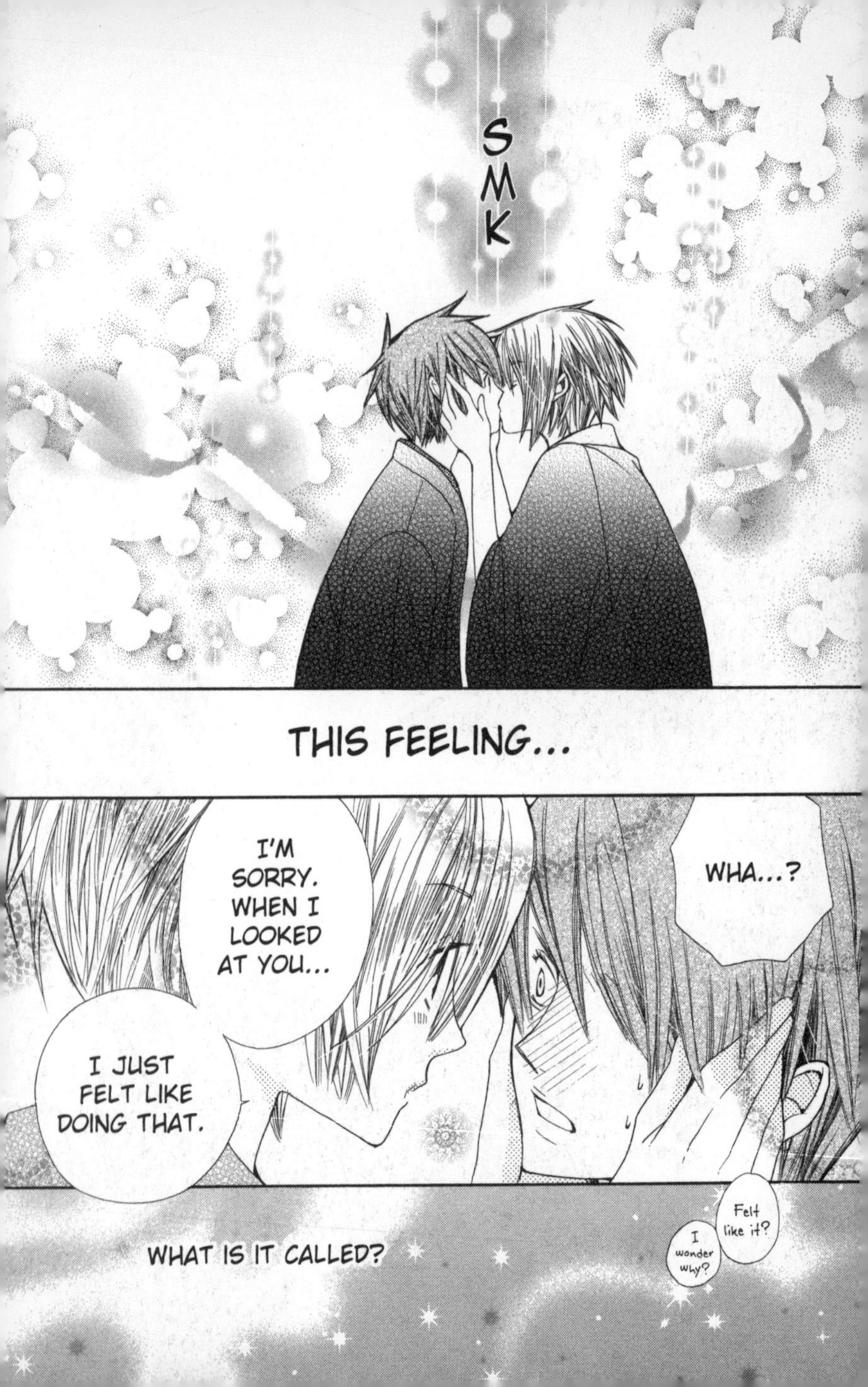
SMK
THIS FEELING...
WHA...?
I'M SORRY. WHEN I LOOKED AT YOU...
I JUST FELT LIKE DOING THAT.
WHAT IS IT CALLED?
Felt like it?
I wonder why?

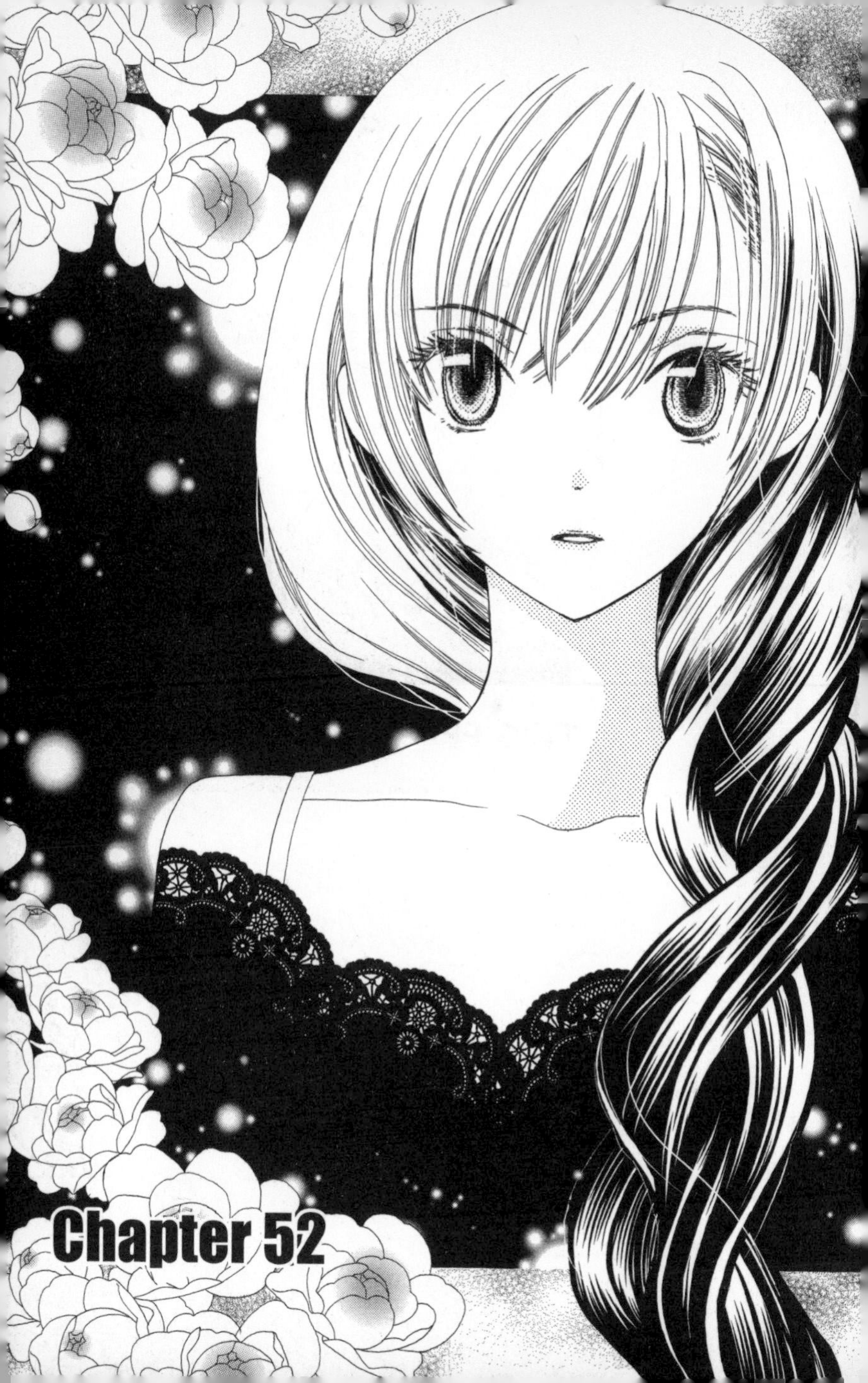
Chapter 52

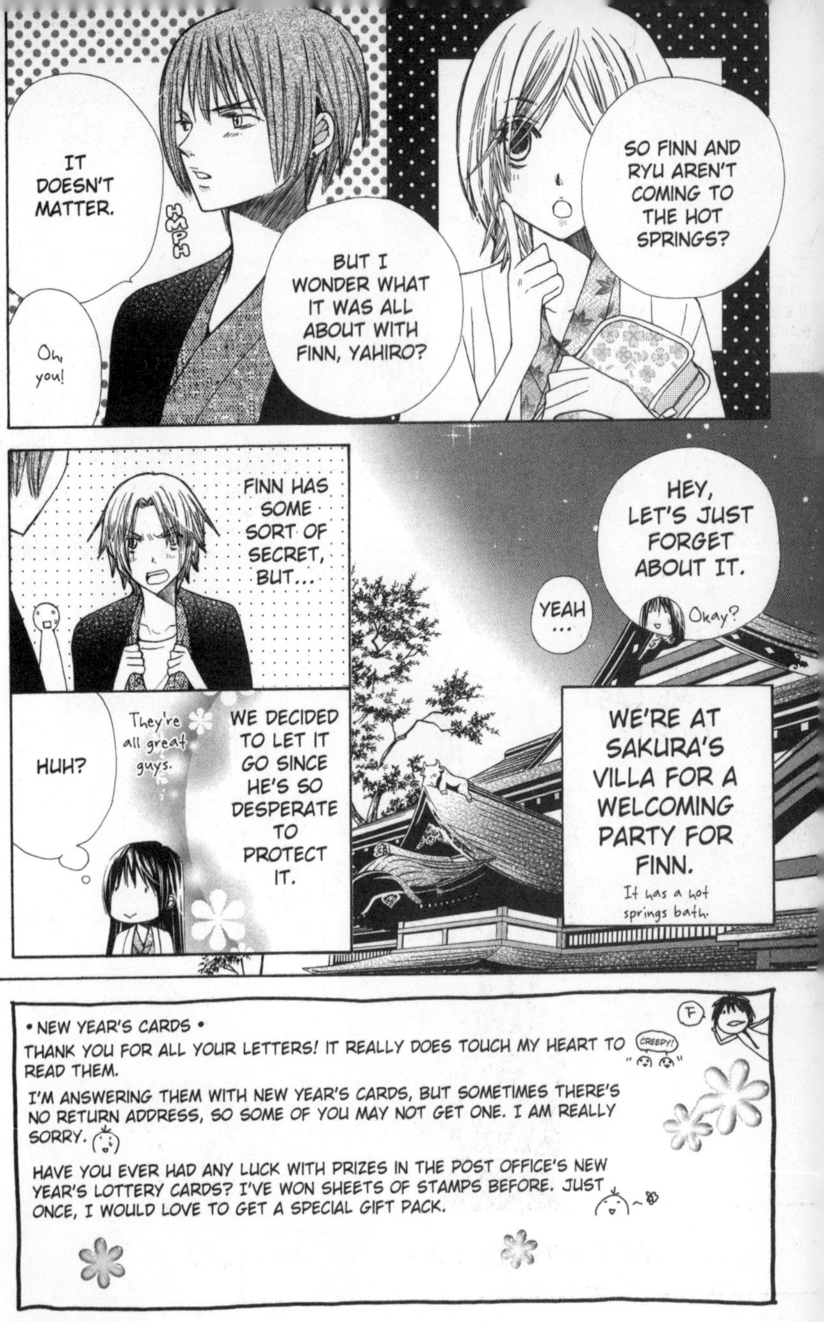
SO FINN AND RYU AREN'T COMING TO THE HOT SPRINGS?
BUT I WONDER WHAT IT WAS ALL ABOUT WITH FINN, YAHIRO?
HMPH
IT DOESN'T MATTER.
Oh, you!
HEY, LET'S JUST FORGET ABOUT IT.
Okay?
YEAH...
WE'RE AT SAKURA'S VILLA FOR A WELCOMING PARTY FOR FINN.
It has a hot springs bath.
FINN HAS SOME SORT OF SECRET, BUT...
WE DECIDED TO LET IT GO SINCE HE'S SO DESPERATE TO PROTECT IT.
They're all great guys.
HUH?

• NEW YEAR'S CARDS •

THANK YOU FOR ALL YOUR LETTERS! IT REALLY DOES TOUCH MY HEART TO READ THEM.

I'M ANSWERING THEM WITH NEW YEAR'S CARDS, BUT SOMETIMES THERE'S NO RETURN ADDRESS, SO SOME OF YOU MAY NOT GET ONE. I AM REALLY SORRY.

HAVE YOU EVER HAD ANY LUCK WITH PRIZES IN THE POST OFFICE'S NEW YEAR'S LOTTERY CARDS? I'VE WON SHEETS OF STAMPS BEFORE. JUST ONCE, I WOULD LOVE TO GET A SPECIAL GIFT PACK.

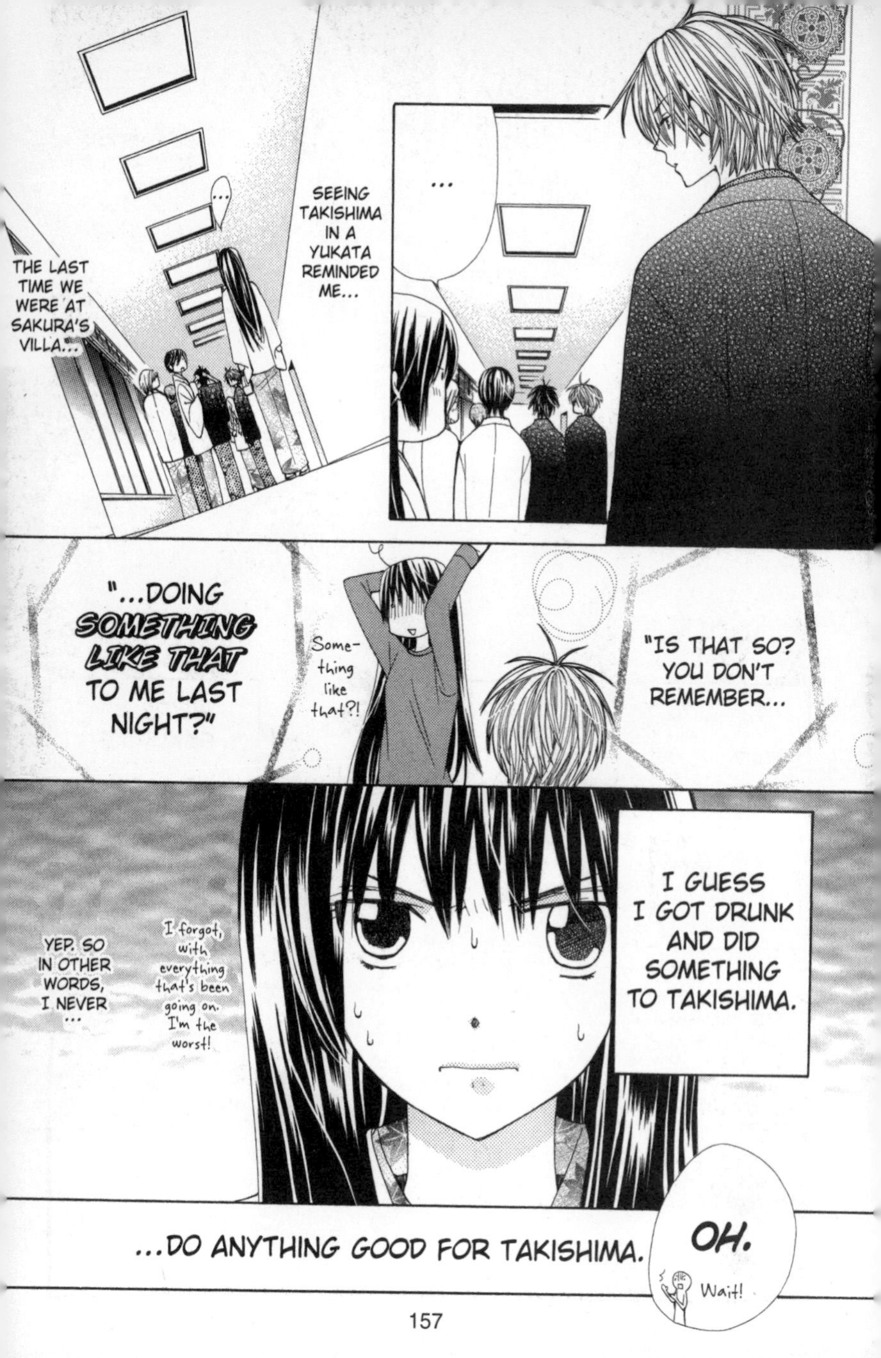
...
SEEING TAKISHIMA IN A YUKATA REMINDED ME...
...
THE LAST TIME WE WERE AT SAKURA'S VILLA...
"IS THAT SO? YOU DON'T REMEMBER...
Something like that?!
"...DOING SOMETHING LIKE THAT TO ME LAST NIGHT?"
I GUESS I GOT DRUNK AND DID SOMETHING TO TAKISHIMA.
I forgot, with everything that's been going on. I'm the worst!
YEP. SO IN OTHER WORDS, I NEVER ...
...DO ANYTHING GOOD FOR TAKISHIMA.
OH.
Wait!

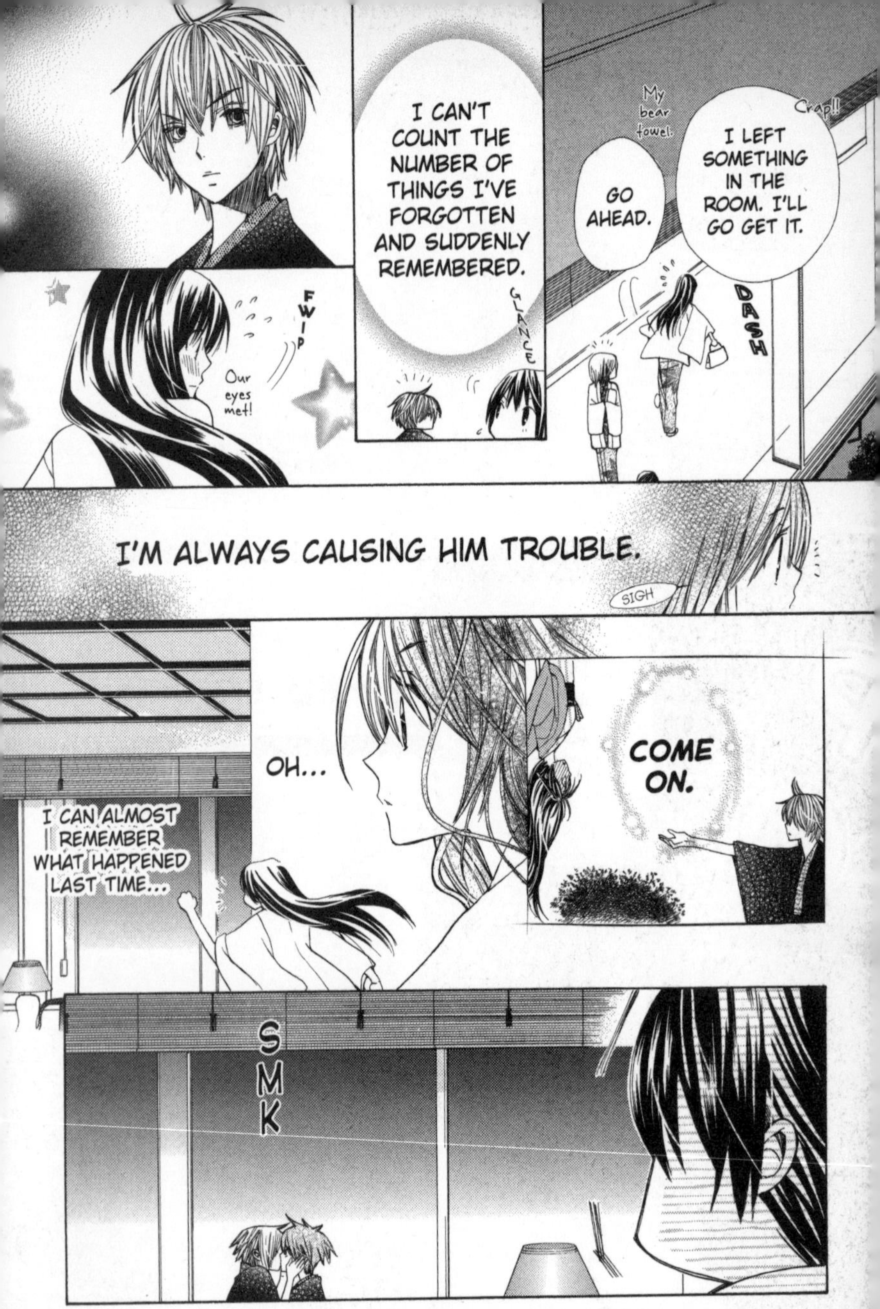

Crap!!
I LEFT SOMETHING IN THE ROOM. I'LL GO GET IT.
My bear towel.
GO AHEAD.
DASH
I CAN'T COUNT THE NUMBER OF THINGS I'VE FORGOTTEN AND SUDDENLY REMEMBERED.
GLANCE
FWIP
Our eyes met!
I'M ALWAYS CAUSING HIM TROUBLE.
SIGH
COME ON.
OH...
I CAN ALMOST REMEMBER WHAT HAPPENED LAST TIME...
SMK

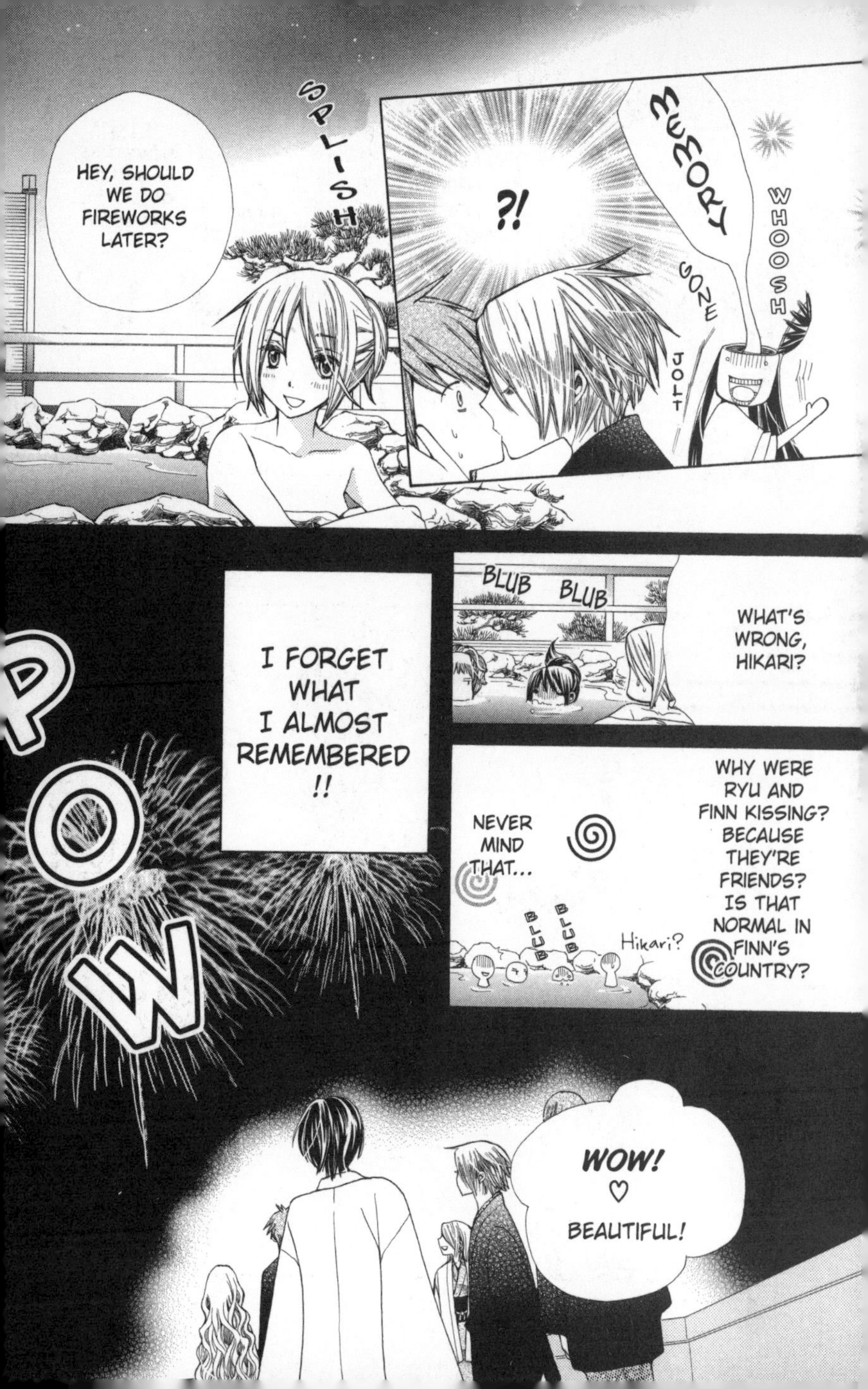

MEMORY GONE
?!
WHOOSH
JOLT
SPLISH
HEY, SHOULD WE DO FIREWORKS LATER?
WHAT'S WRONG, HIKARI?
BLUB BLUB
WHY WERE RYU AND FINN KISSING? BECAUSE THEY'RE FRIENDS? IS THAT NORMAL IN FINN'S COUNTRY?
NEVER MIND THAT...
Hikari?
BLUB BLUB
I FORGET WHAT I ALMOST REMEMBERED !!
POW
WOW! ♡ BEAUTIFUL!

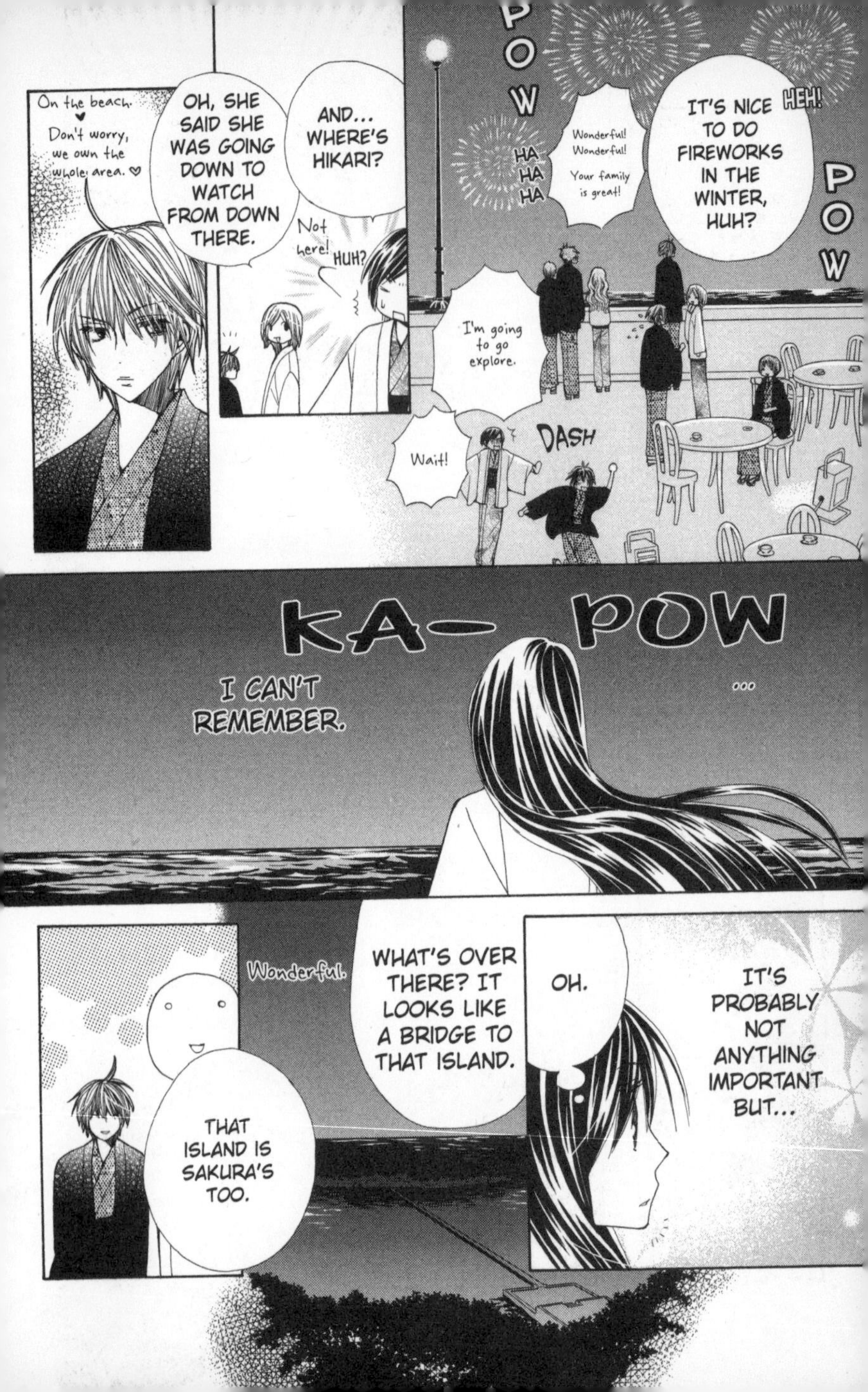
POW
POW
IT'S NICE TO DO FIREWORKS IN THE WINTER, HUH?
HEH!
POW
POW
Wonderful! Wonderful!
Your family is great!
HA HA HA
I'm going to go explore.
DASH
Wait!
AND... WHERE'S HIKARI?
Not here!
HUH?
OH, SHE SAID SHE WAS GOING DOWN TO WATCH FROM DOWN THERE.
On the beach. ♥
Don't worry, we own the whole area. ♡
KA— POW
...
I CAN'T REMEMBER.
IT'S PROBABLY NOT ANYTHING IMPORTANT BUT...
OH.
WHAT'S OVER THERE? IT LOOKS LIKE A BRIDGE TO THAT ISLAND.
Wonderful.
THAT ISLAND IS SAKURA'S TOO.

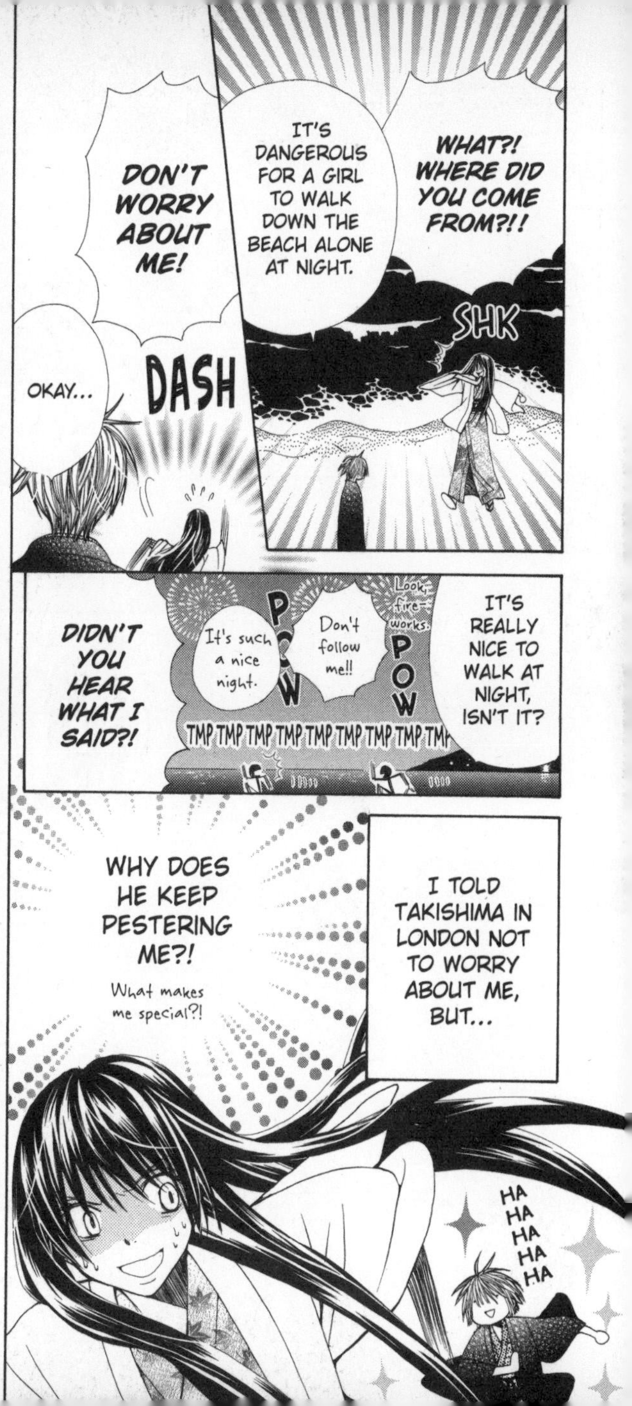
WHAT?! WHERE DID YOU COME FROM?!!
SHK
IT'S DANGEROUS FOR A GIRL TO WALK DOWN THE BEACH ALONE AT NIGHT.
DON'T WORRY ABOUT ME!
DASH
OKAY...
IT'S REALLY NICE TO WALK AT NIGHT, ISN'T IT?
Look, fire-works.
POW
POW
Don't follow me!!
It's such a nice night.
TMP TMP TMP TMP TMP TMP TMP TMP
DIDN'T YOU HEAR WHAT I SAID?!
I TOLD TAKISHIMA IN LONDON NOT TO WORRY ABOUT ME, BUT...
WHY DOES HE KEEP PESTERING ME?!
What makes me special?!
HA HA HA HA HA

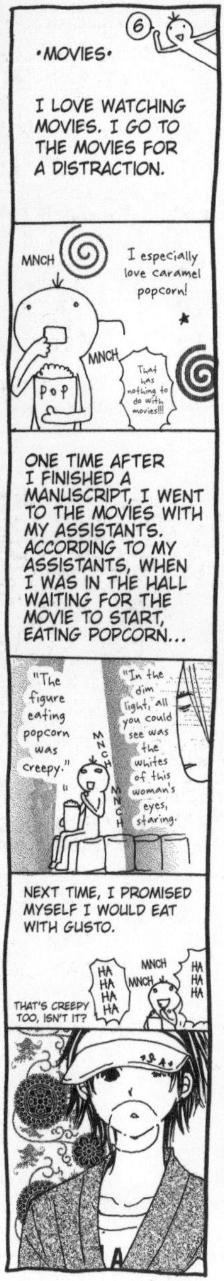
6
•MOVIES•
I LOVE WATCHING MOVIES. I GO TO THE MOVIES FOR A DISTRACTION.
MNCH
I especially love caramel popcorn!
MNCH
POP
That has nothing to do with movies!!!
ONE TIME AFTER I FINISHED A MANUSCRIPT, I WENT TO THE MOVIES WITH MY ASSISTANTS. ACCORDING TO MY ASSISTANTS, WHEN I WAS IN THE HALL WAITING FOR THE MOVIE TO START, EATING POPCORN...
"In the dim light, all you could see was the whites of this woman's eyes, staring.
"The figure eating popcorn was creepy."
MNCH
MNCH
NEXT TIME, I PROMISED MYSELF I WOULD EAT WITH GUSTO.
HA HA HA
MNCH
MNCH
HA HA HA HA
THAT'S CREEPY TOO, ISN'T IT?

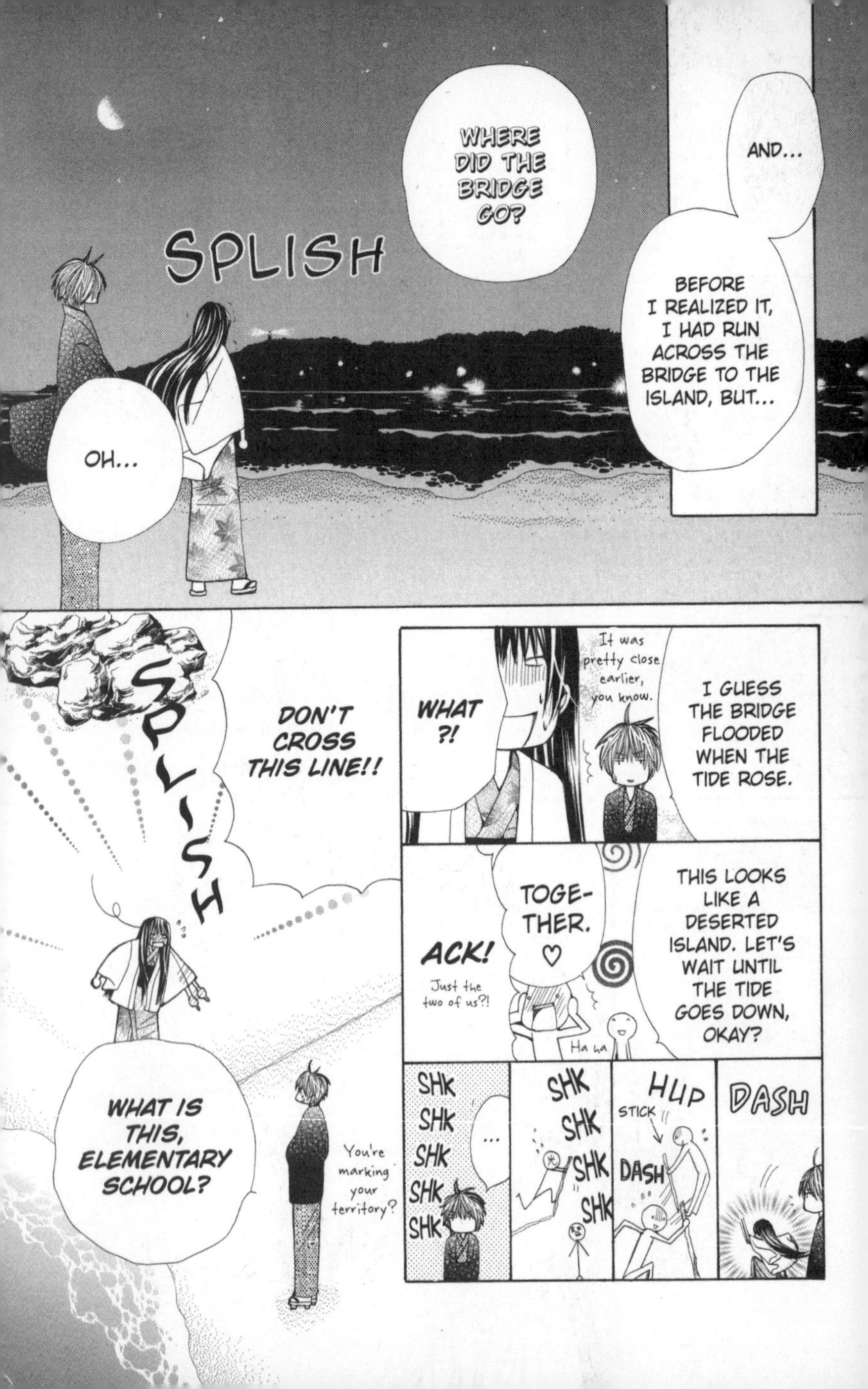
AND...
BEFORE I REALIZED IT, I HAD RUN ACROSS THE BRIDGE TO THE ISLAND, BUT...
WHERE DID THE BRIDGE GO?
SPLISH
OH...
I GUESS THE BRIDGE FLOODED WHEN THE TIDE ROSE.
It was pretty close earlier, you know.
WHAT ?!
THIS LOOKS LIKE A DESERTED ISLAND. LET'S WAIT UNTIL THE TIDE GOES DOWN, OKAY?
TOGE-THER. ♡
Ha ha
ACK!
Just the two of us?!
DASH
HUP
STICK
DASH
SHK SHK SHK SHK
SHK SHK SHK SHK SHK
...
SPLISH
DON'T CROSS THIS LINE!!
You're marking your territory?
WHAT IS THIS, ELEMENTARY SCHOOL?

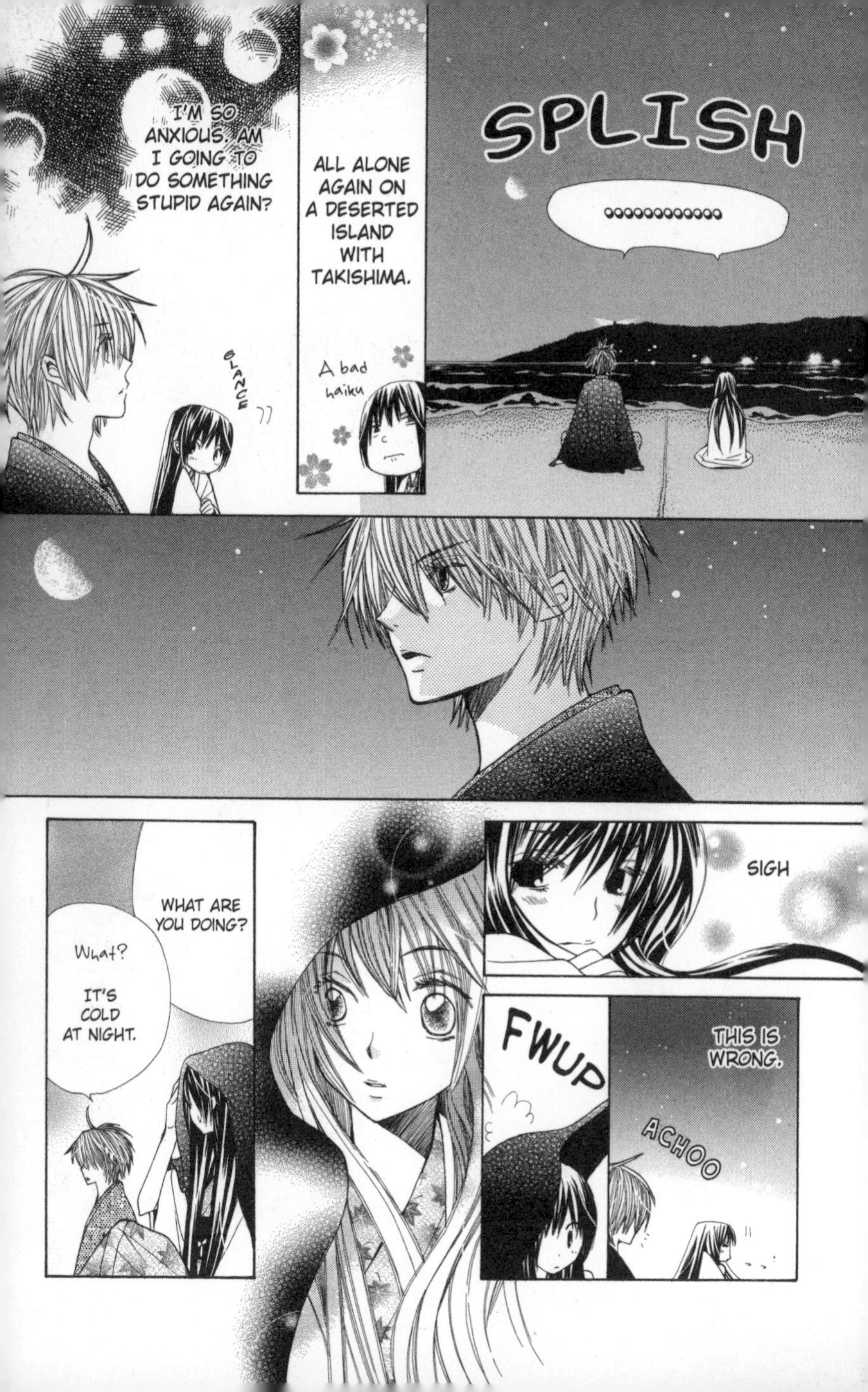
SPLISH
....
ALL ALONE AGAIN ON A DESERTED ISLAND WITH TAKISHIMA.
A bad haiku
I'M SO ANXIOUS. AM I GOING TO DO SOMETHING STUPID AGAIN?
GLANCE
SIGH
THIS IS WRONG.
FWUP
ACHOO
WHAT ARE YOU DOING?
What?
IT'S COLD AT NIGHT.

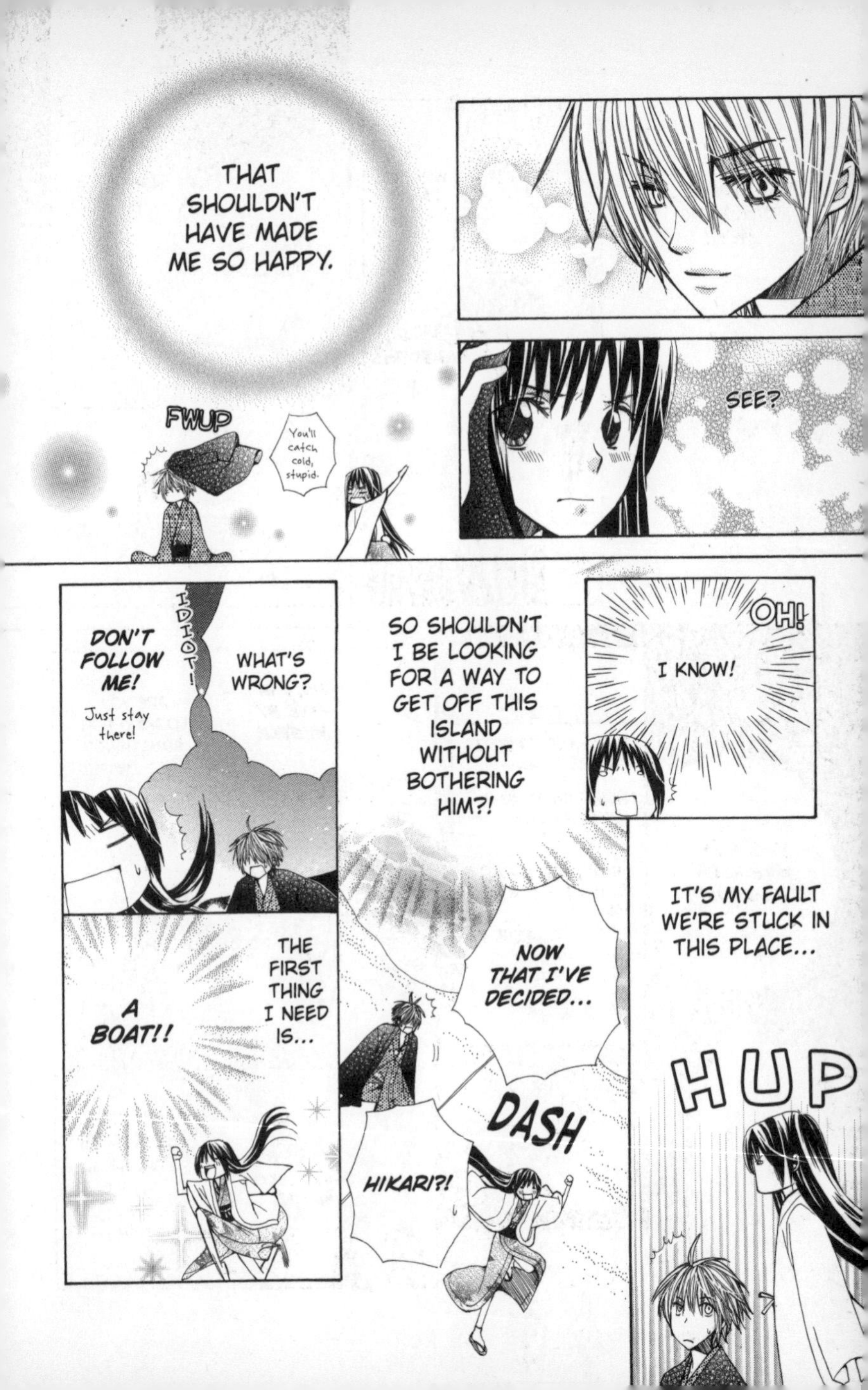
SEE?
THAT SHOULDN'T HAVE MADE ME SO HAPPY.
FWUP
You'll catch cold, stupid.
IT'S MY FAULT WE'RE STUCK IN THIS PLACE...
HUP
SO SHOULDN'T I BE LOOKING FOR A WAY TO GET OFF THIS ISLAND WITHOUT BOTHERING HIM?!
OH!
I KNOW!
NOW THAT I'VE DECIDED...
DASH
HIKARI?!
WHAT'S WRONG?
DON'T FOLLOW ME!
Just stay there!
IDIOT!
THE FIRST THING I NEED IS...
A BOAT!!

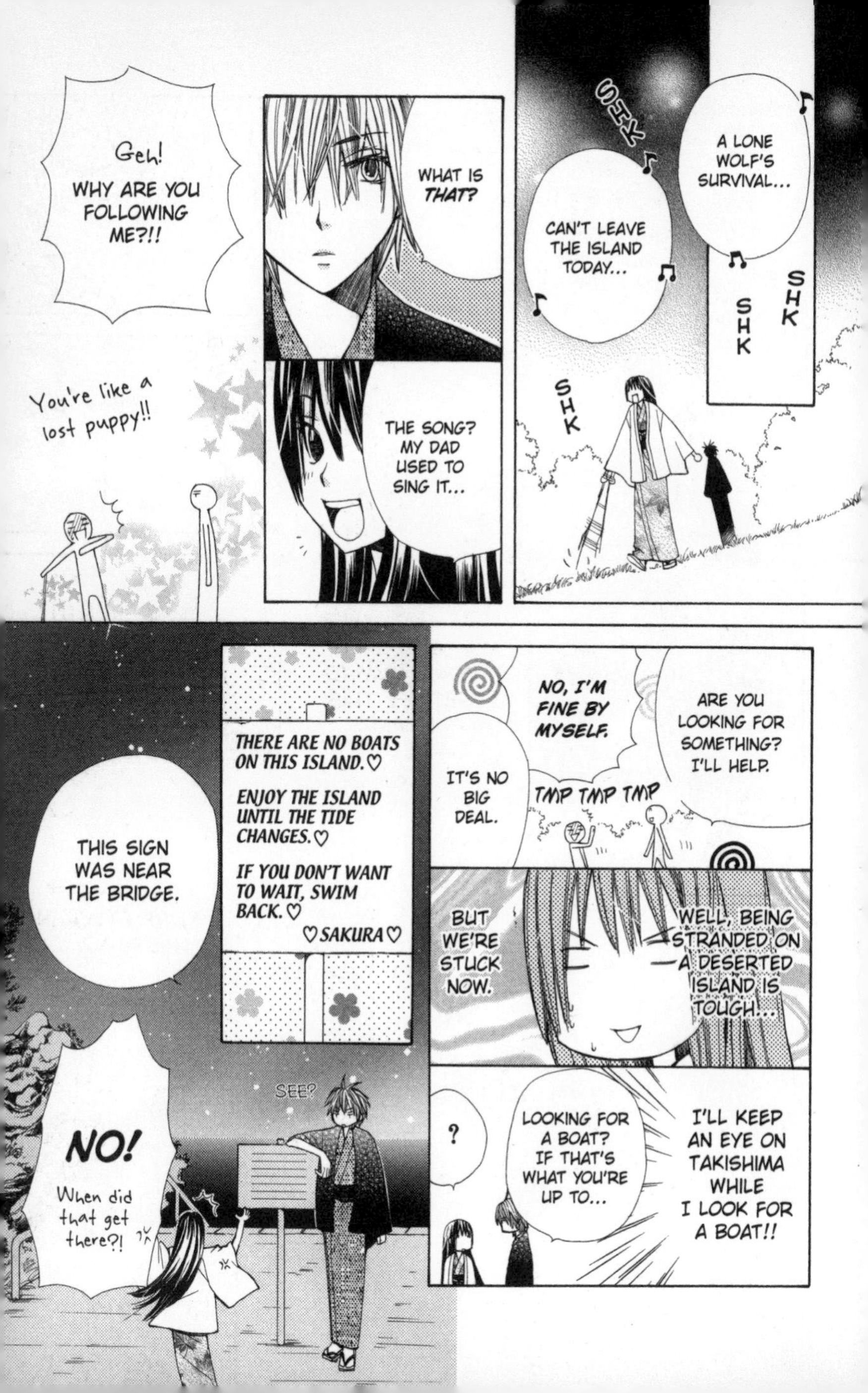
A LONE WOLF'S SURVIVAL...
CAN'T LEAVE THE ISLAND TODAY...
SHK
SHK
SHK
SHK
WHAT IS THAT?
THE SONG? MY DAD USED TO SING IT...
Geh! WHY ARE YOU FOLLOWING ME?!!
You're like a lost puppy!!
ARE YOU LOOKING FOR SOMETHING? I'LL HELP.
NO, I'M FINE BY MYSELF.
IT'S NO BIG DEAL.
TMP TMP TMP
WELL, BEING STRANDED ON A DESERTED ISLAND IS TOUGH...
BUT WE'RE STUCK NOW.
I'LL KEEP AN EYE ON TAKISHIMA WHILE I LOOK FOR A BOAT!!
LOOKING FOR A BOAT? IF THAT'S WHAT YOU'RE UP TO...
?
THERE ARE NO BOATS ON THIS ISLAND.♡
ENJOY THE ISLAND UNTIL THE TIDE CHANGES.♡
IF YOU DON'T WANT TO WAIT, SWIM BACK.♡
♡SAKURA♡
THIS SIGN WAS NEAR THE BRIDGE.
SEE?
NO!
When did that get there?!

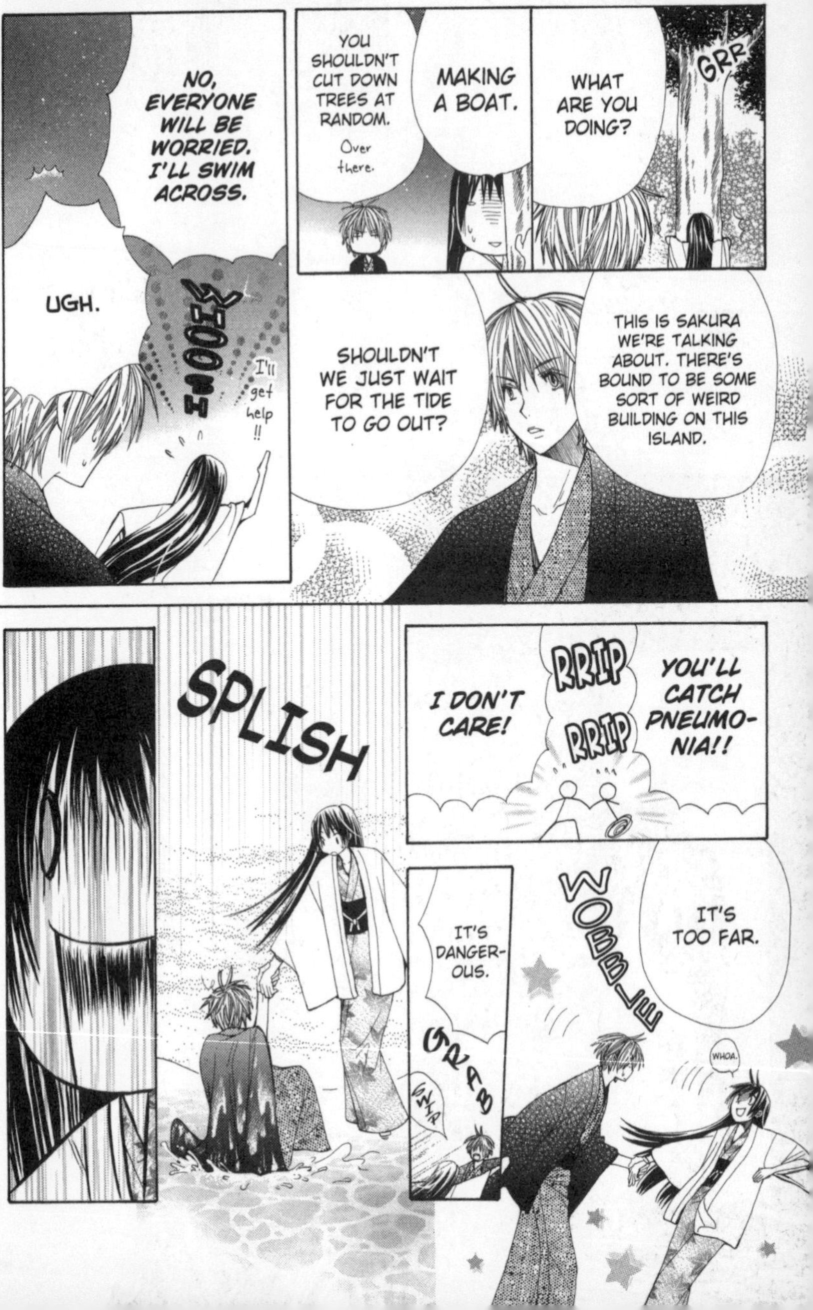
GRR
WHAT ARE YOU DOING?
MAKING A BOAT.
YOU SHOULDN'T CUT DOWN TREES AT RANDOM.
Over there.
THIS IS SAKURA WE'RE TALKING ABOUT. THERE'S BOUND TO BE SOME SORT OF WEIRD BUILDING ON THIS ISLAND.
SHOULDN'T WE JUST WAIT FOR THE TIDE TO GO OUT?
NO, EVERYONE WILL BE WORRIED. I'LL SWIM ACROSS.
UGH.
WHOOSH
I'll get help!!
YOU'LL CATCH PNEUMONIA!!
RRIP
RRIP
I DON'T CARE!
IT'S TOO FAR.
WOBBLE
WHOA.
IT'S DANGEROUS.
GRAB
SWIP
SPLISH

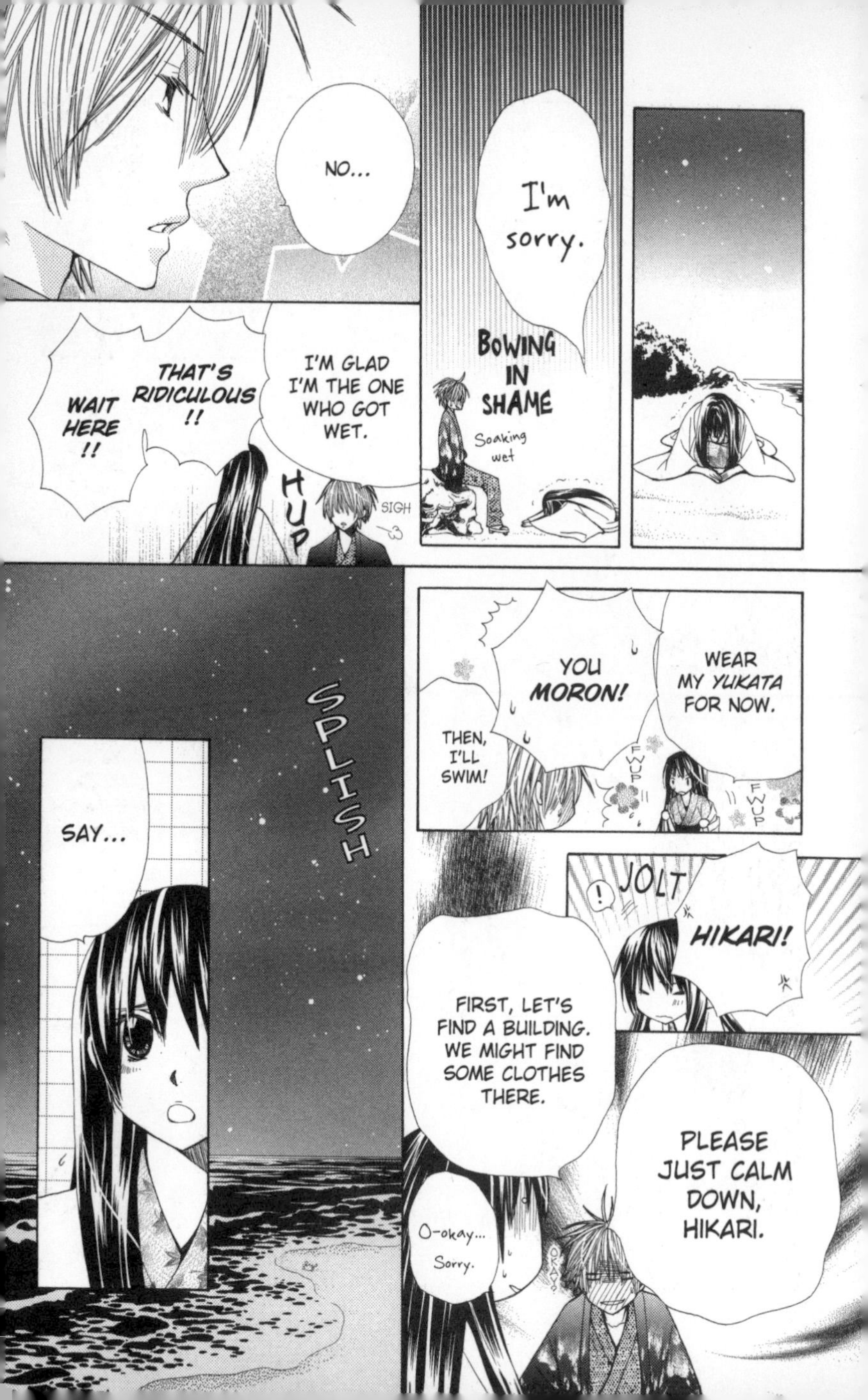

I'm sorry.
BOWING IN SHAME
Soaking wet
NO...
I'M GLAD I'M THE ONE WHO GOT WET.
THAT'S RIDICULOUS!!
WAIT HERE!!
HUP
SIGH
WEAR MY YUKATA FOR NOW.
YOU MORON!
FWUP
FWUP
THEN, I'LL SWIM!
HIKARI!
JOLT
!
PLEASE JUST CALM DOWN, HIKARI.
FIRST, LET'S FIND A BUILDING. WE MIGHT FIND SOME CLOTHES THERE.
OKAY
O-okay... Sorry.
SPLISH
SAY...

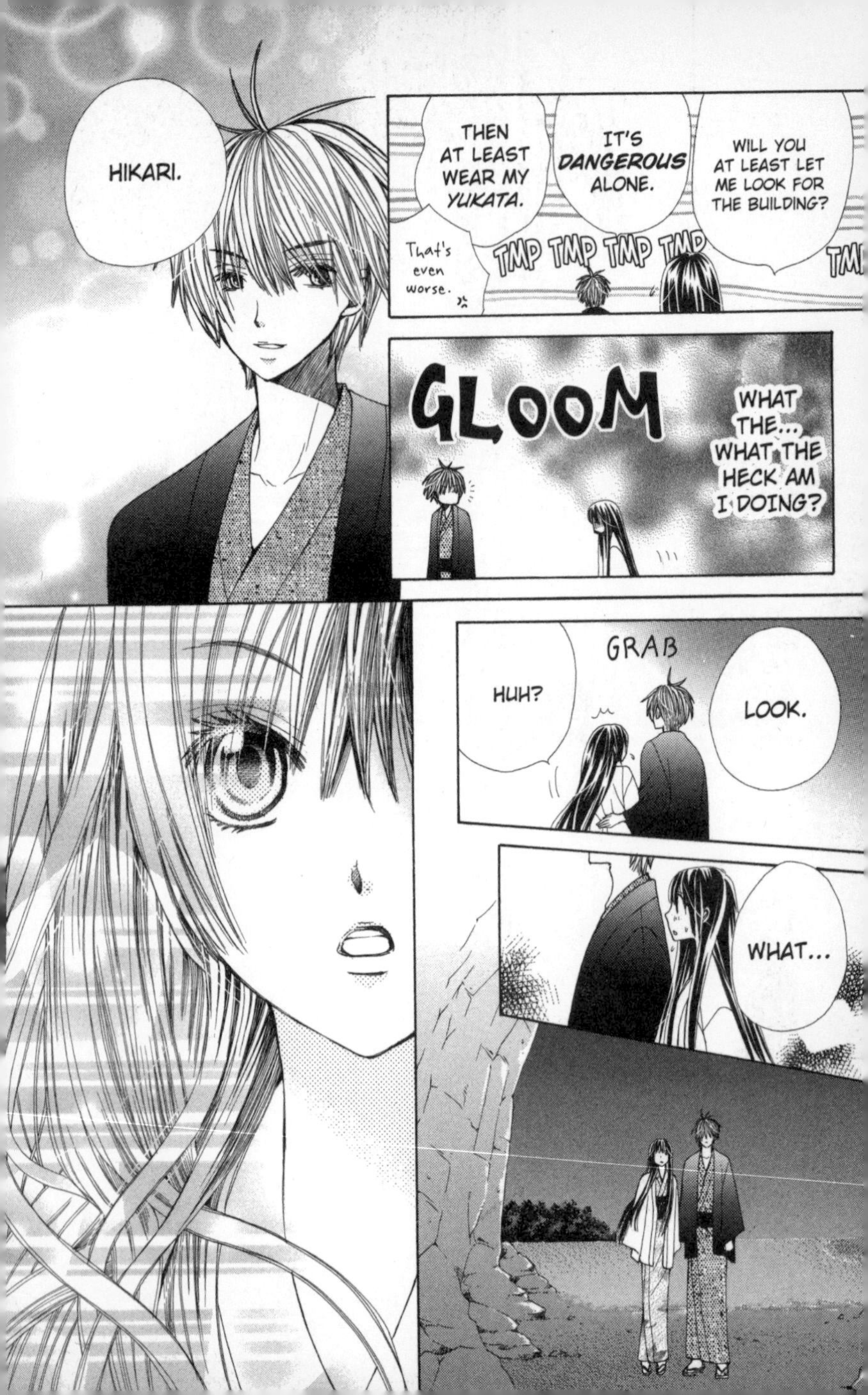
WILL YOU AT LEAST LET ME LOOK FOR THE BUILDING?
TMP
IT'S DANGEROUS ALONE.
THEN AT LEAST WEAR MY YUKATA.
TMP TMP TMP TMP
That's even worse.
WHAT THE... WHAT THE HECK AM I DOING?
GLOOM
HIKARI.
LOOK.
GRAB
HUH?
WHAT...

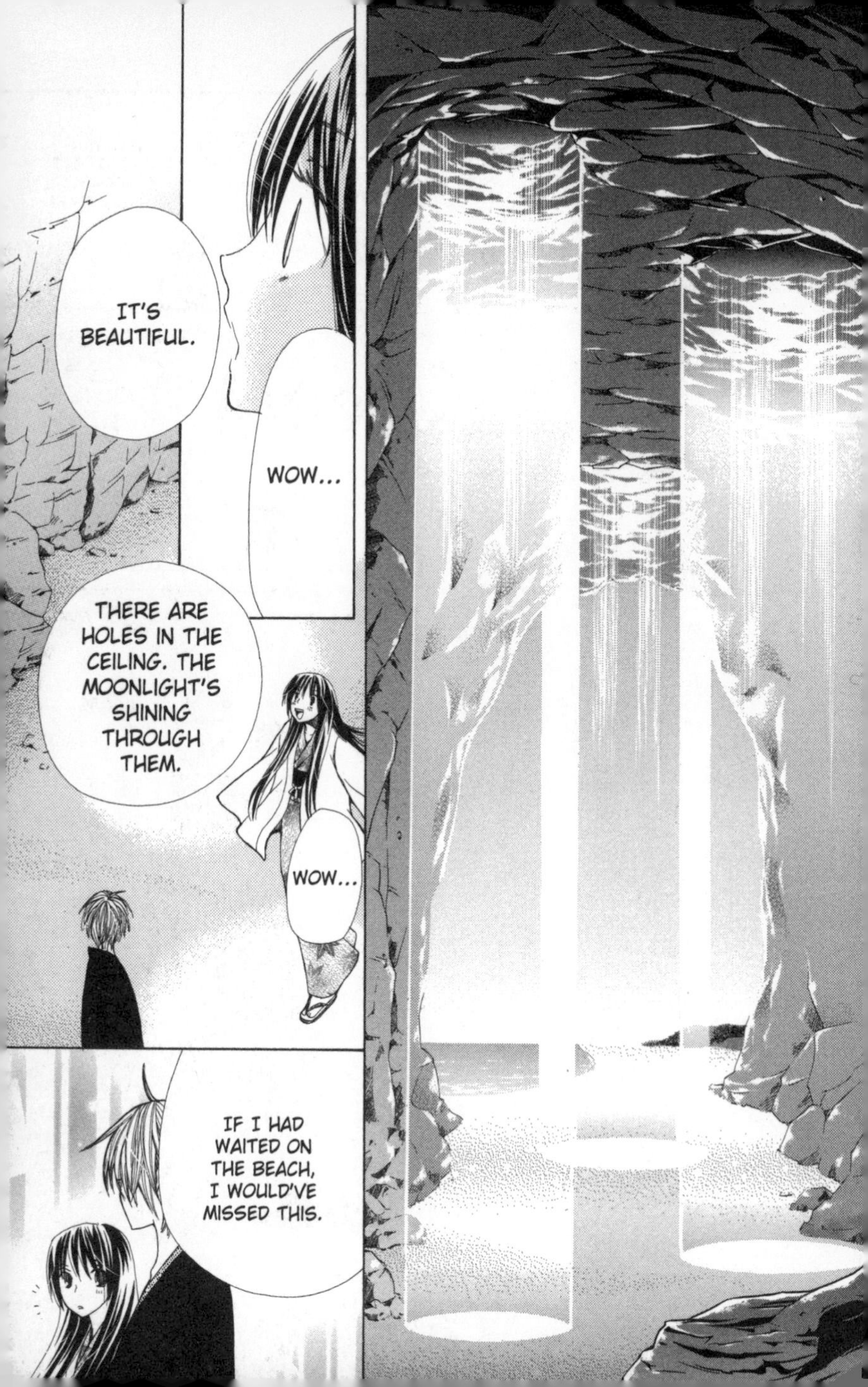
WOW...
IT'S BEAUTIFUL.
WOW...
THERE ARE HOLES IN THE CEILING. THE MOONLIGHT'S SHINING THROUGH THEM.
IF I HAD WAITED ON THE BEACH, I WOULD'VE MISSED THIS.

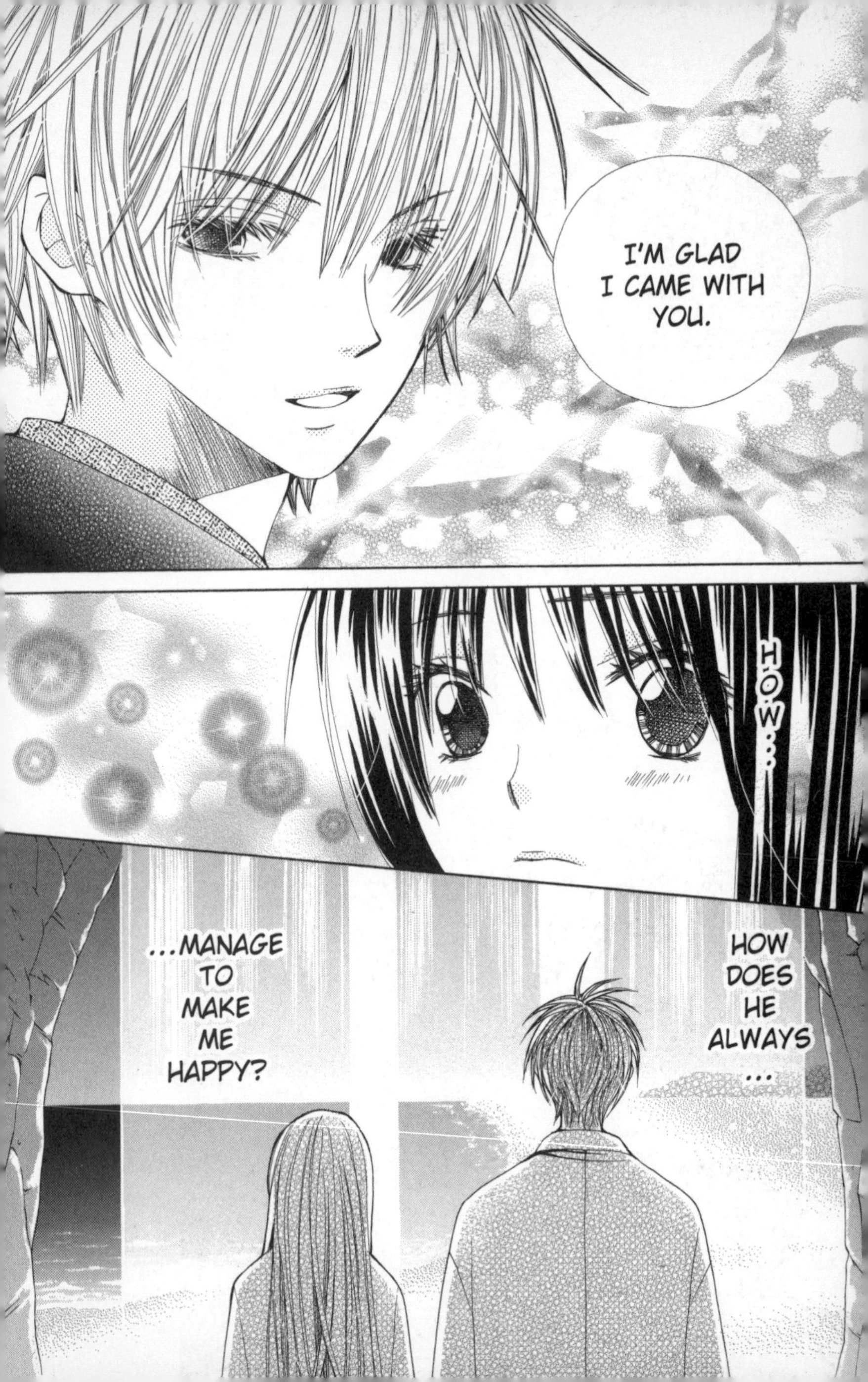
I'M GLAD I CAME WITH YOU.
HOW...
HOW DOES HE ALWAYS ...
...MANAGE TO MAKE ME HAPPY?

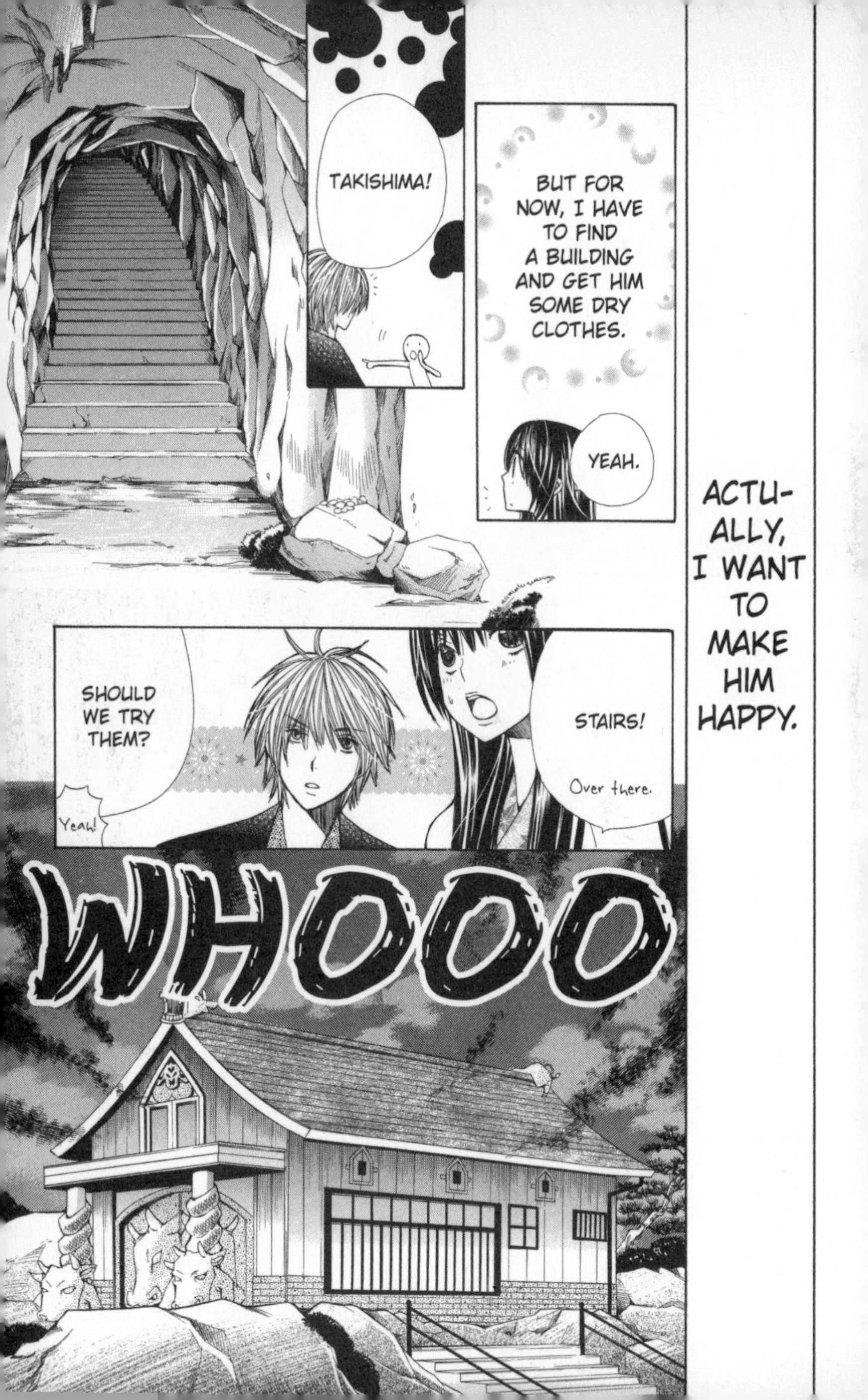
ACTU-
ALLY,
I WANT
TO
MAKE
HIM
HAPPY.
TAKISHIMA!
BUT FOR NOW, I HAVE TO FIND A BUILDING AND GET HIM SOME DRY CLOTHES.
YEAH.
STAIRS!
Over there.
SHOULD WE TRY THEM?
Yeah!
WHOOO

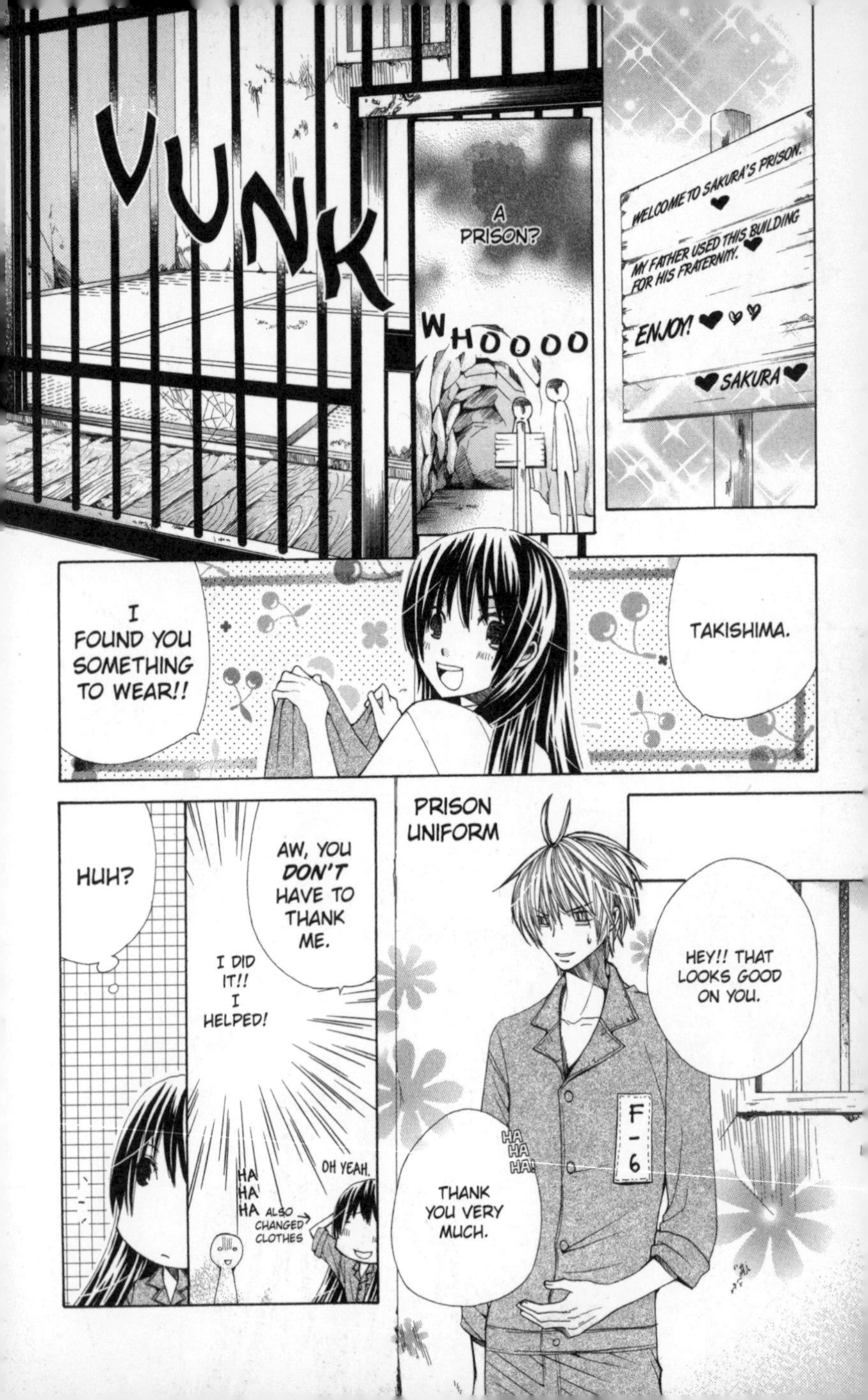
WELCOME TO SAKURA'S PRISON.
MY FATHER USED THIS BUILDING FOR HIS FRATERNITY.
ENJOY!
SAKURA
A PRISON?
WHOOOO
VUNK
TAKISHIMA.
I FOUND YOU SOMETHING TO WEAR!!
PRISON UNIFORM
HEY!! THAT LOOKS GOOD ON YOU.
F-6
HA HA HA!
THANK YOU VERY MUCH.
AW, YOU DON'T HAVE TO THANK ME.
HUH?
I DID IT!! I HELPED!
OH YEAH.
HA HA HA
ALSO CHANGED CLOTHES

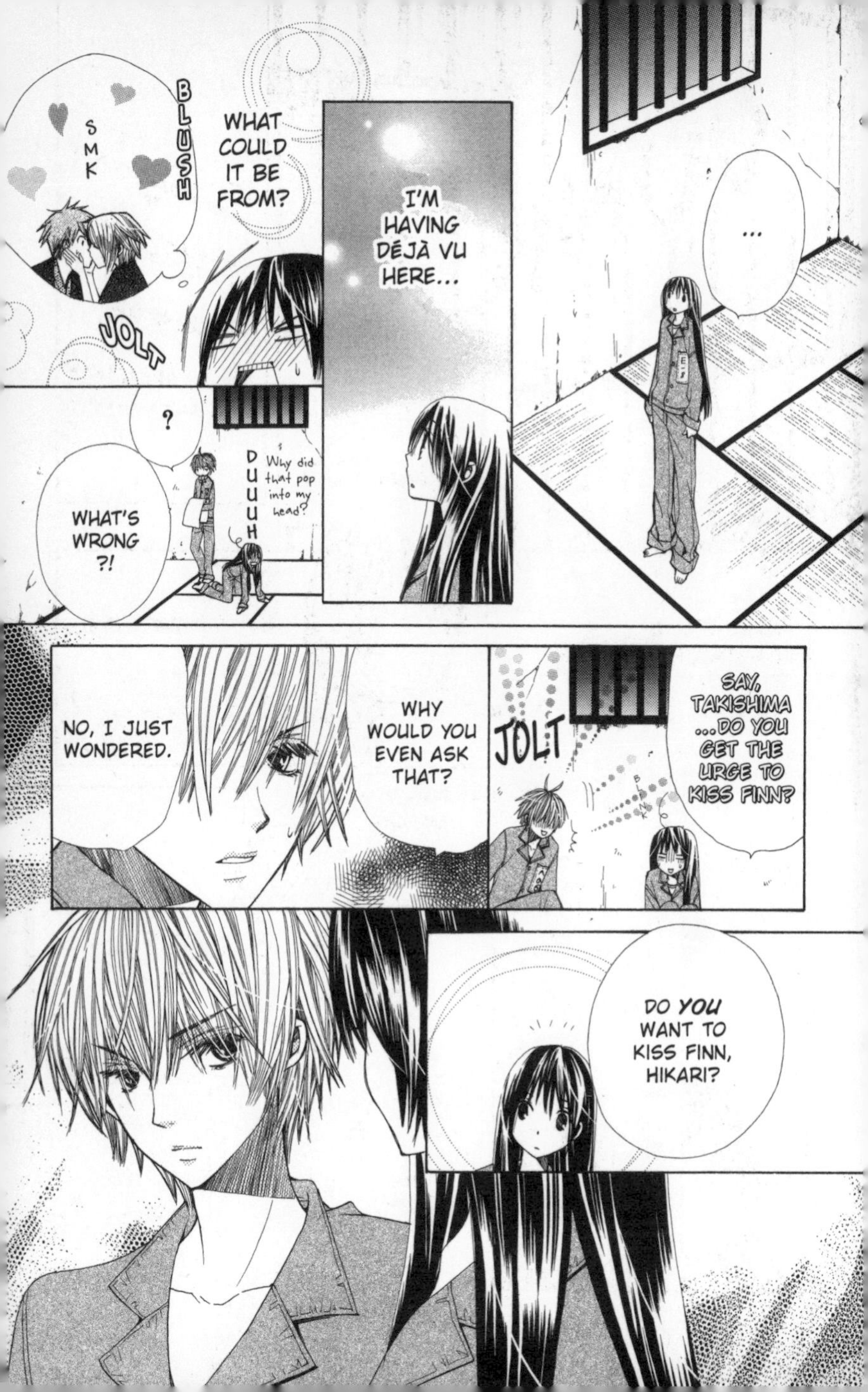
...
I'M HAVING DÉJÀ VU HERE...
WHAT COULD IT BE FROM?
BLUSH
SMK
JOLT
?
WHAT'S WRONG ?!
DUUUH
Why did that pop into my head?
SAY, TAKISHIMA ...DO YOU GET THE URGE TO KISS FINN?
JOLT
BLINK
WHY WOULD YOU EVEN ASK THAT?
NO, I JUST WONDERED.
DO *YOU* WANT TO KISS FINN, HIKARI?

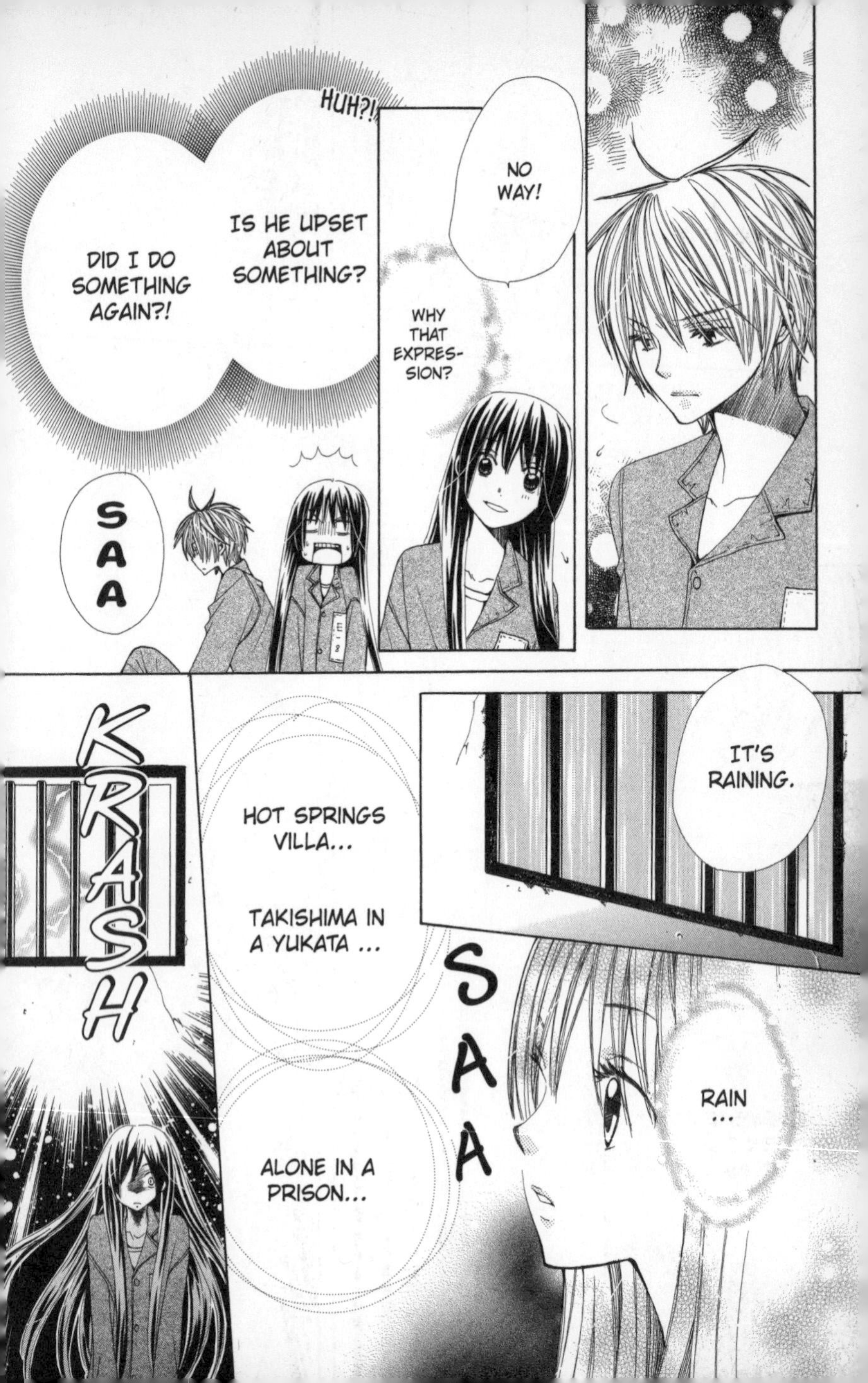
NO WAY!
WHY THAT EXPRES-SION?
HUH?!
IS HE UPSET ABOUT SOMETHING?
DID I DO SOMETHING AGAIN?!
SAA
IT'S RAINING.
SAA
RAIN ...
HOT SPRINGS VILLA...
TAKISHIMA IN A YUKATA ...
ALONE IN A PRISON...
KRASH

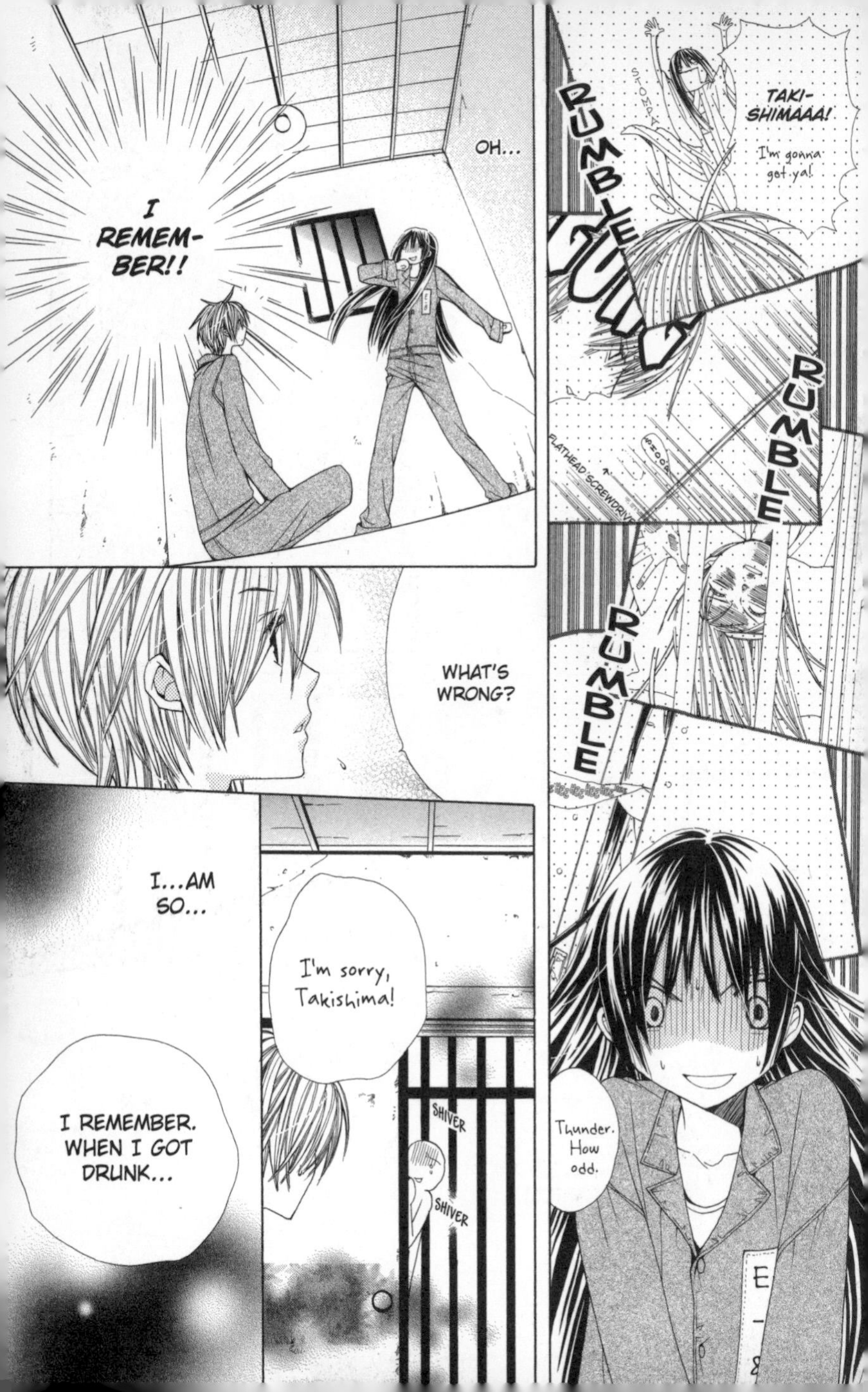
STOMP
TAKI-SHIMAAA!
I'm gonna get ya!
RUMBLE
RUMBLE
FLATHEAD SCREWDRIVE
RUMBLE
Thunder. How odd.
OH...
I REMEMBER!!
WHAT'S WRONG?
I'm sorry, Takishima!
SHIVER
SHIVER
I...AM SO...
I REMEMBER. WHEN I GOT DRUNK...

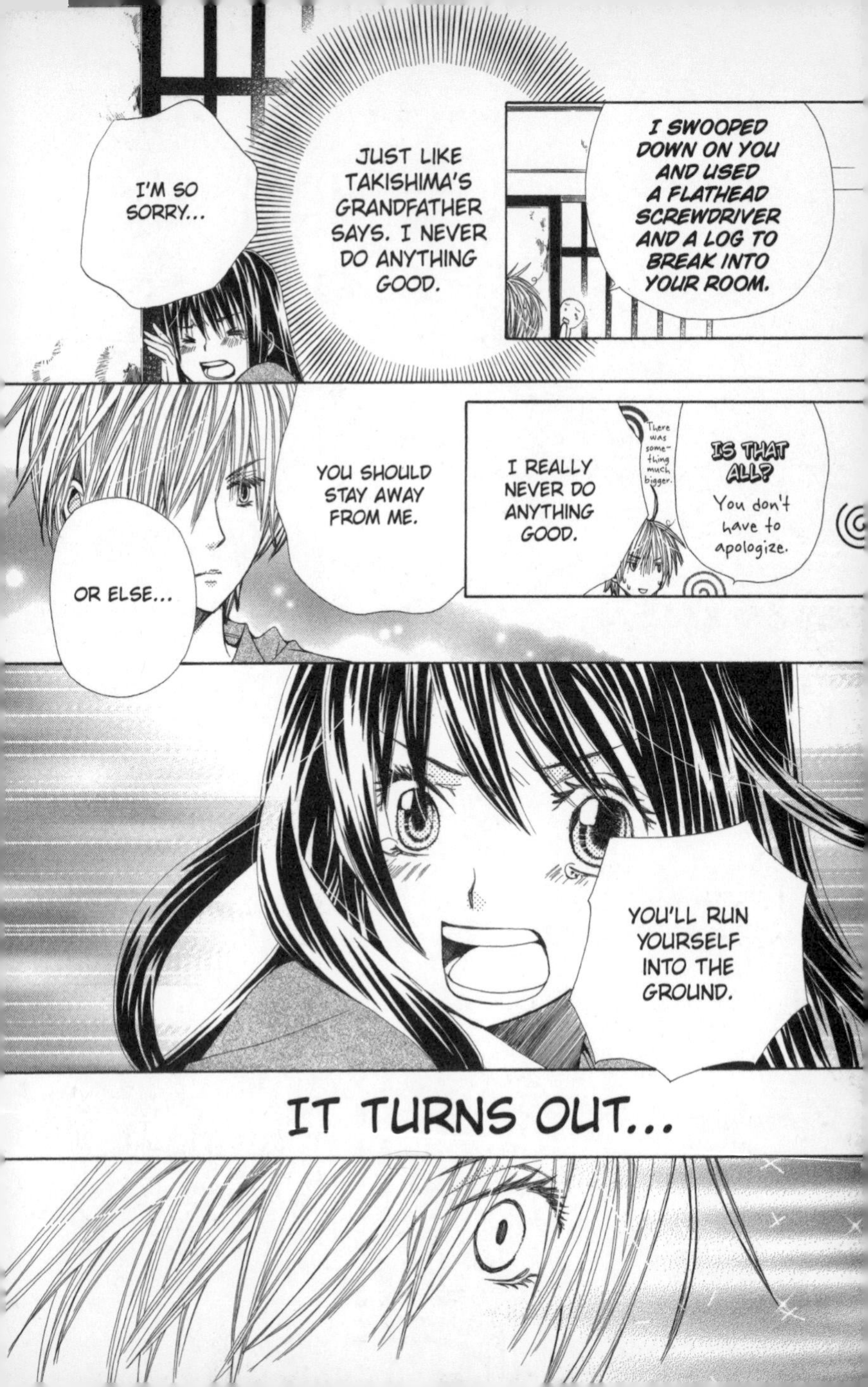
I SWOOPED DOWN ON YOU AND USED A FLATHEAD SCREWDRIVER AND A LOG TO BREAK INTO YOUR ROOM.
JUST LIKE TAKISHIMA'S GRANDFATHER SAYS. I NEVER DO ANYTHING GOOD.
I'M SO SORRY...
IS THAT ALL? You don't have to apologize.
There was something much bigger.
I REALLY NEVER DO ANYTHING GOOD.
YOU SHOULD STAY AWAY FROM ME.
OR ELSE...
YOU'LL RUN YOURSELF INTO THE GROUND.
IT TURNS OUT...

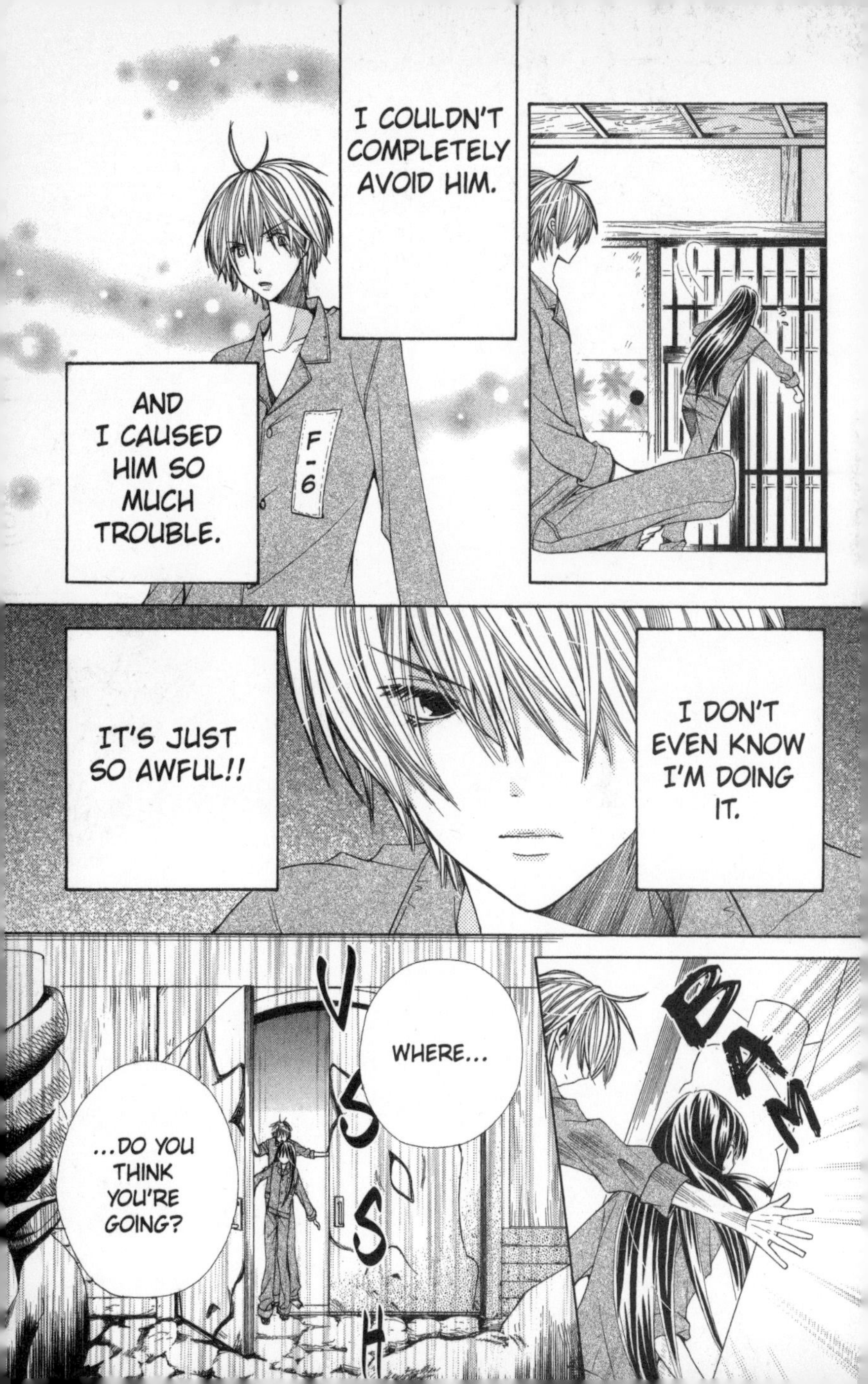
I COULDN'T COMPLETELY AVOID HIM.
AND I CAUSED HIM SO MUCH TROUBLE.
I DON'T EVEN KNOW I'M DOING IT.
IT'S JUST SO AWFUL!!
BAM
WHERE...
...DO YOU THINK YOU'RE GOING?

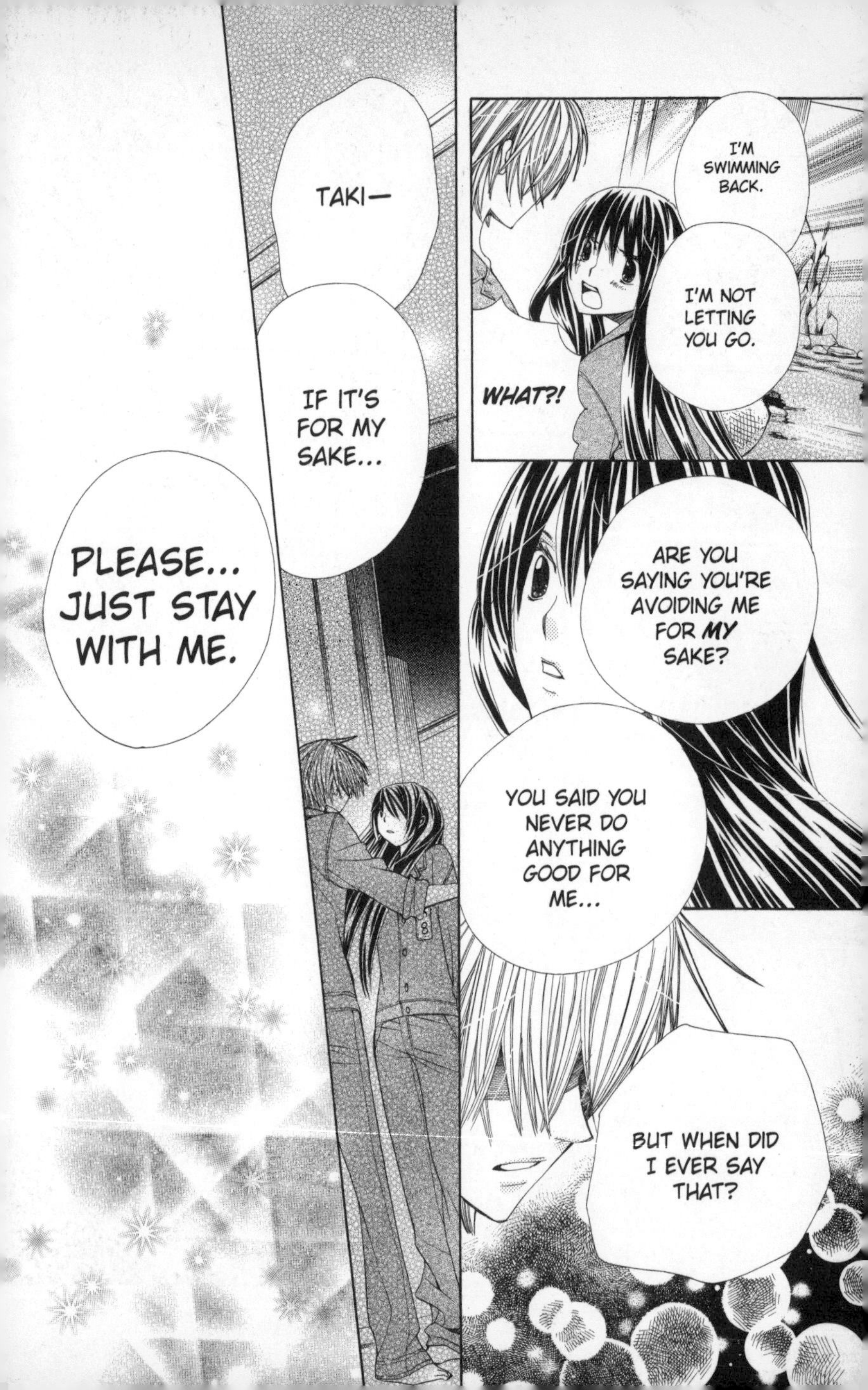
I'M SWIMMING BACK.
I'M NOT LETTING YOU GO.
WHAT?!
ARE YOU SAYING YOU'RE AVOIDING ME FOR *MY* SAKE?
YOU SAID YOU NEVER DO ANYTHING GOOD FOR ME...
BUT WHEN DID I EVER SAY THAT?
TAKI—
IF IT'S FOR MY SAKE...
PLEASE... JUST STAY WITH ME.

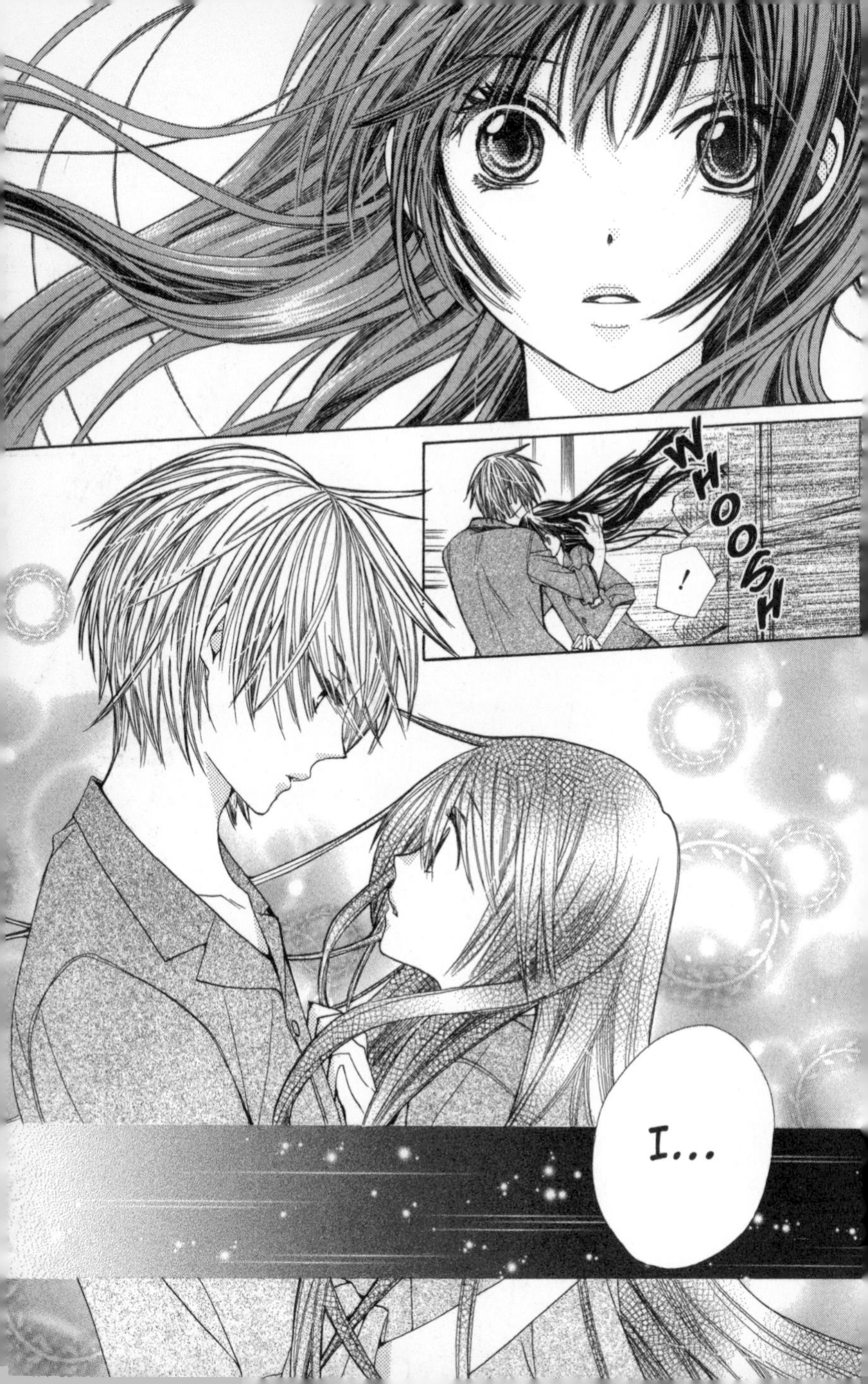
WHOOSH
!
I...

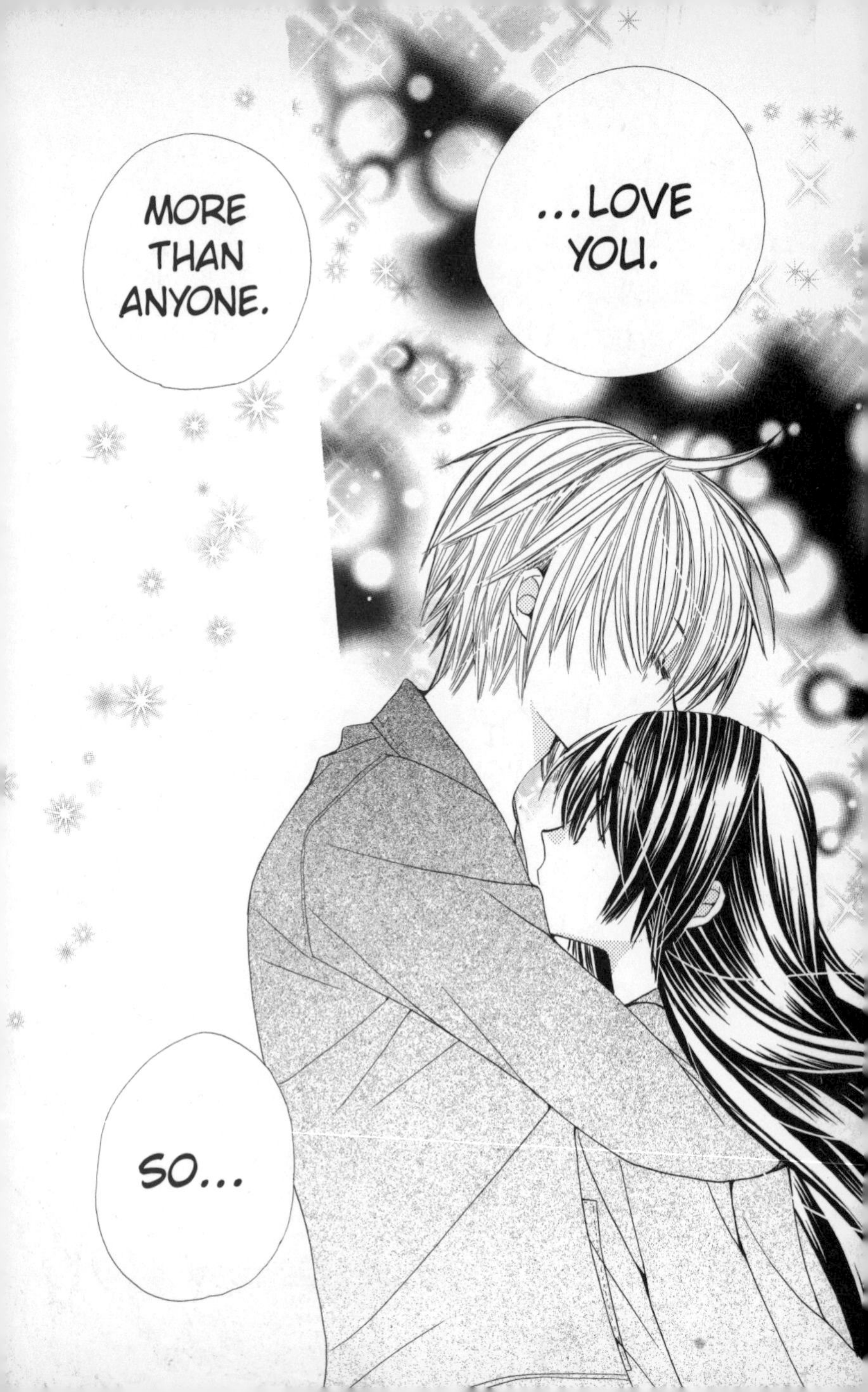
...LOVE YOU.
MORE THAN ANYONE.
SO...

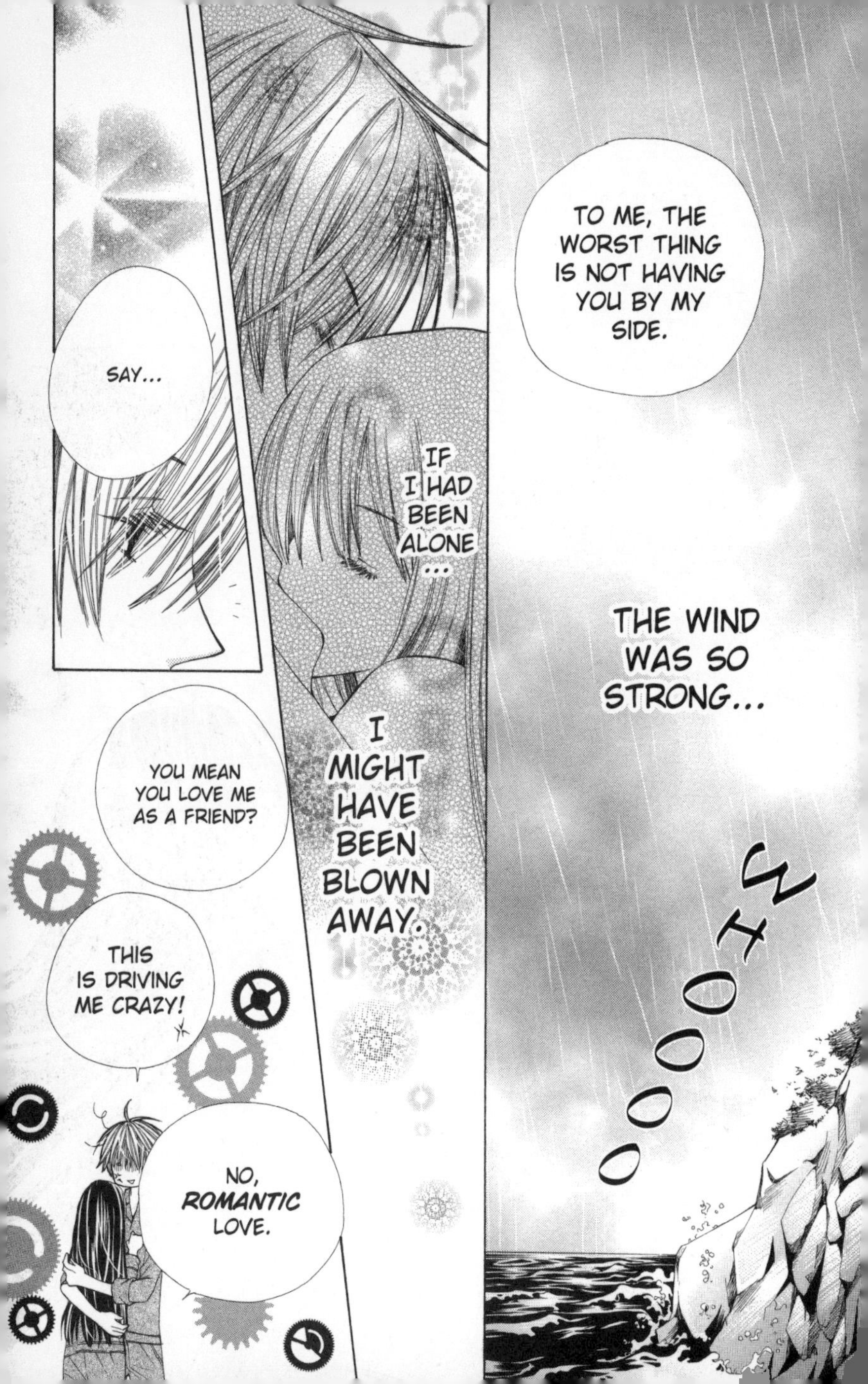
TO ME, THE WORST THING IS NOT HAVING YOU BY MY SIDE.
THE WIND WAS SO STRONG...
WHOOOOO
IF I HAD BEEN ALONE...
I MIGHT HAVE BEEN BLOWN AWAY.
SAY...
YOU MEAN YOU LOVE ME AS A FRIEND?
THIS IS DRIVING ME CRAZY!
NO, ROMANTIC LOVE.

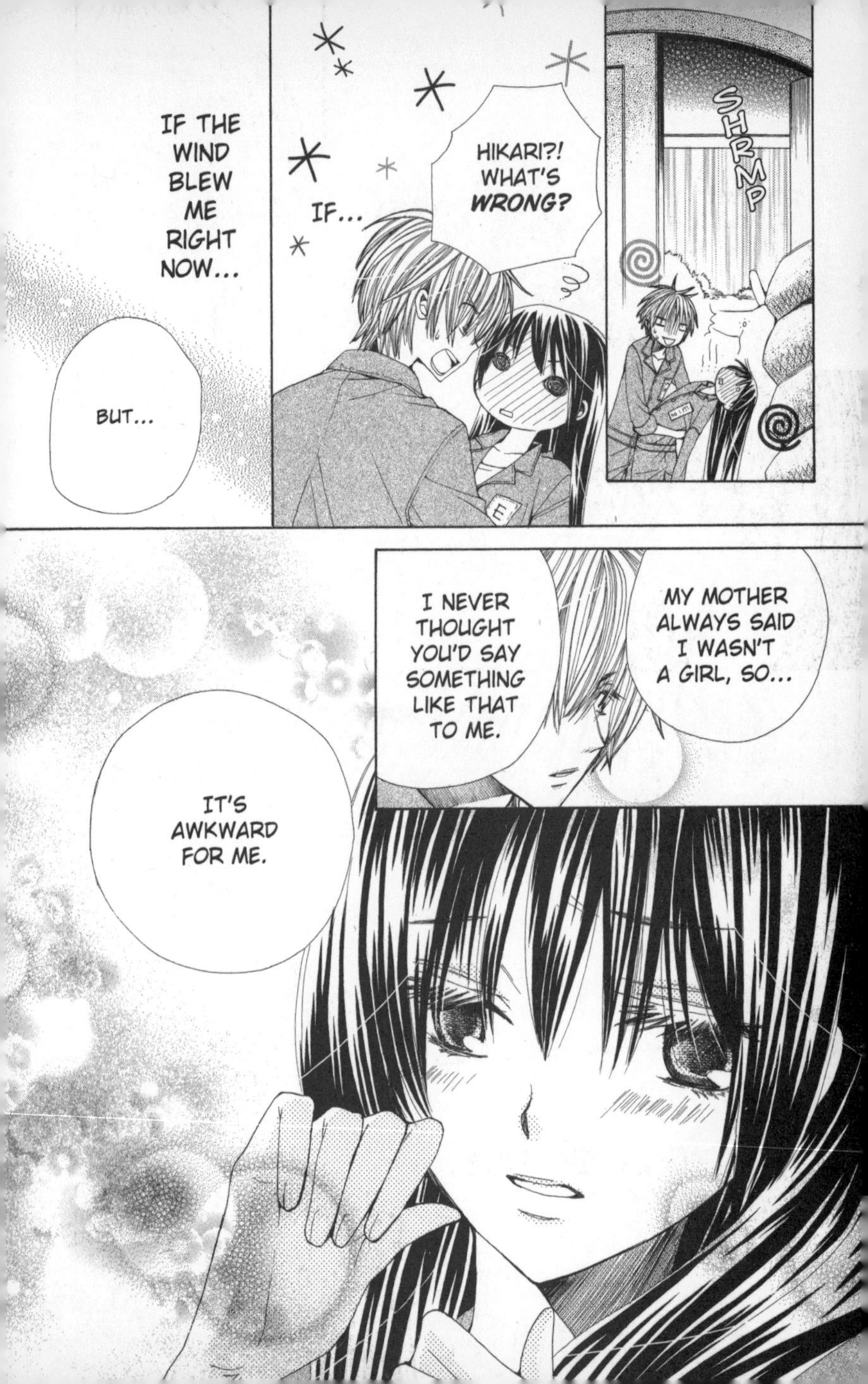
SHRMP
HIKARI?! WHAT'S **WRONG?**
IF...
IF THE WIND BLEW ME RIGHT NOW...
BUT...
MY MOTHER ALWAYS SAID I WASN'T A GIRL, SO...
I NEVER THOUGHT YOU'D SAY SOMETHING LIKE THAT TO ME.
IT'S AWKWARD FOR ME.

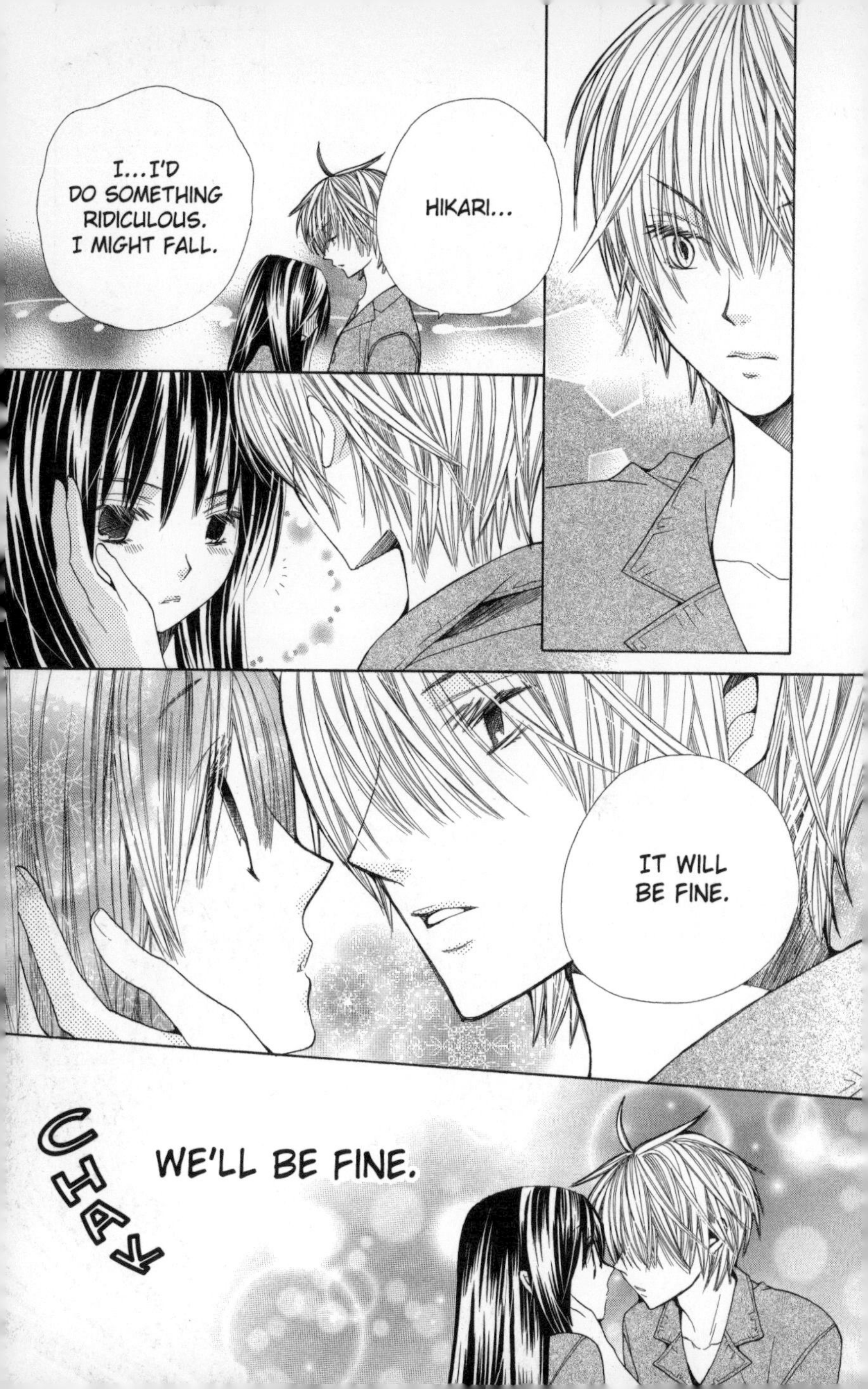
HIKARI...
I...I'D DO SOMETHING RIDICULOUS. I MIGHT FALL.
IT WILL BE FINE.
WE'LL BE FINE.
CHAY

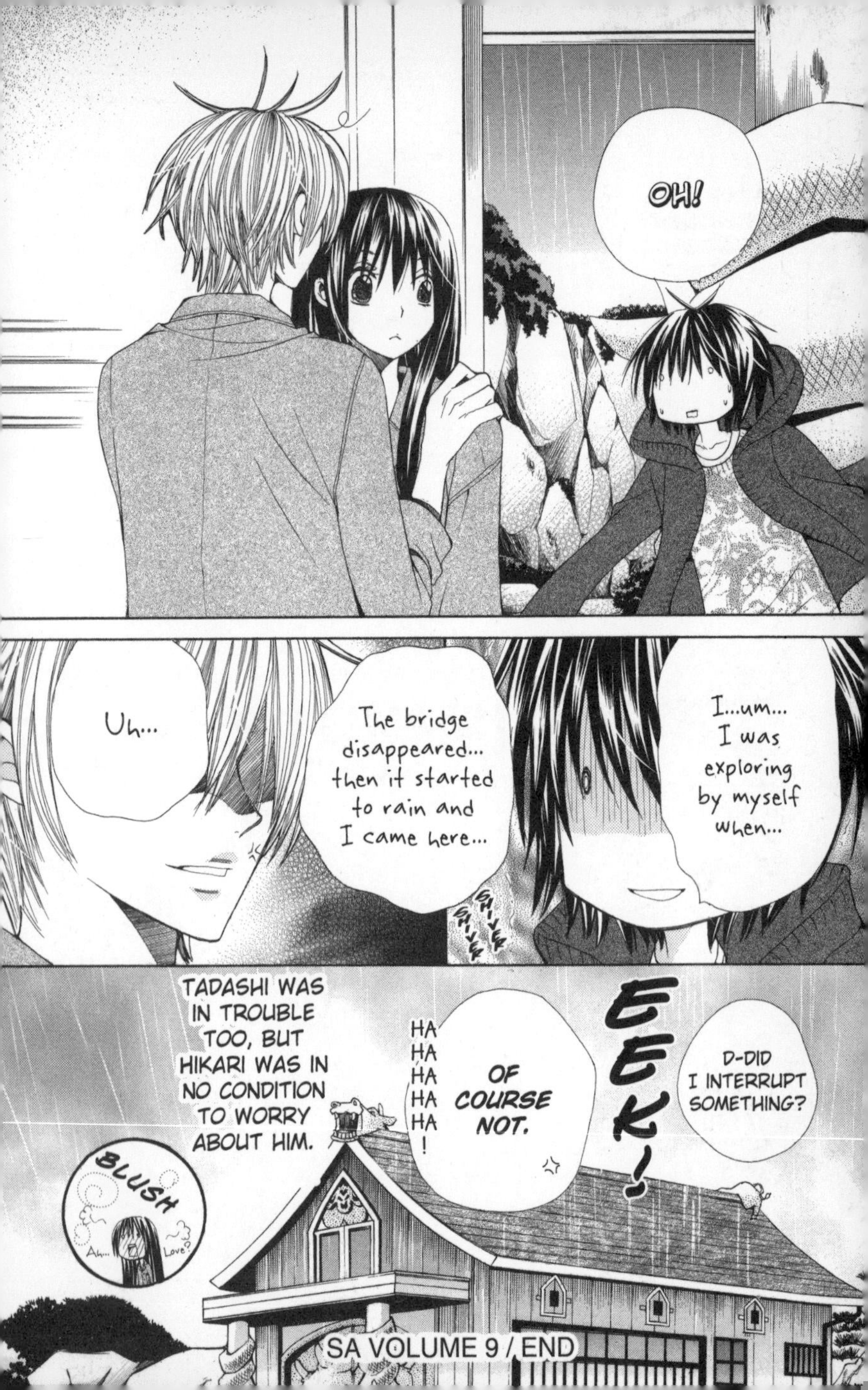
OH!
I...um... I was exploring by myself when...
The bridge disappeared... then it started to rain and I came here...
SHIVER SHIVER
Uh...
D-DID I INTERRUPT SOMETHING?
EEK!
OF COURSE NOT.
HA HA HA HA HA!
TADASHI WAS IN TROUBLE TOO, BUT HIKARI WAS IN NO CONDITION TO WORRY ABOUT HIM.
BLUSH
Ah...
Love?

SA VOLUME 9 / END

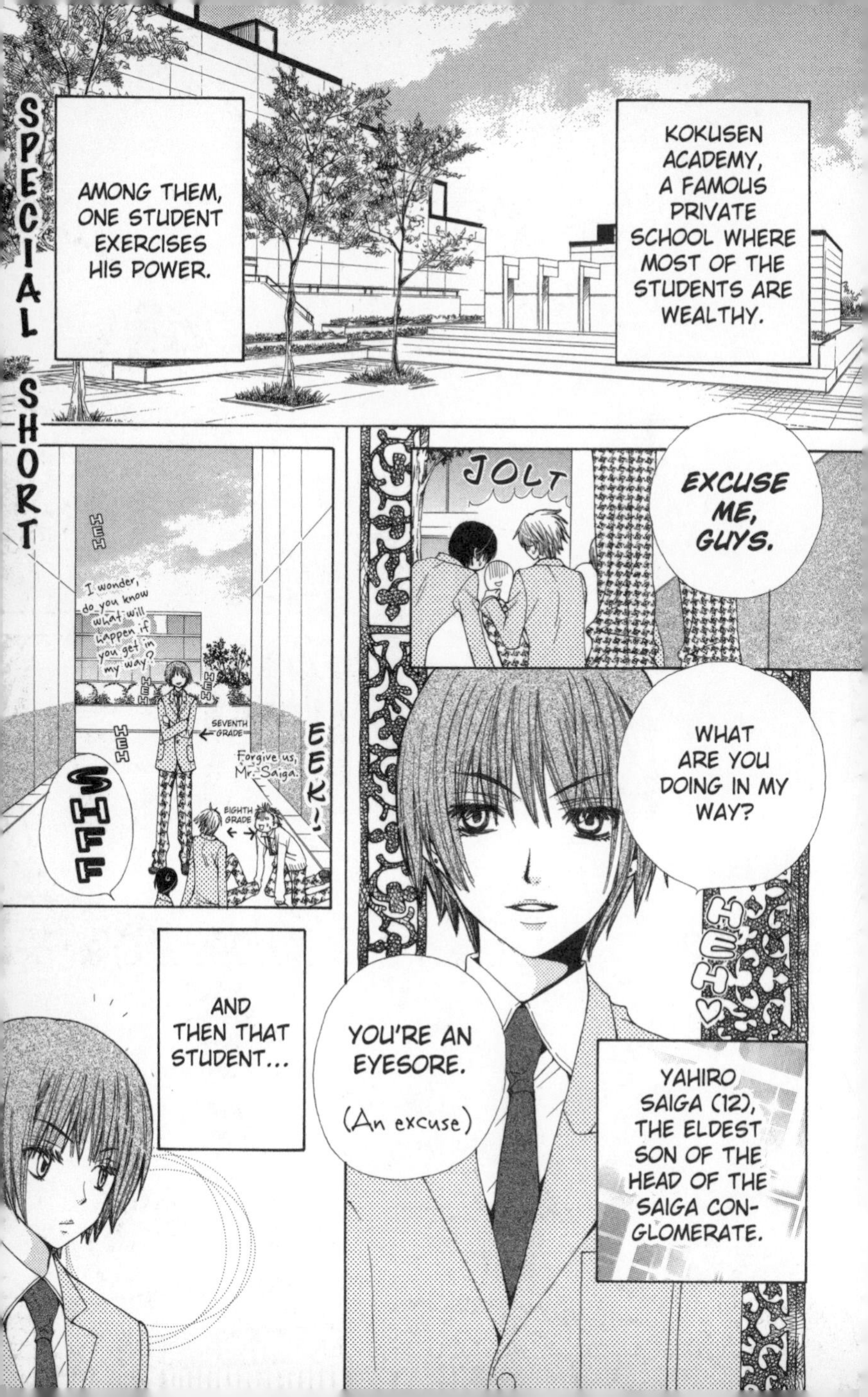
SPECIAL SHORT
KOKUSEN ACADEMY, A FAMOUS PRIVATE SCHOOL WHERE MOST OF THE STUDENTS ARE WEALTHY.
AMONG THEM, ONE STUDENT EXERCISES HIS POWER.
JOLT
EXCUSE ME, GUYS.
HEH
I wonder, do you know what will happen if you get in my way?
HEH HEH
HEH
SEVENTH GRADE
EEK!
Forgive us, Mr. Saiga.
EIGHTH GRADE
SHFF
WHAT ARE YOU DOING IN MY WAY?
HEH HEH
YOU'RE AN EYESORE.
(An excuse)
YAHIRO SAIGA (12), THE ELDEST SON OF THE HEAD OF THE SAIGA CON-GLOMERATE.
AND THEN THAT STUDENT...

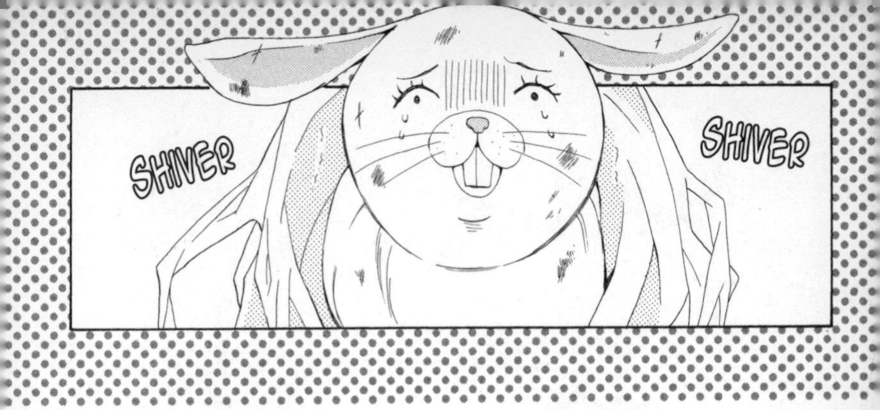
SHIVER
SHIVER
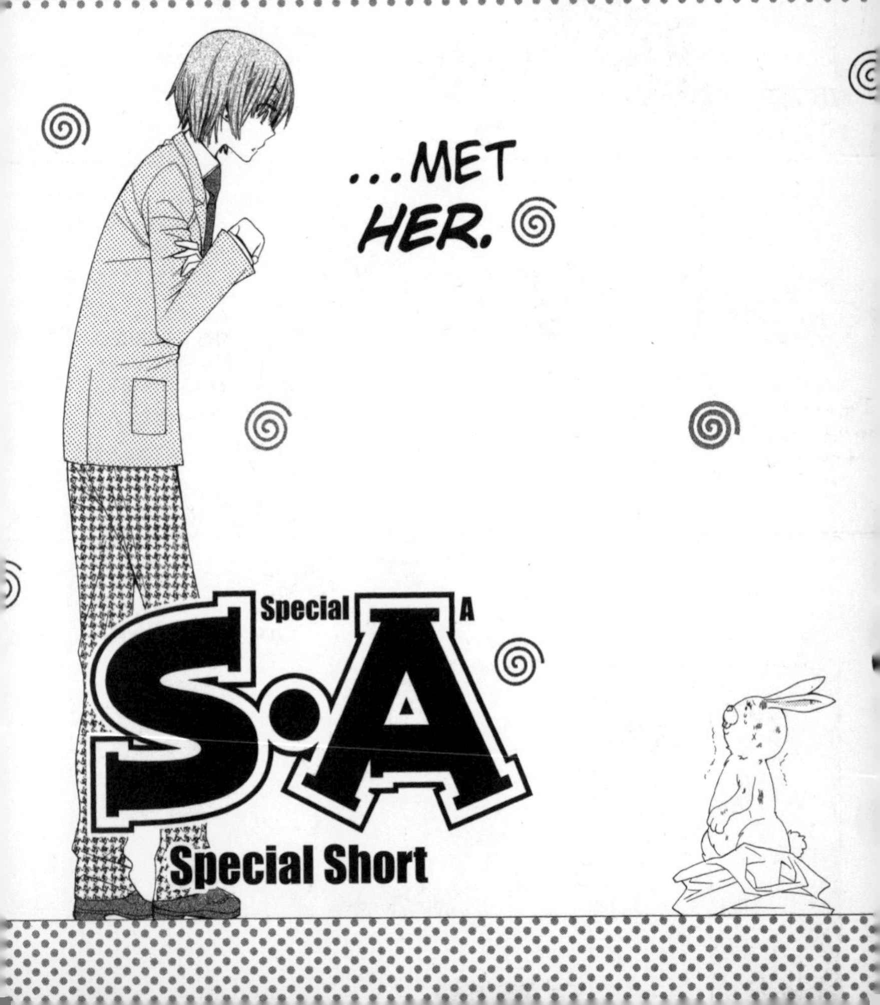
...MET HER.
Special A
S.A
Special Short

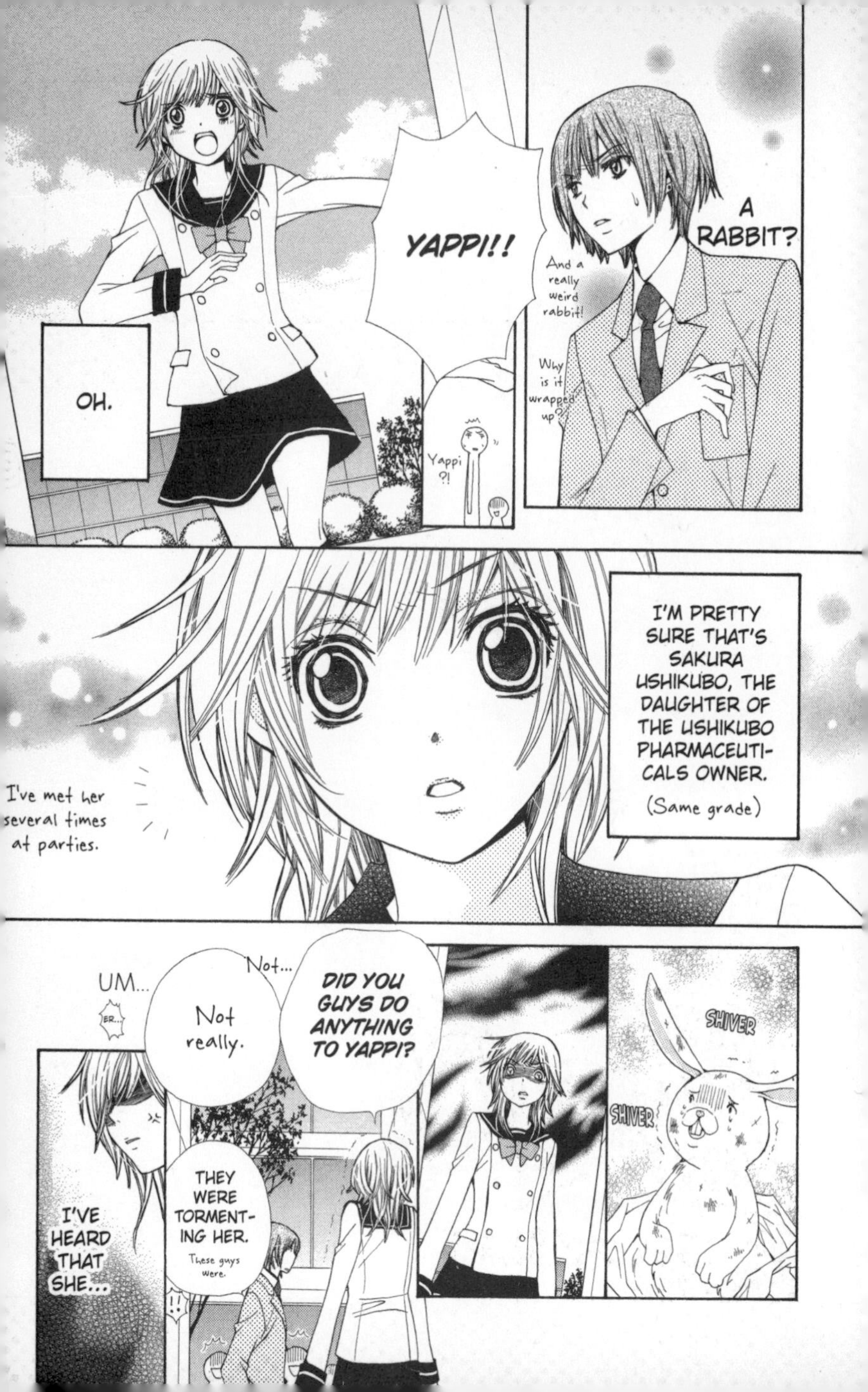
A RABBIT?
And a really weird rabbit!
Why is it wrapped up?
YAPPI!!
Yappi ?!
OH.
I'M PRETTY SURE THAT'S SAKURA USHIKUBO, THE DAUGHTER OF THE USHIKUBO PHARMACEUTI-CALS OWNER.
(Same grade)
I've met her several times at parties.
SHIVER
SHIVER
DID YOU GUYS DO ANYTHING TO YAPPI?
Not...
Not really.
UM...
ER...
THEY WERE TORMENT-ING HER.
These guys were.
I'VE HEARD THAT SHE...
!!

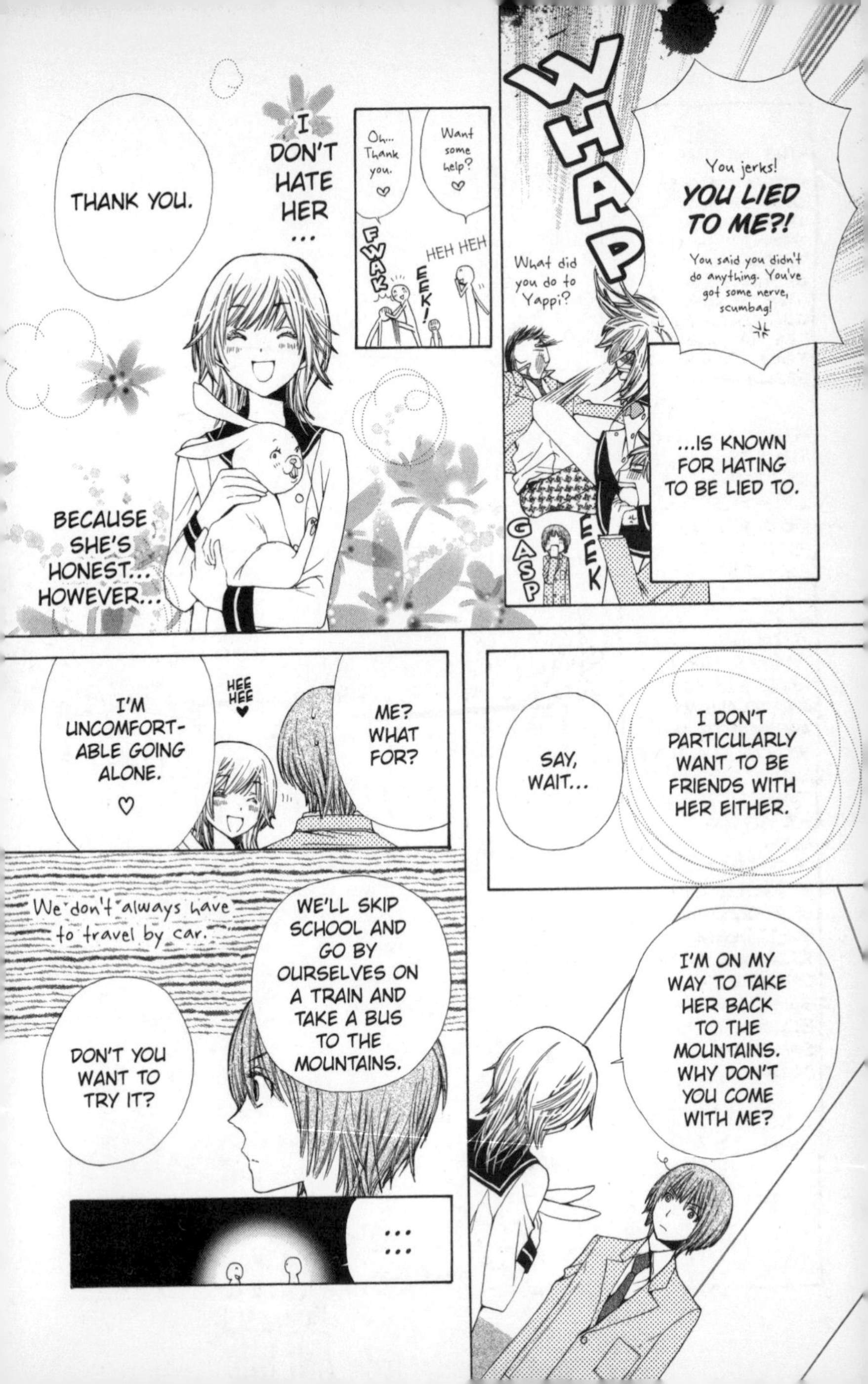
THANK YOU.
I DON'T HATE HER...
BECAUSE SHE'S HONEST... HOWEVER...
Want some help? ♡
Oh... Thank you. ♡
FWAK
EEK!
HEH HEH
WHAP
What did you do to Yappi?
You jerks! YOU LIED TO ME?! You said you didn't do anything. You've got some nerve, scumbag!
GASP
EEK
...IS KNOWN FOR HATING TO BE LIED TO.
I DON'T PARTICULARLY WANT TO BE FRIENDS WITH HER EITHER.
SAY, WAIT...
I'M ON MY WAY TO TAKE HER BACK TO THE MOUNTAINS. WHY DON'T YOU COME WITH ME?
ME? WHAT FOR?
HEE HEE ♥
I'M UNCOMFORTABLE GOING ALONE. ♡
WE'LL SKIP SCHOOL AND GO BY OURSELVES ON A TRAIN AND TAKE A BUS TO THE MOUNTAINS.
DON'T YOU WANT TO TRY IT?
We don't always have to travel by car.
... ...

7

•THIS AND THAT•

•THIS IS THE LAST QUARTER PAGE. THANK YOU FOR STAYING WITH ME THROUGHOUT ALL 13 OF THEM!!

•THE THEME FOR THE QUARTER PAGES THIS TIME WAS "KIMONO." THANK YOU FOR THE REQUEST!

LOVE IT. LOVE IT

•THANK YOU FOR THE BONUS PAGE IDEAS TOO.
I CHANGED THE IDEAS YOU SENT QUITE A BIT.
I'M SORRY...
I WILL TRY HARDER.

•NOW, NOW.
TO EVERYONE WHO READ THIS FAR AND TO ALL MY ASSISTANTS AND MY EDITOR AND MY FAMILY AND MY FRIENDS, THANK YOU SO VERY MUCH!
LET'S MEET AGAIN IN VOLUME 10!!

✿IF YOU'D LIKE, PLEASE SEND US YOUR THOUGHTS.✿
C/O VIZ MEDIA
S.A EDITOR
P.O. BOX 77010
SAN FRANCISCO,
CA 94107

With all...
...my heart.

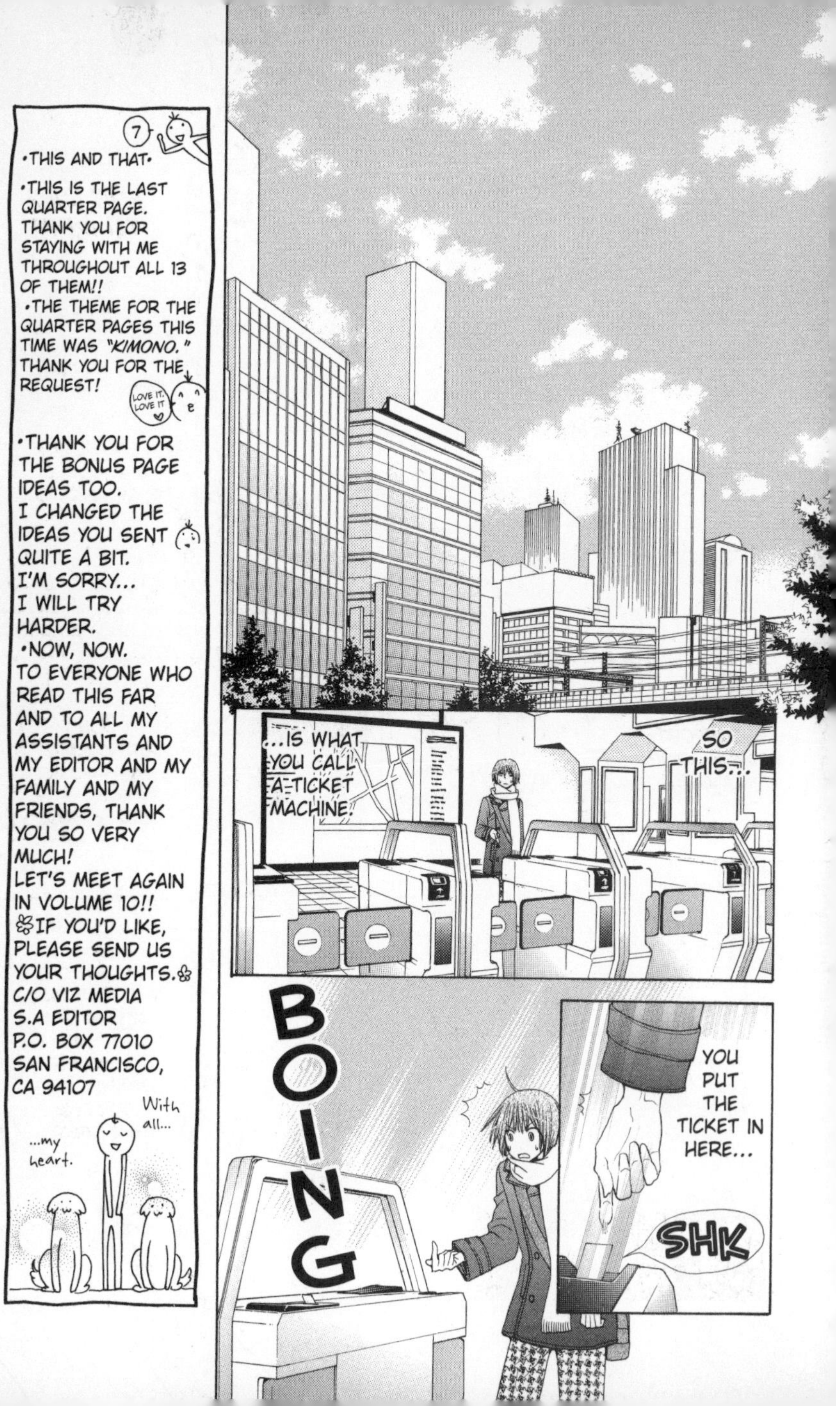
SO THIS...
...IS WHAT YOU CALL A TICKET MACHINE.
YOU PUT THE TICKET IN HERE...
SHK
BOING

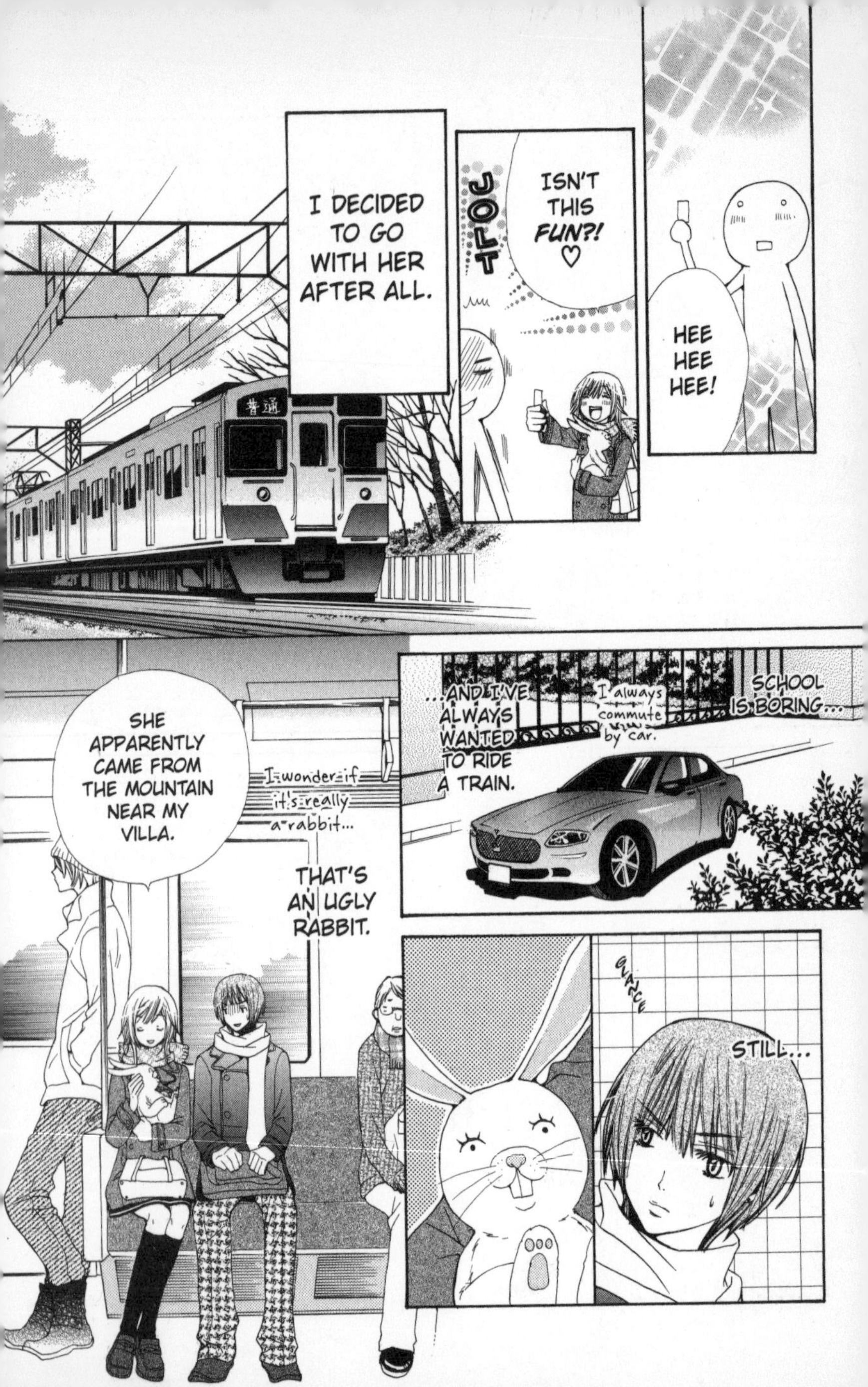
HEE HEE HEE!
ISN'T THIS FUN?! ♡
JOLT
I DECIDED TO GO WITH HER AFTER ALL.
SCHOOL IS BORING...
I always commute by car.
...AND I'VE ALWAYS WANTED TO RIDE A TRAIN.
THAT'S AN UGLY RABBIT.
I wonder if it's really a rabbit...
SHE APPARENTLY CAME FROM THE MOUNTAIN NEAR MY VILLA.
GLANCE
STILL...

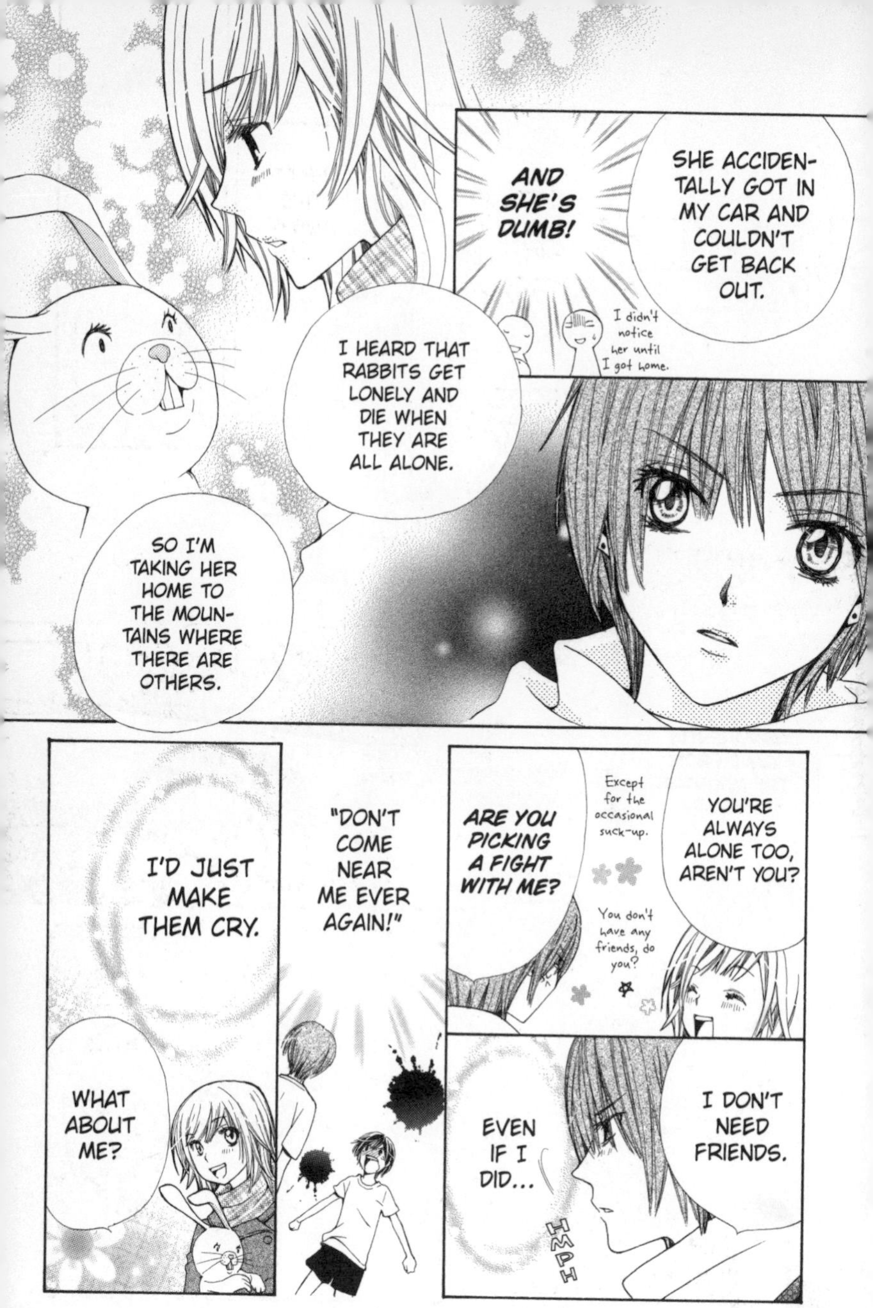
SHE ACCIDENTALLY GOT IN MY CAR AND COULDN'T GET BACK OUT.
AND SHE'S DUMB!
I didn't notice her until I got home.
I HEARD THAT RABBITS GET LONELY AND DIE WHEN THEY ARE ALL ALONE.
SO I'M TAKING HER HOME TO THE MOUNTAINS WHERE THERE ARE OTHERS.
YOU'RE ALWAYS ALONE TOO, AREN'T YOU?
Except for the occasional suck-up.
You don't have any friends, do you?
ARE YOU PICKING A FIGHT WITH ME?
I DON'T NEED FRIENDS.
EVEN IF I DID...
HMPH
I'D JUST MAKE THEM CRY.
"DON'T COME NEAR ME EVER AGAIN!"
WHAT ABOUT ME?

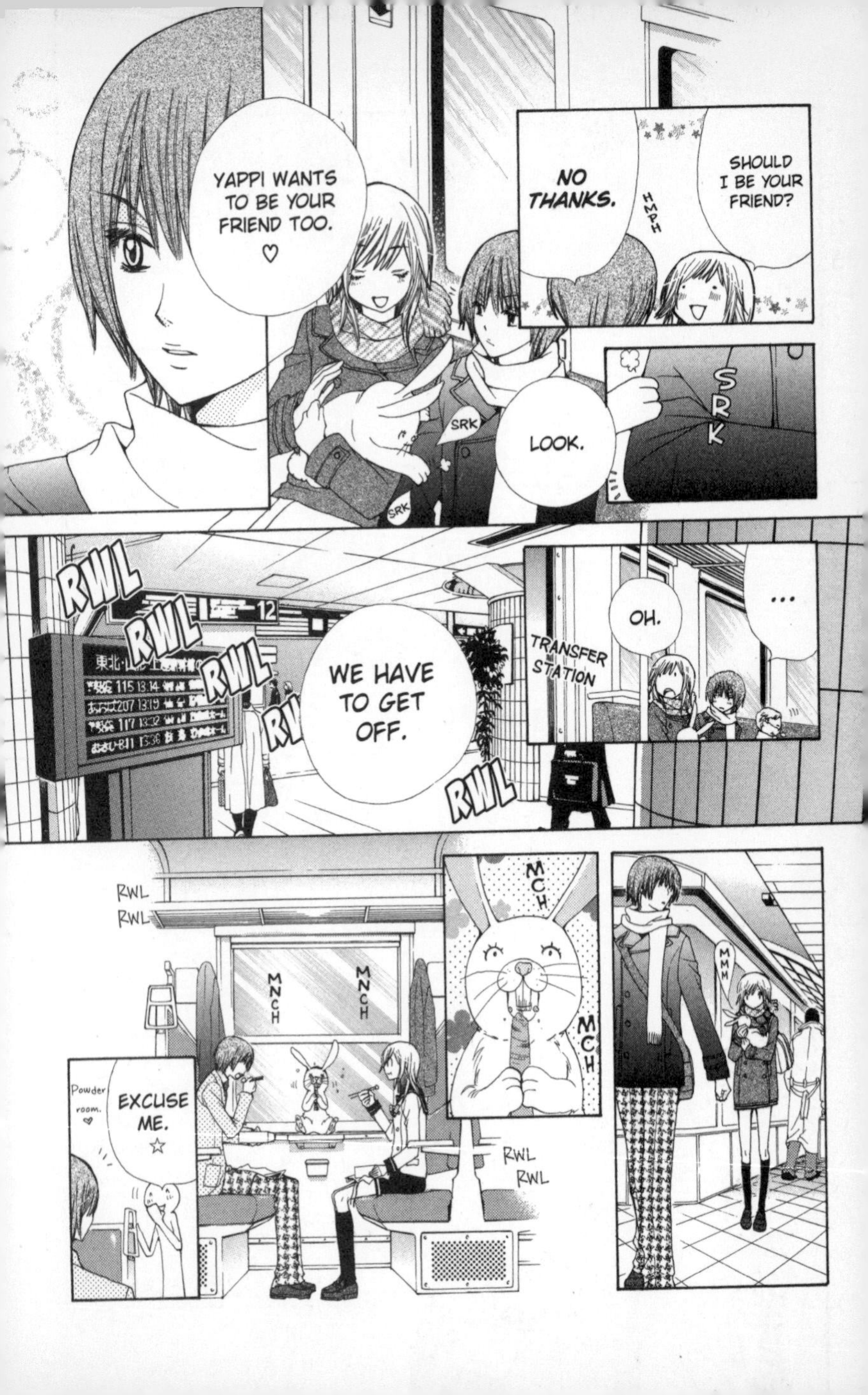
SHOULD I BE YOUR FRIEND?
HMPH
NO THANKS.
SRK
LOOK.
YAPPI WANTS TO BE YOUR FRIEND TOO. ♡
SRK
SRK
...
OH.
TRANSFER STATION
WE HAVE TO GET OFF.
RWL
RWL
RWL
RWL
RWL
MMM
MCH
MCH
RWL
RWL
MNCH
MNCH
RWL
RWL
EXCUSE ME. ☆
Powder room. ♡

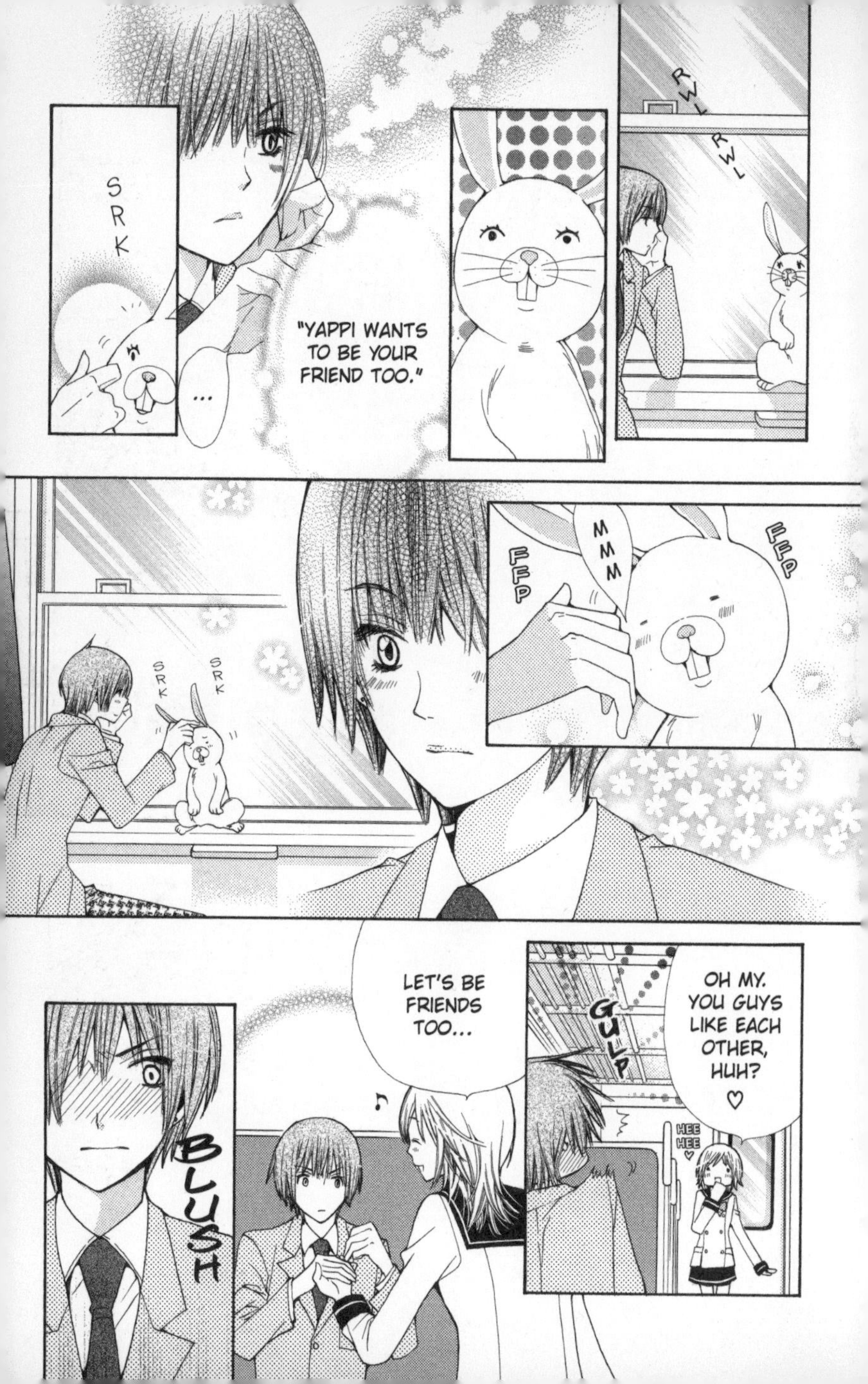
RWL RWL
"YAPPI WANTS TO BE YOUR FRIEND TOO."
...
SRK
FFP
MMM
FFP
SRK SRK
OH MY. YOU GUYS LIKE EACH OTHER, HUH? ♡
GULP
HEE HEE ♡
LET'S BE FRIENDS TOO...
BLUSH

OH... GIMME A BREAK!

WHAP

OH.

8 | 15
9 |
10 |
11 |
12 |
13 |
14 |
15 |
16 |
17 |
18 |
19 | 10

...

TWO BUSES PER DAY...
NEXT BUS IN 3 HOURS.

DON'T APOLO-GIZE.

I'M SORRY.

IT'S MY FAULT.

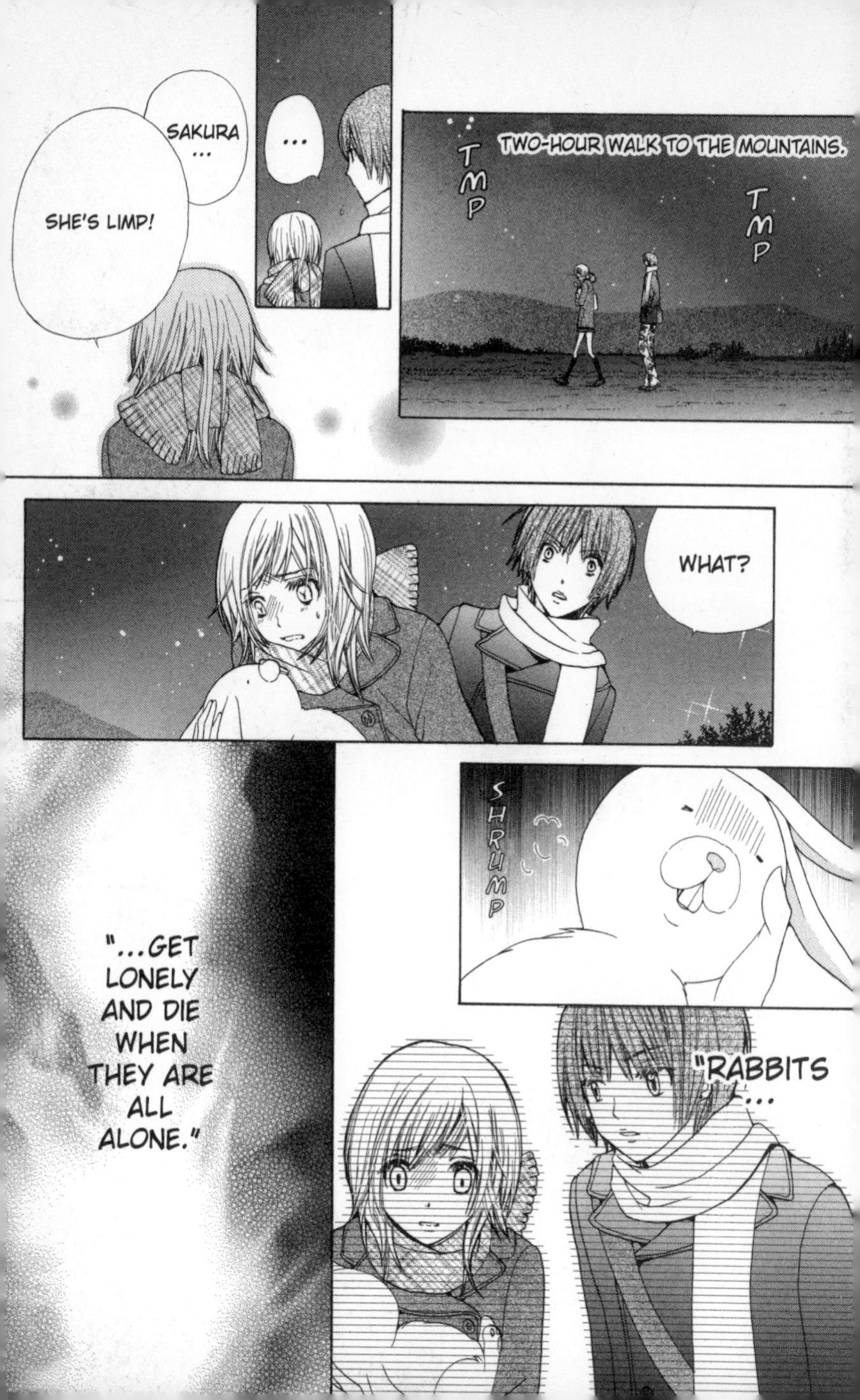
TWO-HOUR WALK TO THE MOUNTAINS.
TMP
TMP
...
SAKURA ...
SHE'S LIMP!
WHAT?
SHRUMP
"RABBITS ...
"...GET LONELY AND DIE WHEN THEY ARE ALL ALONE."

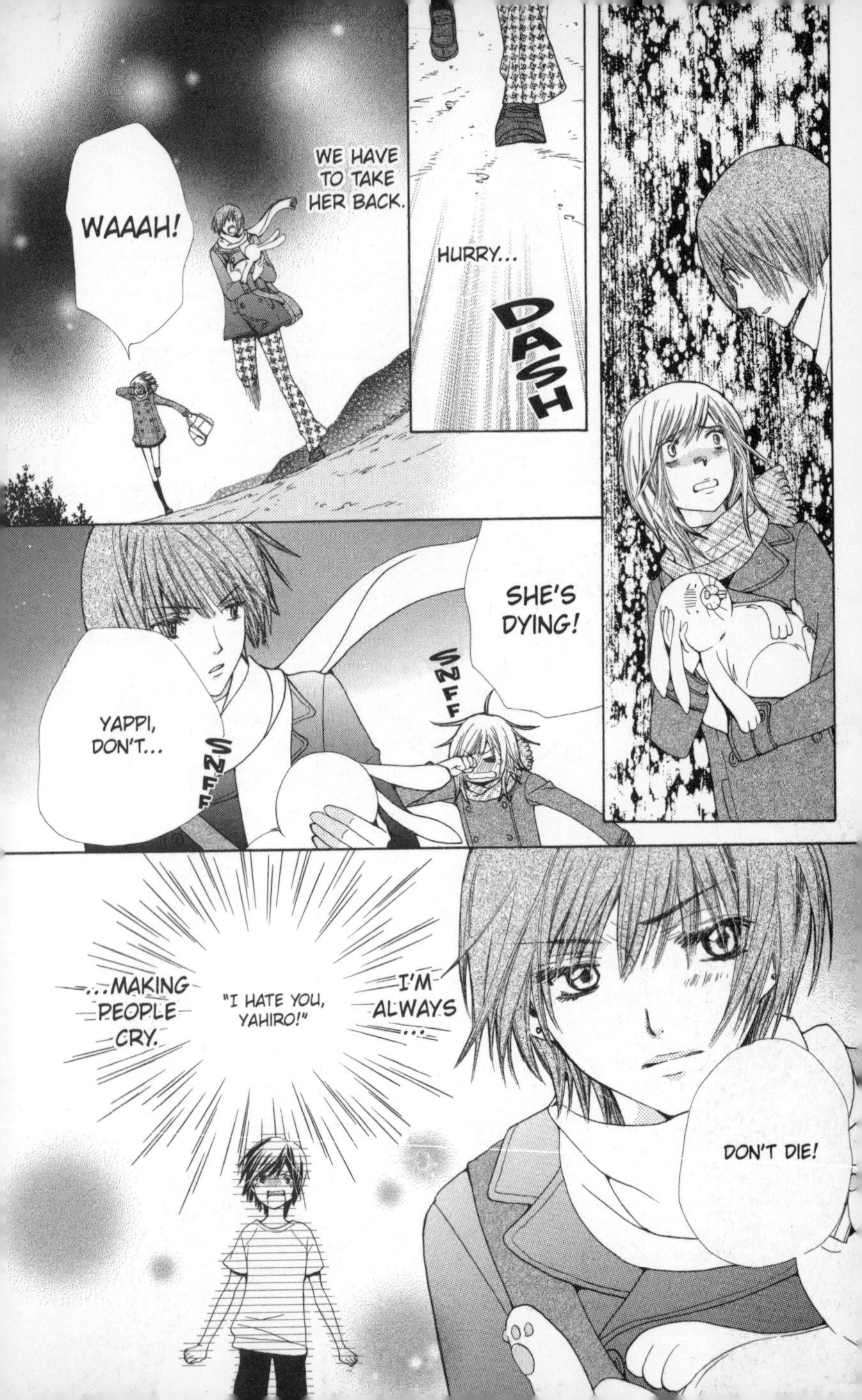
HURRY...
DASH
WE HAVE TO TAKE HER BACK.
WAAAH!
SHE'S DYING!
SNFF
YAPPI, DON'T...
SNFF
DON'T DIE!
I'M ALWAYS...
"I HATE YOU, YAHIRO!"
...MAKING PEOPLE CRY.

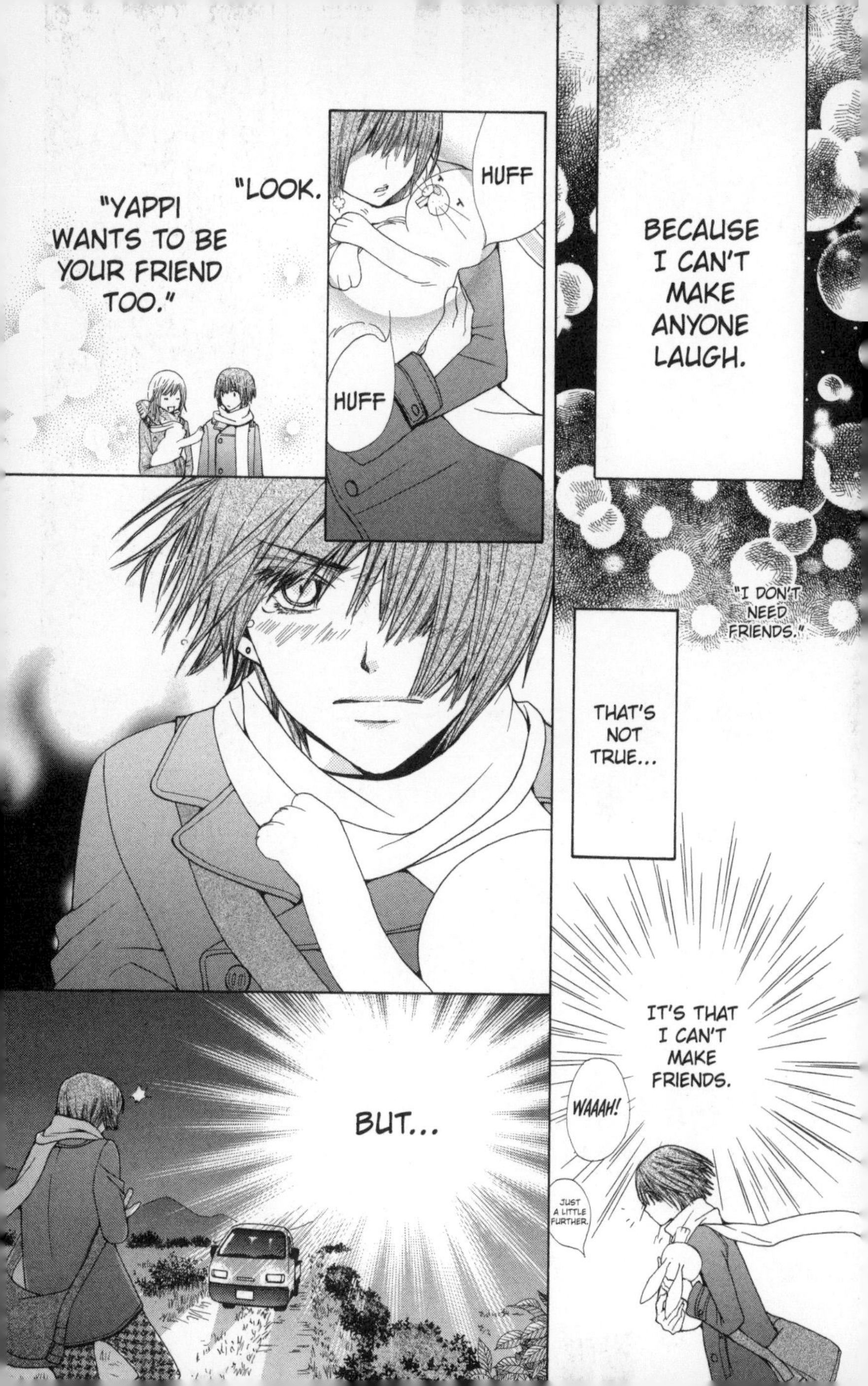
BECAUSE I CAN'T MAKE ANYONE LAUGH.
"I DON'T NEED FRIENDS."
THAT'S NOT TRUE...
IT'S THAT I CAN'T MAKE FRIENDS.
WAAAH!
JUST A LITTLE FURTHER.
HUFF
HUFF
"LOOK.
"YAPPI WANTS TO BE YOUR FRIEND TOO."
BUT...

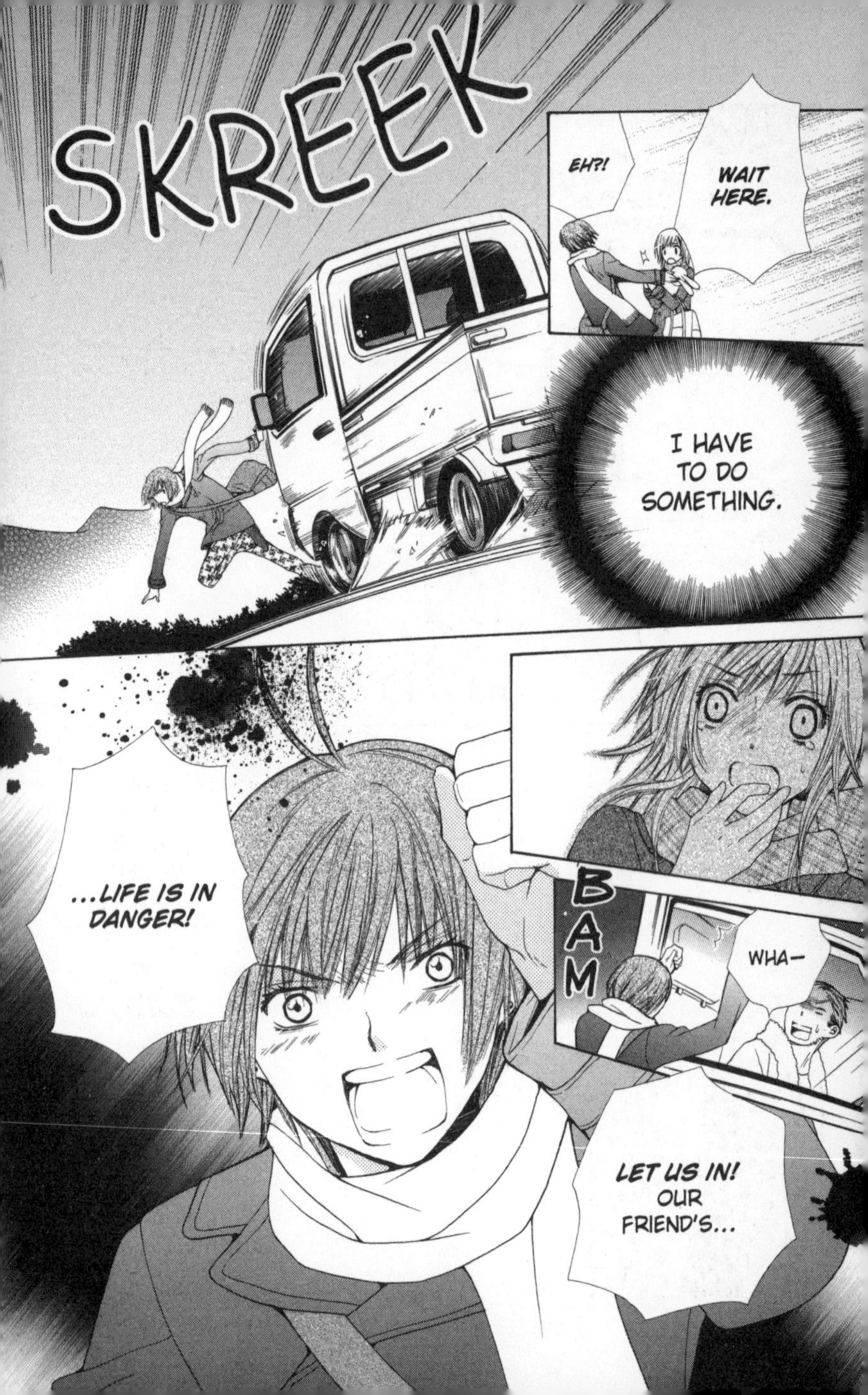
WAIT HERE.
EH?!
I HAVE TO DO SOMETHING.
SKREEK
BAM
WHA-
LET US IN! OUR FRIEND'S...
...LIFE IS IN DANGER!

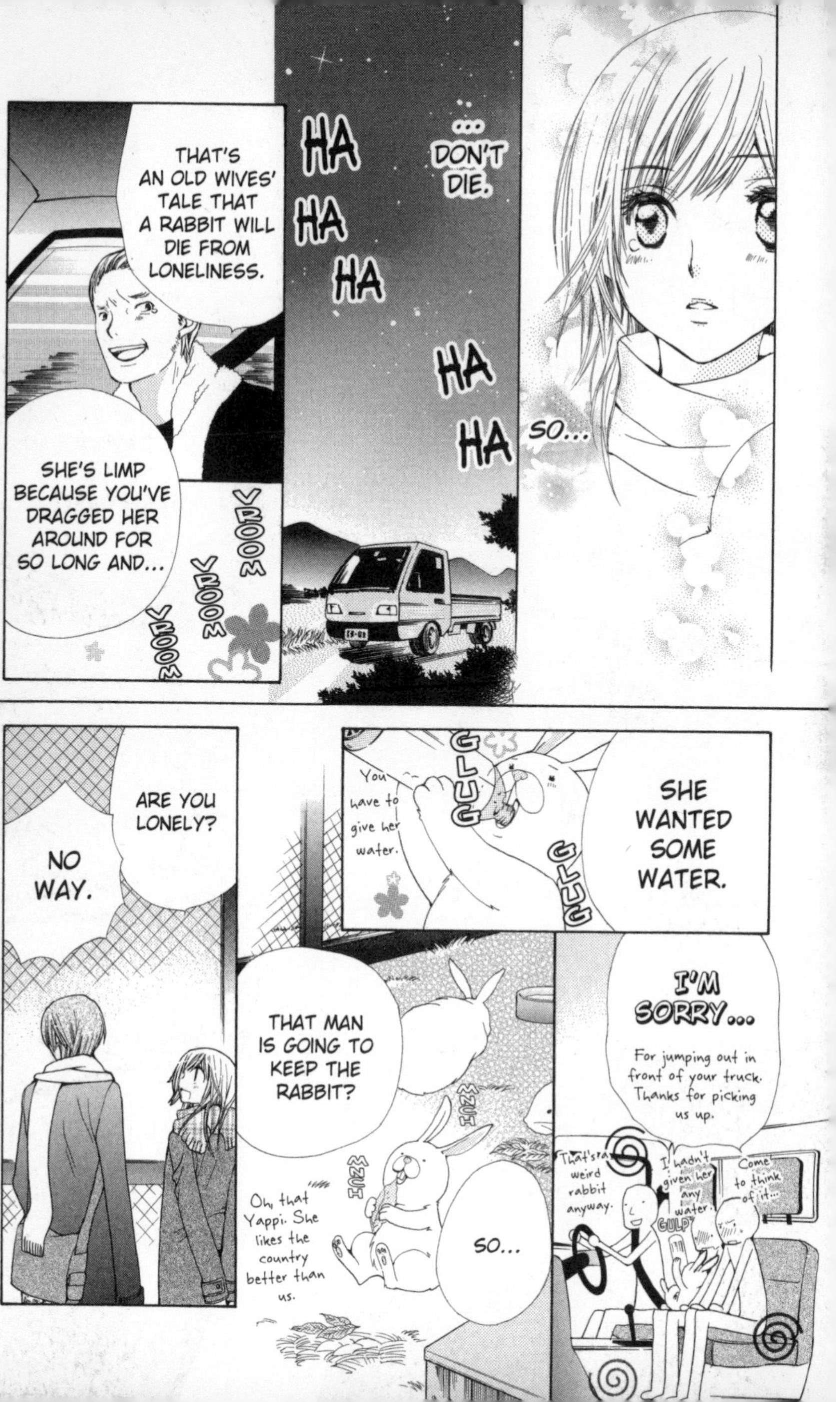
SO...
...DON'T DIE.
HA HA HA HA HA
THAT'S AN OLD WIVES' TALE THAT A RABBIT WILL DIE FROM LONELINESS.
SHE'S LIMP BECAUSE YOU'VE DRAGGED HER AROUND FOR SO LONG AND...
VROOM VROOM VROOM
SHE WANTED SOME WATER.
GLUG GLUG
You have to give her water.
I'M SORRY...
For jumping out in front of your truck. Thanks for picking us up.
Come to think of it...
I hadn't given her any water.
GULP
That's a weird rabbit anyway.
THAT MAN IS GOING TO KEEP THE RABBIT?
MNCH MNCH
SO...
Oh, that Yappi. She likes the country better than us.
ARE YOU LONELY?
NO WAY.

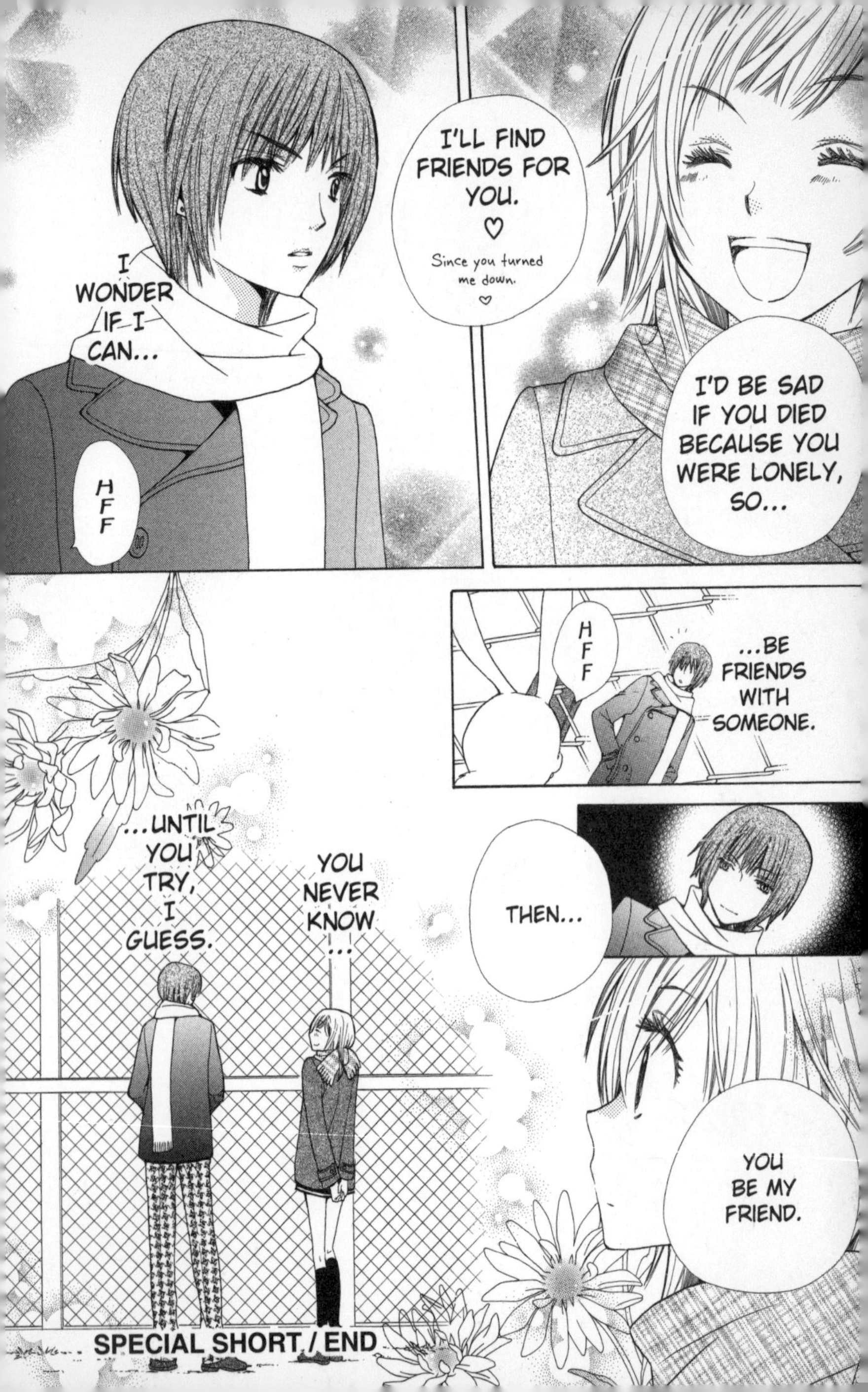
I'D BE SAD IF YOU DIED BECAUSE YOU WERE LONELY, SO...
I'LL FIND FRIENDS FOR YOU. ♡
Since you turned me down. ♡
I WONDER IF I CAN...
HFF
HFF
...BE FRIENDS WITH SOMEONE.
THEN...
YOU BE MY FRIEND.
YOU NEVER KNOW...
...UNTIL YOU TRY, I GUESS.
SPECIAL SHORT / END

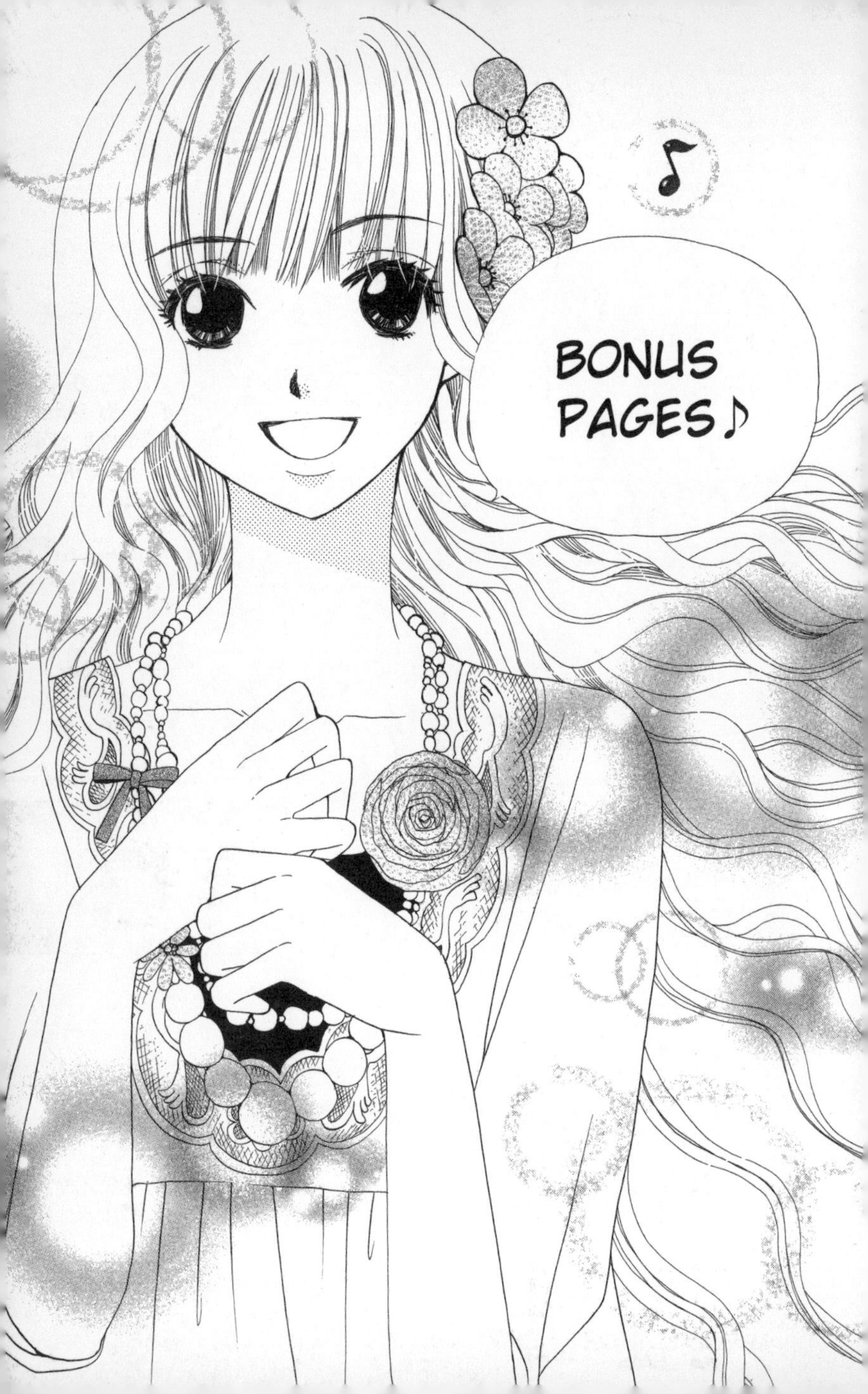
BONUS PAGES♪

Without warning,
a three-page manga.

GO, TADASHI! PART 9!

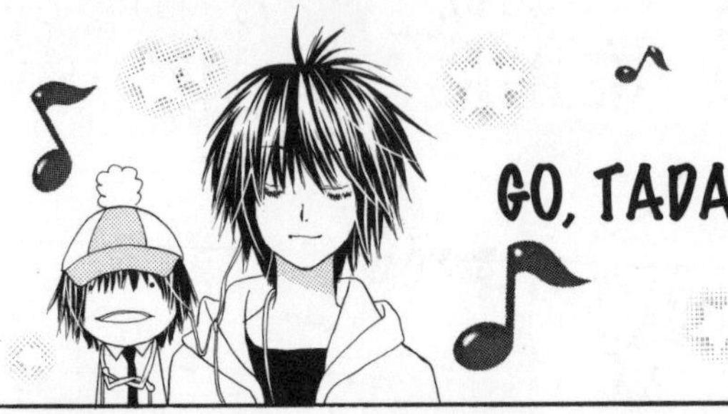

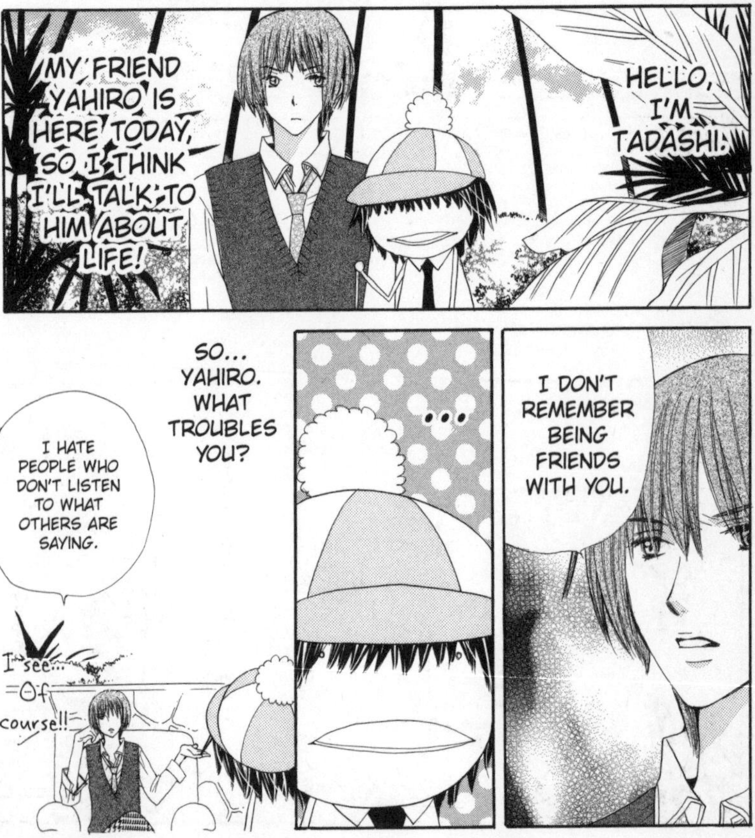
HELLO, I'M TADASHI.
MY FRIEND YAHIRO IS HERE TODAY, SO I THINK I'LL TALK TO HIM ABOUT LIFE!
I DON'T REMEMBER BEING FRIENDS WITH YOU.
...
SO... YAHIRO. WHAT TROUBLES YOU?
I HATE PEOPLE WHO DON'T LISTEN TO WHAT OTHERS ARE SAYING.
I see... Of course!!

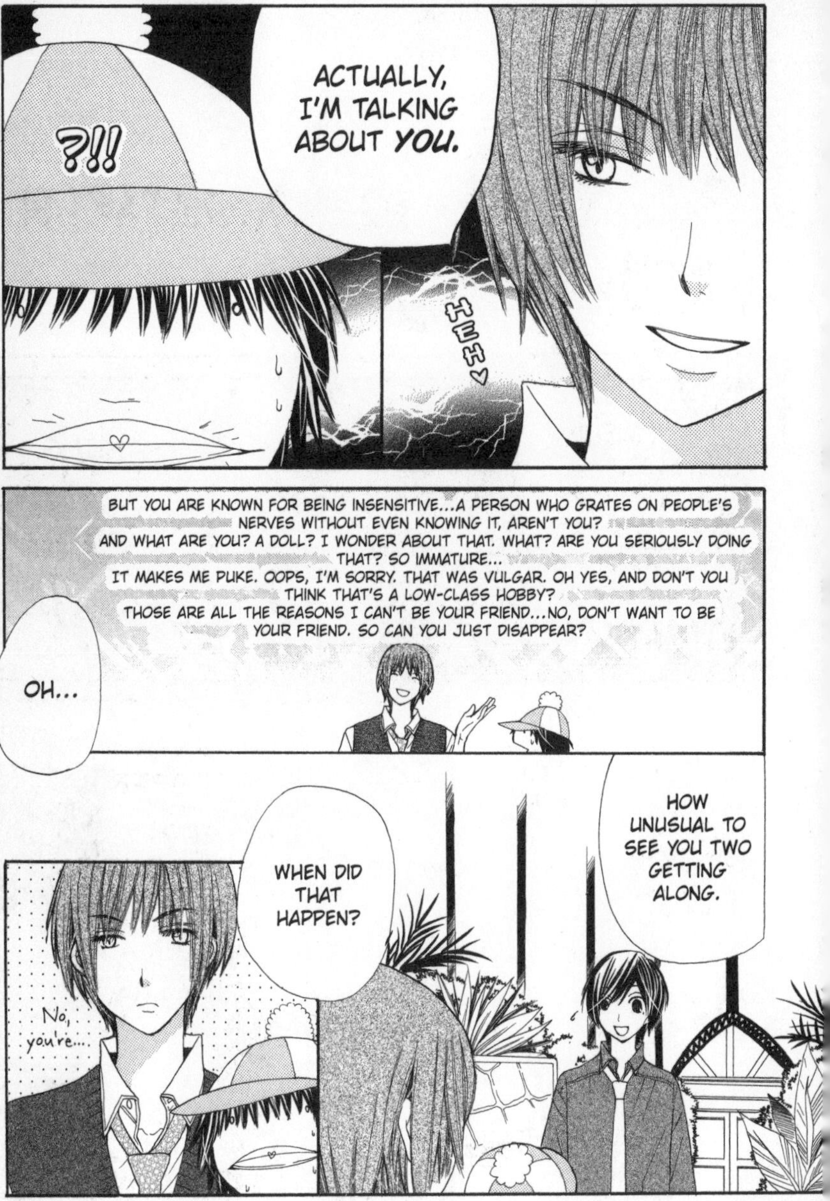
ACTUALLY, I'M TALKING ABOUT *YOU.*
HEH♥
?!!
BUT YOU ARE KNOWN FOR BEING INSENSITIVE...A PERSON WHO GRATES ON PEOPLE'S NERVES WITHOUT EVEN KNOWING IT, AREN'T YOU? AND WHAT ARE YOU? A DOLL? I WONDER ABOUT THAT. WHAT? ARE YOU SERIOUSLY DOING THAT? SO IMMATURE... IT MAKES ME PUKE. OOPS, I'M SORRY. THAT WAS VULGAR. OH YES, AND DON'T YOU THINK THAT'S A LOW-CLASS HOBBY? THOSE ARE ALL THE REASONS I CAN'T BE YOUR FRIEND...NO, DON'T WANT TO BE YOUR FRIEND. SO CAN YOU JUST DISAPPEAR?
OH...
HOW UNUSUAL TO SEE YOU TWO GETTING ALONG.
WHEN DID THAT HAPPEN?
No, you're...

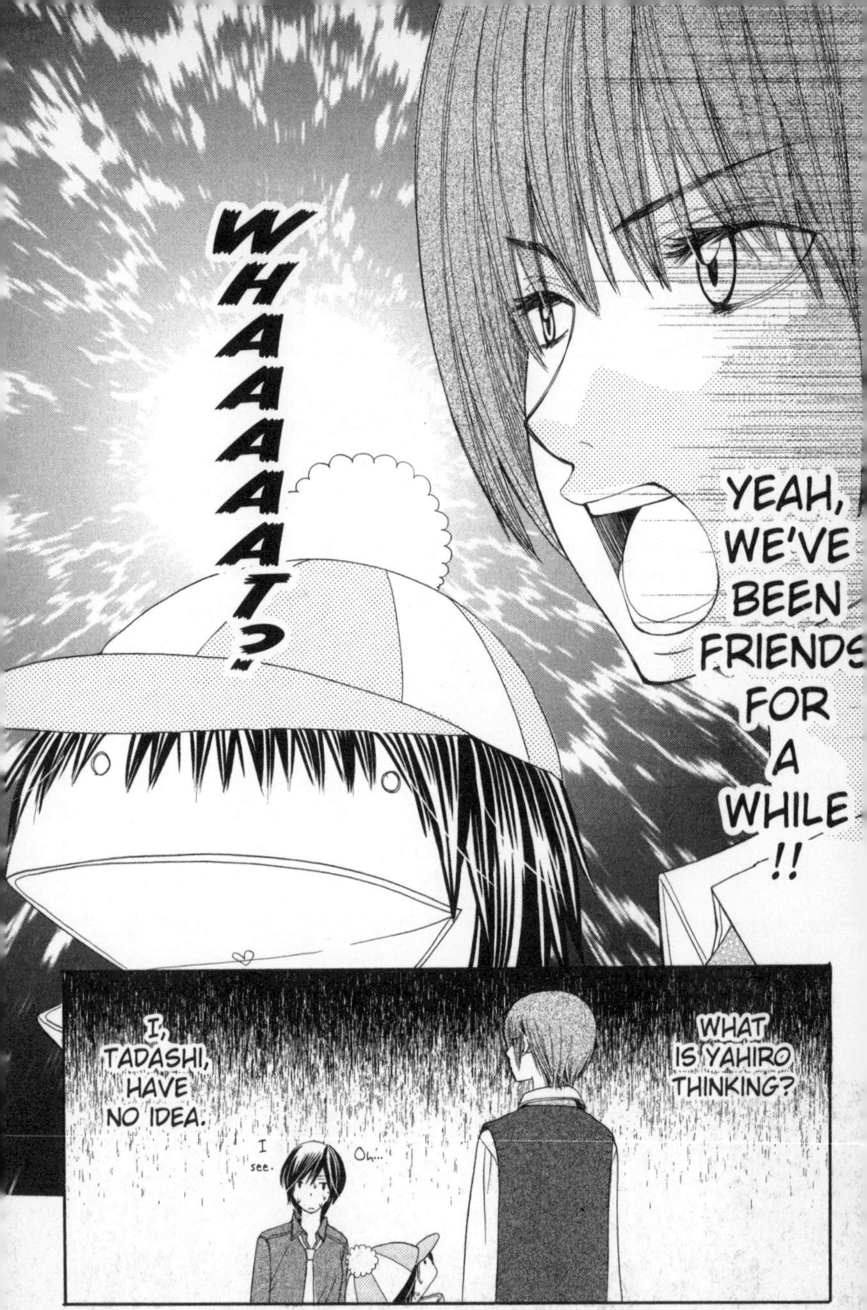
YEAH, WE'VE BEEN FRIENDS FOR A WHILE!!
WHAAAAAT?!
WHAT IS YAHIRO THINKING?
Oh...
I see.
I, TADASHI, HAVE NO IDEA.

BONUS PAGES / END

Maki Minami is from Saitama Prefecture in Japan. She debuted in 2001 with *Kanata no Ao* (Faraway Blue). Her other works include *Kimi wa Girlfriend* (You're My Girlfriend), *Mainichi ga Takaramono* (Every Day Is a Treasure) and *Yuki Atataka* (Warm Winter). *S•A* was serialized in Japan's *Hana to Yume* magazine and made into an anime in 2008.

S·A

Vol. 9
The Shojo Beat Manga Edition

STORY & ART BY
MAKI MINAMI

English Adaptation/Amanda Hubbard
Translation/JN Productions
Touch-up Art & Lettering/HudsonYards
Design/Izumi Hirayama
Interior Design/Deirdre Shiozawa
Editor/Jonathan Tarbox

Editor in Chief, Books/Alvin Lu
Editor in Chief, Magazines/Marc Weidenbaum
VP, Publishing Licensing/Rika Inouye
VP, Sales & Product Marketing/Gonzalo Ferreyra
VP, Creative/Linda Espinosa
Publisher/Hyoe Narita

Printed in Canada

Published by VIZ Media, LLC
P.O. Box 77010
San Francisco, CA 94107

Shojo Beat Manga Edition
10 9 8 7 6 5 4 3 2 1
First printing, March 2009

PARENTAL ADVISORY
S•A is rated T for Teen
and is recommended for
ages 13 and up.

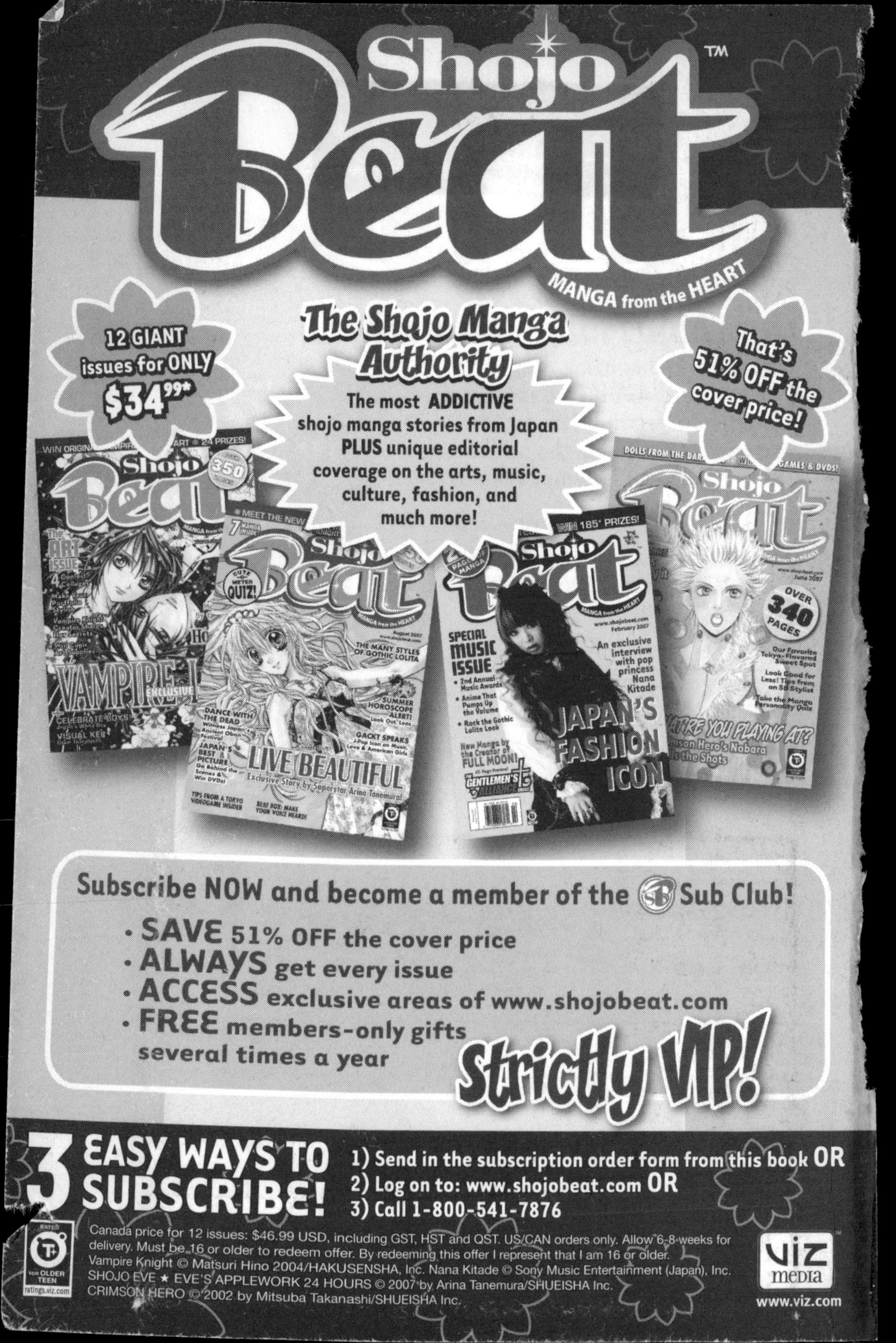
Shojo Beat™
MANGA from the HEART
The Shojo Manga Authority
The most ADDICTIVE shojo manga stories from Japan PLUS unique editorial coverage on the arts, music, culture, fashion, and much more!
12 GIANT issues for ONLY $34.99*
That's 51% OFF the cover price!
Subscribe NOW and become a member of the SB Sub Club!
• SAVE 51% OFF the cover price
• ALWAYS get every issue
• ACCESS exclusive areas of www.shojobeat.com
• FREE members-only gifts several times a year
Strictly VIP!
3 EASY WAYS TO SUBSCRIBE!
1) Send in the subscription order form from this book OR
2) Log on to: www.shojobeat.com OR
3) Call 1-800-541-7876
Canada price for 12 issues: $46.99 USD, including GST, HST and QST. US/CAN orders only. Allow 6-8 weeks for delivery. Must be 16 or older to redeem offer. By redeeming this offer I represent that I am 16 or older.
Vampire Knight © Matsuri Hino 2004/HAKUSENSHA, Inc. Nana Kitade © Sony Music Entertainment (Japan), Inc.
SHOJO EVE ★ EVE'S APPLEWORK 24 HOURS © 2007 by Arina Tanemura/SHUEISHA Inc.
CRIMSON HERO © 2002 by Mitsuba Takanashi/SHUEISHA Inc.
RATED T+ FOR OLDER TEEN
ratings.viz.com
VIZ media
www.viz.com